Lecture Notes in Computer Science 14467

Founding Editors

Gerhard Goos
Juris Hartmanis

The series Lecture Notes in Computer Science (LNCS), including its subseries Lecture Notes in Artificial Intelligence (LNAI) and Lecture Notes in Bioinformatics (LNBI), has established itself as a medium for the publication of new developments in computer science and information technology research, teaching, and education.

LNCS enjoys close cooperation with the computer science R & D community, the series counts many renowned academics among its volume editors and paper authors, and collaborates with prestigious societies. Its mission is to serve this international community by providing an invaluable service, mainly focused on the publication of conference and workshop proceedings and postproceedings. LNCS commenced publication in 1973.

Bo Nørregaard Jørgensen ·
Luiz Carlos Pereira da Silva · Zheng Ma
Editors

Energy Informatics

Third Energy Informatics Academy Conference, EI.A 2023
Campinas, Brazil, December 6–8, 2023
Proceedings, Part I

 Springer

Editors
Bo Nørregaard Jørgensen 🆔
University of Southern Denmark
Odense, Denmark

Luiz Carlos Pereira da Silva 🆔
University of Campinas
Campinas, São Paulo, Brazil

Zheng Ma 🆔
University of Southern Denmark
Odense, Denmark

ISSN 0302-9743   ISSN 1611-3349 (electronic)
Lecture Notes in Computer Science
ISBN 978-3-031-48648-7   ISBN 978-3-031-48649-4 (eBook)
https://doi.org/10.1007/978-3-031-48649-4

This Springer imprint is published by the registered company Springer Nature Switzerland AG
The registered company address is: Gewerbestrasse 11, 6330 Cham, Switzerland

Paper in this product is recyclable.

Preface

The Energy Informatics.Academy Conference 2023 (EI.A 2023) collected great contributions from researchers and practitioners in various scientific, technological, engineering, and social fields to disseminate original research on the application of digital technology and information management theory and practice to facilitate the global transition towards sustainable and resilient energy systems.

With the whole technical program committee's effort, in total thirty-nine (39) high-quality papers (including full papers and short papers) and three (3) abstract papers were accepted and presented at the conference.

These 42 papers covered the following eight themes, elucidating the breadth and depth of research and development in the energy sector and its convergence with digital technologies:

- AI Methods in Energy
- Data-Driven Smart Buildings
- Energy and Industry 4.0
- Energy and Smart Cities
- Energy Forecasting
- Smart Electricity System
- Smart Energy Device Management
- Smart Heating and Cooling System

Each theme brought forward a wealth of knowledge and novel ideas that promise to shape the future trajectory of energy systems and their integration into digitalization. From exploring innovative technologies and methodologies to discussing practical challenges and future perspectives, the papers enriched the conference's discourse, offering attendees a comprehensive overview of the latest in the field. Consequently, the conference became a fertile ground for exchanging ideas, fostering collaborations, and catalyzing future advancements in the energy sector.

Furthermore, eight keynote speeches provided deep insights and diverse perspectives into the evolving realm of energy and technology:

- "Energy transition in Brazil", by Luiz Carlos Pereira da Silva, University of Campinas, Brazil
- "Artificial Intelligence Applied in the Electricity Sector as a Strategic Investment Theme in the Research, Development and Innovation Program of ANEEL" by Paulo Luciano de Carvalho, Brazilian Electricity Regulatory Agency, Brazil
- "Explainable AI for energy and smart grids: from concepts to real-world applications", by Zita A. Vale, Polytechnic of Porto, Portugal
- "Hierarchies of Controllers for the Future Weather-Driven Smart Energy System", by Henrik Madsen, Technical University of Denmark
- "The importance of supervising energy consumption and production", by Marcelo Stehling de Castro, Federal University of Goiás, Brazil

- "Application of Data Analytics to Electrical Energy Systems", by Walmir Freitas, University of Campinas, Brazil
- "Energy & Digital Agroindustry", by Barbara Teruel, University of Campinas, Brazil
- "Energy Informatics Educational Design", by Bo Nørregaard Jørgensen, University of Southern Denmark, Denmark

Each speaker, with their expertise in various facets of energy systems and technology, enriched the dialogue, fostering a multi-dimensional discussion on the challenges, solutions, and future pathways in the energy sector. Engaging Q&A sessions followed the speeches, further elaborating on the pertinent themes and facilitating an exchange of ideas among the participants and speakers alike.

December 2023

Bo Nørregaard Jørgensen
Luiz Carlos Pereira da Silva
Zheng Ma

Organization

Program Committee Chairs

Jørgensen, Bo Nørregaard   University of Southern Denmark, Denmark
Ma, Zheng   University of Southern Denmark, Denmark
Pereira da Silva, Luiz Carlos   University of Campinas, Brazil

Technical Program Committee Chairs

Attux, Romis   University of Campinas, Brazil
Madsen, Henrik   Technical University of Denmark, Denmark
Rider, Marcos J.   University of Campinas, Brazil
Stehling de Castro, Marcelo   University of Goiás, Brazil
Teruel, Bárbara   University of Campinas, Brazil
Vale, Zita   Polytechnic of Porto, Portugal

Technical Program Committee Members

Ai, Qian   Shanghai Jiao Tong University, China
Angelino de Souza, Wesley   Federal University of Technology, Brazil
Aris, Hazleen Binti   Universiti Tenaga Nasional, Malaysia
Arjunan, Pandarasamy   Indian Institute of Science, Robert Bosch Centre for Cyber-Physical Systems, India

Bergel, Alexandre   RelationalAI, Switzerland
Bonatto, Benedito Donizeti   Universidade Federal de Itajubá, Brazil
Bordin, Chiara   Arctic University of Norway, Norway
Chew, Irene   Monash University, Australia
Christensen, Kristoffer   University of Southern Denmark, Denmark
Dai, Wanyang   Nanjing University, China
Fernandes, Ricardo   Federal University of São Carlos, Brazil
Guillardi Júnior, Hildo   São Paulo State University, Brazil
Howard, Daniel Anthony   University of Southern Denmark, Denmark
Huang, Zhilin   Huaqiao University, China
Liang, An   Hong Kong Polytechnic University, China
Liberado, Eduardo   São Paulo State University, Brazil
Lilliu, Fabio   Aalborg University, Denmark

López, Juan Camilo	Universidade Estadual de Campinas, Brazil
Marafão, Fernando	São Paulo State University, Brazil
Othman, Marini	INTI International University, Malaysia
Qu, Ying	University of Southern Denmark, Denmark
Rajasekharan, Jayaprakash	Norwegian University of Science and Technology, Norway
Roomi, Muhammad M.	Illinois at Singapore Pte Ltd, Singapore
Santos, Athila Quaresma	University of Southern Denmark, Denmark
Shaker, Hamid Reza	University of Southern Denmark, Denmark
Vergara, Pedro P.	Delft University of Technology, The Netherlands
Værbak, Magnus	University of Southern Denmark, Denmark
Watson, Richard T.	University of Georgia, USA
Yussof, Salman	Universiti Tenaga Nasional, Malaysia
Swarup, Shanti	IIT Madras, India

Organizing Committee for Special Session - Digitalization of District Heating and Cooling

Brüssau, Martin	SAMSON Aktiengesellschaft, Germany
Nord, Natasa	Norwegian University of Science and Technology, Norway
Saloux, Etienne	Natural Resources Canada, Canada
Schmidt, Dietrich	Fraunhofer IEE, Germany
Shaker, Hamid Reza	University of Southern Denmark, Denmark
Vallée, Mathieu	National Institute for Solar Energy, France
Yang, Xiaochen	Tianjin University, China

Organizing Committee for Special Session - Data-Driven Smart Buildings

Borkowski, Esther	Institute of Technology in Architecture, Switzerland
Jørgensen, Bo Nørregaard	University of Southern Denmark, Denmark
Saloux, Etienne	Natural Resources Canada, Canada
So, Patrick	Hong Kong Electrical and Mechanical Services Department, China
White, Stephen	CSIRO, Australia

Organizing Committee for Special Session - Digitalization, AI and Related Technologies for Energy Efficiency and GHG Emissions Reduction in Industry

Amazouz, Mouloud   Natural Resources Canada, Canada
Levesque, Michelle   Natural Resources Canada, Canada
Ma, Zheng   University of Southern Denmark, Denmark

Reviewers

Acuña Acurio, Byron Alejandro   University of Campinas, Brazil
Chérrez Barragán, Diana Estefania   University of Campinas, Brazil
Clausen, Christian Skafte Beck   University of Southern Denmark, Denmark
Fatras, Nicolas   University of Southern Denmark, Denmark
Hidalgo Leite, Nathalia   University of Campinas, Brazil
Ito Cypriano, Joao Guilherme   University of Campinas, Brazil
Ma, Zhipeng   University of Southern Denmark, Denmark
Mirshekali, Hamid   University of Southern Denmark, Denmark
Mortensen, Lasse Kappel   University of Southern Denmark, Denmark
Santos, Luiza   University of Campinas, Brazil
Silva, Jessica   University of Campinas, Brazil
Søndergaard, Henrik Alexander   University of Southern Denmark, Denmark
   Nissen
Tolnai, Balázs András   University of Southern Denmark, Denmark
Vanting, Nicolai Bo   University of Southern Denmark, Denmark

Contents – Part I

Energy and Industry 4.0

Contents – Part II

Smart Electricity System

Smart Energy Device Management

Smart Heating and Cooling System

AI Methods in Energy

Managing Anomalies in Energy Time Series for Automated Forecasting

Marian Turowski$^{(\boxtimes)}$ (iD), Oliver Neumann (iD), Lisa Mannsperger, Kristof Kraus,
Kira Layer, Ralf Mikut (iD), and Veit Hagenmeyer (iD)

Institute for Automation and Applied Informatics, Karlsruhe Institute of Technology,
Hermann-von-Helmholtz-Platz 1, 76344 Eggenstein-Leopoldshafen, Germany
marian.turowski@kit.edu

Abstract. The increasing number of recorded energy time series enables
the automated operation of smart grid applications such as load analysis, load forecasting, and load management. However, to perform well,
these applications usually require clean data that well represents the
typical behavior of the underlying system. Unfortunately, recorded time
series often contain anomalies that do not reflect the typical behavior of
the system and are, thus, problematic for automated smart grid applications such as automated forecasting. While various anomaly management strategies exist, a rigorous comparison is lacking. Therefore, in the
present paper, we introduce and compare three different general strategies for managing anomalies in energy time series forecasting, namely the
raw, the detection, and the compensation strategy. We compare these
strategies using a representative selection of forecasting methods and
real-world data with inserted synthetic anomalies. The comparison shows
that applying the compensation strategy is generally beneficial for managing anomalies despite requiring additional computational costs because
it mostly outperforms the detection and the raw strategy when the input
data contains anomalies.

Keywords: Anomalies · Anomaly management · Forecasting · Energy
time series

1   Introduction

Since energy systems around the world transition to an increasing share of renewable energy sources in energy supply, the implementation of smart grids supporting this transition also advances. Smart grid implementation implies a growing
number of smart meters that record power or energy consumption and generation as time series [4]. These recorded energy time series are characterized by
a multi-seasonality, an aggregation-level dependent predictability, and a depen-
dence on exogenous influences such as weather [16]. The increasing number of
recorded energy time series enables a wide range of possible applications for this
data and the goal of their automated operation. Exemplary applications for the
smart grid that support the transition to renewable energy sources include customer profiling, load analysis, load forecasting, and load management [39,47].

© The Author(s) 2024
B. N. Jørgensen et al. (Eds.): EI.A 2023, LNCS 14467, pp. 3–29, 2024.
https://doi.org/10.1007/978-3-031-48649-4_1

However, to perform well, these applications usually require clean data that represents the typical behavior of the underlying system well [30, 47].

Unfortunately, recorded time series are usually not clean, but contain anomalies [13]. Anomalies are patterns that deviate from what is considered normal [10]. They can occur in energy time series for many reasons, including smart meter failures [46], unusual consumption [32, 40], and energy theft [24]. All anomalies have in common that they potentially contain data points or patterns that represent false or misleading information, which can be problematic for any analysis of this data performed by the mentioned applications [47]. For example, anomalies such as positive or negative spikes may strongly deviate from what is considered normal, and a subsequent forecasting method that uses the data as input in an automated manner may generate an incorrect forecast. This forecast could in turn lead to an inappropriate energy schedule and ultimately affect the stability of the energy system in an automated smart grid setting.

Therefore, managing anomalies in energy time series – in the sense of dealing with their presence – is an important issue for applications in the energy system such as billing and forecasting [47]. In energy time series forecasting, the importance of an adequate anomaly management is generally known, e.g. [2, 3, 36]. For this reason, various anomaly management strategies exist, including the use of robust forecasting methods [23, 28], the use of information on detected anomalies [43], and the compensation of detected anomalies [9, 14, 37, 50]. However, it is not clear which strategy is the best for managing anomalies in energy time series forecasting regarding the obtained accuracy and also the associated necessary effort, which is why a rigorous comparison of available strategies is needed.

Therefore, the present paper introduces and compares different general strategies for managing anomalies in energy time series forecasting. For this purpose, we build on the typically used strategies mentioned above and describe three different general strategies based on them, namely the raw, the detection, and the compensation strategy. While the raw strategy applies forecasting methods directly to the data input without any changes, the detection strategy provides information on anomalies detected in the input data to the forecasting method. The compensation strategy cleans the input data by detecting and thereafter compensating anomalies in the input data before applying a forecasting method.

To comparatively evaluate these strategies, we use a representative selection of forecasting methods, including naive, simple statistical, statistical learning, and machine learning methods. We also make use of real-world energy time series with inserted synthetic anomalies derived from real-world data. Given these forecasting methods and data, we compare the obtained forecast accuracy of all proposed strategies and present an example of how these strategies work and perform.

The remainder of the present paper is structured as follows: After describing related work in Sect. 2, Sect. 3 introduces the strategies for managing anomalies in energy time series forecasting. In Sect. 4, we evaluate the presented strategies. Finally, we discuss the results and the strategies in Sect. 5 and conclude the paper in Sect. 6.

2   Related Work

Since anomalies are potentially limiting the performance of any downstream application, dealing with their presence is generally a well-known topic. For example, all kinds of pre-processing methods aim to raise data quality to ensure the validity and reliability of data analysis results, e.g. [5,19,37]. Similarly, the influence of the choice of preprocessing methods on the accuracy of forecasting methods is also known, e.g. [1,3]. In energy time series forecasting, several works also address how to deal with the presence of anomalies. We organize these works along three strategies.

Works of the first strategy focus on the robustness of forecasting methods. These works, for example, develop forecasting methods that are robust against anomalies, e.g. [23,28,29,51,53], strengthen existing forecasting methods, e.g. [54], or at least investigate the robustness of forecasting methods with respect to anomalous data, e.g. [27,52]. The second strategy consists of works that make use of information on detected anomalies. In [43], for example, the information on predicted anomalies is used to adapt the energy production. Works of the third strategy detect anomalies and replace the detected anomalies with appropriate values, e.g. [9,14,30,33], or even remove the detected anomalies, e.g. [11].

Despite these works on specific anomaly management strategies, it is not known which strategy is the best for managing anomalies in energy time series forecasting. For this reason, a rigorous comparison of the available strategies – as done in the present paper – is lacking.

3   Strategies for Managing Anomalies in Energy Time Series Forecasting

In this section, we present three general strategies for managing anomalies in energy time series forecasting, which build on the previously described anomaly management strategies in literature.[1] All of these strategies apply a forecasting method $f(\circ)$ to create a forecast for an input power time series $\mathbf{y} = \{y_t\}_{t \in T}$ with T measured values. This forecasting method creates a forecast based on historical values of the input power time series and exogenous features $\mathbf{e}$ such as calendar information or weather forecasts. More specifically, the forecasting method combines the most recent N historical values of the input power time series $\mathbf{y}_t = y_{t-(N-1)}, \ldots, y_t$ with the exogenous features $\mathbf{e}_{t+H} = e_{t+1}, \ldots e_{t+H}$ for the forecasting horizon H. Using this combination, the forecasting method then generates a forecast at time point t

$$\hat{\mathbf{y}}_{t+H} = f(\mathbf{y}_t, \mathbf{e}_{t+H}), \tag{1}$$

where $\hat{\mathbf{y}}_{t+H} = \hat{y}_{t+1}, \ldots \hat{y}_{t+H}$ is the forecast value for the input power time series for each time step in the forecast horizon. Nevertheless, the considered strategies

---

[1] The implementation of the proposed and evaluated strategies is available at https://github.com/KIT-IAI/ManagingAnomaliesInTimeSeriesForecasting.

comprise different steps and thus differ in the inputs to the applied forecasting method (see Fig. 1). We thus describe the included steps, the used input, and the underlying assumptions for each strategy in the following.

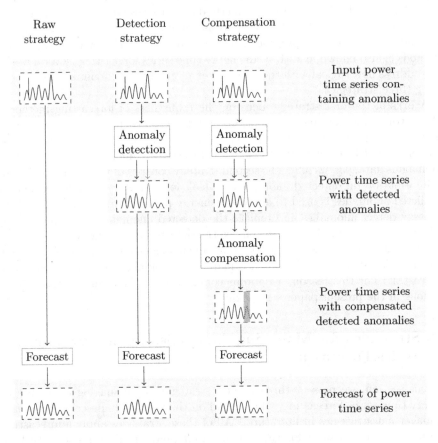

Fig. 1. The three strategies for managing anomalies in energy time series forecasting. The raw strategy directly uses the input power time series to create a forecast. The detection strategy first detects anomalies in the input power time series, before providing a forecast using the information on the detected anomalies from the power time series with detected anomalies. The compensation strategy detects anomalies and additionally compensates the detected anomalies before performing a forecast based on the power time series with compensated detected anomalies.

Raw Strategy. The first strategy is the so-called raw strategy. It directly uses a power time series containing anomalies as input to a forecasting method. Given this input, the applied forecasting method provides a forecast of the input power time series. Formally, the raw strategy thus creates a forecast at time point t

$$\hat{\mathbf{y}}_{t+H}^{\text{raw}} = f(\mathbf{y}_t, \mathbf{e}_{t+H}), \tag{2}$$

where $\mathbf{y}_t$ are the historical values of the input power time series containing anomalies and H, $\mathbf{e}_{t+H}$, and $\hat{\mathbf{y}}_{t+H}$ are defined as above.

The raw strategy assumes that the anomalies contained in the input time series do not strongly affect the forecast of the applied forecasting method or that the applied forecasting method is robust against anomalies. Therefore, the applied forecasting method is assumed to still achieve an accurate forecast.

Detection Strategy. The second strategy is the so-called detection strategy. This strategy first applies an anomaly detection method to the power time series containing anomalies to detect contained anomalies whereby the anomaly detection method can be supervised or unsupervised. The resulting power time series with detected anomalies serves as input to the forecasting method that then provides the forecast of the power time series. Formally, the detection strategy, therefore, results in a forecast at time point t

$$\hat{\mathbf{y}}_{t+H}^{\text{detection}} = f(\mathbf{y}_t, \mathbf{d}_{t+H}, \mathbf{e}_{t+H}), \tag{3}$$

where $\mathbf{d}_{t+H} = d_{t+1}, \ldots d_{t+H}$ are the labels of the detected anomalies for the forecasting horizon H and $\mathbf{y}_t$, $\mathbf{e}_{t+H}$, and $\hat{\mathbf{y}}_{t+H}$ are defined as above.

The assumption of the detection strategy is that the applied forecasting method can incorporate information about detected anomalies in its model so that the consideration of detected anomalies leads to an accurate forecast.

Compensation Strategy. The third strategy is the so-called compensation strategy. It also first applies a supervised or unsupervised anomaly detection method to the power time series containing anomalies to identify the contained anomalies. However, this strategy then uses the power time series with detected anomalies as input to an anomaly compensation method $c(\circ)$ that replaces the detected anomalies with realistic values, i.e.,

$$\tilde{\mathbf{y}}_{t+H} = c(\mathbf{y}_t, \mathbf{d}_{t+H}, \circ), \tag{4}$$

where $\tilde{\mathbf{y}}_{t+H}$ is the power time series with compensated detected anomalies and $\circ$ are additional parameters of the compensation method. This power time series with compensated detected anomalies $\tilde{\mathbf{y}}_{t+H}$ serves as input to the forecasting method that provides the forecast of the power time series. Formally, we describe the forecast of the compensation strategy at time point t with

$$\hat{\mathbf{y}}_{t+H}^{\text{compensation}} = f(\tilde{\mathbf{y}}_t, \mathbf{e}_{t+H}), \tag{5}$$

where $\tilde{\mathbf{y}}_t$ are the historical values of the input power time series with compensated detected anomalies and H, $\mathbf{e}_{t+H}$, and $\hat{\mathbf{y}}_{t+H}$ are defined as above.

The compensation strategy assumes that anomalies have to be detected and compensated in order to enable the applied forecasting method to provide an accurate forecast.

4   Evaluation

To evaluate the proposed strategies for managing anomalies in energy time series forecasting, we compare the forecasting accuracy of all strategies using different forecasting methods. Before presenting the results, we detail the performed evaluation: We introduce the used data and the inserted synthetic anomalies, the anomaly detection methods applied in the detection and compensation strategies, and the anomaly compensation method applied in the compensation strategy. We also describe the used forecasting methods and the experimental setting.

4.1 Data and Inserted Synthetic Anomalies

For the evaluation, we use real-world data in which we insert synthetic anomalies. The chosen data set is the "ElectricityLoadDiagrams20112014 Data Set"[2] from the UCI Machine Learning Repository [18]. It includes electrical power time series from 370 clients with different consumption patterns [38]. The 370 time series are available in a quarter-hourly resolution for a period of up to four years, namely from the beginning of 2011 until the end of 2014. We choose the power time series MT_200 for the evaluation to cover the entire four-year period, to account for the electrical load of a typical client, and to consider a time series that is anomaly-free compared to other time series in the data set (see Fig. 2).

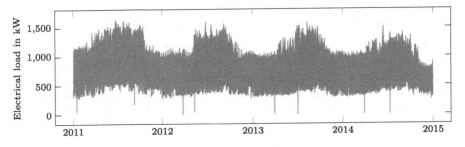

Fig. 2. Overview of the data used for the evaluation.

Since the chosen time series does not include labeled anomalies and thus do not allow for controlled experimental conditions, we insert synthetic anomalies in the complete chosen time series. For this, we consider the two anomaly groups used in [44], namely technical faults in the metering infrastructure and unusual consumption. Using the corresponding available anomaly generation method[3], we insert four types of anomalies from each group: Anomalies of types 1 to 4 are from the group of technical faults and based on anomalies identified in real-world power time series in [45]. These anomalies violate the underlying distribution corresponding to normal behavior. Anomalies of types 5 to 8 are from the group of unusual consumption and represent unusual behavior as described in [44]. These anomalies are characterized by unusually low or high power consumption. We give formulas and examples for all types of anomalies in Appendix 1.

---

[2] https://archive.ics.uci.edu/ml/datasets/ElectricityLoadDiagrams20112014.
[3] https://github.com/KIT-IAI/EnhancingAnomalyDetectionMethods.

For the evaluation, we insert once 20 anomalies of types 1 to 4 each from the group of technical faults and once 20 anomalies of types 5 to 8 each from the group of unusual consumption into the selected time series. We insert 20 anomalies per type to consider a reasonable number of anomalies and we insert all four types of anomalies from a group at once to consider their simultaneous occurrence [44,45]. The inserted anomalies correspond to 5% of the data for the technical faults and 11% of the data for the unusual consumption.

4.2   Applied Anomaly Detection Methods

For the evaluation of the detection and compensation strategies, we choose anomaly detection methods based on the evaluation results in [44], where a variety of anomaly detection methods is already evaluated on the selected data. More specifically, we choose the method from the evaluated supervised and unsupervised anomaly detection methods that overall performs best for the considered groups of anomalies. For both groups of anomalies, the best-performing method is an unsupervised anomaly detection method, namely the Variational Autoencoder (VAE) for the technical faults and the Local Outlier Factor (LOF) for the unusual consumption. We briefly introduce both chosen anomaly detection methods, before we describe their application.

The Variational Autoencoder (VAE) learns to map its input to its output using the probability distribution of ideally anomaly-free data in the latent space, so it is trained to only reconstruct non-anomalous data [26]. The Local Outlier Factor (LOF) estimates the local density of a sample by the distance to its k-nearest neighbors and uses low local densities compared to its neighbors to determine anomalies [8].

To enhance the detection performance of the selected anomaly detection methods, we apply them to the latent space representation of the selected data as suggested in [44] and visualized in Fig. 8 in Appendix 2. We choose the generative method to create these latent space representations for each selected anomaly detection method based on the evaluation results in [44]: We create the latent space data representations for the vae with a conditional Invertible Neural Network (cINN) [6] and the latent space data representation for the LOF with a conditional Variational Autoencoder (cVAE) [41]. We detail the architecture and training of the used cINN and cVAE in Appendix 2. Given the created latent space representation, we apply the selected anomaly detection methods to the entire selected time series of the chosen data as in [44].

4.3   Applied Anomaly Compensation Method

For the anomaly compensation in the evaluation of the proposed compensation strategy, we use a Prophet-based imputation method because of its superior imputation performance for power time series determined in [48]. The Prophet-based imputation method [48] is built on the forecasting method Prophet which is capable of estimating a time series model on irregularly spaced data [42].

Prophet uses a modular regression model that considers trend, seasonality, and holidays as key components. It can be described as

$$y(t) = g(t) + s(t) + h(t) + \varepsilon_t, \tag{6}$$

where g models the trend, s the seasonality, h the holidays, and ε_t all other changes not represented in the model. The Prophet-based imputation method trains the regression model using all values available in the power time series. Given the trained regression model, the Prophet-based imputation method considers all anomalies in the power time series as missing values and imputes them with the corresponding values from the trained regression model.

4.4   Anomaly-Free Baseline Strategy

In the evaluation, we examine the proposed raw, detection, and compensation strategies all based on the selected data containing inserted synthetic anomalies. For the evaluation of these strategies, we additionally provide an anomaly-free baseline. This baseline strategy comprises forecasts that are calculated on that selected data but without any inserted anomalies (see Fig. 3).

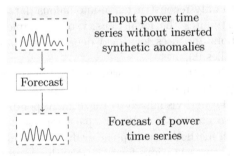

Fig. 3. For evaluating the proposed strategies on the data with inserted synthetic anomalies, we use the forecast calculated on the input power time series without inserted anomalies as an anomaly-free baseline strategy.

4.5   Applied Forecasting Methods

For the evaluation of the proposed strategies, we consider a multi-step 24 h-ahead forecast with a multiple output strategy for which we apply a representative selection of forecasting methods to the selected data. Due to the quarter-hourly resolution of the selected data, the forecast comprises 96 values. For forecasting methods with hyperparameters, we use hyperparameters that we initially choose based on best practices and then verify. We first present the selected forecasting methods and their input data for the raw and compensation strategies, before we describe them for the detection strategy and the anomaly-free baseline strategy. We lastly present the used train-test split.

Methods Applied in Raw and Compensation Strategies. To examine the raw and compensation strategies comprehensively, we consider methods with different learning assumptions. We apply eight forecasting methods, namely two naive and six advanced methods. The advanced methods comprise a simple statistical method, a simple and two more complex machine learning methods, and two statistical learning methods.

The first naive method is the Last Day Forecast. It uses the values of the previous 24 h for the values to be predicted, i.e.,

$$\hat{y}_{t,h} = y_{t-96+h}, \tag{7}$$

where $\hat{y}_{t,h}$ is the forecast value of the electrical load for the forecast horizon h at time t and y_t is the electrical load at time t.

The second naive method is the Last Week Forecast. It takes the corresponding values of the last week as the forecast values, i.e.,

$$\hat{y}_{t,h} = y_{t-672+h}, \tag{8}$$

where $\hat{y}_{t,h}$ is the forecast value of the electrical load for the forecast horizon h at time t and y_{t-672} is the electrical load one week ago at time $t - 672$.

The first advanced method is the Linear Regression (LinR). As a statistical method, it models the forecast values as a linear relationship between the historical load values and calendar information and determines the corresponding parameters using ordinary least squares. It is defined as

$$\hat{y}_{t,h} = c_h + \sum_j \beta_{h,j} \cdot y_{t-j} + \sum_k \gamma_{h,k} \cdot C_{t,k} + \varepsilon, \tag{9}$$

where c is a constant, index j iterates over the lagged load features y_{t-j}, index k iterates over the calendar information $C_{t,k}$, and ε is the error.

The second advanced method is a commonly applied simple machine learning method, namely a Neural Network (NN). It organizes a network of interconnected nodes in input, hidden, and output layers to apply different functions that activate the corresponding nodes to learn the relationship between input and output (e.g., [31,49]). The implementation of the used NN is detailed in Table 6 in Appendix 3. For its training, we use a batch size of 64, the Adam optimizer [25] with default parameters, and a maximum of 50 epochs.

The third advanced method is the Profile Neural Network (PNN) [21] as a state-of-the-art and more complex machine learning method. It combines statistical information in the form of standard load profiles with convolutional neural networks (CNNs) to improve the forecasting accuracy. For this, it decomposes a power time series into a standard load profile module, a trend module, and a colorful noise module, before aggregating their outputs to obtain the forecast

[21]. For the training, the PNN uses a batch size of 512, the Adam optimizer [25], and a maximum of 50 epochs.

The fourth advanced method is the Random Forest (RF) Regressor representing a statistical learning method. It creates several randomly drawn regression trees and takes the mean of each individual tree's forecast as forecast [7], i.e.,

$$\hat{y}_{t,h} = \frac{1}{B} \sum_{b=1}^{B} t_{b,h}(x), \tag{10}$$

where B is the number of bootstrap samples of the training set, t_b is an individual fitted tree, and x are the values from the test set. For the evaluation, we use $B = 100$.

The fifth advanced method is the Support Vector Regression (SVR) and represents another statistical learning method. It determines a regression plane with the smallest distance to all data points used for the training. The data points closest to the regression plane on both sides are the so-called support vectors [17]. We apply the SVR with a linear kernel, $C = 1.0$, and $\epsilon = 1.0$.

The sixth advanced method is the XGBoost Regressor, which represents a more complex machine learning method. It iteratively creates regression trees and uses gradient descent to minimize a regularized objective function [12].

All introduced forecasting methods use the historical values of the selected power time series that contains inserted synthetic anomalies. The advanced methods also consider calendar information as input (see Table 5 in Appendix 3 for more details). While the naive methods directly use the mentioned historical load values, all other methods obtain the normalized load of the last 24 h and the calendar information for the first value to be predicted.

Methods Applied in Detection Strategy. For the detection strategy that can use the information on the detected anomalies for the forecast, we apply the forecasting methods introduced for the raw and compensation strategies. This way, we also evaluate the detection method using forecasting methods with different learning assumptions. However, we adapt the previously introduced methods as follows: We change the Last Day Forecast so that it uses the value from a week ago in the case of a detected anomaly. Similarly, we modify the Last Week Forecast so that it uses the corresponding value of the second to last week as the forecast value if the value to be predicted is a detected anomaly. In accordance with the detection strategy, all other forecasting methods obtain the information on the detected anomalies of the last 24 h as additional features.

Methods Applied in Anomaly-Free Baseline Strategy. To calculate the anomaly-free baseline strategy for the data containing synthetic anomalies, we apply all forecasting methods described for the raw and compensation strategies to the same data but without inserted synthetic anomalies. These forecasting methods obtain the inputs in the way described for the raw and compensation strategies.

Train-Test Split. Regardless of the considered strategy, we use the same train-test split for all evaluated forecasting methods. Each forecasting method is trained on

80% of the available data and tested on the remaining 20%. For all strategies, the available data is the selected time series without the first 96 data points. When calculating the anomaly-free baseline strategy for this data, we use the same period of time, i.e., all values except the first 96 data points.

4.6 Experimental Setting

For evaluation, we use evaluation metrics in a defined hard- and software setting.

Metrics. In order to evaluate the proposed strategies for managing anomalies in energy time series forecasting, we examine the accuracy of the obtained forecasts compared to the data without inserted synthetic anomalies using two metrics.

The first metric is the commonly used root mean squared error (RMSE). Given N data points to be predicted, it is defined as

$$\mathrm{RMSE} = \sqrt{\frac{1}{N} \sum_{t=1}^{N} (y_t - \hat{y}_t)^2}, \tag{11}$$

with the actual value y_t of the anomaly-free time series and the forecast value $\hat{y}_t$. Due to the squared differences considered, the RMSE is sensitive to outliers.

Therefore, we also consider a second commonly used metric, the mean absolute error (MAE), which is robust to outliers. It is defined as

$$\mathrm{MAE} = \frac{1}{N} \sum_{t=1}^{N} |y_t - \hat{y}_t| \tag{12}$$

with N data points to be forecast, the actual value y_t of the anomaly-free time series, and the forecast value $\hat{y}_t$.

Hard- and Software. In order to obtain comparable results, we use the same hardware throughout the evaluation and implement all evaluated strategies and used anomaly detection, anomaly compensation, and forecasting methods in Python (see Appendix 4 for more details).

4.7 Results

To examine the presented strategies, we compare their accuracy on the selected time series with the described inserted synthetic anomalies and using the described anomaly detection, anomaly compensation, and forecasting methods. After presenting the results of this comparison for the technical faults and unusual consumption, we show a part of the selected time series as an example of how the different strategies work and perform.

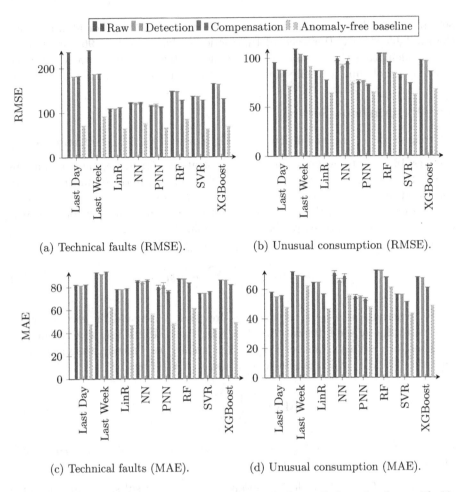

(a) Technical faults (RMSE).   (b) Unusual consumption (RMSE).

(c) Technical faults (MAE).   (d) Unusual consumption (MAE).

Fig. 4. The accuracy of the eight forecasting methods applied to the data with 20 synthetic anomalies of each type from the technical faults and unusual consumption. For each forecasting method introduced in Sect. 4.5, the bars indicate the average RMSE or MAE for the raw strategy, detection strategy, compensation strategy, and anomaly-free baseline strategy. The error bars show the observed standard deviation across all runs on the test data set. Note that the anomaly-free baseline strategy generally performs best because it uses data that does not contain inserted synthetic anomalies.

Comparison. For the comparison, we apply all proposed strategies to the selected data with synthetic anomalies from the technical faults and unusual consumption. For both groups of anomalies, we insert 20 anomalies of each type belonging to this group. Figure 4a and 4c show the resulting RMSE and MAE for the technical faults and Fig. 4b and 4d for the unusual consumption. For each considered forecasting method, the bars indicate the average RMSE or MAE for the raw strategy, the detection strategy, the compensation strategy, and the anomaly-free baseline strategy. The error bars show the observed standard deviation across all runs on the test data set.

Technical Faults. Regarding the technical faults, all considered forecasting methods except the Last Day Forecast, the Last Week Forecast, the LinR, and the NN have both the lowest RMSE and MAE when using the compensation strategy. The SVR has only the lowest RMSE with the compensation strategy but the lowest MAE with the raw strategy. Even though the difference to the compensation strategy is only small, the Last Day Forecast, the Last Week Forecast, and the NN achieve their lowest RMSE and MAE using the detection strategy and the LinR with the raw strategy. Moreover, the difference between the RMSE when using the compensation strategy and the RMSE using the second best strategy is largest for the XGBoost Regressor, the RF Regressor, and the SVR. Similarly, the difference between the MAE when using the compensation strategy and the MAE using the second best strategy is largest for the XGBoost Regressor, the PNN, and the RF Regressor. Additionally, we see the largest difference between the RMSEs in the use of the raw, detection, and compensation strategies for the Last Day Forecast and the Last Week Forecast, followed by the XGBoost Regressor. With respect to the MAE, we observe the largest differences for the PNN, the XGBoost Regressor, and RF Regressor.

Compared to the anomaly-free baseline strategy, the RMSE of all forecasting methods, especially of the Last Day Forecast, the Last Week Forecast, the SVR, and the XGBoost Regressor, is also noticeably greater for all three strategies. Concerning the MAE, we also see large differences between the anomaly-free baseline strategy and the three other strategies for all forecasting methods but especially the Last Day Forecast, the XGBoost Regressor, the LinR, and the SVR. Considering the actual accuracy, the LinR, the PNN, and the NN form the group of forecasting methods that achieve the lowest RMSE and the SVR, the PNN, and the LinR the group with the lowest MAE.

Unusual Consumption. For the unusual consumption, all considered forecasting methods except the NN achieve both the lowest RMSE and MAE using the compensation strategy. The NN has its lowest RMSE with the detection strategy. The Last Day Forecast also has its lowest RMSE using the compensation strategy but its lowest MAE using the detection strategy. The difference in the RMSE and MAE between using the compensation strategy and using the second best strategy is large for the XGBoost Regressor, the LinR, the RF Regressor, the SVR, and small for the NN, the PNN, the Last Day Forecast, and the Last Week Forecast. Moreover, we observe the largest differences between the RMSEs for using the raw, detection, and compensation strategies for the LinR, the RF Regressor, and the SVR. The largest observed differences in the MAE of these three strategies are for the LinR, the XGBoost Regressor, and the NN.

In comparison to the anomaly-free baseline strategy, the RMSE and MAE of all forecasting methods is clearly larger for all three strategies. With regard to their actual accuracy, the PNN achieves the lowest RMSE, followed by the SVR and the LinR. Considering the accuracy in terms of the MAE, the SVR, the PNN, and the Last Day Forecast achieve the lowest MAE.

Example. To demonstrate how the different strategies work and perform, we finally look at a part of the time series used for the evaluation in more detail. Using three days of this time series from June 2014, Fig. 5 illustrates an inserted synthetic anomaly, how this anomaly is detected, and what the resulting forecasts of the different strategies look like.

More specifically, Fig. 5a illustrates the selected original time series, which we assume to be anomaly-free, and the time series with inserted synthetic anomalies. In the latter, we observe an anomaly of type 8 which increases the load values for about one of the three days. In addition to these two time series, Fig. 5b shows the data points of the time series with inserted synthetic anomalies that are detected as anomalous by the LOF, which is the applied anomaly detection method. We observe that the LOF, detects various but not all data points of the inserted synthetic anomaly as anomalous. Figure 5c then illustrates how these detected anomalous data points are compensated using the Prophet-based imputation method. With regard to the compensated detected anomalous data points, our observation is that compensated values are all close to the original anomaly-free time series.

Finally, Fig. 5d additionally shows the multi-step 24 h-ahead forecasts of the four different strategies using the PNN and given the previously described information. We observe that all strategies result in different forecasts: The forecast of the compensation strategy, that is based on the time series with compensated synthetic anomalies introduced in Fig. 5c, is closest to the forecast of the anomaly-free baseline strategy. Moreover, the forecast of the detection strategy, that uses the information on the detected anomalous data points introduced in Fig. 5b, is closer to the forecast of the anomaly-free baseline strategy than the forecast of the raw strategy.

5   Discussion

In this section, we first discuss the results from the evaluation of the proposed strategies for managing anomalies in energy time series forecasting, before reviewing the evaluation regarding its limitations and insights.

In the comparison of the accuracy of the proposed strategies, we observe that using the compensation strategy yields the lowest RMSE and MAE for most forecasting methods and both groups of anomalies. However, while the results are generally consistent across both accuracy metrics, some forecasting methods benefit from the two other strategies with respect to the RMSE, the MAE, or both: The NN and the Last Day Forecast perform best using the detection strategy for the technical faults and unusual consumption, the Last Week Forecast using the detection strategy for only the technical faults, and the LinR and the SVR using the raw strategy for the technical faults. However, it is worth noting that the compensation strategy is often the second-best strategy in these cases with similar accuracy, so it could serve as a default strategy.

Nevertheless, using the compensation and also the detection strategy is associated with additional computational costs because of the necessary anomaly

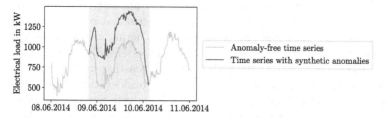

(a) Anomaly-free time series and time series with inserted synthetic anomalies.

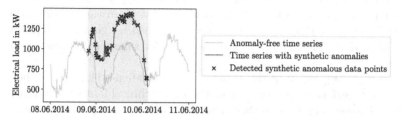

(b) Anomaly-free time series, time series with inserted synthetic anomalies, and the anomalous data points of the synthetic anomaly that are detected using the LOF.

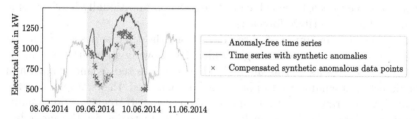

(c) Anomaly-free time series, time series with inserted synthetic anomalies, and the detected anomalous data points of the synthetic anomaly that are compensated using the Prophet-based imputation method.

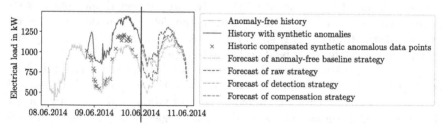

(d) Forecasts of four all strategies using the PNN, the anomaly-free history, the history with synthetic anomalies, and the historic compensated synthetic anomalous data points.

Fig. 5. Three exemplary days of the power time series used for the evaluation, where a synthetic anomaly of type 8 is inserted, detected, and compensated. Finally, the inserted anomaly is dealt with differently in the forecast depending on the strategy.

detection and anomaly compensation. In case of the anomaly detection, the computational costs also include the creation of the latent space representation that we use to enhance the detection performance. Whether the improvement in accuracy over the raw strategy of using the data essentially as-is justifies this additional computational cost depends on the forecasting method and the anomalies contained in the data and requires careful consideration. From these results, one could infer that applying strategies that actively handle anomalies, namely the compensation and the detection strategies, is generally beneficial and, more specifically, that using the compensation strategy is mostly benefi-cial. Based on this inference, a best practice could be to apply the compensation strategy in energy time series forecasting. Additionally, given the nature of the data used for the evaluation, we assume that the gained insights also apply to similar periodic data, for example, from the areas of solar power generation, mobility, and sales.

Moreover, the comparison of the accuracy of all strategies shows that there is no clearly best-performing forecasting method for technical faults and unusual consumption. Instead, there are rather groups of similarly well-performing fore-casting methods, for example, the LinR and the PNN for the technical faults and the PNN and the SVR for the unusual consumption. Additionally, regard-ing their actual accuracy, we observe that even naive forecasting methods can provide reasonable forecasts, which can serve as a computationally light baseline when looking for competitive forecasts.

Furthermore, the example of three days from the time series used for the evaluation illustrates how the strategies differ. By showing an inserted synthetic anomaly, the data points of this anomaly that are detected as anomalous, and how the detected anomalous data points are compensated, the example presents the inputs for the raw, detection, and compensation strategies. Additionally, the example includes the resulting forecasts of all strategies for the next day. Thereby, the influence of the different inputs on the forecast accuracy of the dif-ferent strategies becomes comprehensible. Considering the results of the example, we also observe that the compensation strategy provides the comparatively best forecast although it is dependent on the only partly detected and compensated inserted synthetic anomaly. With regard to the detection performance of the detection method, however, it should be noted that anomaly types of unusual consumption are difficult to be detected from experience.

Nevertheless, we note that these results are associated with certain limi-tations. One limitation is that we only evaluate the proposed strategies with the selected anomaly detection, anomaly compensation, and forecasting meth-ods since the performance of the proposed strategies highly depends on these methods. For example, forecasting methods vary by design in their sensitivity to anomalies and detection methods may not detect all anomalous data points. While we believe that the different selected methods are a representative sample of existing methods, it would be interesting to extend the evaluation to fur-ther anomaly detection, anomaly compensation, and forecasting methods. The performance of the selected methods additionally depends on the used hyperparameters. Although the hyperparameters used are carefully selected, their optimal choice could be investigated. Moreover, the reported results are based on the selected data. Although we perceive the selected time series based on our domain knowledge as comparatively anomaly-free, it could contain anomalies that influence the results. For example, the contained anomalies could worsen the results of the raw strategy and improve the results of the detection and compensation strategies. However, in this case, the relative comparison of the strategies would remain the same. Nevertheless, future work could examine more closely whether anomalies are contained and affect the results. In addition to contained anomalies, the results also depend on the inserted anomalies and might change with different numbers and types of inserted anomalies. Future work could thus also examine the influence of the inserted anomalies on the results. Furthermore, the data used for the evaluation represents the electrical power consumption on a client level. In future work, it might, therefore, be interesting to use other data to investigate how the aggregation level of the data influences the results.

Overall, we conclude from the performed evaluation that the compensation strategy is generally beneficial as it mostly allows for better or at least similar forecasting results as the other evaluated strategies when the input data contains anomalies. By favoring precise forecasts, the compensation strategy provides a means for appropriately managing anomalies in forecasts using energy time series, which could also be beneficial for automated machine learning forecasting.

6   Conclusion

In the present paper, we evaluate three general strategies for managing anomalies in automated energy time series forecasting, namely the raw, the detection, and the compensation strategy. For the evaluation, we apply a representative selection of forecasting methods to real-world data containing inserted synthetic anomalies in order to compare these strategies regarding the obtained forecast accuracy. We also present an example of how these strategies work and perform.

Despite requiring additional computational costs, the compensation strategy is generally beneficial as it mostly outperforms the detection and the raw strategy when the input data contains anomalies.

Given the proposed strategies for managing anomalies in energy time series, future work could address several follow-up questions. For example, future work could verify the results by applying other data including labeled data, anomaly detection methods, and anomaly compensation methods. Similarly, future work could evaluate the proposed strategies with further forecasting methods. Furthermore, future work could integrate the proposed strategies into existing approaches for automated machine learning to include them in the optimization problem of finding the best forecast for a given data set.

Acknowledgments. This project is funded by the Helmholtz Association's Initiative and Networking Fund through Helmholtz AI and the Helmholtz Association under the Program "Energy System Design". The authors thank Nicole Ludwig, Benedikt Heidrich, and Kaleb Phipps for their valuable input during the work on this project.

Appendix 1: Inserted Synthetic Anomalies

For the evaluation, we insert anomalies of the two anomaly groups used in [44], namely technical faults in the metering infrastructure and unusual consumption. For both groups, we consider four types of anomalies each. Each anomaly $\hat{p}_{j,i}$ of type j has a start index i and is inserted in the given power time series $P = p_1, p_2, ...p_N$ with length N.

Technical Faults

The considered technical faults comprise the anomalies of types 1 to 4 taken from [45]. Figure 6 shows an example of each of these types, which we define in the following.

Anomaly Type 1

$$\hat{p}_{1,i+n} = \begin{cases} -1 \cdot \mathrm{mean}(P) + r_s \cdot \mathrm{std}(P), & n = 0 \\ 0, & 0 < n < l - 1 \\ \sum_{t=1}^{i+l-1} p_t, & n = l - 1, \end{cases} \tag{13}$$

where the length $l \sim \mathcal{U}_{[5,24]}$ and the random scaling factor $r_s = 2 + r \cdot 3$ with $r \sim \mathcal{U}_{[0,1]}$.

Anomaly Type 2

$$\hat{p}_{2,i+n} = \begin{cases} 0, & 0 \leq n < l - 1 \\ \sum_{t=i}^{i+l-1} p_t, & n = l - 1, \end{cases} \tag{14}$$

where the length $l \sim \mathcal{U}_{[5,24]}$.

Anomaly Type 3

$$\hat{p}_{3,i} = -r_s \cdot \mathrm{mean}(P), \tag{15}$$

where the random scaling factor $r_s = 0.01 + r \cdot 3.99$ with $r \sim \mathcal{U}_{[0,1]}$.

Anomaly Type 4

$$\hat{p}_{4,i} = r \cdot \mathrm{mean}(P), \tag{16}$$

where the random scaling factor $r_s = 3 + r \cdot 5$ with $r \sim \mathcal{U}_{[0,1]}$.

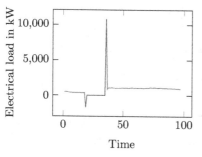

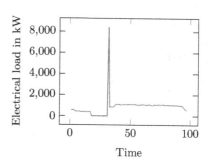

(a) Anomaly type 1: negative power spike followed by zero values and positive spike.

(b) Anomaly type 2: zero power values followed by a positive spike.

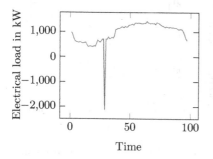

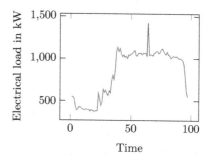

(c) Anomaly type 3: negative power spike.

(d) Anomaly type 4: positive power spike.

Fig. 6. Examples of the anomaly types 1 to 4 from the technical faults taken from [45] that we insert as synthetic anomalies into the selected data. The anomalies are plotted in red. Note that the anomalies of types 3 and 4 actually have a length of one but are marked together with their previous value to be recognizable. (Color figure online)

Unusual Consumption

The considered unusual consumption comprise the anomalies of types 5 to 8 taken from [44]. Figure 7 shows an example of each of these types, which we define in the following.

Anomaly Type 5

$$\hat{p}_{5,i+n} = p_i - r \cdot p_{\min}, \quad 0 < n < l - 1, \tag{17}$$

where the length $l \sim \mathcal{U}_{[48,144]}$, the random scaling factor $r \sim \mathcal{U}_{[0.3,0.8]}$, and $p_{\min} = \min\{p_i, p_{i+1}, \ldots, p_{i+l-1}\}$.

Anomaly Type 6

$$\hat{p}_{6,i+n} = p_i + r \cdot p_{\min}, \quad 0 < n < l - 1, \tag{18}$$

where the length $l \sim \mathcal{U}_{[48,144]}$, the random scaling factor $r \sim \mathcal{U}_{[0.5,1]}$, and $p_{\min} = \min\{p_i, p_{i+1}, \ldots, p_{i+l-1}\}$.

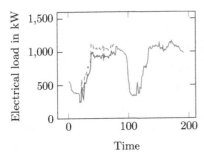

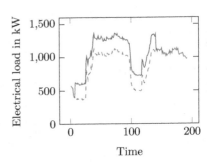

(a) Anomaly type 5: abrupt small temporary reduction in the power values.

(b) Anomaly type 6: abrupt small temporary increase in the power values.

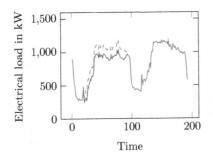

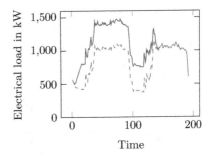

(c) Anomaly type 7: small temporary reduction in the power values with a gradual start and end.

(d) Anomaly type 8: small temporary increase in the power values with a gradual start and end.

Fig. 7. Examples of the anomaly types 5 to 8 from the unusual consumption taken from [44] that we insert as synthetic anomalies into the selected data. The anomalies are plotted in red. (Color figure online)

Anomaly Type 7

$$
\hat{p}_{7,i} = \begin{cases} p_i - r \cdot p_{\min} \cdot \frac{l}{10} \cdot i, & 0 < n < \frac{l}{10} \\ p_i - r \cdot p_{\min}, & \frac{l}{10} \le n \le 1 - \frac{l}{10} \\ p_i - r \cdot p_{\min} \cdot \frac{l}{10} \cdot (1 - i), & 1 - \frac{l}{10} < n < l - 1, \end{cases} \tag{19}
$$

where the length $l \sim \mathcal{U}_{[48,144]}$, the random scaling factor $r \sim \mathcal{U}_{[0.3,0.8]}$, and $p_{\min} = \min\{p_i, p_{i+1}, \ldots, p_{i+l-1}\}$.

Anomaly Type 8

$$
\hat{p}_{8,i} = \begin{cases} p_i + r \cdot p_{\min} \cdot \frac{l}{10} \cdot i, & 0 < n < \frac{l}{10} \\ p_i + r \cdot p_{\min}, & \frac{l}{10} \le n \le 1 - \frac{l}{10} \\ p_i + r \cdot p_{\min} \cdot \frac{l}{10} \cdot (1 - i), & 1 - \frac{l}{10} < n < l - 1, \end{cases} \tag{20}
$$

where the length $l \sim \mathcal{U}_{[48,144]}$, the random scaling factor $r \sim \mathcal{U}_{[0.5,1]}$, and $p_{\min} = \min\{p_i, p_{i+1}, \ldots, p_{i+l-1}\}$.

Appendix 2: Applied Anomaly Detection

Applied Latent Space-Based Anomaly Detection. To enhance their detection performance, we apply the selected anomaly detection methods to the latent space representation of the selected data which we create by a trained generative method (see Fig. 8).

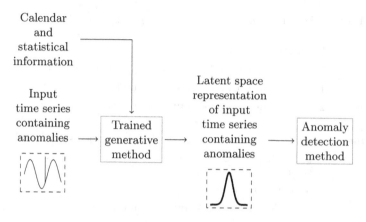

Fig. 8. According to the selected anomaly detection approach from [44], a trained generative method creates the latent space data representation of an input time series containing anomalies. The latent space data representation then serves as input to an anomaly detection method.

Architecture of Generative Methods. For our evaluation, we use the conditional Invertible Neural Network (cINN) [6] and the conditional Variational Autoencoder (cVAE) [41] as described in [22, 44] and as detailed in Tables 1 and 4.

Table 1. Architecture of the used cINN [44].

Element	Description
Number of blocks	10
Layers per block	Glow coupling layer and random permutation
Subnetwork in each block	Fully connected NN (see Table 2)
Conditioning network	Fully connected NN (see Table 3)

Training of Generative Methods. The training of the used cINN and cVAE follows the training described in [44]: We apply the unsupervised cINN and cVAE to the data with inserted synthetic anomalies under the assumption of 10% of the data points are anomalies by setting the contamination parameter of the unsupervised cINN and cVAE to 0.1. Both generative methods obtain standardized data points of the selected time series as samples with a size of 96. Both generative methods also use the mean of the considered time series sample as statistical information as well as the hour of the day, the month of the year, and the weekday as calendar information.

Table 2. Details of the subnetwork in the used cINN [44].

Layer	Description
Input	[Output of previous coupling layer, conditional information]
1	Dense 32 neurons; activation: tanh
2	Dense horizon neurons; activation: linear

Table 3. Details of the conditioning network in the used cINN [44].

Layer	Description
Input	[Calendar information, statistical information]
1	Dense 8 neurons; activation: tanh
2	Dense 4 neurons; activation: linear

Table 4. Architecture of the encoder and decoder in the used cVAE [44].

(a) Encoder	
Layer	Description
Input	[Normal data, conditional information]
1	Dense 64 neurons; activation: tanh
2	Dense 32 neurons; activation: tanh
3	μ: dense latent dimension; activation: linear
4	σ: dense latent dimension; activation: linear

(b) Decoder	
Layer	Description
Input	[Latent data, conditional information]
1	Dense 32 neurons; activation: tanh
2	Dense 64 neurons; activation: tanh
3	Dense horizon neurons; activation: linear

Appendix 3: Applied Forecasting Methods

Table 5. Overview of the used calendar information.

Calendar information	Implementation
Weekday	Boolean
Workdays (Monday to Friday)	Boolean
Hour of the day	$\sin(2 \cdot \pi \cdot \text{hour}/24)$ and $\cos(2 \cdot \pi \cdot \text{hour}/24)$
Day of the month	$\sin(2 \cdot \pi \cdot \text{day}/\text{days of the month})$
Month of the year	$\sin(2 \cdot \pi \cdot \text{month}/12)$ and $\cos(2 \cdot \pi \cdot \text{month}/12)$

Table 6. Details of the applied NN.

Layer	Description
Input	[Load data, encoded calendar information]
1	Dense 256 neurons; activation: relu
2	Dense 128 neurons; activation: relu
Output	Dense 96 neuron; activation: linear

Appendix 4: Hard- and Software

Hardware. The used hardware is an HPC system with two Intel Xeon Gold 5118 CPUs and with 256 GB RAM.

Software. For the anomaly detection using the respective latent space data representation created by the selected cINN or cVAE, we apply the implementation described in [44]. It uses FrEIA[4] and PyTorch[5] [34] for the cINN, PyTorch [34] for the cVAE, Keras[6] [15] for the VAE, and scikit-learn[7] [35] for the LOF.

For the anomaly compensation, we apply the implementation of the Prophet-based method described in [48] that is based on the available Prophet implementation[8] [42].

For the forecasting methods, we use Keras for the NN and scikit-learn for the LinR, SVR, and RF Regressor. Additionally, we apply the available implementation[9] [12] for the XGBoost Regressor, and adapt the available implementation of the PNN[10] [21] to work without weather data.

We finally use pyWATTS[11] [20] to implement the proposed strategies and to automate their evaluation.

References

1. Ahmed, N.K., Atiya, A.F., El Gayar, N., El-Shishiny, H.: An empirical comparison of machine learning models for time series forecasting. Economet. Rev. **29**(5–6), 594–621 (2010). https://doi.org/10.1080/07474938.2010.481556
2. Akouemo, H.N., Povinelli, R.J.: Probabilistic anomaly detection in natural gas time series data. Int. J. Forecast. **32**(3), 948–956 (2016). https://doi.org/10.1016/j.ijforecast.2015.06.001

---

[4] https://github.com/VLL-HD/FrEIA.
[5] https://pytorch.org/.
[6] https://keras.io/.
[7] https://scikit-learn.org/.
[8] https://facebook.github.io/prophet/.
[9] https://xgboost.ai/.
[10] https://github.com/benHeid/Profile-Neural-Network.
[11] https://github.com/KIT-IAI/pyWATTS.

3. Akouemo, H.N., Povinelli, R.J.: Data improving in time series using ARX and ANN models. IEEE Trans. Power Syst. **32**(5), 3352–3359 (2017). https://doi.org/10.1109/TPWRS.2017.2656939
4. Alahakoon, D., Yu, X.: Smart electricity meter data intelligence for future energy systems: a survey. IEEE Trans. Industr. Inf. **12**(1), 425–436 (2016). https://doi.org/10.1109/TII.2015.2414355
5. Alasadi, S.A., Bhaya, W.S.: Review of data preprocessing techniques in data mining. J. Eng. Appl. Sci. **12**(16), 4102–4107 (2017). https://doi.org/10.36478/jeasci.2017.4102.4107
6. Ardizzone, L., Lüth, C., Kruse, J., Rother, C., Köthe, U.: Guided image generation with conditional invertible neural networks. arXiv:1907.02392 (2019)
7. Breiman, L.: Random forests. Mach. Learn. **45**, 5–32 (2001). https://doi.org/10.1023/A:1010933404324
8. Breunig, M.M., Kriegel, H.P., Ng, R.T., Sander, J.: LOF: identifying density-based local outliers. In: Proceedings of the 2000 ACM SIGMOD International Conference on Management of Data, pp. 93–104. ACM (2000). https://doi.org/10.1145/342009.335388
9. Chakhchoukh, Y., Panciatici, P., Mili, L.: Electric load forecasting based on statistical robust methods. IEEE Trans. Power Syst. **26**(3), 982–991 (2011). https://doi.org/10.1109/TPWRS.2010.2080325
10. Chandola, V., Banerjee, A., Kumar, V.: Anomaly detection: a survey. ACM Comput. Surv. **41**(3), 15:1–15:58 (2009). https://doi.org/10.1145/1541880.1541882
11. Charlton, N., Singleton, C.: A refined parametric model for short term load forecasting. Int. J. Forecast. **30**(2), 364–368 (2014). https://doi.org/10.1016/j.ijforecast.2013.07.003
12. Chen, T., Guestrin, C.: XGBoost: a scalable tree boosting system. In: Proceedings of the ACM SIGKDD International Conference on Knowledge Discovery and Data Mining, pp. 785–794. ACM (2016). https://doi.org/10.1145/2939672.2939785
13. Chen, W., Zhou, K., Yang, S., Wu, C.: Data quality of electricity consumption data in a smart grid environment. Renew. Sustain. Energy Rev. **75**, 98–105 (2017). https://doi.org/10.1016/j.rser.2016.10.054
14. Chen, X., Kang, C., Tong, X., Xia, Q., Yang, J.: Improving the accuracy of bus load forecasting by a two-stage bad data identification method. IEEE Trans. Power Syst. **29**(4), 1634–1641 (2014). https://doi.org/10.1109/TPWRS.2014.2298463
15. Chollet, F., et al.: Keras (2015). https://keras.io
16. Dannecker, L.: Energy Time Series Forecasting. Springer Fachmedien, Wiesbaden (2015). https://doi.org/10.1007/978-3-658-11039-0
17. Drucker, H., Burges, C.J.C., Kaufman, L., Smola, A., Vapnik, V.: Support vector regression machines. In: Mozer, M.C., Jordan, M., Petsche, T. (eds.) Advances in Neural Information Processing Systems, vol. 9. MIT Press, Cambridge (1996)
18. Dua, D., Graff, C.: UCI machine learning repository (2019). https://archive.ics.uci.edu/ml
19. Fan, C., Chen, M., Wang, X., Wang, J., Huang, B.: A review on data preprocessing techniques toward efficient and reliable knowledge discovery from building operational data. Front. Energy Res. **9**, 652801 (2021). https://doi.org/10.3389/fenrg.2021.652801
20. Heidrich, B., et al.: pyWATTS: Python workflow automation tool for time series. arXiv:2106.10157 (2021)

21. Heidrich, B., Turowski, M., Ludwig, N., Mikut, R., Hagenmeyer, V.: Forecasting energy time series with profile neural networks. In: The Eleventh ACM International Conference on Future Energy Systems (e-Energy '20), pp. 220–230 (2020). https://doi.org/10.1145/3396851.3397683

22. Heidrich, B., et al.: Controlling non-stationarity and periodicities in time series generation using conditional invertible neural networks. Appl. Intell. **53**, 8826–8843 (2023). https://doi.org/10.1007/s10489-022-03742-7

23. Jiao, J., Tang, Z., Zhang, P., Yue, M., Yan, J.: Cyberattack-resilient load forecasting with adaptive robust regression. Int. J. Forecast. **38**(3), 910–919 (2022). https://doi.org/10.1016/j.ijforecast.2021.06.009

24. Jokar, P., Arianpoo, N., Leung, V.C.M.: Electricity theft detection in AMI using customers' consumption patterns. IEEE Trans. Smart Grid **7**(1), 216–226 (2016). https://doi.org/10.1109/TSG.2015.2425222

25. Kingma, D.P., Ba, J.L.: Adam: a method for stochastic optimization. In: 3rd International Conference on Learning Representations (ICLR 2015) (2015)

26. Kingma, D.P., Welling, M.: Auto-encoding variational Bayes. arXiv:1312.6114v10 (2014)

27. Luo, J., Hong, T., Fang, S.C.: Benchmarking robustness of load forecasting models under data integrity attacks. Int. J. Forecast. **34**(1), 89–104 (2018). https://doi.org/10.1016/j.ijforecast.2017.08.004

28. Luo, J., Hong, T., Fang, S.C.: Robust regression models for load forecasting. IEEE Trans. Smart Grid **10**(5), 5397–5404 (2018). https://doi.org/10.1109/TSG.2018.2881562

29. Luo, J., Hong, T., Gao, Z., Fang, S.C.: A robust support vector regression model for electric load forecasting. Int. J. Forecast. **39**(2), 1005–1020 (2023). https://doi.org/10.1016/j.ijforecast.2022.04.001

30. Luo, J., Hong, T., Yue, M.: Real-time anomaly detection for very short-term load forecasting. J. Mod. Power Syst. Clean Energy **6**(2), 235–243 (2018). https://doi.org/10.1007/s40565-017-0351-7

31. Mitchell, T.M.: Machine Learning. McGraw-Hill, New York (1997)

32. Nordahl, C., Persson, M., Grahn, H.: Detection of residents' abnormal behaviour by analysing energy consumption of individual households. In: 2017 IEEE International Conference on Data Mining Workshops (ICDMW), pp. 729–738. IEEE (2017). https://doi.org/10.1109/ICDMW.2017.101

33. Park, S., Jung, S., Jung, S., Rho, S., Hwang, E.: Sliding window-based LightGBM model for electric load forecasting using anomaly repair. J. Supercomput. **77**(11), 12857–12878 (2021). https://doi.org/10.1007/s11227-021-03787-4

34. Paszke, A., et al.: PyTorch: an imperative style, high-performance deep learning library. In: Wallach, H., Larochelle, H., Beygelzimer, A., D'Alché-Buc, F., Fox, E., Garnett, R. (eds.) Advances in Neural Information Processing Systems, vol. 32 (2019)

35. Pedregosa, F., et al.: Scikit-learn: machine learning in Python. J. Mach. Learn. Res. **12**, 2825–2830 (2011)

36. Quintana, M., Stoeckmann, T., Park, J.Y., Turowski, M., Hagenmeyer, V., Miller, C.: ALDI++: automatic and parameter-less discord and outlier detection for building energy load profiles. Energy Build. **265**, 112096 (2022). https://doi.org/10.1016/j.enbuild.2022.112096

37. Ranjan, K.G., Prusty, B.R., Jena, D.: Review of preprocessing methods for univariate volatile time-series in power system applications. Electr. Power Syst. Res. **191**, 106885 (2021). https://doi.org/10.1016/j.epsr.2020.106885

38. Rodrigues, F., Trindade, A.: Load forecasting through functional clustering and ensemble learning. Knowl. Inf. Syst. **57**(1), 229–244 (2018). https://doi.org/10.1007/s10115-018-1169-y

39. Rossi, B., Chren, S.: Smart grids data analysis: a systematic mapping study. IEEE Trans. Industr. Inf. **16**(6), 3619–3639 (2020). https://doi.org/10.1109/TII.2019.2954098

40. Seem, J.E.: Using intelligent data analysis to detect abnormal energy consumption in buildings. Energy Build. **39**(1), 52–58 (2007). https://doi.org/10.1016/j.enbuild.2006.03.033

41. Sohn, K., Yan, X., Lee, H.: Learning structured output representation using deep conditional generative models. In: Cortes, C., Lawrence, N., Lee, D., Sugiyama, M., Garnett, R. (eds.) Advances in Neural Information Processing Systems, vol. 28, pp. 3483–3491 (2015)

42. Taylor, S.J., Letham, B.: Forecasting at scale. Am. Stat. **72**(1), 37–45 (2018). https://doi.org/10.1080/00031305.2017.1380080

43. Teng, S.Y., Máša, V., Touš, M., Vondra, M., Lam, H.L., Stehlík, P.: Waste-to-energy forecasting and real-time optimization: an anomaly-aware approach. Renew. Energy **181**, 142–155 (2022). https://doi.org/10.1016/j.renene.2021.09.026

44. Turowski, M., et al.: Enhancing anomaly detection methods for energy time series using latent space data representations. In: The Thirteenth ACM International Conference on Future Energy Systems (e-Energy '22), pp. 208–227. ACM (2022). https://doi.org/10.1145/3538637.3538851

45. Turowski, M., et al.: Modeling and generating synthetic anomalies for energy and power time series. In: The Thirteenth ACM International Conference on Future Energy Systems (e-Energy '22), pp. 471–484. ACM (2022). https://doi.org/10.1145/3538637.3539760

46. Wang, L., et al.: Point and contextual anomaly detection in building load profiles of a university campus. In: 2020 IEEE PES Innovative Smart Grid Technologies Europe (ISGT-Europe), pp. 11–15 (2020). https://doi.org/10.1109/ISGT-Europe47291.2020.9248792

47. Wang, Y., Chen, Q., Hong, T., Kang, C.: Review of smart meter data analytics: applications, methodologies, and challenges. IEEE Trans. Smart Grid **10**(3), 3125–3148 (2019). https://doi.org/10.1109/TSG.2018.2818167

48. Weber, M., Turowski, M., Çakmak, H.K., Mikut, R., Kühnapfel, U., Hagenmeyer, V.: Data-driven copy-paste imputation for energy time series. IEEE Trans. Smart Grid **12**(6), 5409–5419 (2021). https://doi.org/10.1109/TSG.2021.3101831

49. Werbos, P.J.: Beyond regression: new tools for prediction and analysis in the behavioral sciences. Ph.D. thesis, Harvard University (1974)

50. Xie, J., Hong, T.: GEFCom2014 probabilistic electric load forecasting: an integrated solution with forecast combination and residual simulation. Int. J. Forecast. **32**(3), 1012–1016 (2016). https://doi.org/10.1016/j.ijforecast.2015.11.005

51. Yue, M., Hong, T., Wang, J.: Descriptive analytics-based anomaly detection for cybersecure load forecasting. IEEE Trans. Smart Grid **10**(6), 5964–5974 (2019). https://doi.org/10.1109/TSG.2019.2894334

52. Zhang, Y., Lin, F., Wang, K.: Robustness of short-term wind power forecasting against false data injection attacks. Energies **13**(15) (2020). https://doi.org/10.3390/en13153780

53. Zheng, R., Gu, J., Jin, Z., Peng, H., Zhu, Y.: Load forecasting under data corruption based on anomaly detection and combined robust regression. Int. Trans. Electr. Energy Syst. **30**(7), e12103 (2020). https://doi.org/10.1002/2050-7038.12103

54. Zhou, Y., Ding, Z., Wen, Q., Wang, Y.: Robust load forecasting towards adversarial attacks via Bayesian learning. IEEE Trans. Power Syst. **8950** (2022). https://doi.org/10.1109/TPWRS.2022.3175252

Illuminating Metaheuristic Performance Using Vortex MAP-Elites for Risk-Based Energy Resource Management

José Almeida⬮, Fernando Lezama⬮, João Soares^(✉)⬮, and Zita Vale⬮

GECAD, LASI, Polytechnic of Porto, 4249 -015 Porto, Portugal
{jorga,flz,jan,zav}@isep.ipp.pt

Abstract. With the current state of the electrical power system, regarding the increase of renewable generation integration and electric vehicle penetration to reduce gas emissions, the energy resource management problem becomes extremely complex to optimize to the significant dimensionality and uncertainty. Metaheuristic optimization algorithms become efficient methods since they guarantee a balance between optimal and practical solutions, but they lack explainability and are treated as black-box techniques. In this work, we introduce an improved version of the Multi-dimensional Archive of Phenotypic Elites (MAP-Elites) algorithm incorporating the Vortex Search to generate new candidate solutions in the iterative process. The VS MAP-Elites is then used to optimize the energy resource management problem for a 13-bus distribution network considering risk analysis due to the existence of extreme scenarios in the day-ahead operation. Two different behaviors of the problem were considered, namely demand response ratio and renewable ratio, and the effect that they have on metaheuristic performance was analyzed through the visualization of the elite archive. Results showed that VS MAP-Elites achieved better cost results compared to MAP-Elites, around a 25 % reduction, since it was able to diversify the search space finding better solutions for the considered problem characteristics.

Keywords: Energy resource management · MAP-Elites · Metaheuristic · Optimization · Visualization · Vortex search

1 Introduction

The current evolution of the energy sector, with the incorporation of modern smart grid (SG) technologies, provides easier integration of distributed energy resources (DER), most noticeable in the penetration of uncertain renewable generation [1]. As such, scheduling energy resources by managing entities such as virtual power players or aggregators so that the proper electrical grid operation is achieved becomes extremely complex, and by considering uncertainty, such entities are subject to the occurrence of extreme events, for example, climate changes which will affect renewable generation [2]. These events are unlikely to occur, so they have a low probability, but if their occurrence is verified, their impact on the grid operation is substantial.

The energy resource management problem (ERM) is a highly constrained problem with many variables, where most traditional mathematical optimization methods fail to find optimal solutions in a short time. When dealing with operation problems, solutions are sometimes needed in a small time window, close to real-time. Metaheuristic optimization approaches are good alternatives regarding energy problems since they can provide near-optimal solutions in useful time [3]. Metaheuristics are increasingly used to solve complex real-world problems, but they still have several significant disadvantages, including the optimality of the provided solution and their explainability [4]. In this work, we intend to make advancements in this regard by taking the Multi-dimensional Archive of Phenotypic Elites (MAP-Elites) to illuminate metaheuristic search space.

The Multi-dimensional Archive of Phenotypic Elites (MAP-Elites) [5] is an illumination algorithm or a quality-diversity (QD) algorithm that identifies a set of solutions covering a space that is known as a behavior space [6]. More specifically, MAP-Elites creates an archive structure that stores the best solutions (or elites) based on the problem behaviors or characteristics the user finds useful to evaluate. This structure acts as an illumination of the search space by giving the user an understanding of how these characteristics affect metaheuristic performance through visualization methods. In the literature, MAP-Elites has been applied to multiple works regarding robot task planning [7,8], video game level generation [9,10], image generation [11] and vehicle routing optimization [12]. From the authors' understanding, there are no works regarding utilizing MAP-Elites or a QD algorithm in problems in the energy domain trying to understand the metaheuristic behavior regarding ERM problem characteristics.

This work proposes a metaheuristic approach due to the problems' large-scale nature and uncertainty, where a MAP-Elites algorithm is implemented for a day-ahead ERM optimization considering risk-based analysis. The proposed MAP-Elites algorithm is improved by incorporating the Vortex Search (VS) metaheuristic [13] to generate new candidate solutions compared to the standard mutation operator used in the standard MAP-Elites algorithm. The VS operators were selected due to their simple implementation with no additional parameters needed. The VS MAP-Elites algorithm optimizes and determines the best elites for this risk-based ERM in a 13-bus distribution network (DN) with significant renewable penetration and electric vehicle integration based on behavior factors. For the risk analysis, extreme event existence, which may jeopardize the proper grid operation, was also considered.

The organization of this paper is as follows. The proposed methodology regarding the mathematical problem formulation and iterated racing approach is presented in Sect. 2. The case study employed in this work, concerning the setting used by irace and the DN, is presented in Sect. 3. The automatic configuration outcomes and the analyses of results are presented in Sect. 4. Finally,

Sect. 5 draws the main takeaways from this work and suggests some possible topics for further research.

2 Proposed Methodology

This section presents the proposed methodology regarding the ERM problem formulation considering a risk analysis through a risk-averse mechanism. In this risk analysis, the aggregator aims to reduce the expected scenario costs and the costs associated with the worst possible scenarios through the conditional value-at-risk ($CVaR$), present in Eq. (1).

Regarding the optimization algorithm, this section also describes the vortex MAP-Elites process, which was used to perform the risk-based ERM problem, illuminating metaheuristic performance.

2.1 Risk-Based Problem Formulation

The objective function for the day-ahead risk-based ERM formulation contemplates the expected costs and the costs associated with the extreme scenarios, in this situation, evaluated through the $CVaR$ method.

Objective Function: The risk-based ERM is a minimization cost problem that can be formulated by Eq. (1), where expected scenario costs and risk aversion costs are considered.

$$min\ v = Ex^{\text{Costs}} + (\gamma \cdot CVaR_\alpha) \tag{1}$$

where γ represents the risk-aversion factor, which varies between $[0,1]$, meaning that 0 no risk-aversion is present in the formulation, and 1 means that the aggregator is taking a 100 % risk-averse approach. This work considers only a γ equal to 1. In the first term, Ex^{Costs} in monetary units (m.u.) represents the expected costs that are given in Eq. (2). The second term presents the costs associated with risk events, evaluated through $CVaR_\alpha$ (m.u.) in the day-ahead operation present in Eq- (3).

$$Ex^{\text{Costs}} = \sum_{s=1}^{N_s} \rho_s \cdot C_s^{\text{Day}+1} \tag{2}$$

$$CVaR_\alpha = VaR_\alpha + \frac{1}{1-\alpha} \sum_{s \in N_x} (C_s^{\text{Day}+1} - Ex^{\text{Costs}} - VaR_\alpha(f_s^{\text{totC}})) \cdot \rho_s \tag{3}$$

where the scenario probability is represented by ρ_s, $C_s^{\text{Day}+1}$ (m.u.) describes the day-ahead scenario costs/profits formulated in Eq. (4). In Eq. (3), VaR_α (m.u.) is the value-at-risk, which evaluates the extreme scenario cost, till the confidence level α ($VaR_\alpha = z - score(\alpha) \cdot std(C_s^{\text{Day}+1})$). In addition to the

VaR_α, the parameter N_x represents the scenarios when the cost is higher than Ex^{Costs} ($C_s^{\text{Day}+1} \geq Ex^{\text{Costs}} + VaR_\alpha \quad \forall s \in N_x$).

$$C_s^{\text{Day}+1} = OC_s^{\text{Day}+1} - In_s^{\text{Day}+1} + B_s \tag{4}$$

where $OC_s^{\text{Day}+1}$ (m.u.) represents the day-ahead operational costs, $In_s^{\text{Day}+1}$ is incomes from day-ahead transactions and B_s represents variables' bound violations.

Operational Costs: The aggregator seeks to reduce the operational costs of the ERM model in Eq. (5) while maximizing the revenues in Eq. (6). The first and second terms of Eq. (5) include the costs of dispatchable distributed generation (DG) and external supplier generation, which are not scenario dependent. The costs associated with the non-dispatchable generation and positive power imbalance are represented in the third and fourth terms of the equation. The fifth and sixth terms demonstrate the costs associated with energy storage systems (ESS) and electric vehicle (EV) discharging. The seventh and eighth terms represent the expenses related to the incentive for demand response (DR) programs and the negative imbalance from load not supplied.

$$OC_s^{\text{Day}+1} = \sum_{t=1}^{N_t} \left(\begin{array}{l} \displaystyle\sum_{i\in\Omega_{DG}^d} DG_{(i,t)}^{\text{Power}} \cdot DG_{(i,t)}^{\text{Cost}} + \sum_{es=1}^{N_{es}} Sup_{(es,t)}^{\text{Power}} \cdot Sup_{(es,t)}^{\text{Cost}} + \\[2mm] \displaystyle\sum_{i\in\Omega_{DG}^{nd}} DG_{(i,t,s)}^{\text{Power}} \cdot DG_{(i,t)}^{\text{Cost}} + \sum_{i=1}^{N_i} Imb_{(i,t,s)}^{\text{Power}^+} \cdot Imb_{(i,t)}^{\text{Cost}^+} + \\[2mm] \displaystyle\sum_{ess=1}^{N_{ess}} ESS_{(ess,t,s)}^{\text{Power}} \cdot ESS_{(ess,t)}^{\text{Cost}} + \sum_{ev=1}^{N_{ev}} EV_{(ess,t,s)}^{\text{Power}} \cdot EV_{(ev,t)}^{\text{Cost}} + \\[2mm] \displaystyle\sum_{l=1}^{N_l} (DR_{(l,t,s)}^{\text{Power}} \cdot DR_{(l,t)}^{\text{Cost}} + Imb_{(l,t,s)}^{\text{Power}^-} \cdot Imb_{(l,t)}^{\text{Cost}^-}) \end{array} \right) \quad \forall s \tag{5}$$

where t represents the index associated with the number of periods N_t, $i \in \Omega_{DG}^d$, is the set representing the number of dispatchable DG units, es represents the index of external suppliers going to N_{es}, $i \in \Omega_{DG}^{nd}$ is the set that represents the number of non-dispatchable DG units. The index ess is the index going through the total number of ESSs (N_{ess}), and ev is the index representing EVs that goes till the total number of EVs considered N_{ev}. The load index is given by l, and N_l demonstrates the total number of loads. Concerning the decision variables in the problem, $DG_{(i,t)}^{\text{Power}}$ (MW) is each dispatchable DG unit's i active power output during the period t, $Sup_{(es,t)}^{\text{Power}}$ (MW) is each external supplier es active power output during the period t. $DG_{(i,t,s)}^{\text{Power}}$ (MW) is the active power output of each non-dispatchable DG unit i during the period t in scenario s, and $Imb_{(i,t)}^{\text{Power}^+}$ (MW) represents the positive active power imbalance due to excess generation of DG unit i for period t. The decision variable $ESS_{(ess,t,s)}^{\text{Power}}$ (MW) represents the discharging power of the ESS unit ess for the period t in scenario s (if $ESS_{(ess,t,s)}^{\text{Power}}$ is negative, 0 otherwise), and similar to EVs, where $EV_{(ev,t,s)}^{\text{Power}}$

(MW) describes the discharging power of each EV unit ev for the period t in scenario s (if $EV_{(ev,t)}^{\text{Power}}$ is negative, 0 otherwise). The decision variables $DR_{(l,t,s)}^{\text{Power}}$ (MW) and $Imb_{(l,t,s)}^{\text{Power}^-}$ (MW) are the active power reduction of load l for the period t in scenario s and the negative power imbalance due to non-supplied power to load l for period t in scenario s. Regarding the parameters, $DG_{(i,t)}^{\text{Cost}}$ (m.u./MWh) is the cost associated with dispatchable DG production in unit i for the period t, $Sup_{(es,t)}^{\text{Cost}}$ (m.u./MWh) is the external supplier es electricity price for the period t. $DG_{(i,t)}^{\text{Cost}}$ (m.u./MWh) represents the associated cost of active power generation from non-dispatchable DG unit i during the period t and $Imb_{(i,t,s)}^{\text{Power}^+}$ (m.u./MWh) represents the cost for positive power imbalance of the excess generation of DG unit i in period t. The costs associated with the active discharging power of EV unit ev and ESS unit ess during the period t are represented by the parameters $ESS_{(ess,t)}^{\text{Cost}}$ (m.u./MWh) and $EV_{(ev,t)}^{\text{Cost}}$ (m.u./MWh). Finally, the parameter $DR_{(l,t)}^{\text{Cost}}$ (m.u./MWh) is related to the cost for active power reduction of load l in period t, and the parameter $Imb_{(l,t)}^{\text{Cost}^-}$ (m.u./MWh) represents the cost associated to the negative imbalance in the system for power not supplied to load l for the period t.

Market Revenues: In Eq. (6), the aggregator earns revenue from electricity market transactions, that is, from selling surplus power in the market. For the day-ahead optimization to be profitable, the aggregator must maximize this function. In other words, the values derived in Eq. (6) must be higher than those in Eq. (5).

$$In_s^{\text{Day}+1} = \sum_{t=1}^{N_t} \sum_{m=1}^{N_m} EM_{(m,t)}^{\text{Power}} \cdot MP_{(m,t,s)} \qquad \forall s \qquad (6)$$

where m represents the index associated with the number of electricity markets N_m. The decision variable $EM_{(m,t)}^{\text{Power}}$ (MW) is the power transacted (offers or bids) in the electricity market m for the period t and the parameter $MP_{(m,t,s)}$ (m.u./MWh) represents price of electricity in market m for period t in scenario s. If $EM_{(m,t)}^{\text{Power}}$ is a positive value, the aggregator sells power in the market. Otherwise, the aggregator needs to buy power, and this variable is considered a cost.

In [14], all of the problem's mathematical formulations can be found, including any resource limitations to which the objective function is subject.

2.2   Vortex MAP-Elites

The MAP-Elites algorithm [5] was used to optimize the previous problem formulation. We improved the standard MAP-Elites algorithm by replacing the normal variation processes of mutation and recombination used with the VS single solution-based variation approach. The VS metaheuristic [13] was incorporated to generate new solutions based on a vortex pattern. Algorithm 1 shows the process of the VS MAP-Elites, where initially, an n dimensional empty archive is created to store the best solutions and corresponding performance (fitness). The next step is randomly initializing the solutions between variables' upper and lower bounds and creating the initial archive. The solutions are stored according to the behavior obtained, which indicates the archive index in which the solution is stored. We considered two different behaviors that are interesting to analyze for the ERM problem. The first is the DR ratio, present in Eq. (7), which is the percentage of DR power present in the total generation, and the second is the renewable generation ratio, formulated in Eq. (8), meaning the percentage of the total production that comes from renewables.

Algorithm 1. Vortex MAP-Elites Algorithm, based on [7]

1: $(\mathcal{X},\mathcal{P}) \leftarrow$ create_empty_archive()   ▷ $\mathcal{X} \leftarrow$ solutions; $\mathcal{P} \leftarrow$ fitness
2: **for all** NP **do**   ▷ Initialization
3:     x' $\leftarrow$ create_random_solutions()
4:     ADD_TO_ARCHIVE(x',$\mathcal{X}$,$\mathcal{P}$)
5: **end for**
6: **while** $it \leq maxIt$ **do**   ▷ Iterative process
7:     x = selection($\mathcal{X}$)   ▷ Select best solution from the archive
8:     $\mu_{it+1} =$ x   ▷ Center
9:     $r_{it+1} =$ Decrease(r_{it})   ▷ Standard deviation (radius)
10:     x' $\leftarrow$ create_candidate_solutions(x)   ▷ N(μ_{it+1},r_{it+1})
11:     x' $\leftarrow$ bound_control_solutions(x')
12:     ADD_TO_ARCHIVE(x',$\mathcal{X}$,$\mathcal{P}$)
13:     $it \leftarrow it + 1$
14: **end while**
15: **return** archive($\mathcal{X}$,$\mathcal{P}$)
16: **procedure** ADD_TO_ARCHIVE(x,$\mathcal{X}$,$\mathcal{P}$)
17:     (p,b) $\leftarrow$ eval(x)   ▷ Evaluate performance and behavior
18:     c $\leftarrow$ get_archive_index(b)
19:     **if** isempty($\mathcal{P}$(b)) —— p ¡ $\mathcal{P}$(b) **then**
20:         $\mathcal{X}$(b) = x   ▷ Store solution in the archive
21:         $\mathcal{P}$(b) = p   ▷ Store fitness in the archive
22:     **end if**
23: **end procedure**

$$DR_{ratio} = \frac{\sum\limits_{s=1}^{N_s}(\sum\limits_{t=1}^{N_t} \sum\limits_{l=1}^{N_l} DR_{(l,t,s)}^{\text{Power}}) \cdot \rho_s}{TotalGen} \qquad (7)$$

$$Renewable_{ratio} = \frac{\sum\limits_{s=1}^{N_s}(\sum\limits_{t=1}^{N_t} \sum\limits_{i \in \Omega_{DG}^{nd}} DG_{(i,t,s)}^{\text{Power}})}{TotalGen} \qquad (8)$$

$$TotalGen = \sum_{s=1}^{N_s} \sum_{t=1}^{N_t} \left(\begin{array}{l} \sum_{i\in\Omega_{DG}^d} DG_{(i,t)}^{\text{Power}} + \sum_{es=1}^{N_{es}} Sup_{(es,t)}^{\text{Power}} + \\ \sum_{i\in\Omega_{DG}^{nd}} DG_{(i,t,s)}^{\text{Power}} + \sum_{ess=1}^{N_{ess}} ESS_{(ess,t,s)}^{\text{Power}} + \\ \sum_{ev=1}^{N_{ev}} EV_{(ess,t,s)}^{\text{Power}} + \sum_{l=1}^{N_l} DR_{(l,t,s)}^{\text{Power}} \end{array} \right) \cdot \rho_s \qquad (9)$$

After storing the initial solutions in the archive, the algorithm enters the iterative process, where the best solution in the archive is selected and considered as the vortex center to generate new candidate solutions. The standard deviation (or radius) is also updated in each iteration according to Eq. (9).

$$r_{it} = \sigma \cdot \frac{1}{0.1} \cdot gammaincinv(0.1, a_{it}) \qquad (10)$$

where $\sigma = \frac{x_i^{\text{upper}} - x_i^{\text{lower}}}{2}$, x_i^{upper} and x_i^{lower} are the variables upper and lower bounds. The process to decrease the radius is given by $a_{it} = \frac{maxIt-it}{maxIt}$. The neighborhood solutions are generated through a Gaussian distribution with mean μ_{it} and standard deviation r_{it}. The next step is to apply a boundary control to check and correct the variables that are outside the stipulated bounds. The final step is to store the best of the candidate solutions in the archive.

Note that all the optimization processes regarding the fitness function procedure and solution vector encoding for the day-ahead problem can be found in [15].

3   Experiment Parameters

The case study that was utilized to support the suggested method is discussed in this section. It describes the resource information of the 13-bus DN and the settings used for the MAP-Elites and VS MAP-Elites algorithms.

3.1   13-Bus Distribution Network

The considered smart grid (SG) is inserted in a mock-up smart city, developed in the BISITE laboratory [16], which was used to create this case study. There are four 1 MVar capacitor banks (which are set to zero in this problem since reactive power is not taken into account), two wind farms, thirteen PV parks (15 renewable DG units), and a 30 MVA substation in bus 1. This DN's consumption comprises 25 distinct loads, including residences, workplaces, and a few service structures (a hospital, a fire station, and a mall). 500 EVs were used in the simulations to represent significant EV adoption, and two energy storage systems are also present in the network.

Using GAMS/SCENRED[1], the initial dataset of 5,000 scenarios is then condensed to 150 scenarios. To cut down on computation time owing to a large

---

[1] https://www.gams.com/latest/docs/T_SCENRED.html.

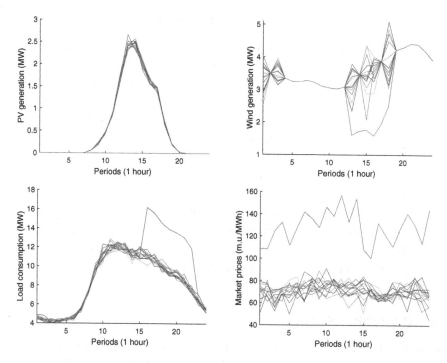

Fig. 1. Scenario variability for day-ahead a) PV Generation; b) wind generation; c) load consumption; electricity market prices.

number of variables, it was eventually reduced to the 15 highest probable scenarios incorporating extreme events. Figure 1a) shows the scenario variation for the PV generation, where one extreme scenario does not have PV generation because non-existent solar radiation can occur. The scenario variability of the generation provided by the wind turbines is presented in Fig. 1b), where one of the extreme events considered has a high reduction of this type of generation. In Fig. 1c) we show the total load consumption from the 25 loads, and from the figure, we can see that one scenario considers a significant increase in load, and in Fig. 1d) the scenarios created for electricity market prices are shown, where we considered one scenario with a vast increase in these prices compared to the remaining. In total, three extreme scenarios were contemplated according to [15].

To meet demand, the aggregator must manage its resources, electricity purchased from an external supplier, and energy purchased/sold on the electricity market. Table 1 shows the energy resource statistics for the day-ahead formulation aggregator using the worst-case scenarios. The capacity, predicted values from renewable sources and loads, minimum and maximum values taken into consideration for resource pricing, and the number of units corresponding to each resource are all distinguished.

Table 1. Energy resource information.

Energy resources		Prices (m.u./MWh) min–max	Capacity (MW) min–max	Forecast (MW) min–max	Units
Photovoltaic		29–29		0.00–0.81	13
Wind		31–31		0.30–3.07	2
External Supplier		50–90	0.00–30.00		1
Storage units	Charge	110–110	0.00–1.25		2
	Discharge	60–60	0.00–1.25		
EVs	Charge	0–0	0.01–0.05		500
	Discharge	60–60	0.01–0.05		
DR		100–100	0.00–1.21		25
Load		0–0		0.01–2.38	25
Electricity market		44.78–156.91	0.00–2.00		1

3.2   MAP-Elites Settings

Regarding the MAP-Elites and VS Map-Elites, a total number of 50 individuals (Pop^{Size}) and 200 iterations ($maxIt$) were considered for the optimization process, equivalent to 10,000 objective function evaluations ($Pop^{Size} \times maxIt$). For both algorithms, a grid size of 20 was set, with two dimensions, regarding the considered behaviors, which means that the algorithms had a total of 400 bins (20^2) in the archive. Additionally, the range of values for the DR ratio was set between [0.22,0.32], and for the renewable generation ratio, the range was set between [0.40,0.46], considering the observed behavior during previous experiments.

We implemented and evaluated both algorithms using MATLAB R2018a on a Windows 10 machine with 16GB of RAM and an Intel Xeon Gold 5120@2.20GHz CPU.

4   Experiments Results

This section presents the simulation results obtained by the proposed VS MAP-Elites, and a comparison is made to the results obtained by the standard MAP-Elites.

The optimization problem is composed of 13,680 variables for each scenario, so a total of 205,200 decision variables. Table 2 shows the average risk-based ERM optimization costs and time for both algorithms over the course of 20 trials. VS MAP-Elites shows a better objective function cost with a reduction of 24.81 % in costs since this algorithm was able to reduce both terms of Eq. (1), regarding the expected costs (Ex^{Costs}) and $CVaR_\alpha$ costs. This is further proved by Fig. 2, which shows the objective function costs in the 20 trials performed, where

Table 2. Average risk-based cost results and optimization time for each algorithm over 20 trials.

Algorithm	v (m.u.)	Ex^{Costs} (m.u.)	$CVaR_\alpha$ (m.u.)	B_s (m.u.)	$max(C_s^{\text{Day}+1})$ (m.u.)	Time (sec)
MAP-Elites	158,740.59	25,005.85	133,734.74	9,106.67	188,007.51	55.18
VS MAP-Elites	119,349.61	20,925.88	98,423.73	5,391.67	140,758.75	668.51

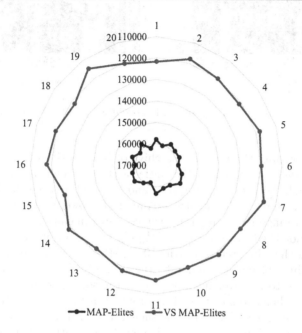

Fig. 2. Radar plot regarding the objective function cost for each optimization trial.

VS MAP-Elites presented a global better performance in all runs compared to MAP-Elites, with lesser costs. Concerning the expected costs, VS MAP-Elites presented a reduction of 16.32 %, and when it comes to $CVaR_\alpha$, the reduction was 26.40 % because of the reduction in worst scenario costs of 25.13 % in case of the worst possible scenario for the aggregator $(max(C_s^{\text{Day}+1}))$.

Since the variation processes in the standard MAP-Elites algorithm are simple and require little computational effort, the optimization time is substantially less than the VS MAP-Elites algorithm. From Table 2, it is possible to conclude that MAP-Elites is around 12 times faster than VS MAP-Elites.

Regarding the best elites, Fig. 3a) shows the initial archive obtained by MAP-Elites, before the algorithm enters the iterative process and muta-tion/recombination occurs. In this figure, it is possible to visualize that the archive presents few solutions and is not diversified. Also, in this archive, the solutions are stored to higher values of DR ratio and medium value of renew-able generation ratio, meaning higher costs since the cost for load reduction is significantly higher than the renewable generation cost. After the iterative pro-

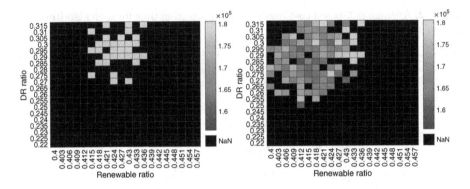

Fig. 3. MAP-Elites a) initial; and b) final solution archive for a single run.

cess of the algorithm, the final elite archive of the algorithm can be obtained, as Fig. 3b) shows. Compared to the initial archive, a higher diversification is achieved through the variation processes, and better elites are stored in the final archive. The best elites in this archive are present for lower to mid-range DR ratio values and mid-range renewable ratio values, which means that the aggregator requested less load reduction through DR programs resulting in lower costs.

Concerning the elite archive for the VS MAP-Elites algorithm, Fig. 4 shows the initial archive of elites. Similar to the initial archive of MAP-Elites, the archive has little to no diversification, where the solutions stored present high costs due to the behaviors of the ERM problem, mainly of the DR ratio. The final elite archive of VS MAP-Elites is shown in Fig. 4b), where in comparison to the final archive of the MAP-Elites, higher diversification of the search space was achieved, resulting in better elites with lower costs. In this archive, the best solutions resulted in lower DR ratio values in the behavior with lower to mid-range values in the renewable generation ratio. Utilizing both resources still presents costs to the aggregator, mainly the DR, where the worst elites stored present high DR ratio values.

Note that the archives for both metaheuristics were presented for a single optimization run. We assumed the best run out of the 20 runs performed in the simulations.

The graphic convergence of both metaheuristics for a total of 200 iterations is presented in Fig. 5, where the black line shows the average convergence over the 20 runs for the MAP-Elites algorithm, and the red line shows the average convergence of the VS MAP-Elites metaheuristic. The graphic also shows the fitness variance in the 20 trials as boxplots. The MAP-Elites algorithm presents higher fitness values compared to VS MAP-Elites, as expected, and some outliers are noticed between iterations 10 and 20, 50 and 90, and 110 and 130. Also, MAP-Elites seems to stabilize the convergence curve around iteration 170 fully. In comparison, VS MAP-Elites presents more dispersed fitness outliers, with larger variance between runs. The VS MAP-Elites seems to not fully converge, as no stabilization in the convergence curve was noticed, so increasing the number

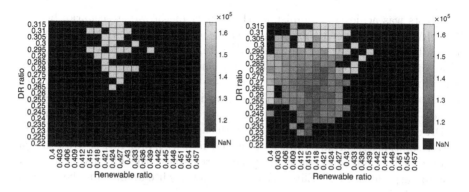

Fig. 4. VS MAP-Elites a) initial; and b) final solution archive for a single run.

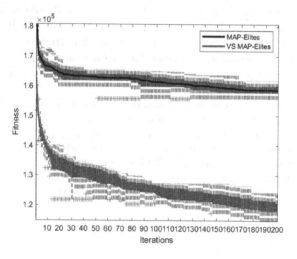

Fig. 5. Convergence plot of the MAP-Elites and VS MAP-Elites algorithms.

of iterations would allow the algorithm to improve the cost results but increase optimization time.

5   Conclusions

An improved MAP-Elites algorithm based on the VS variation processes was proposed in this work for centralized day-ahead risk-based ERM problem considering extreme events for a distribution network with high integration of renewables and EVs. This version, what we called VS MAP-Elites, was then compared to the standard version of the algorithm regarding cost results and elite archive diversity considering two different problem characteristics or behaviors (DR ratio and renewable ratio).

Regarding cost results, the VS Map-Elites algorithm showed lower objective function costs when compared to MAP-Elites, around 25 %, since a reduction in risk costs was achieved, diminishing the impact of the worst scenario, because VS MAP-Elites reduced this scenario costs by around 25 % also. When analyzing the elite archives of both tested metaheuristics, VS MAP-Elites has a more diverse elite archive with better solutions when compared to MAP-Elites, regarding solutions with lower DR ratio, since the use of DR brings higher costs to the aggregator and also renewable generation ratio with lower to mid-range values. In the latter, even though renewable generation costs are low compared to DR costs, they still represent a cost to the aggregator, so it was expected that better solutions regarding total costs would fit with lower ratios. We can conclude that through diversification of the search space, the VS MAP-Elites was able to outperform MAP-Elites, achieving a better elite archive for the problem characteristics.

Concerning future research, additional behaviors interesting to analyze in the day-ahead risk-based ERM problem could be considered, and how they would affect the performance of the algorithms, since in this work, only two different problem behaviors were analyzed. Another venue that could be explored is the integration of other variation processes based on other metaheuristics, which already showed good performance for this type of energy problem.

Acknowledgments. The present work has received funding from the Brazilian Federal Agency for Support and Evaluation of Graduate Education (CAPES) and through the FCT Portuguese Foundation for Science and Technology (2019.00141.CBM). José Almeida is supported by FCT with Ph.D. Grant 2022.09590.BD. João Soares has received funding from FCT, namely CEECIND/00420/2022. The authors acknowledge the work facilities and equipment provided by the GECAD research center (UIDB/00760/2020 and UIDP/00760/2020) to the project team.

References

1. Wang, C., Zhang, Z., Abedinia, O., Farkoush, S.G.: Modeling and analysis of a microgrid considering the uncertainty in renewable energy resources, energy storage systems and demand management in electrical retail market. J. Energy Storage **33**, 102111 (2021)
2. Perera, A.T.D., Nik, V.M., Chen, D., Scartezzini, J.-L., Tianzhen Hong, T.: Quantifying the impacts of climate change and extreme climate events on energy systems. Nature Energy **5**(2), 150–159 (2020)
3. Soares, J., Pinto, T., Lezama, F., Morais, H.: Survey on complex optimization and simulation for the new power systems paradigm. Complexity **2018**, 1–32 (2018)
4. Bacardit, J., Brownlee, A.E.I., Cagnoni, S., Iacca, G., McCall, J., Walker, D.: The intersection of evolutionary computation and explainable AI. In: Proceedings of the Genetic and Evolutionary Computation Conference Companion, pp. 1757–1762, Boston Massachusetts. ACM (2022)
5. Mouret, J.-B., Clune, J.: Illuminating search spaces by mapping elites (2015). arXiv:1504.04909
6. Pugh, J.K., Soros, L.B., Stanley. K.O.: Quality Diversity: a new frontier for evolutionary computation. Front. Robot. AI **3**, 40 (2016)

7. Vassiliades, V., Chatzilygeroudis, K., Mouret, J.-B.: Using centroidal voronoi tessellations to scale up the multidimensional archive of phenotypic elites algorithm. IEEE Trans. Evol. Comput. **22**(4), 623–630 (2018)
8. Pierrot, T., Richard, G., Beguir, K., Cully, A.: Multi-objective quality diversity optimization. In: Proceedings of the Genetic and Evolutionary Computation Conference, pp. 139–147, Boston Massachusetts. ACM (2022)
9. Fontaine, M.C.: Mapping hearthstone deck spaces through MAP-elites with sliding boundaries. In: Proceedings of the Genetic and Evolutionary Computation Conference, pp. 161–169, Prague Czech Republic. ACM (2019)
10. Fontaine, M.C., et al.: Illuminating Mario Scenes in the Latent Space of a Generative Adversarial Network. In: Proceedings of the AAAI Conference on Artificial Intelligence, vol. 35, no. 7, pp. 5922–5930 (2021)
11. Basher, S.F., Ross, B.J.: Managing diversity and many objectives in evolutionary design. In: 2022 IEEE Congress on Evolutionary Computation (CEC), pp. 1–8, Padua, Italy, IEEE (2022)
12. Urquhart, N., Höhl, S., Hart, E.: An illumination algorithm approach to solving the micro-depot routing problem. In: Proceedings of the Genetic and Evolutionary Computation Conference, pp. 1347–1355, Prague Czech Republic, ACM (2019)
13. Doğan, B., Ölmez, T.: A new metaheuristic for numerical function optimization: vortex Search algorithm. Inf. Sci. **293**, 125–145 (2015)
14. Almeida, J., Soares, J., Lezama, F., Vale, Z.: Robust energy resource management incorporating risk analysis using conditional value-at-risk. IEEE Access **10**, 16063–16077 (2022)
15. Almeida, J., Soares, J., Canizes, B., Razo-Zapata, I., Vale, Z.: Day-ahead to intraday energy scheduling operation considering extreme events using risk-based approaches. Neurocomputing **543**, 126229 (2023)
16. Canizes, B., Soares, J., Vale, Z., Corchado, J.: Optimal distribution grid operation using DLMP-based pricing for electric vehicle charging infrastructure in a smart city. Energies **12**(4), 686 (2019)

Comparing Manual vs Automatic Tuning of Differential Evolution Strategies for Energy Resource Management Optimization

José Almeida⬤, Fernando Lezama⬤, João Soares$^{(\boxtimes)}$⬤, and Zita Vale⬤

GECAD, LASI, Polytechnic of Porto, 4249-015 Porto, Portugal
{jorga,flz,jan,zav}@isep.ipp.pt

Abstract. The energy resource management problem in energy systems is hard to optimize, mainly due to non-linear restrictions and a large number of variables involved. This is partly because of the increased integration of distributed energy resources. Computational intelligence optimization techniques, namely evolutionary algorithms, are regarded as efficient techniques for identifying optimal and near-optimal solutions. However, these algorithms usually have in their design several parameters that need to be set and, in most cases, tuned for a given problem to find good solutions. This work proposes an automatic configuration approach of different differential evolution strategies using the irace package to solve a centralized day-ahead energy resource management problem. The problem considers an aggregator managing multiple resources, such as renewable generation, battery energy systems, electric vehicles, and loads with demand response capabilities. The aggregator aims to minimize operational costs and maximize revenues to obtain a profit. We compare the results of a "manual" tuning of parameters with the results obtained with the auto-tuned parameters using irace. Results show that the automatic configuration improves the profits of the aggregator in almost all strategies (except for DE/either-or-algorithm/1), getting the best results, an improvement of around 7%, with the automatically tuned DE/target-to-best/1 mutation strategy.

Keywords: Automatic tuning · Differential evolution · Energy resource management · Evolutionary algorithms · Iterated racing · Optimization

1 Introduction

The socio-economic situation of the energy sector is complex, necessitating extensive research and planning. In reality, many of the issues in this area are complicated and have traits like high dimensionality, a large number of restrictions, lack of information, and noisy and corrupted data due to the large uncertainty in the energy system [1,2]. Also, these problems frequently involve temporal limits

B. N. Jørgensen et al. (Eds.): EI.A 2023, LNCS 14467, pp. 44–59, 2024.
https://doi.org/10.1007/978-3-031-48649-4_3

that require solutions to operate in almost real-time [3]. Consequently, finding effective and exact solutions in a reasonable amount of time is still an issue that needs to be addressed for many energy problems.

Consider, for example, the energy resource management (ERM) in distribution networks. In such a problem, due to the grid constraints, we are dealing with a mixed-integer non-linear programming (MINLP) formulation, which is tough for mathematical methods to solve. Algorithms based on computational intelligence (CI), in this context evolutionary algorithms (EAs), have shown to be particularly well suited for this type of problem since they produce good results in a useful time. As such, they provide an effective optimization alternative to mathematical methods for problems in the energy domain [4]. These algorithms are also more tolerant to uncertainty and more suitable for addressing the nonlinearities prevalent in energy problems [5]. EAs are in their majority population-based algorithms with several associated parameters. Due to their stochastic nature, fine-tuning these parameters becomes essential to achieve feasible solutions to a wide range of problems with a minimum requirement for robustness [6]. This tuning can be done in different ways, but many authors have performed this tuning manually through a sensitivity analysis of the parameters [7]. Manual configuration is extremely time-consuming and needs the developers' expertise and knowledge of the specific problem to be solved [8]. Therefore, exploring automatic configuration methods that efficiently search the parameter space to find high-performing configurations and removing the drawbacks from manual configuration is essential in the design of optimizers. Automatic configuration methods can be divided into simple generate-evaluate methods (Brute force [9], and F-Race [10]), high-level generate-evaluate methods (Post-selection [11]), and iterative generate-evaluate methods (CALIBRA [12], Iterated F-Race [13], and others) [14]. To our knowledge, such automatic configuration methods regarding EA optimization for ERM problems have yet to be applied in the literature, so we believe this work will significantly contribute to this field.

In this paper, we propose an automatic tuning of the parameters of multiple differential evolution (DE) strategies considering the iterated racing F-race approach present in the irace package in [13] to solve an ERM problem [15]. The irace package was chosen for its customization (multiple automatic configuration procedures) and simplicity. In a smart grid problem (SG), a 33-bus distribution network (DN) is considered with distributed generation sources, electric vehicles (EVs), battery energy systems (BES), and demand response (DR) programs for load reduction. An aggregator optimizes resource allocation, minimizing electricity market purchases during peak hours while maximizing power sales to the market and meeting the needs of residential customers, EV users, and the BES. We analyze the experiments made by the irace package to find the best configuration for the parameters of different DE strategies and present the best configuration (final elite configuration) for each. In addition, we compare the results with those obtained with manual tuning made in [15]. The results are compared in terms of operational costs and the incomes of the aggregator.

The organization of this paper is as follows. The proposed methodology regarding the mathematical problem formulation and iterated racing approach is presented in Sect. 2. The case study employed in this work, concerning the setting used by irace and the DN, is presented in Sect. 3. The automatic configuration outcomes and the analyses of results are presented in Sect. 4. Finally, Sect. 5 draws the main takeaways from this work and suggests some possible topics for further research.

2 Proposed Methodology

The aggregator intends to reduce the operational costs in Eq. 1 for day-ahead management while maximizing electricity selling to consumers and market transactions in Eq. 2. The decision variables for energy resource generation power, DG unit commitment, BES and EV schedules, and DR loads, among others, are all included in the ERM model under study for each unit and each period considered. The voltage and angles in each bus must also be considered during scheduling.

2.1 Problem Formulation

The objective function for the day-ahead ERM formulation contemplates the operational costs associated with multiple resources (previously mentioned) for the 24-hour horizon with a time step of 1 h.

Operational Costs. Eq. 1 models the operational costs of the ERM model that the aggregator aims to minimize while maximizing the incomes in Eq. 2. The first and second terms of Eq. 1 include the costs of DG and excess of generation imbalance. The third and fourth terms of the equation represent the costs associated with BES and EV discharging. The fifth and sixth terms represent the costs associated with the incentive for DR programs and the negative imbalance from load not supplied. Finally, the income from selling electricity in the market is represented in the last term.

$$
min f_{OC}^{\text{Day}+1} = \sum_{t \in T} \cdot \left(\begin{array}{l} \displaystyle\sum_{i \in I} (p_{(i,t)}^{\text{DG}} \cdot C_{(i,t)}^{\text{DG}} + p_{(i,t)}^{\text{imb}^+} \cdot C_{(i,t)}^{\text{imb}^+}) + \\[6pt] \displaystyle\sum_{s \in S} p_{(s,t)}^{\text{Sup}} \cdot C_{(s,t)}^{\text{Sup}} + \\[6pt] \displaystyle\sum_{b \in B} p_{(b,t)}^{\text{dis}} \cdot C_{(b,t)}^{\text{dis}} + \sum_{v \in V} p_{(v,t)}^{\text{dis}} \cdot C_{(v,t)}^{\text{dis}} + \\[6pt] \displaystyle\sum_{l \in L} (p_{(l,t)}^{\text{Red}} \cdot C_{(l,t)}^{\text{Red}} + p_{(l,t)}^{\text{imb}^-} \cdot C_{(l,t)}^{\text{imb}^-}) \end{array} \right) \cdot \Delta t \qquad (1)
$$

where T is the set of the number of periods $(1, 2, 3, ..., 24)$, I is the set of DG units $(1, 2, 3, ..., N_i)$, S the set of external suppliers $(1, 2, 3, ..., N_s)$ B represents the set of BES $(1, 2, 3, ..., N_b)$, V demonstrates the set of EVs $(1, 2, 3, ..., N_v)$, L is the set of different loads participating in the DR program $(1, 2, 3, ..., N_l)$ and M is the set of electricity markets available for the aggregator transactions $(1, 2, 3, ..., N_m)$. Regarding the parameters, Δt represents the time step which in this case is considered to be one hour. $C_{(i,t)}^{DG}$ is the cost associated with DG production in unit i for the period t (m.u./kWh), $C_{(i,t)}^{imb^+}$ represents the cost of the exceeding power of DG unit i in periods t (m.u./kWh) and $C_{(s,t)}^{Sup}$ the external supplier s electricity price for the period t (m.u./kWh). The discharging costs of the BES and EVs are the parameters $C_{(b,t)}^{dis}$, and $C_{(v,t)}^{dis}$ for BES b and EV v, respectively for the period t (m.u./kWh). $C_{(l,t)}^{Red}$ is the DR cost of the load l (m.u./kWh), and $C_{(l,t)}^{imb^-}$ is the cost associated with the demand not-supplied to the respective load (m.u./kWh). The decision variables in this equation are the following, $p_{(i,t)}^{DG}$, which is the active power produced by each DG unit i for the period t (kW), $p_{(i,t)}^{imb^+}$ describes the exceed active power of each DG unit (kW), $p_{(s,t)}^{Sup}$ is the active power supplied by external supplier s in period t (kW). The active discharging power of each BES and EV is given by $p_{(b,t)}^{dis}$ and $p_{(v,t)}^{dis}$ respectively (kW). The load curtailment power of load l for period t is represented by the variable $p_{(l,t)}^{Red}$ (kW) and the non-supplied power is given by $p_{(l,t)}^{imb^-}$ (kW).

Aggregator's Incomes. In Eq. 2, the aggregator earns revenue from BES and EV charging, modeled with the first and second terms; revenue from selling electricity to residential loads with the third term; and offers for the electricity market with the fourth term. The aggregator needs to maximize this function to achieve profits in the day-ahead optimization. That is, the values obtained in Eq. 2 need to be superior to those in Eq. 1.

$$max f_{In}^{Day+1} = \sum_{t \in T} \cdot \left(\begin{array}{l} \sum_{b \in B} p_{(b,t)}^{cha} \cdot S_{(b,t)}^{cha} + \sum_{v \in V} p_{(v,t)}^{cha} \cdot S_{(v,t)}^{cha} + \\ \sum_{l \in L} p_{(l,t)}^{Load} \cdot S_{(l,t)}^{Load} + \sum_{m \in M} p_{(m,t)}^{Sell} \cdot S_{(m,t)}^{Sell} \end{array} \right) \cdot \Delta t \quad (2)$$

where $S_{(b,t)}^{cha}$ and $S_{(v,t)}^{cha}$ are the parameters associated with the prices of BES and EV charging (m.u./kWh). $S_{(l,t)}^{Load}$ represents the tariff of load l in period t (m.u./kWh) and $S_{(m,t)}^{Sell}$ is the price of selling electricity in market m in each period t (m.u./kWh). $p_{(l,t)}^{Load}$ is the parameter of day-ahead load forecast in period t (kW). $p_{(b,t)}^{cha}$ and $p_{(v,t)}^{cha}$ are the variables of active charging power of each BES b and EV v (kW). The variable associated with power sold in the electricity market m in each period t is $p_{(m,t)}^{Sell}$ (kW).

Objective Function. The cost minimization problem is defined in Eq. 3, where the aggregator subtracts the incomes from the operational costs to obtain a profit.

$$minimize \ z(\boldsymbol{x}) = -f_{In}^{Day+1} + f_{OC}^{Day+1} \quad (3)$$

The complete mathematical formulations of the problem regarding all grid constraints and resource constraints that the objective function (Eq. 3) is subject to can be found in [16]. In this paper, only the main network constraints are shown as follows:

Active and reactive power balance:

$$
\begin{pmatrix}
\sum_{i \in \Omega_I^j} (p_{(i,t)}^{DG} - p_{(i,t)}^{imb^+}) + \sum_{s \in \Omega_S^j} p_{(s,t)}^{Sup} + \\
\sum_{b \in \Omega_B^j} (p_{(b,t)}^{dis} - p_{(b,t)}^{cha}) + \sum_{v \in \Omega_V^j} (p_{(v,t)}^{dis} - p_{(v,t)}^{cha}) + \\
\sum_{l \in \Omega_L^j} (p_{(l,t)}^{Red} + p_{(l,t)}^{imb^-} - p_{(l,t)}^{Load}) - \sum_{m\Omega_M^j} p_{(m,t)}^{Sell} - \\
V_{(j,t)} \cdot \sum_{k \in K} V_{(k,t)} (G_{(j,k,t)} \cdot cos\theta_{(j,k,t)} + \\
B_{(j,k,t)} \cdot sin\theta_{(j,k,t)})
\end{pmatrix} = 0 \qquad (4)
$$
$$\forall t, \forall j, k \neq j$$

$$
\begin{pmatrix}
\sum_{i \in \Omega_I^j} Q_{(i,t)}^{DG} + \sum_{s \in \Omega_s^j} Q_{(s,t)}^{Sup} - \sum_{l \in \Omega_L^j} Q_{(l,t)}^{Load} - \\
V_{(j,t)} \cdot \sum_{k \in K} V_{(k,t)} (G_{(j,k,t)} \cdot sin\theta_{(j,k,t)} - \\
B_{(j,k,t)} \cdot cos\theta_{(j,k,t)})
\end{pmatrix} = 0 \qquad (5)
$$
$$\forall t, \forall j, k \neq j$$

where K is the set of buses $(1, 2, 3, ..., N_k)$, Ω_I^j is the set of DG units at bus j of the network, Ω_S^j the set of external suppliers at bus j, Ω_B^j is the set of BES at bus j, Ω_V^j is the set of EVs at bus j, Ω_L^j represents the set of loads at bus j, and Ω_M^j is the set of electricity market buyers at bus j. Regarding $V_{(j,t)}$ represents the voltage magnitude at bus j in the period t (p.u.). $G_{(j,k,t)}$ and $B_{(j,k,t)}$ represent the real and imaginary part of the line admittance from bus j to bus k for the period t (Ω^{-1}). $Q_{(i,t)}^{DG}$ (kvar), $Q_{(s,t)}^{Sup}$ and $Q_{(l,t)}^{Load}$ are the reactive powers of DG unit i for period t (kvar), the reactive power of external supplier s in period t and the reactive load power l for the period t (kvar).

Voltage magnitude and angle levels:

$$V_{(j,t)}^{min} \leq V_{(j,t)} \leq V_{(j,t)}^{max} \qquad\qquad \forall t, \forall j \qquad (6)$$

$$\theta_{(j,t)}^{min} \leq \theta_{(j,t)} \leq \theta_{(j,t)}^{max} \qquad\qquad \forall t, \forall j \qquad (7)$$

where $V_{(j,t)}^{min}$ and $V_{(j,t)}^{max}$ represent the minimum and maximum limits for the voltage magnitude at bus j for the period t (p.u.). The $\theta_{(j,t)}^{min}$ and $\theta_{(j,t)}^{max}$ are the minimum and maximum voltage phase angles at bus j in period t (rad).

Thermal line limits:

$$
\left| \begin{array}{c} V_{(j,t)}([(V_{(j,t)} - V_{(k,t)})y_{(j,k,t)}]^* + \\ [V_{(j,t)} \cdot \frac{1}{2} y_{Shunt\_j}]^*) \end{array} \right| \leq S_{(j,k,t)}^{max} \qquad (8)
$$
$$\forall t, \forall j, k \neq j$$

where $y_{(j,k,t)}$ is the line admittance from bus j to bus k for the period t t (Ω^{-1}), y_{Shunt_j} is the shunt admittance of the line connected to bus j t (Ω^{-1}) and $S_{(j,k,t)}^{\max}$ is the maximum apparent power flow in the line from bus j to bus k in period t (kVA).

2.2   Differential Evolution Strategies

DE is a population-based EA for continuous optimization. DE combines solutions from the population using a linear operator. New solutions are generated at each iteration and evaluated in a given fitness function to optimize a particular problem. The algorithm retains the solutions with better performance, and solutions with lower fitness values are replaced in the iterative process. The phases of this method are as follows: first, a solution (target vector) is formed; next, a donor vector is generated by mutation (by a combination of different solutions in the population); and last, a trial vector is generated through a recombination operator between the target vector and the donor vector. The way in which the donor vector is created can have variations that give rise to different DE strategies. The reader can consult [15] to get specifics on these DE strategies.

We briefly discuss four well-known DE mutation strategies applied in this work to address the ERM problem and to apply the automatic configuration package. The first DE strategy is the DE/rand/1 strategy, where a linear combination of three randomly selected solutions creates the donor vector. In the second strategy, the DE/target-to-best/1, the base vectors are chosen following a line formed by the target vector and the best-so-far vector (i.e., the best-so-far solution found in the iterative process). In the third strategy, the DE/rand/1 with dither, the operator uses a random variation of the scale factor (dither), which is incorporated in the formulation of the donor vector. Finally, in the DE/rand/1/either-or, either a three-vector pure mutation method (like standard DE), with probability p_m, or a random recombination technique, with probability $1-p_m$, is used to create the mutant vector.

For a full explanation of the solution encoding used for DE optimization and the formulations of the different DE strategies, the reader can be directed to [15].

2.3   Iterated Racing

Figure 1 shows the automatic configuration approach based on iterated racing for the multiple DE strategies. Initially, irace needs an input scenario that allows irace to run and evaluate the various configurations based on iterated racing. The finite number of configurations to start the race is related to the maximum experiment budget given in the scenario. Additionally, each DE parameter for irace to configure (i.e., name, type, range) is also set in the scenario, together with an initial configuration that irace first evaluates and forbidden configurations in terms of logical expressions between parameters, which irace does not consider. Each DE strategy is also passed as input to obtain the auto-tuning parameters for the respective strategy.

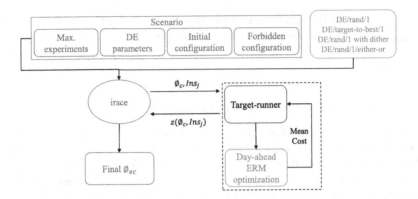

Fig. 1. Proposed method for automatic configuration of the multiple DE strategies using irace.

Irace then calls the target-runner, which is in charge of analyzing a specific target algorithm configuration (ϕ_c) of a particular instance ($Ins_j(instance, seed)$) and returning the appropriate cost value ($z(\phi_c, Ins_j)$). In this case, since we omitted different training instances due to the characteristics of the problem in [15], irace only considers different random seeds as instances. The target-runner evokes the DE day-ahead ERM optimization problem (implemented in MATLAB) to obtain the respective mean cost results over several runs.

After irace finishes the iterative process, it selects the best-performing configurations and the so-called elite configurations (ϕ_{ec}) based on the lowest mean cost values.

3   Case Study

This section describes the case study used to validate the proposed approach. The case study includes data regarding energy resources and the parameterization needed for irace to perform auto-tuning.

3.1   33-Bus Distribution Network

The SG consists of a medium voltage 12.66 kV 33-bus distribution network [17] used to test the multiple DE strategies and automatic tuning of irace. The 33-bus network scenario includes 1800 EVs with V2G capabilities, 67 DGs (including a sizable wind turbine), 10 external providers, and 15 BES. In bus 33, external suppliers are represented as a substation linked to the main grid. Figure 2 shows the total forecasted load demand comprising 32 residential consumers and the total forecasted renewable generation (PV and wind) for the day-ahead optimization. Direct Load Control (DLC) contracts as low as 0.02 m.u./kWh are also considered. Consumers receive this advantage for each lowered energy unit

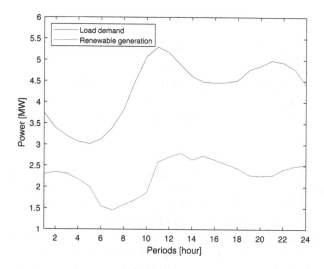

Fig. 2. Total forecasted day-ahead load demand and renewable generation.

instead of paying the 0.14 m.u./kWh supply price agreed upon by the aggregator. The selling price for energy is also fixed at 0.14 m.u./kWh. Additionally, a fleet of 1800 EVs with V2G capabilities is considered, with a forecast of 13.77 MWh total energy needed for 2553 trips. EV and BES have a discharge cost of 0.19 m.u./kWh. EV and BES have charging/discharging efficiencies set at 70% and 90%, respectively.

Modeling these EV trips was done using an EV travel behavior simulator tool suggested in [18]. With the aid of this simulator, we can gather information about each EV's trip, including the maximum charge and discharge rates, the minimal amount of charging necessary for the EV to complete its journey in the upcoming hour (or hours), as well as many other variables that are used as input for the optimization.

3.2   Irace Parameterization

The DE algorithm used in this work only needs four different parameters to be set. Table 1 shows each parameter, where NP is the population size, $maxIt$ is the maximum number of iterations the algorithm performs, and F and Cr are the scale factor and crossover probability, respectively. These parameters must be set and passed to irace, giving the software the type of each parameter (e.g., NP and $maxIt$ are integer parameters). It is also needed to set the range of values for each parameter, i.e., the search space that the irace algorithm uses to find the best configurations. We set these ranges according to the manual tuning performed in [15] and also consider the computation effort in the search space.

Irace starts with an initial configuration to be set and tested first; if results are satisfactory, similar configurations will be generated and tested. Table 1 presents

Table 1. DE parameters.

Parameter	Type	Parameter range	Initial value
NP	i	(10,100)	20
$maxIt$	i	(1,500)	100
F	r	(0.00,1.00)	0.30
Cr	r	(0.00,1.00)	0.50

the values for the initial configuration given to irace, starting from the initial point considered in the previous work where F, Cr, NP, and $maxIt$ were set to 0.3, 0.5, 20, and 100, respectively. These values did not result from an a priori tuning. They were just randomly set and given to irace.

Additionally, to be in conformity with [15], we set the maximum number of function evaluations (FEs) that the algorithm can test to 10,000 ($NP \times maxIt \leq$ 10,000). We set this restriction as a forbidden configuration to avoid testing combinations of NP and $maxIt$ that result in a large number of FEs. Finally, a maximum of 300 experiments, which sets the tuning budget, limiting the total number of executions. This number represents the maximum tuning budget used for irace, i.e., the number of configurations evaluated for each instance. We noticed that increasing this value would greatly increase simulation time since more configurations would need to be tested.

We implement and evaluate the irace package on a Linux virtual machine running Ubuntu 22.04.1 LTS equipped with an Intel Xeon Gold 5120 processor operating at 2.20GHz and 16GB of RAM. The irace package used a target-runner developed in Python 3.6.10, and the DE optimization strategies were implemented in MATLAB R2018a.

4   Results and Discussion

This section presents the results and the experiments made using irace for the parameter auto-tuning of the multiple DE strategies. Also, we compare the best-obtained automatic tuning configurations with those found with the manual tuning in [15].

4.1   Auto-tuning Experiments

Irace simulations were done for a total of 10 runs and 10,000 function evaluations (FEs) for each DE optimization in MATLAB. That is, the MATLAB code is run for 10 trials when it is called by the target-runner in irace.

Concerning the experiment process, Fig. 3 shows the performance of the elite configurations in each iteration of irace for the DE/rand/1 strategy. The figure shows the best configurations for ten instances (random seeds) evaluated. The final best configuration found by irace for this strategy was configuration 24,

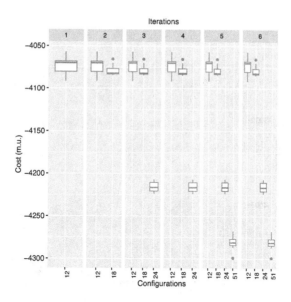

Fig. 3. Elite configuration performance by iteration of irace for DE/rand/1 strategy (in green the best configuration). (Color figure online)

which presented the lowest mean cost value (-4,215.31 m.u.). Notice that, even though configuration 51 gives lower values, irace did not obtain cost results for this configuration in all the ten tested instances (only for 8 of those), which is why this configuration was not chosen as the best. That is, in two out of ten evaluated instances, irace did not obtain any cost results (presented NA results), disregarding this configuration as the best (more robust) for this DE strategy because the race terminated before the instances were considered for this configuration. Figure 4 presents the performance of the best elite configurations for the DE/target-to-best/1 strategy, similar to the preceding case. In this situation, only configuration 49 was considered elite in the final iteration, with the others being discarded by the statistical test done by irace. This configuration presented a mean cost value of -4,053.93 m.u. for nine seeds, a reduction of 189.08 m.u. compared to configuration 2 (best elite in iteration 4).

Figure 5 shows the iterative process regarding the elite configurations for the DE/rand/1 with dither mutation strategy. The figure shows that configuration 27 was the best-performing configuration with the lowest mean cost value compared with configurations 9 and 13, which were also elites in the last iteration. Configuration 27 obtained −4,173.36 m.u., a decrease of 2.78% compared to configuration 13 and 11.38% compared to configuration 9. Similar to the DE/target-to-best/1, only one elite configuration was obtained with DE/rand/1/either-or strategy in the last iteration of irace, with the rest being discarded, as Fig. 6 shows. In this strategy, the best-performing configuration was configuration 52 (the last configuration evaluated by irace), with a mean cost value of −4,144.43 for 9 instances.

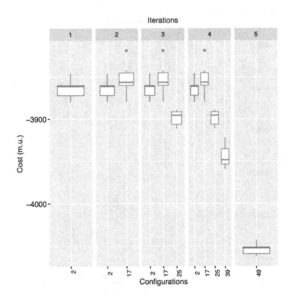

Fig. 4. Elite configuration performance by iteration of irace for DE/target-to-best/1 strategy (in green the best configuration). (Color figure online)

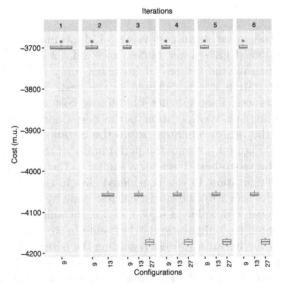

Fig. 5. Elite configuration performance by iteration of irace for DE/rand/1-with-dither strategy (in green the best configuration). (Color figure online)

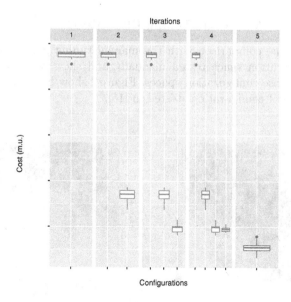

Fig. 6. Elite configuration performance by iteration of irace for DE/rand/1/either-or strategy (in green the best configuration). (Color figure online)

Table 2. Best elite configurations obtained by irace.

Strategy	NP	$maxIt$ (60k FEs)	F	Cr
DE/rand/1	37	249 (1,622)	0.28	0.39
DE/target-to-best/1	21	425 (2,857)	0.57	0.10
DE/rand/1 with dither	27	428 (2,222)	0.03	0.25
DE/either-or-algorithm/1	49	181 (1,224)	0.25	0.33

We took the final best elite configurations for each proposed DE mutation strategy. The parameters of the best elite configurations given by irace are presented in Table 2.

The DE/rand/1 and DE/either-or-algorithm/1 strategies performed better for higher values of NP and lower values of $maxIt$ compared to the other two strategies. Notice that the obtained parameters were found for 10,000 FEs due to the computational effort, which is a smaller number of FEs than the one used in [15] for the final result comparison. Thus, for a more realistic comparison of the final results presented in Sect. 4.2 of [15], we updated the number of iterations based on the NP parameter to match the 60,000 FEs used to solve the ERM optimization problem in the cited paper.

4.2   Manual vs. Automatic Tuning ERM Results

Before starting the comparison with the manual tuning performed in [15], we take the configuration space tested manually and show where our automatic tuning lays in those configuration spaces. Figure 7 show heatmaps representing the performance of configurations tested in [15].

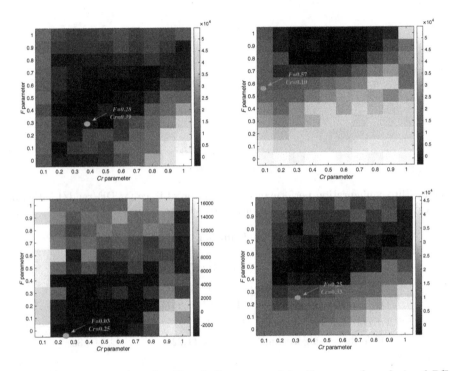

Fig. 7. Auto-tuning points for F and Cr compared to the manual analysis of DE strategies. (a) DE/rand/1. (b) DE/target-to-best/1. (c) DE/rand/1 with dither. (d) DE/rand/1/either-or (in blue, the best F and Cr parameters found with auto-tuning). (Color figure online)

A darker color represents a better performance of a specific combination of F and Cr parameters. We then plot the best configuration found with irace automatic tuning as a blue point in that figure. It can be noticed in Fig. 7(a) that the manual tuning for DE/rand/1 showed good performances for Cr between [0.3,0.8] and F in the range of [0.3,07], whereas irace obtained values for F and Cr near that area. In contrast, Fig. 7(b) shows that for the DE/target-to-best/1 strategy, the F and Cr point acquired by irace does not fall inside the ranges where the manual tuning showed good fitness results (specifically found for higher values of F (between 0.7 and 1) and [0.3,0.7] for Cr). Figure 7(c) shows that, again, the auto-tuning configuration of DE/rand/1 with dither strategy obtained is within the range of values for F and Cr recommended

Table 3. Comparison of each algorithm's manual and automatic profit and cost results.

Strategy	Manual tuning (m.u.)			Automatic tuning (m.u.)		
	Avg. Profits ± std	In	OC	Avg. Profits ± std	In	OC
DE/rand/1	4,458.99 ± 20.48	19,939.98	15,480.99	4,705.11 ± 9.63	19,724.46	15,019.35
DE/target-to-best	4,151.39 ± 28.46	20,356.94	16,205.55	4,465.51 ± 13.26	19,699.04	15,233.53
DE/rand/1 with dither	4,610.24 ± 19.15	19,798.25	15,188.02	4,633.38 ± 14.78	19,809.28	15,175.91
DE/either-or-algorithm/1	4,746.70 ± 6.46	19,624.75	14,878.05	4,307.64 ± 42.00	19,001.98	14,694.34

by the manual tuning. Finally, similarly to what occurred with the DE/target-to-best/1 strategy, Fig. 7(d) shows an automatic tuning configuration for the DE/rand/1/either-or strategy a bit out of the recommended ranges of the manual tuning. Note that in the manual tuning, the NP and $maxIt$ parameters were fixed values, but in irace, these parameters are optimized together with F and Cr, so these figures do not ideally represent the performance of irace since the other parameters also need to be taken into account.

Comparing the manual tuning of the DE strategies for the NP parameter to the automatic configuration, the manual tuning obtained the best results for a NP value of 30 in all strategies. In contrast, the automatic configuration obtained more specific values for each strategy, as shown previously, and the number of iterations was uploaded accordingly to the maximum number of FEs. Table 3 gives the average profit results (Eq. (3)) obtained with the best manual configuration found in [15] and the automatic configuration found using irace. 50 trials were done using the best automatic configurations found (remember that 60,000 FEs were considered for a fair comparison). The table shows that the automatic configuration for each DE strategy showed better results, except for the DE/either-or-algorithm/1, where a decrease of 9.25% compared to the manual configuration was registered. Regarding the average optimization time, the automatic tuning was faster in all strategies. The running time for the manual tuning took around 60 min in all algorithms, while the automatic tuning took about 40 min.

The decrease in performance for the automatic tuning of the DE/either-or-algorithm/1 strategy is justified by the low incomes obtained, shown in Table 3, compared to the manual configuration. The parameters provided by irace for DE/rand/1 showed an increase in profits of 246.12 m.u. in the ERM optimization compared to the original work. This improvement is given mostly by a decrease in operational costs of 2.98% compared to the costs obtained by the manual configuration (Table 3). Concerning the DE/target-to-best/1 strategy, the automatic configuration found a solution that increases the profits by 314.12 m.u. compared to the manual configuration. This increase is accomplished by the reduction in operational costs of 972.02 m.u., even though the auto-tuned obtained less income (657.90 m.u.) compared to the manual tuning, evidenced in Table 3. Regarding the DE/rand/1 with dither mutation strategy, the auto-tuning provided a slightly better solution, with the incomes and operational costs being similar.

5   Conclusions

In this work, we proposed automatically tuning multiple parameters for diverse DE mutation strategies using irace. Irace is a software package that utilizes iterated racing for automatic configuration evaluations. We compared the results obtained with the auto-tuning with those obtained using a manual configuration in a centralized day-ahead ERM optimization problem.

Results showed that the parameters obtained in the automatic configuration found better optimization solutions for all proposed DE strategies except for DE/either-or-algorithm/1. The decrease in performance for this strategy (worse profit results) can be justified by the number of maximum experiments established in the setting of the irace software. An increase in this specific parameter would allow irace to test more configurations, allowing it to test and find better configurations with this strategy (and with the rest of the tested strategies). However, increasing this parameter would also increase execution time as more optimization trials would be required. This is important to recall since automatic tuning is intended to be a more efficient method to configure our algorithms; thus, performing an adequate number of tests is key to achieving such efficiency. Still, the automatic tuning was insufficient to find a better configuration than the one found with the manual tuning for the DE/either-or-algorithm/1. Nevertheless, the automatic tuning found an acceptable solution with DE/rand/1 strategy, a solution that is just 0.88% worse than the best solution found with the manual tuning configuration. These results show that despite the advantages of automatic tuning, there is still room for improvement when using such methods.

As interesting venues for future research, new tests could be implemented with an increase in the maximum tuning budget, increasing the number of evaluated configurations, and increasing the computational time. Also, we could explore the efficiency of the method when initial configurations for each strategy, based, for example, on the best configuration found with the manual tuning, are provided as starting points. Additionally, more instances of the problem with modified characteristics would be required to validate the algorithms' performance and guarantee a more general algorithm parameterization.

Acknowledgments. The present work has received funding from the Brazilian Federal Agency for Support and Evaluation of Graduate Education (CAPES) and through the FCT Portuguese Foundation for Science and Technology (2019.00141.CBM). José Almeida is supported by FCT with Ph.D. Grant 2022.09590.BD. João Soares has received funding from FCT, namely CEECIND/00420/2022. The authors acknowledge the work facilities and equipment provided by the GECAD research center (UIDB/00760/2020 and UIDP/00760/2020) to the project team.

References

1. Yazdanie, M., Orehounig, K.: Advancing urban energy system planning and modeling approaches: gaps and solutions in perspective. Renew. Sustain. Energy Rev. **137**, 110607 (2021)

2. Milford, J., Henrion, M., Hunter, C., Newes, E., Hughes, C., Baldwin, S.F.: Energy sector portfolio analysis with uncertainty. Appl. Energy **306**, 117926 (2022)
3. Hossain, M.A., Pota, H.R., Squartini, S., Abdou, A.F.: Modified PSO algorithm for real-time energy management in grid-connected microgrids. Renew. Energy **136**, 746–757 (2019)
4. Soares, J., Pinto, T., Lezama, F., Morais, H.: Survey on complex optimization and simulation for the new power systems paradigm. Complexity **2018**, 1–32 (2018)
5. Songyuan, Yu., Fang, F., Liu, Y., Liu, J.: Uncertainties of virtual power plant: problems and countermeasures. Appl. Energy **239**, 454–470 (2019)
6. Kazikova, A., Pluhacek, M., Senkerik, R.: Why tuning the control parameters of metaheuristic algorithms is so important for fair comparison? MENDEL **26**(2), 9–16 (2020)
7. Vieira, M., Faia, R., Lezama, F., Vale, Z.: A sensitivity analysis of PSO parameters solving the P2P electricity market problem. In: 2022 IEEE Congress on Evolutionary Computation (CEC), pp. 1–7, Padua, Italy, July (2022). IEEE
8. Stützle, T., López-Ibáñez, M.: Automated design of metaheuristic algorithms. In: Gendreau, M., Potvin, J.-Y. (eds.) Handbook of Metaheuristics. ISORMS, vol. 272, pp. 541–579. Springer, Cham (2019). https://doi.org/10.1007/978-3-319-91086-4_17
9. Birattari, M.: Tuning metaheuristics: a machine learning perspective. Tuning Metaheuristics **197**, 221 (2009)
10. Birattari, M., Stützle, T., Paquete, L., Varrentrapp, K.: A racing algorithm for configuring metaheuristics. In: Proceedings of the 4th Annual Conference on Genetic and Evolutionary Computation, GECCO 2002, pp. 11–18, San Francisco, CA, USA (2002). Morgan Kaufmann Publishers Inc
11. Yuan, Z., Stützle, T., Montes de Oca, M.A., Lau, H.C., Birattari, M.: An analysis of post-selection in automatic configuration. In: Proceeding of the Fifteenth Annual Conference on Genetic and Evolutionary Computation Conference - GECCO 2013, pp. 1557, Amsterdam, The Netherlands (2013). ACM Press
12. Adenso-Díaz, B., Laguna, M.: Fine-tuning of algorithms using fractional experimental designs and local search. Oper. Res. **54**(1), 99–114 (2006)
13. López-Ibáñez, M., Dubois-Lacoste, J., Cáceres, L.P., Birattari, M., Stützle, T.: The irace package: iterated racing for automatic algorithm configuration. Oper. Res. Perspect. **3**, 43–58 (2016)
14. Huang, C., Li, Y., Yao, X.: A survey of automatic parameter tuning methods for metaheuristics. IEEE Trans. Evol. Comput. **24**(2), 201–216 (2020)
15. Lezama, F., Sucar, E., de Cote, E.M., Soares, J., Vale, Z.: Differential evolution strategies for large-scale energy resource management in smart grids. In: Proceedings of the Genetic and Evolutionary Computation Conference Companion, pp. 1279–1286, Berlin Germany, July (2017). ACM
16. Soares, J., Ghazvini, M.A.F., Silva, M., Vale, Z.: Multi-dimensional signaling method for population-based metaheuristics: solving the large-scale scheduling problem in smart grids. Swarm Evol. Comput. **29**, 13–32 (2016)
17. Baran, M.E., Wu, F.F.: Network reconfiguration in distribution systems for loss reduction and load balancing. IEEE Trans. Power Deliv. **4**(2), 1401–1407 (1989)
18. Soares, J., Canizes, B., Lobo, C., Vale, Z., Morais, H.: Electric vehicle scenario simulator tool for smart grid operators. Energies **5**(6), 1881–1899 (2012)

Standard Energy Data Competition Procedure: A Comprehensive Review with a Case Study of the ADRENALIN Load Disaggregation Competition

Balázs András Tolnai[1,2] , Zheng Ma[1,2(✉)] , and Bo Nørregaard Jørgensen[1,2]

[1] SDU Center for Energy Informatics, Maersk Mc-Kinney Moeller Institute, 5230 Odense, Denmark
bat@mmmi.sdu.dk

[2] The Faculty of Engineering, University of Southern Denmark, 5230 Odense, Denmark

Abstract. Crowdsourcing data science competitions has become popular as a cost-effective alternative to solving complex energy-related challenges. However, comprehensive reviews on hosting processes remain scarce. Therefore, this paper undertakes a detailed review of 33 existing data competitions and 12 hosting platforms, complemented by an in-depth case study of the ADRENALIN load disaggregation competition. The review identifies essential elements of competition procedure, including platform selection, timeline, datasets, and submission and evaluation mechanisms. Based on proposed 16 evaluation criteria, the similarities and differences between data competition hosting platforms can be categorized into platform scoring and popularity, platform features, community engagement, open-source platforms, region-specific platforms, platform-specific purposes, and multi-purpose platforms. The case study underscores strategic planning's critical role, particularly platform selection. The case study also shows the importance of defining competition scope which influences the whole competition content and procedure, especially the datasets.

Keywords: Data science competition · Data competitions · Competition Platforms · Competition timelines

1 Introduction

The phenomenon of crowdsourcing solutions to data problems through competitive platforms has grown immensely popular over the last decade. These competitions serve as a cost-effective alternative to traditional hiring, fostering a broad spectrum of innovative solutions by harnessing the collective intelligence of global participants. For competitors, these events offer a remarkable opportunity to learn new techniques, refine their skills, and augment their professional portfolios.

This trend is particularly vital in the energy sector, where data-driven solutions are crucial for addressing complex energy-related challenges and problems {Christensen,

© The Author(s), under exclusive license to Springer Nature Switzerland AG 2024
B. N. Jørgensen et al. (Eds.): EI.A 2023, LNCS 14467, pp. 60–76, 2024.
https://doi.org/10.1007/978-3-031-48649-4_4

2019 #62}. From energy efficiency and load forecasting to renewable energy integration and grid stability, data competitions play a significant role in generating groundbreaking solutions and accelerating the energy transition {Vanting, 2021 #109}.

Numerous companies and platforms, such as Kaggle, specialize in hosting these competitions. The selection ranges from free platforms to premium services, where professional teams aid in the competition's management. Choosing the hosting platform is one of the many pivotal decisions that underpin the successful execution of a data science competition.

While guidelines for hosting or setting up these competitions do exist, such as Kaggle's community competition setup guide [7] and Chalearn's guide [9], there is a notable lack of a comprehensive review that considers the entire process. This paper aims to fill this gap by thoroughly examining the hosting process of data science competitions, drawing insights from 33 prior competitions hosted in 2021 and 2022 by the NeurIPS 2022 conference (25 out of 33 competitions) [12] and other conferences on the AIcrowd platform. These competitions were collected in 2022 and they tackle a large variety of topics, including reinforcement learning, computer vision and forecasting.

To enrich our exploration, we present a case study - the ADRENALIN load disaggregation competition [14]. This competition is an integral part of the ADRENALIN project, a strategic initiative to crowdsource energy solutions for buildings. This paper provides a comprehensive review of standard energy data competition procedures and their importance in addressing energy-related challenges, with a spotlight on the ADRENALIN case.

The paper is organized as follows: The paper will first review the process of competition hosting. First, it looks at the official websites and platforms for competition hosting, and then analyses the stages, and durations of the competitions. Afterward, it looks into the technical parts of a competition, by reviewing the datasets, the starter kit, the submission, the evaluation, and the competition description. After the review, the paper showcases the case study of the ADRENALIN load disaggregation competition.

2 Review of Data Competition Procedures

The review of the 33 data competitions shows that a data competition includes the following 7 elements:

2.1 Official Website

Every online competition necessitates an official website. These websites serve as the primary source for sharing up-to-date information about the competition, equipping participants with everything they need to compete. They provide background information, the problem statement, evaluation procedures, prizes, and details about sponsors and hosting organizations. They also offer guidance on the submission process, where to submit, and access to the dataset.

In addition to these websites, many competitions maintain a GitLab or GitHub page, as observed in 17 of the investigated competitions [17]. These platforms primarily function as repositories for sharing information. The competition description is usually incorporated in the readme.md file, displayed on the GitHub page. They can also host datasets, starting kits, reinforcement learning environments, or any other necessary tools. These resources can be effortlessly downloaded or forked by Git users. AIcrowd, for example, frequently utilizes its own GitLab to manage code submissions [17].

Among the 33 examined competitions, 27 maintained more than one website. However, it is not uncommon to solely use a data competition hosting platform for all purposes. Of the 33 competitions, six employed one of the hosting platforms as their official website. Of these, two used AIcrowd [18, 19], two used Kaggle [20, 21], and one-one used Codalab [22] and EvalAI [23].

2.2 Hosting Platforms

Figure 1 shows the distribution of the used platforms in the 33 analyzed competitions. The figure shows that 10 of the competitions did not use a hosting platform. These used their own websites to organize the competition, handling submissions by uploading on the website, or through other means, such as Google Drive. Three of these were hosted by the Institute of Advanced Research in Artificial Intelligence [24–26], which has hosted multiple competitions on its own website. The most used platform was Codalab, used 8 times, followed by AI crowd, used 7 times. The other three platforms used in the sample of 33 competitions, were EvalAI 4 times, Kaggle 3 times, and DrivenData once.

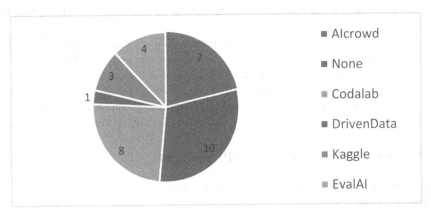

Fig. 1. Platforms used for the 33 reviewed data competitions.

There are many platforms designed to host data science competitions. One of the most important features of these platforms is the automatic evaluation of the submissions. Using the automatic scoring, a live leaderboard can be maintained throughout the competition. This helps competitors see how well their solution fares compared to the others. Since the evaluation is done automatically, it also ensures that the rankings are unbiased.

This paper applies 16 criteria (as shown in Table 1) to evaluate the 12 data competition hosting platforms, extending, and updating a comparison previously made by David Rousseau and Andrey Ustyuzhanin [27]. These hosting platforms are AiCrowd,

Table 1. Platforms comparison criteria

	Criteria	Description
1	Code-sharing	Code sharing gives participants an opportunity to share their work. This can help the community to find better solutions and increase the reproducibility of the winning solutions
2	Code submission	Platforms that allow code submission can automatically run the submitted code to produce the predictions. Code submission has some advantages over result submission
3	Active community	Does the platform have an active community, that will join the competition, and actively participate in it
4	Staged challenge	Is it possible to create a competition with multiple different stages
5	Custom metrics	Does the platform allow the hosts to define their own evaluation metrics or is it only possible to select from a list of predefined metrics
6	Private evaluation	Private evaluation allows the competition hosts to evaluate the submissions without sharing the test data with the hosting platform. This is useful if the privacy of the test set needs to be protected
7	Multi score leader board	Multi-score leaderboards allow the competitions to have multiple scores calculated from the submissions and posted on the leaderboard
8	Human evaluation	Some sites allow the hosting of competitions, where automatic scoring is replaced with human-in-the-loop evaluation
9	Open-source	Open-source platforms have higher transparency of their workings, and hosts have the option to set up their own servers by using the source code
10	RL-friendly	Reinforcement learning is a unique type of ML, where the agents need to communicate with the environment. This requires a unique setup, not supported by all platforms

(*continued*)

Table 1. (*continued*)

	Criteria	Description
11	Run for free	Some platforms allow the hosting of competitions free of charge
12	Discussion forum	Most platforms provide a forum for each competition, where the contestants can communicate with each other and with the organizers. Common topics include sharing ideas, looking for teammates, or discussing issues they came across
13	Technic support	Platforms marked as "certain" are designed for the users to set up technical support by themselves, relying only on the documentation. Despite this, the platform's creators and operators can be contacted directly with inquiries
14	Arrangement and management services	Does the platform provide services for arranging and managing data competition events
15	Ease of use for hosting	How easy is it to host and set up a data science competition on the platform
16	Ease of use for participation	How easy is it to join and participate in a competition. This includes registration, submission, etc

CodaLab, CrowdAnalytiX, EvalAI, Kaggle, RAMP, Tianchi, Driven Data, Zindi, Topcoder, Bitgrit, and HackerEarth. This comparison is shown in Table 2.

The comparison shows that the similarities and differences among the reviewed 12 platforms can be categorized into:

Platform Scoring and Popularity. In this comparison, Kaggle was the highest-scoring platform, with 14 points. As Kaggle is the most known and most used platform, competitions hosted here normally attract the most participants. AIcrowd follows as the second scoring 13.5 points. With 13.25 points, the third competition in ranking is Eval.AI, one of the fully open-source and free competition hosting platforms on this list. Ranking fourth with 12.75 points is Codalab. Driven Data also has an active community, though not quite as large as some other platforms.

Platform Features. Kaggle has also become more flexible over time, and competitions of all categories can be found on the platform. It is important to note, that Kaggle has both free and paid competitions. A free competition is very easy to host, but it has some restrictions compared to the paid version and would score lower. This version lacks some features, such as custom metrics (although there are many metrics to choose from), human evaluation, and technical support. AIcrowd does not have a free version. It is a flexible platform, with many different competitions hosted, which is the main reason for its high score. Codalab allows hosts to make significant changes to almost all aspects of the competition after its initial setup, using the dashboard on the website.

Community Engagement. Kaggle, AIcrowd, and Driven Data have active communities, with Kaggle attracting the most participants. AIcrowd usually has a few hundred competitors, and a few threads in the discussion forums. Driven Data, while not as large as some other platforms, hosts large competitions with substantial prize money.

Open-source Platforms. Eval.AI and Codalab are fully open-source and free competition hosting platforms. Eval.AI offers an email where it is possible to get in contact for those who have questions or have run into problems with the setup. A documentation can also be found, which includes a guide on how to set up competitions. Codalab also has good documentation online, and multiple example competitions can be found on Codalab's GitHub page.

Region-Specific Platforms. Tianchi, operated by Alibaba Cloud, is considered the Chinese equivalent of Kaggle. Ramp is an open-source platform, developed by the Paris-Saclay Center for Data Science and is mainly used by the University of Paris-Saclay to host competitions. Zindi is a platform that aims to support the African data science community.

Platform-Specific Purposes. Kaggle, Tianchi, and Zindi are not only about the competition but a central hub for learning and networking. The website for Tianchi serves as a sharing point for datasets, data science learning, and getting in touch with other computer scientists through the forums. Zindi also facilitates learning and job searching.

Multi-purpose Platforms. Topcoder, unlike the other platforms, is not specialized to host Data science competitions. It offers different tracks, such as ones called development, design, and QA (Quality assurance).

2.3 Competition Descriptions

The information shared on the websites and the official competition platform is important, as the participants read these to decide if they want to join the competition, or not. This is also their source of information, for what the competition is about, what they should do, and what they should expect from the competition. Competition descriptions usually have the following parts:

Background Information. This explains what the purpose of the competition is and what is the importance of the task the participants are trying to solve.

Problem formulation explains what the task is, and what is the target column in the dataset. It needs to be clear, so the participants know what they are going to be working on for the duration of the competition.

The timeline of the competition describes all of the deadlines, starts, and end dates of each competition phase.

The prizes section describes what prizes are available at the competition. This is usually prize money, split between the top finish contestants, but it can also be a publication opportunity or a conference or workshop invitation. In one competition the

Table 2. Comparison of data competition event hosting platforms

Criteria	AICrowd [1]	CodaLab Competitions [2]	CrowdAnalytiX [3]	EvalAI [4]	Kaggle [5]	RAMP [6]	Tianchi [8]	DrivenData [10]	Zindi [11]	Topcoder [13]	Bitgrit [15]	HackerEarth [16]
1	Y	Y	X	Y	Y	Y	Y	Y	Y	X	X	?
2	Y	Y	X	Y	Y	Y	Y	Y	X	Y	X	Y
3	***	***	*	**	****	*	*****	***	****	**	**	**
4	Y	Y	X	Y	Y	Y	Y	Y	X	X	Y	Y
5	Y	Y	Y	Y	Y	Y	?	Y	?	X	?	?
6	Y	Y	X	Y	Y	X	X	X	?	X	?	?
7	Y	Y	X	Y	X	X	Y	Y	X	X	X	X
8	Y	X	X	Y	Y	X	X	Y	X	X	X	X
9	X	Y	X	Y	X	Y	X	X	X	X	X	X
10	Y	Y	X	Y	Y	X	X	X	X	X	X	X
11	X	Y	X	Y	Y	Y	?	X	X	X	X	X
12	Y	Y	Y	Y	Y	X	Y	Y	Y	Y	Y	Y
13	Y	Y (certain)	Y	Y (certain)	Y	Y	Y	Y	Y	Y	Y	?
14	Y	X	Y	X	Y	X	Y	Y	Y	Y	Y	Y
15	****	**	****	*	****	***	****	****	****	****	****	****
16	***	**	**	**	****	**	**	***	***	**	**	**
Total score	13.5	12.75	5.75	13.25	14	8.5	9.5	11.5	6.5	6	6	6

The last row is a score calculated from the other criteria. It was calculated as every Y is one point, and every * is 0.25 points.

top finishers got offered a position, and in another one items were given out as special prizes.

The dataset description explains what the available dataset contains. Usually explains each file, and each column in the dataset.

The submission section describes the submission process, whether it is code or result, what needs to be uploaded, and where.

A description of the evaluation process usually discusses the evaluation metric, and how the private evaluation takes place.

Competitions usually need **a set of rules**, this usually asks the competitors to avoid things that could be considered cheating. Such as privately sharing code to take multiple top positions, and trying to find ways to abuse the submission system, such as creating multiple accounts to circumvent the submission limits.

2.4 Timeline and Stages

Competitions have a timeline, marking the most important dates of the competitions. Although the timelines are normally set before the competition starts, deadline extensions do occasionally happen. Competitions can have multiple stages, with different data availability, and different submission types.

Pre-phase. Some competitions have a stage before the main event of the competition takes place. In this study, these are referred to as a "pre-phase". Out of the analyzed competitions, 13 had a pre-phase. Twelve of these were an announcement, or a similar pre-phase with a different name. These usually include the release of part of the data, such as the training set without the test set, the release of the starter kit, and the announcement of the full details of the competition. This includes phases with different names, but similar purposes, such as quick start, registration, data, or starting kit release.

Two competitions have a warm-up phase, which this study also considers as a pre-phase. During this phase, most necessary information is already released, but the leaderboard is either not open, or the submissions are tested against the training data.

These phases are usually intended to help competitors familiarize themselves with the dataset, and the problem at hand. It is also a good opportunity for the organizers, to take some feedback from the participants, and potentially make adjustments before the competition starts at its earnest.

Main Phases. Eight out of the 33 competitions have only one main phase. These are the simplest competitions. For example, the majority of the competitions hosted on Kaggle fall into this category. These competitions usually have a start date, a final submission deadline, and often a team merger deadline or a rule acceptance deadline.

Seven of the analyzed competitions have 2 stages. In the second stage of the competition, the organizers often release additional data. This can serve multiple purposes, such as lowering the time participants get with the entire dataset and lowering the ability to purposefully overfit the dataset. Competitions often have a final phase, where the evaluation is held on a previously not used part of the dataset, with a very limited number of submissions. This is necessary to make sure that it is protected from leaderboard probing, and that the models are not overfitting by being finetuned, based on the results of the submission.

Some platforms, notably Kaggle, use the Private leaderboard system instead of a separate private evaluation round. In this setup, the test set is separated into a private and a public subset. Submissions are made on the entire test set, but feedback is only provided about the results on the public part. After the end of the competition, the leaderboard based on the private part is released, which reflects the results of the competition. The Ariel Machine Learning Data Challenge [28] competition had both a final submission and a second data release phase, making it the only three-phase competition with standard phases.

Competitions can have unique phases, and sometimes have multiple tracks. PETs Prize Challenge: Advancing Privacy-Preserving Federated Learning [29] had three phases unique to the problem. Participants could register as either a team that created a privacy-preserving federated system, or a team that tested these systems by trying to devise attacks on them. In the first phase, participants had to submit a concept paper for their federated system ideas. In the second phase, these concepts were developed and scored by judges, while the last phase was for the testing of these systems, by the tester teams. The Reconnaissance Blind Chess [30] was a competition, that was hosted as a tournament. There were two, optional test tournaments, and a real tournament. The Real Robot Challenge 2022 had a simulated qualification phase first, which was designed to limit the number of runs necessary on the real robots, in the second phase.

Competitions have multiple tracks, when there are multiple, closely correlated problems the organizers would like to solve. In these cases, often they chose to organize one competition, with multiple tracks, instead of a series of separate ones. The NeurIPS 2022 IGLU Challenge [18] had two tracks, the first one was about creating an AI that can follow instructions given in a natural language, to build structures. In the second task, an AI had to ask clarifying questions, when the instructions given are not enough to construct the structure. The Trojan Detection Challenge [31] had 3 tracks for three tasks. The first task was to identify trojaned networks while the second task was to classify trojaned networks into different categories. The last task was to create trojaned networks, that are difficult to identify. The Neural MMO challenge [32] had two tracks, in one of them the agents had to play the game alone, while on the other track, the agents had to play the game together, interacting with each other.

Most competitions have some form of activities after the competition has ended. This includes the announcement of the winners and contacting the winning teams to hand in further information about their solutions, such as documentation, papers, and program code. Some competitions are followed by a conference, or a workshop, where the winning teams are invited to present their solutions.

2.5 Competition Durations

The duration of each competition can vary, sometimes with large differences. The length of the one main stage competitions can be seen in Table 3. Their average length is about 77 days. Commonly the main stage of the competitions is around 90, roughly three months.

It is shown in Table 4. That two-stage competitions usually have a longer first stage. On average the length of the first stage is 74 days, while the second stage is only 19 days.

This is especially true when the second stage is the private test phase. This usually does not need a long time, as it is intended for submission of final models previously created, rather than for further development. Overall, the length of the competitions tends to be somewhere between two and four months.

Table 3. Duration of One-stage competitions

Event	Days
Discover the mysteries of the Maya - ECML PKDD 2021 - Discovery Challenge [33]	91
Feedback Prize – Predicting Effective Arguments. [20]	91
RSNA 2022 Cervical Spine Fracture Detection Identify cervical fractures from scans [21]	91
Global Challenge 2021 [34]	61
ADDI Alzheimer's Detection Challenge [35]	43
BASALT Competition 2022 [19]	98
OGB Large-Scale Challenge (OGB-LSC) [36]	161
AutoML Decathlon 2022 [37]	118
Natural Language for Optimization (NL4Opt) NeurIPS 2022 [38]	92
Second AmericasNLP Competition: Speech-to-Text Translation for Indigenous Languages of the Americas [39]	10
Open Catalyst Challenge [23]	16
Multimodal Single-Cell Integration Across Time, Individuals, and Batches [40]	92
Sensorium 2022 Competition [41]	117
Visual Domain Adaptation Challenge [42]	10
Habitat Rearrangement Challenge 2022 [43]	59

2.6 Data and Starter Kit

Starter Kit. Starter kits often accompany competitions, proving particularly crucial for those involving complex submission requirements, code submissions, and notably, reinforcement learning contests. These kits should contain all the necessary resources for making a submission, generally including a functional example. Occasionally, a baseline model may be included to provide competitors with a solid starting point, encouraging them to modify the baseline model according to their approach. The primary aim of these kits is to ensure that participants can correctly submit their entries by swapping the model in the starting kit with their own.

Out of the 33 competitions analyzed, 26 provided a starter kit. Sixteen of these were available through GitHub, four via GitLab, and the remaining six could be found on the hosting platform or website.

Table 4. Duration of two-stage competitions

Event	Stage 1 (days)	Stage 2 (days)
CityLearn Challenge 2022 - Multi-Agent Reinforcement Learning for energy management in cities [17]	46	30
EURO Meets NeurIPS 2022 Vehicle Routing Competition [44]	91	27
Weather4cast Multi-sensor Weather Forecast Competition [26]	110	6
Data Purchasing Challenge 2022 [45]	24	35
Cross-Domain MetaDL 2022 [46]	62	30
2022 NeurIPS Driving SMARTS Competition [47]	92	10
Weather4cast 2022 [24]	80	8
MyoChallenge [48]	69	6
Weakly Supervised Cell Segmentation [49]	93	19

Dataset. Datasets are usually shared through the Competition hosting platforms, as they normally offer the possibility to upload the dataset on their platform, where the competitors can download it. Some competitions use other ways for dataset sharing, for example, GitHub or GitLab. The dataset is normally available alongside the starter kit or example submission.

The dataset is one of the most important parts of every data science problem, and as such, it is important for hosting a data science competition as well. The organizers must make sure that there is sufficient data available to teach machine learning models. A general rule of thumb is that the more data is the better. There are a few additional things that must be kept in mind when creating the dataset for the competition:

- In standard data science competitions featuring a private testing phase, the dataset must be divided into three parts: training, public validation, and private validation. When the competition employs a public and private leaderboard system, only two splits are necessary - one for training and one for validation. The training split should include the solutions column.
- In high-stakes competitions with monetary rewards, it is crucial to keep the test set concealed and devoid of leaks. If some participants gain access, it could compromise the competition's results.

2.7 Submission and Evaluation

Submission. There are two main ways a competition can take submissions. These are result submission and code submission. Out of the 33 competitions looked at in this paper, 16 used result submission, and 14 used code submission. Additionally, The Real Robot Challenge 2022 [50] used a system, where in the first round, participants had to submit their achieved score, and the code was only rerun for the top teams to verify their score. The Reconnaissance Blind Chess competition [30] did not require submission, as the tournament was played online. If a competition uses result submission, the test data must be shared with the participants, without the target column. The competitors have to locally compute their predictions, and submit it in tabular format. Afterward, the submission can be directly evaluated against the ground truth.

With code submission, the participants must submit their code, which is re-run on the competition's server to compute the predictions. This requires more computational power from the server. In exchange, it allows the test set to remain entirely hidden. In addition, it also allows further options for the evaluation of the submission, notably the measurement of the code's runtime. Code submission competitions normally have a runtime limit. This has the technical purpose of not allowing single submission to occupy a computational unit for an indefinite duration, but it can also help create more practical models, for real-life applications.

Evaluation. Normally, evaluation is the automatic calculation of a score, by comparing the predictions with the ground truth. Usually, there are two test sets, to calculate a public, and a private score. The public score serves as feedback for the competitors, which appears on the public leaderboard. The private score is used to calculate the outcome of the competition. This is either computed parallelly with the public score, at each submission or calculated in a final, separate round. This is important to avoid overfitting on the test data. The public dataset is also vulnerable to leaderboard probing, where the participants use various methods to infer information about the data based on the returned scores. This can in extreme cases lead to revealing the ground truth.

The comparison of the ground truth and the prediction is done via a mathematical formula, often called metric, or score. There have been many metrics developed over the years, with different goals in mind. For example, a simple F1 score is used in [22], and mean intersection over union for evaluation is used in a computer vision competition [42]. Furthermore, in the CityLearn Challenge [17], the average of 6 metrics is calculated in order to evaluate electricity consumption and carbon emissions. These metrics include ramping, 1-load factor, average daily peak demand, maximum peak electricity demand, total electricity consumed and carbon emissions. These Metrics are not unique to competitions, as it is always desirable to measure the accuracy of the machine learning model, in a way that they can be compared to each other. Loss functions are similar, often the same formulas, which are used during the learning process of an algorithm, though they usually have different criteria to fulfill. As loss functions are used during the training process, they usually need to be fast to compute, and gradient descent-based learning can only be performed on differentiable formulas. Evaluation metrics usually aim to be easy to understand for humans, and to capture and emphasize the most important aspects of the model.

3   Case Study

This case study centers around the organization of the "ADRENALIN 2023: Building Energy Load Disaggregation Challenge", a competition embedded in the ADRENALIN project with the aim of developing energy load disaggregation algorithms.

3.1 Competition Scope Definition

The overall theme of the competition is non-intrusive load disaggregation. Load disaggregation deals with the problem of discovering the sub-loads that make up a central, aggregated load. This can be beneficial for multiple reasons, e.g., to propagate energy saving behavior, or to create more precise demand response algorithms {Ma, 2021 #110}.

To determine the scope of the competition, a scoping review was also conducted [51]. Based on this review, it was decided that the competition will use low-frequency data, and aim to produce lightweight models. Furthermore, the literature also shows that the transferability of the developed forecasting models in buildings is a challenge, therefore the competitions also aim to test the applicability of the proposed solutions on different buildings.

3.2 Official Website

Similarly to the majority of the analyzed competitions, the case will also have multiple websites. The official website of the competition (https://adrenalin.energy/adrenalin-2023-building-energy-load-disaggregation-challenge) is on the ADRENALIN project's website [14]. The competition's other website is hosted on Codalab, which will handle submissions and maintain the leaderboard. The description of the competition's details is available on both sites.

3.3 Hosting Platforms

The selection of a hosting platform necessitated an evaluation of various options. Given the project's limited funding, the decision was made to utilize a free hosting service. Kaggle, known for its user-friendly interface, was one of the options, along with Eval.AI, and Codalab. However, Kaggle's restrictions, including the prohibition of prize offerings in the free version, led to its exclusion. After experimenting with Codalab and Eval.AI, Codalab was chosen due to its relative simplicity.

3.4 Competition Timeline, Stages, and Durations

Based on prior investigations, a three-stage competition was designed, which comprises a pre-phase, and two main phases. It commences with a **warm-up phase** from the 1st of February to the 15th of March 2024. This gives about 1.5 months (43 days) for participants to familiarize themselves with the problem.

The second phase is the **development phase**, stretching from the 15th of March to the 14th of June 2024, lasting 91 days. This corresponds to the duration of the development phase in the reviewed competitions. This is when participants refine their models, experiment with solutions, and struggle to achieve the best solution.

Given that Codalab does not support a private leaderboard system, the competition ends with the **private test phase**, lasting from the 15th of June to the 31st of July. This 1.5 month gives plenty of time for the participants to make a final submission, and for the organizers to validate the submissions. During this phase, the submissions are evaluated against previously unseen data to test their ability to generalize. This phase determines the final leaderboard positions and competition winners.

3.5 Data and Starter Kit

Starter Kit. The competition will feature a starter kit. This will include an example of a correct submission, and the evaluation program that will be used on Codalab to calculate the scores. This will help contestants locally test their submissions, ensuring their correctness. The starter kit might also include a working baseline model, chosen based on a scoping review, as an example.

Data. The competition will feature a diverse dataset, collected by the ADRENALIN project partners, from various countries across the world. This will provide a sufficient amount of data to facilitate learning. At least three datasets will be created: training data, test data for the development phase, and test data for the private test phase.

The dataset will include main- and sub-meter measurements from different buildings, including multiple different features, using low-frequency sampling. Supplementary information on the building's properties and weather information will also be included where available.

Furthermore, the usage of external data is allowed in this competition, as long as it is free and publicly available. The competitors must ensure that all data they use is freely available to all participants, and post access to the dataset on the competition forum before the end of the competition.

3.6 Submission and Evaluation

Submission. The submission of solutions will take place through the Codalab platform, using Codalab's submission system. The submission will be a result submission. Result submission is generally simpler to set up and guarantees that the submissions will have the same result as on the participant's own computer.

Metric. Deciding the metric for the competition is not a simple task. To see what evaluation metrics are used, a further study was conducted on a large number of competitions (130), to determine what are the most popular metrics used in current data science competitions. Furthermore, the literature review of load disaggregation also revealed the most popular metrics in the scope.

The most relevant metric was determined to be mean absolute error (MAE). MAE can be used to calculate the average difference between the predictions and the ground truth for the entire predicted time period. Based on the literature, it is preferred over Root mean squared error, as it does not emphasize larger errors disproportionately compared to smaller errors. Since Codalab can display multiple scores on the leaderboard, it is possible to add further metrics. Relative Mean Absolute Error and Mean Absolute Percentage Error are two averaged versions of MAE, which can provide further information, for human interpretation of the results.

3.7 Competition Descriptions

The descriptions of the competition will be available through both the official website and the Codalab platform. The descriptions include the sections identified during the revision.

It starts with the background, explaining the importance of energy disaggregation. This is followed by the problem statement, stating the goals and the task of the competition, based on the literature review. The following dataset description first gives an overview of the datasets, discusses its main features, and finally each file, and their contained features separately. The submission and the evaluation and metrics sections present the submission and the evaluation processes. The timeline section displays the information presented earlier. To help with getting in touch, a link to the discussion forum is also provided. Finally, the rules of the competition are provided, and acknowledgment to the sponsors of the competition.

4 Discussion and Conclusion

This paper conducts a comprehensive review on the procedure of data science competitions. This review uncovers the key elements involved, which include the construction of official websites, the selection of hosting platforms, timelines, datasets, starter kits, submission and evaluation protocols, and competition descriptions.

In a comparative analysis of various data science competition platforms, Kaggle was found to be the highest-scoring and most popular platform due to its flexibility, variety of competitions, and active community. AIcrowd, Eval.AI, Codalab, and Driven Data also scored high, offering a range of features and community engagement opportunities. Eval.AI and Codalab stand out as open-source platforms, while Tianchi, Ramp, and Zindi cater specifically to certain regions. Kaggle, Tianchi, and Zindi also serve as hubs for learning and networking, extending beyond just hosting competitions. Unlike the other platforms, Topcoder has a broader focus, offering tracks in development, design, and quality assurance alongside data science.

The case study of organizing a competition such as the Building Energy Load Disaggregation Challenge reveals the importance of careful planning and strategic decision-making in structuring the competition, choosing the hosting platform, and defining the submission and evaluation mechanisms. Especially the definition of competition scope which are not yet discussed in the literature. The competition scope influences the whole competition content and procedure, especially the datasets. The choice of Codalab for this competition exemplifies how factors such as cost and usability can significantly influence the hosting platform selection.

The insights gained from this study carry important implications for stakeholders in the energy sector seeking to organize data competitions to address pressing challenges. These stakeholders can range from academic institutions, industry professionals, government entities, to non-profit organizations. By applying the findings of this paper, they can more effectively set up competitions that not only crowd-source innovative solutions but also foster a culture of learning and creativity within the sustainable energy domain.

However, it is important to consider the limitations of this study. As it only samples 33 competitions, it captures just a fraction of the data competitions being hosted. Future research should include a larger sample size and a wider range of competitions to provide a more comprehensive understanding of best practices in data competition hosting.

Acknowledgment. This paper is part of the Project "Data-dreven smarte bygninger: data sandkasse og konkurrence" (Journal-nummer: 64021–6025) funded by EUDP (Energy Technology

Development and Demonstration Program) and IEA EBC Annex 81 Data-Driven Smart Buildings project funded by EUDP (case number: 64019–0539), Denmark.

References

1. AIcrowd (2023). https://www.aicrowd.com/
2. CodaLab (2023). https://codalab.lisn.upsaclay.fr/
3. CrowdANALYTIX (2023). https://www.crowdanalytix.com/community
4. EvalAI (2023). https://eval.ai/
5. Kaggle (2023). https://www.kaggle.com/
6. RAMP (2023). https://ramp.studio/
7. Kaggle community competitions setup guide (2023). https://www.kaggle.com/community-competitions-setup-guide
8. Tianchi (2023). https://tianchi.aliyun.com/
9. Chlearn competition guide (2023). http://www.chalearn.org/tips.html
10. DrivenData (2023). https://www.drivendata.org/
11. Zindi (2023). https://zindi.africa/
12. NurIPS (2023). https://nips.cc/virtual/2022/events/competition
13. Topcoder (2023). https://www.topcoder.com/
14. ADRENALIN project (2023). https://adrenalin.energy/
15. bitgrit (2023). https://bitgrit.net/
16. HackerEarth (2023). https://www.hackerearth.com/
17. CityLearn challenge 2022 (2023). https://www.aicrowd.com/challenges/neurips-2022-citylearn-challenge
18. NeurIPS 2022 IGLU challenge (2023). https://www.drivendata.org/competitions/98/nist-federated-learning-1/page/522/
19. BASALT competition 2022 (2023). https://www.aicrowd.com/challenges/neurips-2022-minerl-basalt-competition
20. Feedback Prize – predicting effective arguments (2023). https://www.kaggle.com/competitions/feedback-prize-effectiveness/
21. RSNA 2022 cervical spine fracture detection (2023). https://www.kaggle.com/competitions/rsna-2022-cervical-spine-fracture-detection/overview
22. NeurIPS 2022 CausalML challenge (2023). https://codalab.lisn.upsaclay.fr/competitions/5626
23. Open catalyst challenge (2023). https://opencatalystproject.org/challenge.html
24. Weather4cast 2022 (2023). https://www.iarai.ac.at/weather4cast/challenge/
25. Traffic4cast 2022 (2023). https://www.iarai.ac.at/traffic4cast/challenge/
26. Weather4cast Multi-sensor weather forecast competition (2023). https://www.iarai.ac.at/weather4cast/2021-competition/
27. Rousseau, D., Ustyuzhanin, A.: Machine learning scientific competitions and datasets (2020)
28. Yip, K.H., et al.: ESA-Ariel data challenge NeurIPS 2022: inferring physical properties of exoplanets from next-generation telescopes (2022)
29. PETs prize challenge (2023). https://www.drivendata.org/competitions/98/nist-federated-learning-1/page/522/
30. Reconnaissance blind chess (2023). https://rbc.jhuapl.edu/tournament
31. Trojan detection challenge (2023). https://trojandetection.ai/
32. The neural MMO challenge (2023). https://www.aicrowd.com/challenges/neurips-2022-the-neural-mmo-challenge

33. Discover the mysteries of the Maya (2023). https://euro-neurips-vrp-2022.challenges.ortec.com/

34. Global wheat challenge 2021 (2023). https://www.aicrowd.com/challenges/global-wheat-challenge-2021

35. ADDI Alzheimer's detection challenge (2023). https://www.aicrowd.com/challenges/addi-alzheimers-detection-challenge#rounds

36. OGB large-scale challenge (2023). https://ogb.stanford.edu/neurips2022/

37. AutoML decathlon 2022 (2023). https://www.cs.cmu.edu/~automl-decathlon-22/

38. Natural language for optimization (2023). https://nl4opt.github.io/

39. Second AmericasNLP competition (2023). https://turing.iimas.unam.mx/americasnlp/st.html

40. Open problems - multimodal single-cell integration (2023). https://www.kaggle.com/competitions/open-problems-multimodal

41. Sensorium 2022 competition (2023). https://github.com/sinzlab/sensorium

42. Visual domain adaptation challenge (2023). https://ai.bu.edu/visda-2022/

43. Habitat rearrangement challenge 2022 (2023). https://aihabitat.org/challenge/rearrange_2022/

44. EURO meets NeurIPS 2022 vehicle routing competition (2023). https://euro-neurips-vrp-2022.challenges.ortec.com/

45. Data purchasing challenge 2022 (2023). https://www.aicrowd.com/challenges/data-purchasing-challenge-2022

46. Cross-domain MetaDL 2022 (2023). https://codalab.lisn.upsaclay.fr/competitions/3627

47. 2022 NeurIPS driving SMARTS competition (2023). https://codalab.lisn.upsaclay.fr/competitions/6618

48. MyoChallenge (2023). https://sites.google.com/view/myochallenge

49. Weakly supervised cell segmentation in multi-modality high-resolution microscopy images (2023). https://neurips22-cellseg.grand-challenge.org/

50. Real robot challenge 2022 (2023). https://real-robot-challenge.com/

51. Tolnai, B.A., Z. Ma, Jørgensen, B.N.: (Accepted) A scoping review of energy load disaggregation. In: The 22nd Portuguese Conference on Artificial Intelligence (2023)

Deep HarDec: Deep Neural Network Applied to Estimate Harmonic Decomposition

Luiz G. R. Bernardino[1], Claudionor F. do Nascimento[2],
Wesley A. Souza[3(✉)], Fernando P. Marafão[1], and Augusto M. S. Alonso[4]

[1] ICTS, São Paulo State University (UNESP), Sorocaba, SP, Brazil
[2] DEE, Federal University of São Carlos (UFSCar), São Carlos, SP, Brazil
[3] DAELE, Federal University of Technology - Paraná (UTFPR), Cornélio Procópio,
PR, Brazil
wesleyangelino@utfpr.edu.br
[4] EESC, University of São Paulo (USP), São Carlos, SP, Brazil

Abstract. A Deep Harmonic Decomposition (Deep HarDec) approach
is proposed in this paper, being developed by means of a deep neural network, allowing to obtain estimations of the amplitude and phase quantities of a given periodic signal. Consequently, harmonic characterization
of periodic signals are explored in this paper, assessing the suitability
of the Deep HarDec. Such a method can be potentially applied to the
real-time management of electric power systems as well as other control applications, supporting the monitoring of harmonic distortions and
providing means to active filtering interventions targeting power quality
improvement. In order to build the Deep HarDec model, a dataset comprising diverse combinations of the fifth, seventh, eleventh, and thirteenth
harmonic orders was considered, covering a wide range of operational
perspectives. A grid search technique was used to find the best configuration for the multi-layer perceptron adopted for the approach, and
the deep neural network was subjected to a training procedure targeting the harmonic estimation. A study case focusing on a selective active
filtering application demonstrates that the Deep HarDec can effectively
decompose harmonics, supporting the synthesis of real-time compensation references to tackle harmonic distortions in an electric grid.

Keywords: artificial neural networks · active power filter · deep
learning · harmonic decomposition · harmonic estimation · multi-layer
perceptron · power quality

1 Introduction

The increasing presence of non-linear loads in electrical systems has raised significant attention in the past decades, mostly due to the resulting harmonic
pollution and its detrimental impact on other electronic equipment and the grid
itself [1].

© The Author(s), under exclusive license to Springer Nature Switzerland AG 2024
B. N. Jørgensen et al. (Eds.): EI.A 2023, LNCS 14467, pp. 77–94, 2024.
https://doi.org/10.1007/978-3-031-48649-4_5

Such loads (e.g., microwave ovens, computers and peripherals, electronic power converters, and so forth) exhibit an intrinsic non-linear characteristic caused by their particular instantaneous energy demand patterns that distort their current waveforms [2]. For instance, the periodic currents drawn from such loads are not proportional to the applied voltage [3], leading to the circulation of harmonic currents that are known for causing power quality (PQ) issues [4] such as resonances, low energy efficiency and many others [5,6]. Therefore, when analyzing current and voltage waveforms from a system comprising non-linear loads, it is common to identify that their signal spectrum consists of a fundamental component as well as other undesired harmonic terms (i.e., which are usually multiple integer frequencies of the former [7]).

Measuring harmonic sources and their impact on the operation of electrical systems is an important aspect of PQ [8], mainly due to the fact that the related distortions to voltages and currents need to be quantified and interpreted prior to deploy a countermeasure action. The treatment of harmonics in a power system concerns consumers, prosumers, and utilities. Standards such as the IEEE Recommendation 519 [9] establish harmonic limits for voltage and current signals. The most commonly used method to identify harmonics is the Fourier transform (FFT), mainly due to its straightforward implementation, that allows to determine the amplitudes and phases of harmonic components from limited signal samples [10]. However, digital instruments generally rely on discrete Fourier transform (DFT) techniques, requiring a measurement window width of 12 cycles (approximately 200 ms) for 60 Hz-based power systems, as presented in [9]. Such a long measurement window may not effectively support decisions for equipment operating with faster dynamics, such as an active power filter (APF) [11]. In particular, although APFs are power conditioners with fast response capabilities, the estimation of the harmonic content can be crucial to achieve proper compensation performance. Consequently, DFT-based strategies can make real-time compensation difficult [12]. Additionally, the literature often lacks comprehensive validation studies and comparisons of different harmonic estimation methods. It is important to comprehend which techniques perform better in distinct scenarios.

Computational techniques applied to harmonic estimation are continuously evolving. Nonetheless, there is a gap in the literature for what concerns the application of modern computational approaches applied to electrical systems: only a few research papers present harmonic analyses based on machine learning, artificial intelligence, or advanced signal processing techniques; although they are usually more effective in obtaining accurate estimation of the harmonic content of current and voltage waveforms. As an alternative for harmonic analyses, the deep neural network (DNN) can be used in the main processing stage to perform pattern recognition [13,14] in power system applications, mainly in distribution systems. DNNs can identify harmonics from distorted waves, enhancing processing speed compared to DFT-based techniques, facilitating and improving harmonic detection [12]. Deep-learning methods are representation-learning methods with multiple levels of representation, obtained by composing simple but non-linear modules that each transform the representation at one level into a representation at a higher and slightly more abstract level [13]. In addition, Artificial neural network (ANN) can be trained to classify the preliminary information extracted in the pre-processing stage of this approach.

Aiming at contributing to the perspective of harmonic estimation in applications related to electrical systems, this work proposes the Deep HarDec: a novel method for harmonic identification that takes advantage of DNNs, resulting in a tool that presents low computational effort and fast convergence capability. The output of such a DNN is a mathematical model capable of assessing current and voltage quantities, allowing the Deep HarDec to only require a quarter of a signal's fundamental cycle to estimate the magnitude (i.e., amplitude) of harmonic components. Thus, harmonics can be effectively estimated, providing means for implementing real-time compensation in APFs (operating as an alternative tool to traditional), developing low-cost electric energy meters, also being suitable to other PQ-related applications.

In addition to this introductory section, this article follows the subsequent structure: Sect. 2 addresses harmonic estimation methods and their related implementation features; Sect. 3 describes the proposed Deep HarDec method; Sect. 4 presents results and discussions; and Sect. 5 brings conclusions related to the findings of this study.

2 Harmonic Estimation Methods and Correlated Studies

Within electrical systems, harmonics are sinusoidal components from waveforms of voltage and/or current, oscillating at integer multiples of the grid's fundamental frequency [15]. A mathematical representation of such harmonic components is presented in Eq. (1). Instantaneous variable $x(t)$ is the time-domain quantity (i.e., signals of current or voltage), X_1 is the magnitude (i.e., peak value) of the fundamental component, X_h is the magnitude of the harmonic signal at order h, ϕ_1 and ϕ_h are the phase shifts of the fundamental and harmonic components respectively, ω is the angular frequency and t is time, and H is the maximum harmonic order to be considered. It is important to mention that the context of interharmonics [16] is out of scope in this paper.

$$x(t) = X_1 \cdot \cos(\omega t + \phi_1) + \sum_{h}^{H} X_h \cdot \cos(h\omega t + \phi_h) \tag{1}$$

Although the literature presents multiple methods to assess harmonic distortion, the most common index adopted is the total harmonic distortion (THD). The total harmonic distortion (THD). represents a ratio between the overall magnitudes of the harmonic components in relation to the fundamental component. For the current THD, for instance, such a definition is given by Eq. (2), where I_h is the root mean square (RMS) value of the harmonic h, and I_1 is the RMS value of the fundamental component.

$$\text{THD} = \frac{\sqrt{\sum_{h=2}^{H} (I_h)^2}}{I_1} \tag{2}$$

Harmonic monitoring is a valuable tool for quantifying the impact of harmonic distortion and, for the power system perspective, this process involves acquiring and computing signals of voltage or current seen at different grid nodes [17]. Several studies have proposed to automate the process of harmonic quantification using ANNs to enhance the speed, reliability, and simplicity of data acquisition and storage [18,19]. In the context of PQ studies, ANNs have been utilized for harmonic identification [20,21]. One of the main advantages of this approach is the ANNs's potential to adapt to various environments and high tolerance to noise [20]. Among various types of ANNs, multi-layer percetron (MLP) is the most commonly used one applied for pattern recognition [17]. The MLP architecture typically comprises an input layer, one or more hidden layers, and an output layer. In addition, MLP implementations are usually trained using supervised learning through the backpropagation algorithm [22,23].

Although harmonic assessment and monitoring can be performed by implementing intelligent computational tools, acting on the mitigation of either harmonic currents or voltages relies on additional electric apparatuses. One of the most effective alternatives for PQ improvement depends on the deployment of an APF connected to the grid [24]. APFs can provide dynamic compensation of harmonics even in scenarios where the harmonic demand imposed by non-linear loads change [15]. However, real-time quantization of harmonics must be used in the control system of such an APF to attain proper operation [25]. An alternative to implement real-time harmonic analysis for an integrated operation with power conditioners is devised by a trained DNN. Besides adding real-time features to the dynamic operation of the APF, such a DNN-based approach offers the advantage of fast computation and low computational effort during the operational stage [26], making it significantly attractive to embedded applications.

In [27], the authors introduced a neural technique for harmonic identification and compensation purposes. In such a compensation method, the harmonic components may be individually selected, and the reactive power can be controlled. In [28–31], the authors applied an ANN in amplitude and phase identification for individual harmonic orders for a condition in which distortions were presented in the measured signals. The results demonstrated that the proposed algorithms were capable of detecting harmonics with high accuracy, fast convergence behavior and satisfactory performance under steady conditions. ANN was also used in [32,33] to identify harmonic current components of single-phase non-linear loads. As previous works from the literature, the proposed ANN could also estimate harmonic currents efficiently.

A parallel perspective found in [34] proposed the use of ANN to estimate the Fourier coefficients corresponding to the fundamental harmonic of any distorted voltage or current signal. Likewise, in [35], the authors presented a procedure to estimate the impacts on voltage harmonic distortion at a given point of interest in the grid.

In [36], the authors considered the real application of a voltage sourced converter (VSC) for an industrial microgrid (MG), in which an ANN-based control method was employed to achieve harmonic identification for implementing a compensation strategy. In [37], the authors detected islanding and PQ issues in a hybrid distributed generation (DG) system composed of photovoltaic (PV) system and wind power plant using Wavelet Transform and ANN.

A novel deep network structure is presented in [38], aiming at the problems of a low convergence speed, low accuracy, and poor generalization ability of traditional power disturbance identification and classification methods. A PQ disturbance identification and classification method for MG based on the new network structure is proposed. The trained and optimized network is applied to PQ disturbance identification and classification. The proposed method reached a higher accuracy, convergence speed, and stronger generalization ability than other methods. In [39], an ANN-based model deals with electric load forecasting. In [5,40,41], a power management strategy based on ANN for solar PV systems is presented to show the benefits of this strategy.

Several studies have shown the effectiveness of ANN in harmonic identification and compensation and in detecting events such as voltage sag, voltage swell, interruption, and harmonics. Moreover, ANN has been successfully applied in amplitude and phase identification and identifying harmonic current components of single-phase nonlinear load currents. The proposed algorithms have shown better accuracy, faster convergence, and stability under steady conditions. Additionally, ANN-based control methods have been employed in practical situations, such as in a VSC for industrial MG and in hybrid DG systems composed of PV and wind power plants. Furthermore, ANN has been used in electric load forecasting and power management strategies for solar PV systems. Novel deep network structures have been proposed for PQ disturbance identification and classification, demonstrating higher accuracy, convergence speed, and generalization ability than other methods.

Despite the ongoing development of techniques for harmonic content identification based on machine learning algorithms, gaps and challenges still need to be addressed. For instance, the accurate identification of harmonics in complex electrical environments, such as when load variations and network distortions occur, remains a challenge. Consequently, artificial intelligence (AI) algorithms need to be robust enough to handle such operational complexities. As far as one can find in the literature, most deep neural network models can be considered black boxes, making it challenging to comprehend how they converged to a specific decision. Hence, such a condition can be a concern when dealing with critical issues in energy security and power quality, where the interpretability of physical phenomena is essential. Obtaining labeled data for training AI algorithms can be challenging and costly. The absence of specific labeled datasets for electrical harmonic analysis can constrain the development of accurate models.

3   The Deep HarDec Method

This section discusses the development of the Deep HarDec method, highlighting the stages of training, validation, testing samples, and the DNN's implementation method. Figure 1 shows the workflow of the Deep HarDec, which requires as input sampling only a quarter of a wave cycle (i.e., in respect to the fundamental frequency) to estimate harmonic amplitudes. The output of the Deep HarDec comprises the values of magnitudes of the fundamental grid frequency harmonics. For the training and stage of the Deep HarDec, a synthetic dataset was built from distorted current waveforms, as presented in the Subsect. 3.1.

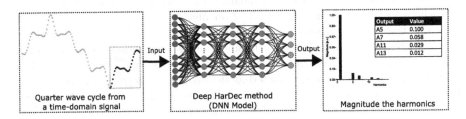

Fig. 1. Deep HarDec workflow.

3.1   Dataset Generation for Training, Validation and Testing

The data samples were generated using an algorithm that sums the fundamental current component with all the pre-established harmonic components using a nested loop, as seen in Fig. 2. The sum of the harmonic components combines all the possibilities of pre-established amplitudes and phase shifts, resulting in a set of 33,177,300 samples. The dataset size is defined exponentially according to the amplitudes and phase shifts possibilities. Current samples are generated with a quarter wave cycle of the fundamental frequency. Each sample has 64 sample values, equivalent to a sampling rate of 15.36 kHz, which is the recommended value for a fundamental frequency of 60 Hz according to IEC 61850 [42].

Figure 2 depicts a nested loop employed in sample generation. This loop serves the purpose of creating a dataset for training the Deep HarDec model. The generated samples constitute combinations of the fifth, seventh, eleventh, and thirteenth harmonic orders. The nesting of this loop is attributed to its concurrent iteration over multiple variables. The outer loop traverses the harmonic orders, whereas the inner loop iterates through amplitude and phase values for each harmonic order. Thus, the generated samples are subsequently applied to train the MLP incorporated within the Deep HarDec approach.

The individual harmonic samples use Eq. (3) to build the nth harmonic samples set. Then, using the nested loop of Fig. 2, we sum each possibility of individual harmonics. Current samples are generated following (3) and considering the quantities obtained from a real non-linear load, presented in Table 1. Such quantities compose a signal as illustrated in Fig. 3. The samples generation algorithm groups 768 samples per batch and stores each batch on disk.

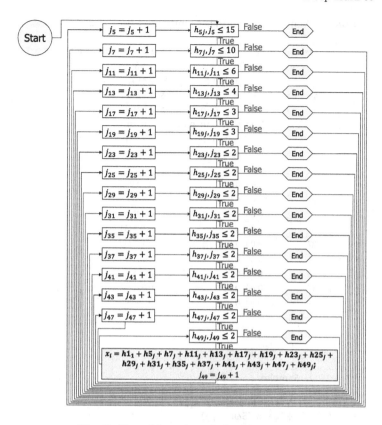

Fig. 2. Nested loop in samples generation.

$$\vec{h_n} = A_n \cdot \cos\left(n\omega\,\vec{t} + \varphi_n\right) \tag{3}$$

It is worth mentioning that it would be possible to build a sample dataset with a wider range of amplitudes and phase shifts. However, we selected only specific harmonic orders due to the limitations of the used computer, which presented 16 GB of RAM and an Intel(R) Core(TM) i7-10750H CPU. For instance, harmonics from 5th, 7th, 11th, and 13th orders with amplitudes and phase shifts suitable for the test load were taken into consideration in this study.

The samples go through a normalization process [43] by applying a transformation that maintains the obtained mean value close to 0, as well as the standard deviation close to 1. Hence, the sample set is used in the training stage for the DNN's modeling and configuration, aiming to estimate harmonics amplitudes.

3.2   Exhaustive Search over Parameters Values for DNN

An exhaustive search for hyperparameters of the deep neural network in the Deep HarDec method was conducted through GridSearchCV [44]. The search implements a fitting process and an evaluation process. The estimator is a DNN

Table 1. Amplitudes and phase shifts used in training samples.

Harmonic	Amplitudes [pu]	Phase shifts [rad]
1	1.00	−1.3979
5	0.00, 0.05, 0.10, ... , 0.70	2.4194
7	0.00, 0.05, 0.10, ... , 0.45	2.8255
11	0.00, 0.05, 0.10, ... , 0.25	0.3619
13	0.00, 0.05, 0.10, 0.15	0.6919
17	0.00, 0.05, 0.10	−1.761
19	0.00, 0.05, 0.10	−1.3728
23	0.00, 0.05	2.4537
25	0.00, 0.05	2.7928
29	0.00, 0.05	0.3532
31	0.00, 0.05	0.6974
35	0.00, 0.05	−1.7451
37	0.00, 0.05	−1.3939
41	0.00, 0.05	2.4388
43	0.00, 0.05	2.8011
47	0.00, 0.05	0.3557
49	0.00, 0.05	0.7058

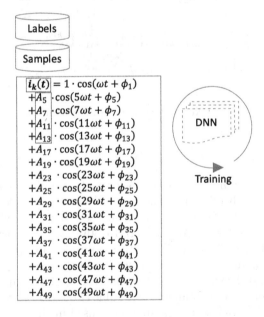

Fig. 3. Deep HarDec diagram.

built with a stack of dense (i.e., fully connected) layers using ReLU (4) activation on the hidden layers. The DNN is implemented into a Keras [45] sequential model. The input layer has 64 input features, and the output layer has 4 neurons, one for each harmonic amplitude. We applied AdaMax [46] as an optimizer,

Table 2. NN models ranking.

Ranking	Neurons (n)	Hidden Layers (i)	Activation (a)	MAE
1	144	4	relu	0.00099
2	152	3	linear	0.00139
3	144	3	linear	0.00139
4	152	2	relu	0.00151
5	88	4	linear	0.00158

having mean squared error (MSE) (5) as the loss function and mean absolute error (MAE) (6) as metrics, assuming that u is the typical neuron output and y_{pred} is the predicted variable for a determined input x in (4).

$$y = \begin{cases} 0, & \text{for } x < 0; \\ u, & \text{for } x \geq 0. \end{cases} \tag{4}$$

$$\text{MSE} = \sqrt{y_{true} - y_{pred}} \tag{5}$$

$$\text{MAE} = |y_{true} - y_{pred}| \tag{6}$$

The sample set was split using the scikit learn Train Test Split function [47]. This function splits arrays into random train/test subsets [48]. We defined that the training set to have 90% of the samples and the test set had 10%. The validation set was then extracted from the training set (15%). Moreover, we configure a kernel initializer [45] with the GlorotUniform [49] function using seed 333 to standardize the model and enable its reproduction.

The parameters sought are the number of hidden layers, the number of neurons in the hidden layers, and the output layer activation. The following scoring methods were analyzed: DNN with an exhaustive search for the best configuration of the number of neurons (n) in the ith hidden layer and for the best output layer activation (a), in which $n = \{32, 40, ..., 144, 152\}$, $i = \{2, 3, 4\}$ and $a = [\text{relu}, \text{linear}]$. The negative mean absolute error was used to rank the DNN models according to their performance by estimating harmonics from the test set. The highest ranked configuration has 4 hidden layers ($i = 4$), 144 neurons in each hidden layer ($i = 144$), and linear activation in the output layer ($a = \text{linear}$).

3.3   Creating the DNN Model

The best-ranked model is implemented in Python 3.9 [50] through Keras API [45]. The GridSearchCV [44] method revealed that the model architecture 4 hidden layers with 144 neurons in each layer is the best among the checked possibilities as presented in Table 3. The DNN's input layer receives 64-position vectors. DNN has 4 hidden layers, each with 144 neurons and an output layer with 4 neurons. Hidden layers use ReLU activation, while the output layer uses linear activation.

The algorithm was configured to train the model for 200 epochs with an early stopping criterion establishing a minimum MAE variance of 0.0001 for 5

Table 3. Summary of the ANN.

Layer (type)	Output Shape	Activation	Param #
input	(None, 64)	-	-
hidden #1 (Dense)	(None, 144)	relu	9360
hidden #2 (Dense)	(None, 144)	relu	20880
hidden #3 (Dense)	(None, 144)	relu	20880
hidden #4 (Dense)	(None, 144)	relu	20880
output (Dense)	(None, 4)	linear	580

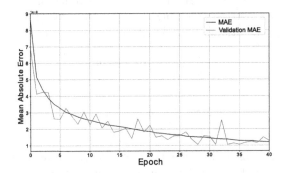

Fig. 4. Mean absolute error while training.

epochs. The proportion of training, validation, and testing samples used in the exhaustive search over parameters was maintained for the DNN training. The optimizer, loss function, and metrics were also kept the same. In addition, to train the DNN with a stratified split of samples, we also trained the DNN with a random split of samples, keeping the same proportions of training, validation, and testing samples.

The MAE in the last trained epoch is similar in both training processes, but the DNN training using a random split of samples achieved a slightly smaller error than using stratified samples. The final MAE in Fig. 4 is 0.001205. The DNN trained using a random split of samples was implemented due to its smaller achieved MAE.

The accuracy of the harmonic estimation performed by the trained DNN is evaluated using the test samples. The achieved mean absolute error is 0.001082.

3.4   Controlled Rectifier Model for Deep HarDec Evaluation

We present some case studies in Sect. 4 aiming at validating the performance of the Deep HarDec on estimating harmonics. The mathematical modeling [51] of the current drawn from a controlled rectifier was used to obtain the distorted waveforms target in this study. Such an instantaneous AC current is given by Eq. (7), in which V is the RMS phase voltage in Volts, α is the firing angle in radians, R is the load resistance in Ohm, and L is the load inductance in Henry. The coefficients CN and Δ_n are given by Eqs. (8) and (9).

$$i(t) = \frac{12\sqrt{6} \cdot V}{\pi} \cdot \frac{\cos\alpha}{R} \cdot \sum_{m=1,3,5...49} \frac{\sin\left(m \cdot \frac{\pi}{3}\right)}{m} \cdot \cos\left(m\left(\omega t - \alpha - \frac{\pi}{3}\right)\right)$$
$$+ \frac{8\sqrt{6} \cdot V}{\pi^2} \cdot \sum_{n=6,12,18...96} \frac{CN}{ZN} \cdot \sin\left(n\omega t + \Delta_n - \arctan\left(\frac{n\omega L}{R}\right)\right) \tag{7}$$

$$CN = \frac{C2}{\sin(\Delta_n)} \tag{8}$$

$$\Delta_n = \arctan\left(\frac{C2}{C1}\right) \tag{9}$$

The coefficients C1 and C2 are given by Eqs. (10) and (11).

$$C1 = \frac{\sin\left(N1\frac{\pi}{6}\right)}{N1} \cdot \left[\cos\left(N1 \cdot \left(\alpha + \frac{\pi}{6}\right) - \frac{\pi}{3}\right) + \cos\left(N1 \cdot \left(\alpha + \frac{5\pi}{6}\right) + \frac{\pi}{3}\right) - \cos\left(N1\left(\alpha - \frac{\pi}{2}\right)\right)\right]$$
$$- \frac{\sin\left(N2\frac{\pi}{6}\right)}{N2} \cdot \left[\cos\left(N2 \cdot \left(\alpha + \frac{\pi}{6}\right) + \frac{\pi}{3}\right) + \cos\left(N2 \cdot \left(\alpha + \frac{5\pi}{6}\right) - \frac{\pi}{3}\right) - \cos\left(N2\left(\alpha - \frac{\pi}{2}\right)\right)\right] \tag{10}$$

$$C2 = -\frac{\sin\left(N1\frac{\pi}{6}\right)}{N1} \cdot \left[\cos\left(N1 \cdot \left(\alpha + \frac{\pi}{6}\right) - \frac{\pi}{3}\right) + \cos\left(N1 \cdot \left(\alpha + \frac{5\pi}{6}\right) + \frac{\pi}{3}\right) - \cos\left(N1\left(\alpha - \frac{\pi}{2}\right)\right)\right]$$
$$+ \frac{\sin\left(N2\frac{\pi}{6}\right)}{N2} \cdot \left[\cos\left(N2 \cdot \left(\alpha + \frac{\pi}{6}\right) + \frac{\pi}{3}\right) + \cos\left(N2 \cdot \left(\alpha + \frac{5\pi}{6}\right) - \frac{\pi}{3}\right) - \cos\left(N2\left(\alpha - \frac{\pi}{2}\right)\right)\right] \tag{11}$$

where:

$$N1 = n - 1$$
$$N2 = n + 1 \tag{12}$$

4   Results and Discussions

We performed harmonic identification tests with different values of load resistance (R) and load inductance (L) in (7), being $R = \{5, 10, 15, 20, ..., 195, 200\}$ and $L = \{0.001, 0.002, 0.003, 0.004, 0.005, 0.006, 0.007, 0.008, 0.009, 0.01\}$, given in Ω and H, respectively. Figure 5 illustrates the mean absolute percentage error in harmonic estimation achieved by the trained DNN. The mean absolute percentage error serves as an indicator of the predictive accuracy of the DNN. Note that Fig. 5 demonstrates variations in mean absolute percentage error behavior across different harmonic orders. Detailed outcomes of individual harmonic assessments for each load combination are presented in Fig. 6.

We also performed an individual harmonic evaluation for each load combination, resulting in Fig. 6. The individual harmonic samples are generated using Eq. (3) to build the n-th harmonic samples set. The nested loop of Fig. 2 is used to sum each possibility of individual harmonics. The current samples are generated following Eq. (3) and considering the quantities obtained from a real non-linear load, which is presented in Table 1. The mean absolute percentage error behavior is different according to the harmonic order.

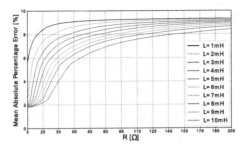

Fig. 5. Mean Absolute Percentage Error

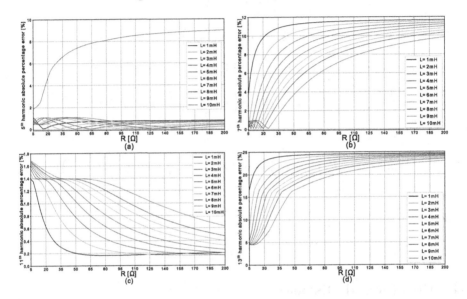

Fig. 6. Individual harmonic absolute percentage error.

4.1 Selective Compensation of Estimated Harmonics by Deep HarDec

A study case based on computational simulations, targeting a harmonic compensation intervention, is presented herein. For this study, the harmonic compensation was performed at a point of common coupling (PCC), which is a grid node connecting the experimental load, a voltage source emulating the grid, and a harmonic current compensator. The latter is emulated in a simulation as an ideal current source, which generates a compensation current based on the amplitude references provided by the DNN. Figure 7 illustrates the implemented simulation scenario. Moreover, Table 4 presents the parameters considered in simulation for the use in (7) to obtain the load AC current waveform.

Note from Fig. 7 that the current at the PCC before compensation is fed into the DNN block. The digitized current signal is used for the harmonic content

Table 4. Parameters for rectifier current waveform.

Parameter	Value
RMS phase voltage (V)	127 V
Fundamental frequency (f)	60 Hz
Firing angle (α)	$\dfrac{\pi}{9}$ rad
Load resistance (R)	10 Ω
Load inductance (L)	5 mH

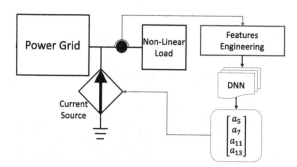

Fig. 7. Conceptual diagram of the harmonic current compensation system.

estimation. The DNN is divided into 3 stages: feature engineering [52], DNN and harmonic amplitude output. The feature engineering stage is responsible for adapting the digital signal to the DNN inputs, which includes the normalization and aggregation of 64 values per quarter cycle in an array (i.e., based on a sampling frequency of 15.36 kHz). This array is then submitted to DNN to estimate amplitudes of the harmonics from the 5th, 7th, 11th, and 13th. then, the DNN returns another array containing the estimated amplitudes, which are used to reconstruct the signal according to the application. Particularly in the considered example case, such a signal is an ideal source's reference current. The current source uses the reconstructed signal as a reference to generate the selective compensation current, which is injected into PCC.

As a reference metric for assessing the compensation actions, according to the IEEE 519:2014 [9], it is considered that a current THD should be limited to up 5%.

The currents seen at the load at the source are illustrated in Fig. 8, as well as the compensation current generated by the proposed method. The source current does not present a sinusoidal waveform due to the non-compensated harmonic orders. However, as we can see in Table 5, the targeted harmonic orders were significantly attenuated when compensation was performed.

The DNN model for estimating harmonic amplitudes was evaluated in this study based on non-linear load currents from literature. The results showed that this model can estimate harmonic amplitudes with relatively high accuracy.

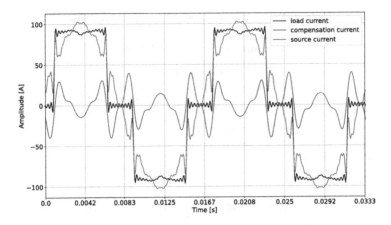

Fig. 8. Compensation waveforms results.

The comparisons performed in this work indicate that the average absolute percentage error varies according to the combination of load resistance and inductance values. The performance of the DNN in estimating the harmonics amplitudes of interest was considered satisfactory since these amplitudes were almost completely null after compensation.

These results comply with the conclusions pointed out in [28–31], with regards to using ANN to estimate individual harmonic amplitudes and using the estimated amplitudes to generate a compensation current reference.

4.2   Discussions, Advantages, and Limitations of the Deep HarDec

Based on the test results and case study of Sect. 4.1, the Deep HarDec presented estimation performance comparable to the FFT decomposition approach, indicating that it can be used to identify harmonics in electrical signals, as well as for compensating harmonics, monitoring, and assessing PQ indexes.

As advantages, the Deep HarDec corresponds to a model based on a deep neural network, which, after being trained, becomes a matrix of weights and connections; when input data is presented, basic mathematical calculations are

Table 5. Compensation individual results.

Harmonic	Before Compensation (%)	After Compensation (%)
1	100	100
5	21.03	0.11
7	13.20	0.08
11	9.30	0.14
13	7.02	0.44

Table 6. Computational time to identify harmonics of one signal using CISC and RISC processors (* Intel Core i9 9880H, ** ESP-32 Tensilica Xtensa LX6 240 MHz).

	Architecture	
Method	CISC*	RISC**
FFT (butterfly)	0.0013	0.0412
Deep HarDec	0.0018	0.0245

performed. As shown in Table 6, this is an advantage for RISC architectures (i.e., for most embedded systems) because assembly instructions are limited. In addition, to calculate the harmonics of interest, the Deep HarDec requires only a quarter cycle, whereas the FFT requires at least one cycle.

With regards to limitations, the Deep HarDec's computational complexity is $\mathcal{O}(n^4)$, whereas an FFT technique has a complexity of $\mathcal{O}(n \log_2 n)$. As shown in Table 6, the Deep HarDec has advantages in RISC architectures, but the FFT is quicker than the Deep HarDec in CISC architectures.

5 Conclusions

The suitability of a multi-layer perceptron ANN approach to estimate harmonic magnitudes from the 5th, 7th, 11th and 13th orders was discussed in this paper, requiring sampling data during a quarter of a fundamental cycle. The training dataset used in the study cases contained 33,177,300 quarter-cycle waves with a sampling rate of 15,360 Hz.

The adopted grid search method revealed that the model architecture with 4 hidden layers, and 144 neurons in each layer, is the best among the checked possibilities. The results show that ANN models are recommended for harmonic estimation, especially for individual low-order frequencies. Moreover, using ANN model in the operational stage could facilitate the implementation of low cost microprocessors in power converters (i.e., due to the simplicity of the proposed mathematical model).

The next step of this work is to improve the accuracy of the ANN model, targeting a more precise obtainment of magnitude estimations for harmonic components.

Acknowledgments. The authors are grateful for the financial support provided by the Coordenação de Aperfeiçoamento de Pessoal de Nível Superior (CAPES) and by the Sao Paulo Research Foundation (FAPESP) under grants 2022/00317-3 and 2016/08645-9.

References

1. Dao, T., Phung, B.T.: Effects of voltage harmonic on losses and temperature rise in distribution transformers. IET Gener. Transm. Distrib. **12**, 347–354 (2018)
2. Hong, W.-C., Fan, G.-F.: Hybrid empirical mode decomposition with support vector regression model for short term load forecasting. Energies **12**, 1996–1073 (2019)

3. Alonso, A.M.S., et al.: Current-based coordination of distributed energy resources in a grid-connected low-voltage microgrid: an experimental validation of adverse operational scenarios. Energies **15**, 6407 (2022)
4. Almohaimeed, S.A., Abdel-Akher, M.: Power quality issues and mitigation for electric grids with wind power penetration. Appl. Sci. **10**, 8852 (2020)
5. Kumar, D., Zare, F.: A comprehensive review of maritime microgrids: system architectures, energy efficiency, power quality, and regulations. IEEE Access **7**, 67249–67277 (2019)
6. Wan, Y., Cui, S., Wu, S., Song, L.: Electromagnetic design and losses analysis of a high-speed permanent magnet synchronous motor with toroidal windings for pulsed alternator. Energies **11**, 562 (2018)
7. Subtirelu, G.-E.: Harmonic distortions analyzer for power rectifiers. Acta Electrotehnica **57** (2016)
8. Viciana, E., et al.: An open hardware design for internet of things power quality and energy saving solutions. Sensors **19**, 627 (2019)
9. IEEE Recommended Practice and Requirements for Harmonic Control in Electric Power Systems. IEEE Std 519-2014 (Revision of IEEE Std 519-1992), 1–29 (2014)
10. Ewert, P., Orlowska-Kowalska, T., Jankowska, K.: Effectiveness analysis of pmsm motor rolling bearing fault detectors based on vibration analysis and shallow neural networks. Energies **14**, 712 (2021)
11. Li, D., Wang, T., Pan, W., Ding, X., Gong, J.: A comprehensive review of improving power quality using active power filters. Electr. Power Syst. Res. **199**, 107389 (2021)
12. Temurtas, F., Gunturkun, R., Yumusak, N., Temurtas, H.: Harmonic detection using feed forward and recurrent neural networks for active filters. Electr. Power Syst. Res. **72**, 33–40 (2004)
13. LeCun, Y., Bengio, Y., Hinton, G.: Deep learning. Nature **521**, 436–444 (2015)
14. Schmidhuber, J.: Deep learning in neural networks: an overview. Neural Netw. **61**, 85–117 (2015)
15. Fuchs, E., Masoum, M.A.S.: Power quality in power systems and electrical machines, p. 1140(2015)
16. Testa, A., et al.: Interharmonics: theory and modeling. IEEE Trans. Power Delivery **22**, 2335–2348 (2007)
17. Arrillaga, J. & Watson, N. R. Power System Harmonics, p. 412 John Wiley & Sons (2004)
18. Fei, J., Chu, Y.: Double hidden layer output feedback neural adaptive global sliding mode control of active power filter. IEEE Trans. Power Electron. **35**, 3069–3084 (2020)
19. Shukl, P., Singh, B.: Delta-bar-delta neural-network-based control approach for power quality improvement of solar-PV-interfaced distribution system. IEEE Trans. Industr. Inf. **16**, 790–801 (2020)
20. Srinivasan, D., Ng, W., Liew, A.: Neural-network-based signature recognition for harmonic source identification. IEEE Trans. Power Delivery **21**, 398–405 (2006)
21. Bernardino, L.G.R., Nascimento, C.F., Tavares, R.F., Souza, W.A., Marafão, F.P.: Neural-network-based approach applied to harmonic component estimation in microgrids. In: Proceedings of the IEEE Brazilian Congress of Power Electronics, pp. 1–6 (2021)
22. Rumelhart, D.E., Hinton, G.E., Williams, R.J.: Learning representations by back-propagating errors. Nature **323**, 533–536 (1986)
23. Haykin, S.: Neural Netw. Learn. Mach. Prentice Hall/Pearson, New York (2009)

24. Akagi, H.: Active Harmonic Filters. Proc. IEEE **93**, 2128–2141 (2005)
25. Fei, J., Liu, L.: Real-time nonlinear model predictive control of active power filter using self-feedback recurrent fuzzy neural network estimator. IEEE Trans. Industr. Electron. 69, 8366–8376 (2021)
26. Nagata, E.A., et al.: Real-time voltage sag detection and classification for power quality diagnostics. Measurement **164**, 108097 (2020)
27. Abdeslam, D.O., Wira, P., Flieller, D., Merckle, J.: Power harmonic identification and compensation with an artificial neural network method in Proceedings of the International Symposium on Industrial. Electronics **3**, 1732–1737 (2006)
28. Temurtas, H., Temurtas, F.: An application of neural networks for harmonic coefficients and relative phase shifts detection. Expert Syst. Appl. **38**, 3446–3450 (2011)
29. Jain, S.K., Singh, S.N.: Fast harmonic estimation of stationary and time-varying signals using EA-AWNN. IEEE Trans. Instrum. Meas. **62**, 335–343 (2013)
30. Garanayak, P., Panda, G.: An adaptive linear neural network with least mean M-estimate weight updating rule employed for harmonics identification and power quality monitoring. Trans. Inst. Meas. Control. **40**, 1936–1949 (2017)
31. Žnidarec, M., Klaić, Z., Šljivac, D., Dumnić, B.: Harmonic distortion prediction model of a grid-tie photovoltaic inverter using an artificial neural network. Energies **12**, 790 (2019)
32. Do Nascimento, C.F., de Oliveira, A.A., Goedtel, A. Serni, P.J.A.: Harmonic identification using parallel neural networks in single-phase systems. Appl. Soft Comput. **11**, 2178–2185 (2011)
33. Nascimento, C.F., Oliveira, A.A., Goedtel, A., Dietrich, A.B.: Harmonic distortion monitoring for nonlinear loads using neural-network-method. Appl. Soft Comput. **13**, 475–482 (2013)
34. Flores-Garrido, J.L., Salmerón, P., Gómez-Galán, J.A.: Nonlinear loads compensation using a shunt active power filter controlled by feedforward neural networks. Appl. Sci. **11**, 7737 (2021)
35. Manito, A., et al.: Evaluating harmonic distortions on grid voltages due to multiple nonlinear loads using artificial neural networks. Energies **11**, 3303 (2018)
36. Xu, J., Wu, Z., Yang, X., Ye, J., Shen, A.: ANN-based Control Method Implemented in a Voltage Source Converter for Industrial Micro-grid. In: Proceedings of the International Conference on Bio-Inspired Computing: Theories and Applications, pp. 140–145 (2011)
37. Puthenpurakel, S.P., Subadhra, P.R.: Identification and classification of microgrid disturbances in a hybrid distributed generation system using wavelet transform. In: Proceedings of the International Conference on Next Generation Intelligent Systems, pp. 1–5 (2016)
38. Gong, R., Ruan, T.: A new convolutional network structure for power quality disturbance identification and classification in micro-grids. IEEE Access **8**, 88801–88814 (2020)
39. Kumar, S., Hussain, L., Banarjee, S., Reza, M.: Energy load forecasting using deep learning approach-LSTM and GRU in spark cluster. In: Proceedings of the International Conference on Emerging Applications of Information Technology, pp. 1–4 (2018)
40. Faria, J., Pombo, J., Calado, M., Mariano, S.: Power management control strategy based on artificial neural networks for standalone PV applications with a hybrid energy storage system. Energies **12**, 902 (2019)
41. Alsaidan, I., Chaudhary, P., Alaraj, M., Rizwan, M.: An Intelligent Approach to Active and Reactive Power Control in a Grid-Connected Solar Photovoltaic System. Sustainability **13**, 4219 (2021)

42. UCA. Implementation Guideline for Digital Interface to Instrument Transformers Using IEC 61850-9-2 (2004)
43. Ba, J. L., Kiros, J. R., Hinton, G.E.: Layer Normalization (2016). arXiv: 1607.06450
44. Ahmad, G.N., Fatima, H., Ullah, S., Saidi, A.S., et al.: Efficient medical diagnosis of human heart diseases using machine learning techniques with and without GridSearchCV. IEEE Access **10**, 80151–80173 (2022)
45. Chollet, F. et al. Keras Available online: https://keras.io. Accessed 29 Aug 2023
46. Kingma, D.P., Ba, J.: Adam: a method for stochastic optimization (2017). arXiv: 1412.6980
47. Buitinck, L., et al.: API design for machine learning software: experiences from the scikit-learn project. In: Proceedings of the ECML PKDD Workshop: Languages for Data Mining and Machine Learning, pp. 108–122 (2013)
48. Pedregosa, F., et al.: Scikit-learn: machine learning in Python. J. Mach. Learn. Res. **12**, 2825–2830 (2011)
49. Glorot, X., Bengio, Y.: Understanding the difficulty of training deep feedforward neural networks. In: Proceedings of the International Conference on Artificial Intelligence and Statistics, vol. 9, pp. 249–256 (2010)
50. Beazley, D.: Python essential reference. Addison-Wesley (2009)
51. Campos, F.P.: Mathematical models for three-phase rectifiers using switching functions Masters thesis, Federal University of Rio de Janeiro (1990)
52. Souza, W.A., et al.: Selection of features from power theories to compose NILM datasets. Adv. Eng. Inform. **52**, 101556 (2022)

Automating Value-Oriented Forecast Model Selection by Meta-learning: Application on a Dispatchable Feeder

Dorina Werling[✉], Maximilian Beichter, Benedikt Heidrich, Kaleb Phipps, Ralf Mikut, and Veit Hagenmeyer

Karlsruhe Institute of Technology, Karlsruhe, Germany
dorina.werling@kit.edu

Abstract. To successfully increase the share of renewable energy sources in the power system and for counteract their fluctuating nature in view of system stability, forecasts are required that suit downstream applications, such as demand side management or management of energy storage systems. However, whilst many forecast models to create these forecasts exist, the selection of the forecast model best suited to the respective downstream application can be challenging. The selection is commonly based on quality measures (such as mean absolute error), but these quality measures do not consider the value of the forecast in the downstream application. Thus, we introduce a meta-learning framework for forecast model selection, which automatically selects the forecast model leading to the forecast with the highest value in the downstream application. More precisely, we use a meta-learning approach that considers the selection task as a classification problem. Furthermore, we empirically evaluate the proposed framework on the downstream application of a smart building's photovoltaic-battery management problem known as dispatchable feeder on building-level with a data set containing time series from 300 buildings. The results of our evaluation demonstrate that the proposed framework reduces the cost and improves the accuracy compared to existing forecast model selection heuristics. Furthermore, compared to a manual forecast model selection, it requires noticeably less computational effort and leads to comparable results.

Keywords: meta-learning · forecast value · forecast model selection

1 Introduction

The increasing share of decentralised, renewable energy sources challenges system operators since they must maintain system stability despite the uncertain

This project is funded by the Helmholtz Association's Initiative and Networking Fund through Helmholtz AI, the Helmholtz Association under the Program "Energy System Design", and the German Research Foundation (DFG) as part of the Research Training Group 2153 "Energy Status Data: Informatics Methods for its Collection, Analysis and Exploitation".

B. N. Jørgensen et al. (Eds.): EI.A 2023, LNCS 14467, pp. 95–116, 2024.
https://doi.org/10.1007/978-3-031-48649-4_6

and fluctuating behaviour of these energy sources. To maintain the system stability and to make optimal use of decentralised sources, smart grids make use of intelligent downstream applications. Such downstream applications include the intelligent management of smart buildings via demand side management [7,16], or dispatchable feeders [4,30,38]. These applications can be connected in a smart grid internet of things (IoT) environment, swiftly communicating with one another via information and communication technology (ICT) to ensure stable system operation. However, despite real-time data via smart meters, these downstream applications often rely on load and renewable energy generation forecasts.

In order to create these forecasts, a number of choices must be made regarding the forecast model, including the selection of the forecast method (e.g. autoregressive integrated moving average (ARIMA), support vector regression, or neural networks). Furthermore, several further decisions must be taken, such as the choice of the method's hyperparameters and the loss function used for training. Whilst many scientific papers promote certain forecast model choices that they claim will lead to good forecasts [2,18,23], it is important to consider and define what constitutes a "good" forecast. Thereby, the "goodness" of a forecast can be measured by its quality and/or its value [25]. The forecast quality evaluates the forecast solely from the forecaster's point of view and is typically measured by metrics such as mean absolute error (MAE) or mean squared error (MSE). On the other hand, the forecast value considers the downstream application's point of view by evaluating the performance of the downstream application based on the forecast. For the smart building optimisation examples described above, the performance of these downstream applications can be evaluated by calculating the economic costs based on the optimisation problem's result to assess the forecast value.

Several studies investigate the quality and the value of forecast methods [11,13,28] and hyperparameters [6,37] for solar, wind, and load forecasting. These studies show that the relation between forecast quality and value does not have to be linear or monotonic [25] and thus, improving the forecast quality may not always lead to a higher value in the downstream application in case of a forecast with remaining uncertainties. Additionally, [37] shows that the downstream application's setting and the considered data influence the forecast value. The authors show for a domestic photovoltaic-battery management problem that the battery capacity, as well as the prosumption profile, can also impact the forecast value.

These findings highlight the complexity of selecting forecast models to improve the value in the downstream application and indicate that the computational effort of a manual, optimal forecast model selection can be tremendous. To reduce the manual forecast model selection's computational burden while achieving comparable results, we propose a solution for automatically selecting forecast models based on the resulting forecast's value in the downstream application using meta-learning. Specifically, we propose a framework for forecast model selection that treats the selection task as a classification problem.

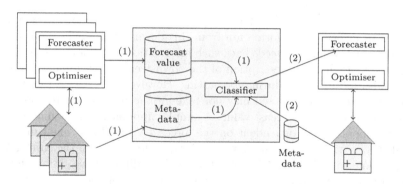

Fig. 1. The schematic representation of the proposed framework for a smart building optimisation as downstream application with the novelty marked in blue. In step (1), a classifier is trained using the buildings' metadata and the buildings' label of the forecast model leading to the forecast with the highest value. In step (2), the trained classifier can be operated to predict the forecast model leading to the highest value forecast for a new building utilising its metadata (marked in green). Then, the smart building optimisation can be executed. (Color figure online)

To achieve this, we train a classifier to select the forecast model leading to the forecast with the highest value in the downstream application, using metadata as input. In the smart building optimisation context, Fig. 1 displays the proposed framework. In step (1), the classifier is trained. For this training, we first execute the building optimisation with varying forecasts from different forecast models and then calculate the value of each forecast. Then, the forecast model leading to the forecast with the highest value is determined and together with metadata of the building used to train a classifier. In step (2), the trained classifier can then predict the forecast model leading to the forecast with the highest forecast value for a new building by utilising the new building's metadata. For evaluation, we apply our framework on the downstream application of a smart building's photovoltaic-battery-management problem - a dispatchable feeder - using real-world time series of 300 buildings.

The remainder of the paper is structured as follows. Section 2 gives a brief overview of the related work. Section 3 introduces the meta-learning framework for forecast model selection, while Sect. 4 presents the considered downstream application of a dispatchable feeder. Section 5 describes the experimental setup for evaluation and presents the corresponding results. Section 6 discusses the results and Sect. 7 wraps up the paper.

2   Related Work

In this section, we position our research compared to existing literature by addressing two aspects. First, we summarize prior work focusing on forecast models designed for the downstream application. Second, we present existing meta-learning approaches for quality-oriented forecast model selection.

One approach to designing forecast models based on the downstream application is to incorporate information from this downstream application into the forecast model. While [41] feeds back such information to the forecasting, [14,15] utilise the mathematical description of the downstream application, in this case an optimisation problem, during forecasting. However, these approaches can be computationally expensive and may not take into account all the relevant information influencing the forecast value. A simpler approach is to assume that the forecast value is solely dependent on the forecast error. Then, one can use the so-called cost-oriented loss function [19,22,24,36,40]. Thereby, the cost-oriented loss function is a piecewise function that assigns different weights to forecast errors, resulting in biased forecasts. While the form of the cost-oriented loss function needs to be known in [22,24,36,40] approximate the form in a computationally expensive manner. However, the cost-oriented loss function is not suitable for complex downstream applications with constraints, such as battery management problems. The approach of customising the loss function to fit the downstream application is also pursued in [1,20]. However, this approach is specifically designed for a single downstream application and cannot necessarily be generalised to create high-value forecasts for other applications.

Approaching the forecast model selection, several works aim to find the best-suited forecast method based on forecast quality measures using meta-learning [31,34,35]. Additionally, [9] directly predicts the RMSE of a forecast using meta-learning. However, these approaches do not consider the value of the forecast in the downstream application.

Summarizing, several existing works present approaches to either design forecasts based on their downstream applications or use meta-learning for forecast model selection with respect to forecast quality. In contrast, our meta-learning framework selects the forecast model with respect to the forecast value while not requiring knowledge of the downstream application during forecasting making it easily usable for various applications.

3 Meta-learning Framework for Forecast Model Selection

The idea of the underlying meta-learning framework for forecast model selection is to find the forecast model leading to the forecast with the highest value in the downstream application for a specific instance, e.g. a specific building. Thereby, the forecast value is a forecast evaluation metric that measures the performance of the downstream application based on the forecast and depends on the quantity of interest e.g. a building's electricity cost or self-sufficiency. Mathematically, the forecast value can be described by a function of the downstream application, its required data, and the information needed to generate the forecasts, namely the forecast model and the specific instance's data. The aim of the proposed framework is then to find the forecast model for each instance that maximises the forecast value, which we will refer to as the best forecast model in the following. Thus, we search for the best forecast model for instance $i \in \mathcal{I}$

$$f_i^* = \operatorname*{argmax}_{f \in \mathcal{F}} \text{Value}\Big(a, D_i, f\Big) \tag{1}$$

from a set of forecast models $\mathcal{F}$ given a downstream application a and the instance's data D_i. Thereby, D_i includes the input data of forecast models in $\mathcal{F}$ as well as additional data required by the downstream application a. Although this best forecast model may be found through a manual search, such a manual selection is cost-intensive and time-consuming. Therefore, we propose a meta-learning framework to identify the best forecast model automatically. In the following, we introduce this meta-learning framework for forecast model selection which interprets the selection task as a classification problem. First, we present the components of the proposed framework. Afterwards, we explain the usage of the framework including the training process and the operation.

3.1   Components of the Proposed Framework

The meta-learning framework for forecast model selection consists of four components. These are the set of forecasts models $\mathcal{F}$, the downstream application a, the metadata extraction component, and the classifier c.

The set of forecast models $\mathcal{F}$ comprises all considered forecast models. To handle the influence of the data D_i of different instances $i \in \mathcal{I}$ on what is the best forecast model, we require that the set of forecast models $\mathcal{F}$ is diverse. Thus, this diversity has to be ensured when $\mathcal{F}$ is created. The second component is the considered downstream application a. This downstream application requires a forecast provided by a forecast model $f \in \mathcal{F}$ as input for execution. The execution's performance determines the forecast value. The third component is the metadata extraction component. This component extracts the metadata m_i from D_i that is used by the classifier to determine the best forecast model. The last component is the classifier c. The task of the classifier is to select the forecast model leading to the forecast with the highest value in the downstream application a. Thus, we need to interpret the selection problem in Eq. (1) as a classification problem by considering each $f \in F$ as a class. Consequently, the target of the classification problem is the class of f_i^*. Given the metadata m_i, the output of the classifier is then

$$\hat{f}_i^* = c(m_i).$$

3.2   Usage of the Proposed Framework

To use the proposed framework, we first need to train the framework in order to operate it afterwards.

Step 1: Training Fig. 2a provides an overview of the proposed framework's training. This training requires the creation of the input features and the target variables. In the following, we present the creation of the input features and target variables as well as the training of the classifier in more detail.

First, to create the input features, we extract the metadata m_i of the data D_i for each instance $i \in \mathcal{I}$. Additionally, to create the target variables, we create a set of forecast models $\mathcal{F}$ and train the forecast models on the data D_i of each instance $i \in \mathcal{I}$. These forecast models provide forecasts to the downstream application a for execution. The execution's performance determines the forecast value for each $f \in F$ and $i \in \mathcal{I}$ from which we derive the target variable $f_i^{\star}$. Second, using these target variables and the corresponding metadata m_i, we train the classifier c.

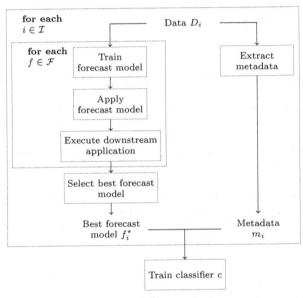

(a) To train the proposed framework, training data needs to be created. Therefore, for the data D_i of each instance $i \in \mathcal{I}$ and each forecast model $f \in \mathcal{F}$ the forecast value in the downstream application is calculated. Based on this, the best forecast model $f_i^{\star}$ for this instance is determined. Afterwards, $f_i^{\star}$ is used as target variable together with the metadata m_i as input data to train the classifier c.

(b) To operate the proposed framework, the metadata $m_{i_{\mathrm{new}}}$ of the data $D_{i_{\mathrm{new}}}$ of a new instance i_{new} is extracted. Based on this, the classifier determines the best forecast model $\hat{f}_{i_{\mathrm{new}}}^{\star}$. This forecast model can be trained and it's forecast provided to the downstream application a.

Fig. 2. The usage of the meta-learning framework for forecast model selection. (a) In the first step, the framework needs to be trained. (b) Afterwards, the framework can be operated.

Step 2: Operation. The operation of the proposed framework is displayed in Fig. 2b. First, for the new instance i_{new} and the corresponding data $D_{i_{\text{new}}}$, we extract the metadata $m_{i_{\text{new}}}$. Using this metadata as input, the classifier's output is the best forecast model $\hat{f}^*_{i_{\text{new}}}$. Based on this output, the corresponding forecast model can be trained, and the resulting forecast provided to the downstream application a.

4 Applying the Proposed Framework: Application on a Dispatchable Feeder

In this section, we apply our framework to the downstream application of a dispatchable feeder as in [37]. We, therefore, first describe the dispatchable feeder before highlighting how we apply our framework to this downstream application.

4.1 Application Dispatchable Feeder

In this section, we introduce the exemplary downstream application on which we apply and evaluate our meta-learning framework for forecast model selection. The exemplary downstream application is a dispatchable feeder, which consists, from the system side, of an inflexible, volatile component and a flexible, but energy-constrained component [4, 30]. The overall aim of the dispatchable feeder is to intelligently manage the flexible component so that the inflexibility inherent in the system is balanced out. Thereby, the management of the flexible component is described via a two-level non-linear optimisation problem. In the following, we first specify the considered system components, before we explain the management.

System Components of the Dispatchable Feeder. We apply a dispatchable feeder in a domestic building setting and consider the prosumption of the building with a rooftop photovoltaic (PV) panel as the inflexible and the domestic battery as the flexible component. To model these components, we consider a discrete system operation with time intervals indexed with $k \in \mathbb{N}$ and duration of $\Delta t \in \mathbb{R}$. Additionally, we consider only active power. To model the battery, we use its power output $P_s(k) \in \mathbb{R}$ and state of energy $E_s(k) \in \mathbb{R}$. Both variables are restricted by lower and upper bounds $\underline{P}_s, \overline{P}_s \in \mathbb{R}$ and $\underline{E}_s, \overline{E}_s \in \mathbb{R}_{\geq 0}$. Further, we model the dynamic evolution of the battery's state of energy via

$$E_s(k+1) = E_s(k) + \Delta t \cdot \left(P_s(k) - \mu P_s^+(k) + \mu P_s^-(k) \right) \tag{2}$$

with loss coefficient $0 \leq \mu \leq 1$ and $P_s^+(k) \in \mathbb{R}_{\geq 0}$ and $P_s^-(k) \in \mathbb{R}_{\leq 0}$ being the positive and negative parts of the battery's power output. The building's prosumption is defined as domestic load minus PV power generation. The power exchange between the grid and the dispatchable feeder is then the sum of the battery's power output and the building's prosumption.

Battery Management of the Dispatchable Feeder. In the following, we briefly introduce the battery management of the dispatchable feeder via a hierarchical optimisation problem with two levels. A detailed mathematical description of the optimisation problems can be found in Appendix A.1.

In the first level, we calculate a cost-minimal dispatch schedule $\tilde{P}_g(k) \in \mathbb{R}$ for the next day using deterministic forecasts of the prosumption $\hat{P}_l(k) \in \mathbb{R}$. As a cost function, we take peak shaving and self-consumption into account:

$$C_{DS}\big(\tilde{P}_g^+(k), \tilde{P}_g^-(k)\big) = c_q^+ \cdot (\tilde{P}_g^+(k))^2 + c_l^+ \cdot \tilde{P}_g^+(k) \\ + c_q^- \cdot (\tilde{P}_g^-(k))^2 + c_l^- \cdot \tilde{P}_g^-(k), \tag{3}$$

with $\tilde{P}_g^+(k) \in \mathbb{R}_{\geq 0}$ and $\tilde{P}_g^-(k) \in \mathbb{R}_{\leq 0}$ being the positive and negative parts of the dispatch schedule and $c_q^+, c_l^+, c_q^-, c_l^- \in \mathbb{R}_{\geq 0}$ being weighting parameters.

In the second level, we minimize the deviation of the dispatch schedule $\Delta P_g(k) \in \mathbb{R}$ with consideration of the realised prosumption $P_l(k) \in \mathbb{R}$, while respecting the battery's technical constraints.

4.2   Applying the Proposed Framework

As described in Sect. 3, the proposed framework interprets the selection of the best forecast model as a classification task. In the downstream application of the dispatchable feeder, we are interested in identifying for each building the prosumption forecast model which provides the forecast with the highest value. As forecast value we consider the average daily total cost, with lower costs corresponding to a higher value [37]. Therefore, we briefly describe these costs below.

The total cost is comprised of two components: the cost associated with the dispatch schedule, as described in Eq. (3), and the cost resulting from the difference between the actual dispatch and the dispatch schedule, referred to as imbalance cost [4]. More precisely, we define the imbalance cost as

$$C_{\text{imb}}\big(\Delta P_g(k)\big) = c_q^\Delta \cdot \mid \Delta P_g(k) \cdot \Delta t \mid^2 + c_l^\Delta \cdot \mid \Delta P_g(k) \cdot \Delta t \mid$$

with $\Delta P_g(k)$ being the difference between the actual dispatch and the dispatch schedule and the weighting parameters c_q^Δ and $c_l^{\Delta 1}$.
The total cost can then be expressed as

$$C_{total}\big(\tilde{P}_g^+(k), \tilde{P}_g^-(k), \Delta P_g(k)\big) = C_{DS}\big(\tilde{P}_g^+(k), \tilde{P}_g^-(k)\big) + \alpha \cdot C_{imb}\big(\Delta P_g(k)\big)$$

with imbalance cost factor[2] α. Further, we sum the total cost over 24 h and average this daily total cost over the considered days to obtain the average daily total cost[3].

5   Evaluation

We evaluate the meta-learning framework for forecast model selection on the previously described downstream application of a dispatchable feeder.

---

[1] In this paper, we select $c_q^\Delta = 0.05 \frac{\text{€}}{\text{kWh}^2}$ and $c_l^\Delta = 0.3 \frac{\text{€}}{\text{kWh}}$ as in [5].

[2] In this paper, we select as imbalance cost factor either 2 or 10 as in [5].

[3] In the following, we use the average daily total cost without its unit (€).

5.1 Experimental Setup

This section presents the experimental setup[4] for the evaluation of the proposed framework.

Forecast Models. Driven by the results of [37], we consider neural networks using varying loss functions as forecast models. More precisely, we use three-layered fully connected neural networks. As input, the neural networks receive the historical prosumption of the past 24 h. The hidden layer has 16 neurons and a ReLU [17] activation function. The output layer provides the prediction of the prosumption for the next 42 h using 42 output neurons and a linear activation function. Furthermore, we use 20% of the training data for validation to apply early stopping, a batch size of 512, and the RMSProb optimiser.

To achieve a diverse set of forecast models, we consider four different loss functions. This set of forecast models is guaranteed to be diverse because the used loss functions are responsible for the resulting forecast's properties. Thereby, a loss function quantifies how well the neural network models the true values $y_t, t \in [1 \ldots N]$, and is minimised in training. The first loss function is the **mean absolute error** (MAE). It is the mean over the absolute errors and defined as

$$\text{MAE} = \frac{1}{N} \sum_{t=1}^{N} |y_t - \hat{y}_t|.$$

The MAE treats large and small errors equally. Second, the **mean squared error** (MSE) is the mean over the sum of the squared errors and defined as

$$\text{MSE} = \frac{1}{N} \sum_{t=1}^{N} (y_t - \hat{y}_t)^2.$$

Due to the squared error term, the loss function is more sensitive to outliers. Third, the **Huber** loss function combines properties of the MSE and the MAE and is defined as

$$\text{Huber} = \frac{1}{N} \sum_{t=1}^{N} \begin{cases} \frac{1}{2}(y_t - \hat{y}_t)^2, & \text{for } |y_t - \hat{y}_t| \leq 1 \\ (|y_t - \hat{y}_t| - \frac{1}{2}), & \text{otherwise} \end{cases}.$$

Therefore, if the absolute of the error is less than one, the squared error loss is used, and if not, an absolute error based loss is used. This error function is therefore less influenced by outliers than the MSE. The **pinball** loss, which is often utilised for generating $\tau \in (0, 1)$ quantile forecasts, has the propensity to produce biased estimates. Specifically, the true values are underestimated with a probability of τ and overestimated with a probability of $\tau - 1$. It is defined as

$$\text{pinball}(\tau) = \frac{1}{N} \sum_{t=1}^{N} \max(\tau \cdot (y_t - \hat{y}_t), (\tau - 1) \cdot (y_t - \hat{y}_t)).$$

In the present paper, we choose τ values of 0.1, 0.25, 0.75, and 0.9.

---

[4] See Appendix A.2 for a detailed description of the implementation.

Classifier Setup. The classifier within our proposed framework requires metadata that captures relevant time series information as input. Thus, we consider a set of statistical features as input features including the mean, standard deviation, minimum, 25th percentile, median, 75th percentile, maximum, skewness, and kurtosis of the prosumption time series. Furthermore, we also include the average daily prosumption profile, i.e. the mean over all considered days for each hour. For further analysis with different input features, the reader is referred to Appendix A.4. To reduce the dimensionality of the input data, we use SKLearn's principal component analysis with 70% of explained variance [26]. Therefore, we scale the input data with SKLearn's standard scaler.

Given the selected metadata, we evaluate our framework with six different classifiers to cover a broad range of classification approaches including tree-, distance-, support vector-, and neural network-based classifiers, which we briefly describe in the following. The first classifier is the XGBoost classifier [10]. XGBoost boosts multiple decision trees iteratively to improve the prediction. The second classifier is the k-nearest neighbour (kNN) [12]. It determines the k nearest neighbours for a given test sample. The final classification is then performed by a majority vote of the k nearest neighbours. The third classifier is the support vector classifier (SVC) [27]. The SVC aims to find a hyperplane between two classes [32]. To apply the SVC in the multi-class scenario of the considered downstream application, the one-vs-one strategy is used. The fourth classifier is the multi-layer perceptron (MLP). The MLP consists of one or more hidden layers of fully connected neurons with a non-linear activation function to approximate arbitrary functions. The fifth classifier is a decision tree (DT) [8]. DTs extract rules from the training data. Based on these rules, DTs predict the class of the given sample. The sixth classifier is the naive Bayes (NB) [39]. NB assumes the conditional independence of the input features and uses them for the prediction of a conditional probability given the prior probability of the output variable.

Data. For our evaluation, we use the "Ausgrid - Solar home electricity data" set [29]. The data set contains load and PV power generation time series from 300 residential buildings in Australia spanning three years from 1st July 2010 to 30th June 2013 in a 30 min resolution. We resample the data to hourly resolution and calculate the prosumption data by subtracting the PV power generation from the load. To compare different ratios of load with regards to the installed PV power generation, we scale the PV power generation with the factors 1, 5, and 10, and the load with factors 1/5, 1/2, 1, 2, and 5.

Further, we use training and test splitting, see Appendix A.3. Thereby, for training the neural networks, we use the first two years of data as training data set. For evaluating the neural networks, we utilise the last year as test data set. Further, for training the classifiers, we use the first 200 buildings. For evaluating the classifiers, we employ the last 100 buildings. Additionally, for all buildings, we extract the metadata based on the first two years and consider the output labels based on the last year.

Benchmarks. To evaluate the performance of our proposed framework, we compare it to two benchmarks. The first benchmark is the **one loss function** benchmark. As suggested by the name, this benchmark applies one forecast model to all buildings. More precisely, we train one neural network with the same loss function for each building on the first two years. As the second benchmark, we consider a **manually selected loss function** for each building. In this benchmark, we calculate which loss function is cost-minimal for each building based on the first two years of data. Then, each building applies this cost-minimal loss function for the last year.

Metrics. For evaluation, we use three metrics. The first metric is the F_1 score as an accuracy measure for the considered classifier. The F_1 score is defined as

$$F_1 = \frac{2 \cdot \mathrm{TP}}{2 \cdot \mathrm{TP} + \mathrm{FP} + \mathrm{FN}},$$

with TP being the true positives, FP being the false positives and FN being the false negatives. For the one loss function benchmark, the F_1 score corresponds to the percentage of buildings for which the loss function is cost-minimal. Second, to measure the forecast value in our downstream application we use the average daily total cost in Sect. 4.2, which take the imbalance and the dispatch schedule cost into account. Thereby, we calculate the mean of the building's average daily total cost over the considered buildings for imbalance cost factors 2 and 10. Third, we measure computational effort by recording the average computation time of each component in seconds and calculate based on this the average forecast model selection time in seconds. Thereby, the latter consists of the time required to select the forecast model and to generate the forecast.

5.2   Results

In this section, we evaluate the performance of the meta-learning framework for forecast model selection. First, we compare the cost and accuracy of our framework with the two selected benchmarks. Second, we evaluate the impact of different classifiers on the forecast model selection performance and, finally, address the computational effort.

Benchmarking. We compare the cost and accuracy of our framework to the two benchmarks with respect to imbalance cost factors 2 and 10 in Table 1.

Starting with imbalance cost factor 2, we observe for the one loss function benchmark that the selected loss function has a noticeable impact on the cost and accuracy. This benchmark achieves the lowest cost (6.09) with MAE as loss function. However, similar costs are obtained when using Huber (6.11) and MSE (6.27). The corresponding accuracies with MSE, MAE, and Huber is 0.25, 0.22, and 0.17 respectively. In contrast, pinball 0.75 results in cost of 8.83 despite being the cost-minimal loss function for the most buildings (namely 34%). In comparison, the proposed framework with SVC as classifier reduces the one loss

Table 1. The average daily total costs and the F_1 scores of the proposed framework and the considered benchmarks for the imbalance cost factors 2 and 10. The metrics are calculated for the test data set with the last year of data and the last 100 buildings. Note, for the average daily total costs lower values are better and for the F_1 scores higher values.

Approaches	Imbalance cost factor 2		Imbalance cost factor 10	
	Average daily total costs (€)	F_1 scores	Average daily total costs (€)	F_1 scores
One loss function with				
MAE	6.09	0.22	20.05	0.16
MSE	6.27	0.25	18.95	0.20
Huber	6.11	0.17	19.05	0.11
Pinball 0.10	9.62	0.00	43.78	0.00
Pinball 0.25	7.41	0.02	30.47	0.01
Pinball 0.75	8.83	0.34	27.04	0.37
Pinball 0.90	18.13	0.00	60.08	0.16
Manually selected loss function	5.92	0.69	17.67	0.73
Proposed framework (SVC)	5.93	0.68	17.80	0.67

function benchmark cost by at least 2.6% to 5.93 and improves the accuracy to 0.68. However, the proposed framework has slightly higher cost (5.92) and lower accuracy (0.69) compared to the manually selected loss function benchmark.

For imbalance cost factor 10, the one loss function benchmark reaches its lowest cost (18.95) using MSE as loss function, with similar costs using Huber (19.05) and MAE (20.05). The corresponding accuracy is 0.20 with MSE, 0.16 with MAE, and 0.11 with Huber. The highest accuracy of 0.37 is reached with pinball 0.75. In comparison, the proposed framework with SVC as classifier, again, reduces the one loss function benchmark cost by at least 6% to 17.80 and improves the accuracy to 0.67. Further, similar to imbalance cost factor 2, the difference in cost and accuracy between the proposed framework and the manually selected loss function benchmark is less than 1% and 10% respectively.

Impact of Classifier. To investigate the impact of the classifier, we compare the performance of the proposed framework with six classifiers. Based on the results for the imbalance cost factors 2 and 10 in Table 2, we present three observations.

First, for with imbalance cost factor 2, we observe that the proposed framework achieves the lowest cost of 5.93 when using SVC and MLP. The classifiers kNN, XGBoost, and decision tree lead to costs of 6.00, 6.03 and 6.07 respectively. With respect to the accuracy, the order of the classifier is similar with SVC/MLP (0.68), XGBoost (0.64), kNN (0.63), and decision tree (0.58). In contrast, naive Bayes leads to the highest cost of 6.21 as well as to the lowest accuracy of 0.6.

Second, for imbalance cost factor 10, SVC and MLP lead to the lowest costs of 17.80 and 17.81 and to accuracy of 0.67. Further, the classifier kNN, XGBoost, and naive Bayes lead to costs of 17.98, 18.13, and 18.21 and accuracies of 0.63,

Table 2. The average daily total costs and the F_1 scores of the proposed framework using different classifiers for the imbalance cost factors 2 and 10. The metrics are calculated for the test data set with the last year of data and the last 100 buildings. Thereby, we calculate the mean over five runs with the values in the brackets being the minimum and maximum. Note, for the average daily total costs lower values are better and for the F_1 scores higher values.

Approaches	Imbalance cost factor 2		Imbalance cost factor 10	
	Average daily total costs (€)	F_1 scores	Average daily total costs (€)	F_1 scores
XGBoost	6.03	0.64	18.13	0.61
kNN	6.00	0.63	17.98	0.63
SVC	5.93	0.68 (0.67,0.68)	17.80	0.67
MLP	5.93 (5.92,5.95)	0.68 (0.67, 0.68)	17.81 (17.76, 18.39)	0.67
Decision tree	6.07 (6.06,6.09)	0.58 (0.57,0.59)	18.35 (18.32, 18.39)	0.56 (0.55,0.57)
Naive Bayes	6.21	0.6	18.21	0.58

0.61, and 0.58 respectively. In contrast to the results for the imbalance cost factor 2, decision tree performs worst with cost of 18.35 and accuracy of 0.56.

Our final observation regarding the classifiers' impact is that each classifier reaches a higher accuracy for imbalance cost factor 2 compared to imbalance cost factor 10.

Computational Effort. We first measure each component's computation time. Afterwards, we calculate the time of the proposed framework and the benchmarks to select the forecast model for a new building.

For each component, Table 3a provides the average computation time in seconds per building. The most time-intensive component is the optimisation problem's run time on the first two years, followed by the neural network's training time. The other components require a negligible amount of time.

Based on the measured components' times, we can estimate the forecast model selection time for a new building. For the one loss function benchmark, the neural network with the considered loss function must be trained on the first two years of the new building's data. For the manually selected loss function benchmark, we need to train neural networks for each loss function, generate forecasts with the trained neural networks and solve the optimisation problem with the resulting forecasts for the first two years. For the proposed framework, we must first extract the metadata based on the first two years, then run the classifier, and, finally, train the neural network with the selected loss function once. Table 3a shows the resulting forecast model selection times. In this table, we make two observations. First, the manually selected loss function benchmark has, noticeably, the highest forecast model selection time with 287.14 s. The one loss function benchmark and the proposed framework require noticeably less time. Second, we observe that despite using a meta-learning approach the forecast model selection time of the proposed framework is only slightly higher than that of the one loss function benchmark.

Table 3. The average computation time of each component and the average forecast model selection time of the proposed framework and the considered benchmarks in seconds for a new building. Note, the times do not depend on the considered imbalance cost factor.

(a) Computation time of the components

Components	Computation time (s)
Classifier inference time	
XGBoost	0.02
kNN	0.08
SVC	0.10
MLP	0.01
Decision tree	0.00
Naive Bayes	0.01
Metadata generation time	0.19
Forecasting NN training time	9.38
Forecasting NN inference time	0.07
Optimisation problem run time	31.57

(b) Forecast model selection time of the proposed framework and the considered benchmarks for a new building.

Approaches	Forecast model selection time (s)
One loss function	9.38
Manually selected loss function	287.14
Proposed framework (SVC)	9.67

6   Discussion

This section discusses the previously reported results in Sect. 5.2, the benefits, and the limitations of the meta-learning framework for forecast model selection.

With regard to the results of the evaluation, we discuss three aspects. First, the results indicate that the proposed framework reduces the cost and improves the accuracy compared to the one loss function benchmark. Thereby, the choice between the classifiers SVC and MLP does not affect the proposed framework's performance. In contrast, for this application, using the naive Bayes and decision tree classifier is not recommended. Furthermore, the performance of the proposed framework with respect to cost and accuracy is comparable to the performance of the manually selected loss function benchmark. However, there is still potential for further improvement, e.g. more advanced classifier as well as hyperparameter optimisation. Second, we observe a non-monotonic, non-linear relation between cost and accuracy. More precisely, improving the accuracy does not necessarily lead to lower cost. For the one loss function benchmark, this means that the cost-minimal loss function for most buildings is not necessarily the cost-minimal loss function for the whole data set. This observation can be explained by extensive costs for the remaining buildings and highlights the complexity of selecting the loss function with respect to the forecast value in the downstream application. Finally, the results show that the proposed framework reduces the computational effort compared to the manually selected loss function benchmark by 97%. That makes the proposed framework particularly interesting for downstream applications for which scalability is essential. For example, in the considered application of the dispatchable feeder, scalability and low computational effort could become important for the joint optimisation of multiple buildings. Additionally, in contrast to the manually selected loss function benchmark, the computational effort of the proposed framework increases negligibly when the set of forecasting models is expanded. Besides the benefit with respect to scalability, we want to highlight a further advantage that comes from the design of the proposed framework. This is, due to its simplicity, it can be easily applied to various applications without extensive knowledge of the optimisation problem.

With regard to the proposed framework's limitations, we discuss three aspects. First, it should be noted that the proposed framework has been evaluated on one application. Second, the proposed framework currently uses two years of historical data for the initial training process. Therefore, further evaluation is required to determine how a reduced training set affects the performance. Third, the proposed framework selects the forecast model for each building once. Further research could extend the framework to an online setting that continually re-classifies each building based on recent information. This extension is especially motivated by the results of the manually selected loss function benchmark that indicates that the forecast value of a forecast model might change over time.

7 Conclusion

The present paper addresses the complexity of selecting a forecast model based on the resulting forecast's value in the downstream application. To automate this selection and avoid a computational expensive manual selection, we propose a meta-learning framework for forecast model selection. More precisely, we consider the selection task as a classification problem and train a classifier based on labels referring to the forecast model which provides the forecast with highest value in the downstream application. We evaluate this meta-learning framework for forecast model selection on the exemplary downstream application of a smart building's domestic photovoltaic-battery management problem known as dispatchable feeder. Therefore, we consider neural networks with different loss functions as forecast models. Thus, the selection task is to select the neural network's loss function providing forecasts with the highest value for the dispatchable feeder. The results show that our framework reduces the cost and improves the accuracy compared to selecting the same loss function for each building. In comparison with selecting the loss function for each building manually, the proposed framework leads to similar cost and accuracy requiring noticeably less computational effort.

In future work, we plan to expand our framework by incorporating the dynamically selection of the forecast model based on recent input data and by increasing the considered set of forecast models.

A Appendix

A.1 Optimisation Problems

In the following, the first and second level optimisation problems of the dispatchable feeder in Sect. 4.1 are described. In the first level, the cost function in Eq. (3) is minimised under consideration of the system constraints. The first level optimisation problem can be described by

$$\min_{\{X\}_\mathcal{K}} \sum_{k\in\mathcal{K}} C_{DS}\left(\tilde{P}_g^+(k), \tilde{P}_g^-(k)\right)$$

s.t. for all $k \in \mathcal{K}$

(2)

$$E_s(k_0) = E_s^0$$
$$\tilde{P}_g(k) = P_s(k) + \hat{P}_l(k)$$
$$\tilde{P}_g(k) = \tilde{P}_g^+(k) + \tilde{P}_g^-(k)$$
$$\tilde{P}_g^-(k) \le 0 \qquad\qquad (4)$$
$$P_s(k) = P_s^+(k) + P_s^-(k)$$
$$P_s^+(k) \ge 0$$
$$P_s^-(k) \le 0$$
$$0 = P_s^+(k) \cdot P_s^-(k)$$
$$\underline{P}_s \le P_s(k) \le \overline{P}_s$$
$$\underline{E}_s \le E_s(k) \le \overline{E}_s$$

with a discrete scheduling horizon $\mathcal{K}$, decision vector $X(k) = \big(\tilde{P}_g(k),\, \tilde{P}_g^+(k),\, \tilde{P}_g^-(k), E_s(k+1), P_s(k),\, P_s^+(k), P_s^-(k)\big)^T$, and parameters $\hat{P}_l(k)$, E_s^0, $\underline{P}_s, \overline{P}_s$, $\underline{E}_s, \overline{E}_s$. Thereby, the state of energy at the start of scheduling $k_0 \in \mathbb{N}$ has to be known or estimated.

In the second level, the deviation of the dispatch schedule $\Delta P_g(k) \in \mathbb{R}$ is minimised while considering the realised prosumption $P_l(k) \in \mathbb{R}$ and the battery's technical constraints. It can be described by

$$\min_{X(k)} \big(\Delta P_g(k)\big)^2$$

(2)

$$E_s(k) = E_s^k$$
$$P_g(k) = P_s(k) + P_l(k)$$
$$P_g(k) = \tilde{P}_g(k) + \Delta P_g(k)$$
$$P_s(k) = P_s^+(k) + P_s^-(k) \qquad (5)$$
$$P_s^+(k) \ge 0$$
$$P_s^-(k) \le 0$$

$$0 = P_s^+(k) \cdot P_s^-(k)$$

$$\underline{P}_s \leq P_s(k) \leq \overline{P}_s$$

$$\underline{E}_s \leq E_s(k) \leq \overline{E}_s$$

with actual dispatch $P_g(k) \in \mathbb{R}$, decision vector $X(k) = \big(\Delta P_g(k), P_g(k),$ $E_s(k+1), P_s(k), P_s^+(k), P_s^-(k)\big)^T$ and parameters $\tilde{P}_g(k)$, $P_l(k)$, E_s^k, $\underline{P}_s, \overline{P}_s$, $\underline{E}_s, \overline{E}_s$. Thereby, the state of energy in $k \in \mathbb{N}$ is known.

A.2   Implementation

In the following, we briefly describe the hard- and software and the optimisation problems' parameter specification used for our evaluation.[5]

All of our experiments are performed on a small server with 32 cores (2.1GHz), 64GB RAM, and a Nvidia Titan RTX. To ensure reproducibility and reusability, we implement the experiments using the pyWATTS library [21]. To solve the optimisation problem in our downstream application, we use the Python version of CasADi [3] with IPOPT [33]. We set the parameters of the optimisation problem in Eq. (4) and Eq. (5) as in [5], see Table 4. Further, we implement all classifiers except XGBoost with implementation provided by SKLearn [26]. For XGBoost, we use the XGBoost library [10]. Furthermore, we use the default hyperparameters for all classifiers apart from the MLP classifier, where we raise the maximum number of epochs to 1000.

Table 4. Parameter specification of the optimisation problems in Eq. (4) and Eq. (5).

Parameter	Value
Δt	1 (hour)
$\mathcal{K}$	$\{k_s, ..., k_s + 29\}^a$
c_q^+	0.05 (€/kWh^2)
c_l^+	0.3 (€/kWh)
c_q^-	0.05 (€/kWh^2)
c_l^-	0.15 (€/kWh)
$\underline{P}_s$	-5 (kW)
$\overline{P}_s$	5 (kW)
$\underline{E}_s$	0 (kWh)
$\overline{E}_s$	13.5 (kWh)
μ	0.05
E_s^0	day 1: 6 (kWh)
	days 2 - 7: estimated^b

^{a} $k_s \in \mathbb{N}$ is the index of the time interval starting at midnight
^{b} The initial state of energy E_s^0 for days two to seven is estimated via an optimisation problem, see [4].

---

[5] The Code is publicly available at https://github.com/KIT-IAI/Automating-Value-Oriented-Forecast-Model-Selection-by-Meta-Learning.

A.3   Training and Test Data Sets

Fig. 3 displays the training and test data set splitting for the forecast models and the classifiers.

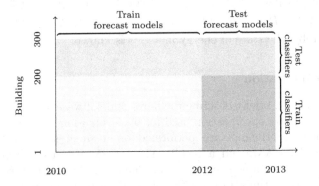

Fig. 3. The training and test data sets for the forecast models and the classifiers. Note, for the classifiers, we extract the metadata from the first two years and consider the output labels based on the last year.

A.4   Input Features

Table 5 shows the costs and accuracies of the proposed framework for different input features.

Table 5. The average daily total costs (left) and the F₁ scores (right) of the proposed meta-learning framework for forecast model selection using different classifiers and different input features for imbalance cost factor 2. Thereby, the metadata is calculated for the prosumption time series and consists of the following statistical features: [B] mean, standard deviation, minimum, 25th percentile, median, 75th percentile, and maximum; [F1] mean over all days for each hour; [F2] mean, minimum, and maximum of each day; [F3] mean over all days of minimum and maximum for each day; [F4] seasonality and trend; [F5] skewness and kurtosis; [F6] autocorrelation. The metrics are calculated for the test data set with the last year of data and the last 100 buildings. Thereby, we calculate the mean over five runs with the values in the brackets being the minimum and maximum. Note, for the average daily total costs lower values are better and for the F₁ scores higher values.

Input features	Classifier											
	XGBoost		kNN		SVC		MLP		Decision Tree		Naïve Bayes	
	(€)	F₁ scores	(€)	F₁ scores	(€)	F₁ scores	(€)	F₁ scores	(€)	F₁ scores	(€)	F₁ scores
B+F1	6.02	0.6	5.99	0.62	5.93	0.68	5.93 (5.93, 5.94)	0.68	6.04 (6.03, 6.05)	0.55 (0.55, 0.56)	6.22	0.6
B+F1+F2	6.0	0.6	5.98	0.62	5.93	0.68	5.96 (5.94, 5.99)	0.66 (0.66, 0.67)	6.1 (6.08, 6.11)	0.56 (0.56, 0.57)	6.27	0.57
B+F1+F3	6.04	0.61	5.99	0.63	5.93	0.68	5.93 (5.92, 5.94)	0.68 (0.68, 0.69)	6.09 (6.07, 6.1)	0.55 (0.54, 0.56)	6.15	0.6
B+F1+F4	6.02	0.61	5.99	0.61	5.93	0.68	5.93 (5.92, 5.94)	0.68 (0.68, 0.69)	6.07 (6.06, 6.07)	0.55 (0.55, 0.56)	6.22	0.6
B+F1+F5	6.03	0.64	6.00	0.63	5.93	0.68	5.93 (5.92, 5.95)	0.68 (0.67, 0.68)	6.07 (6.06,6.09)	0.58 (0.57, 0.59)	6.21	0.6
B+F1+F6	6.03	0.63	5.98	0.63	5.93	0.68	5.93 (5.92, 5.93)	0.69 (0.68, 0.69)	6.05 (6.04, 6.07)	0.56 (0.55, 0.57)	6.21	0.6
B+F1+F2+F5	5.99	0.62	5.98	0.61	5.93	0.68	5.95 (5.94, 5.98)	0.67 (0.66, 0.68)	6.09 (6.08, 6.11)	0.56 (0.55, 0.57)	6.27	0.57
B+F1+F3+F5	6.01	0.64	5.98	0.64	5.93	0.68	5.94 (5.92, 5.97)	0.68 (0.67, 0.7)	6.06 (6.05, 6.06)	0.58 (0.58, 0.59)	6.21	0.61
B+F1+F2+F3+F5	5.99	0.62	5.98	0.61	5.93	0.68	5.96 (5.94, 5.97)	0.67 (0.66, 0.67)	6.09 (6.09, 6.11)	0.56 (0.55, 0.58)	6.27	0.57
B+F1+F2+F3+F4+F5+F6	5.99	0.61	5.98	0.61	5.93	0.68	5.96 (5.95, 5.97)	0.66 (0.66, 0.67)	6.1	0.56	6.27	0.57

References

1. Abdulla, K., Steer, K., Wirth, A., Halgamuge, S.: Improving the on-line control of energy storage via forecast error metric customization. J. Energy Storage **8**, 51–59 (2016)
2. Ahmad, T., Zhang, H., Yan, B.: A review on renewable energy and electricity requirement forecasting models for smart grid and buildings. Sustain. Urban Areas **55**, 102052–102082 (2020)
3. Andersson, J.A.E., Gillis, J., Horn, G., Rawlings, J.B., Diehl, M.: CasADi - a software framework for nonlinear optimization and optimal control. Math. Program. Comput. **11**, 1–36 (2019)
4. Appino, R.R., González Ordiano, J.Á., Mikut, R., Faulwasser, T., Hagenmeyer, V.: On the use of probabilistic forecasts in scheduling of renewable energy sources coupled to storages. Appl. Energy **210**, 1207–1218 (2018)
5. Appino, R.R., González Ordiano, J.Á., Mikut, R., Hagenmeyer, V., Faulwasser, T.: Storage scheduling with stochastic uncertainties: feasibility and cost of imbalances. In: 2018 Power Systems Computation Conference (PSCC), pp. 1–7 (2018)
6. Bessa, R.J., Miranda, V., Botterud, A., Wang, J.: 'Good' or 'bad' wind power forecasts: a relative concept. Wind Energy **14**(5), 625–636 (2011)
7. Biyik, E., Kahraman, A.: A predictive control strategy for optimal management of peak load, thermal comfort, energy storage and renewables in multi-zone buildings. J. Build. Eng. **25**, 100826–100836 (2019)
8. Breiman, L., Friedman, J.H., Olshen, R.A., Stone, C.J.: Classification and Regression Trees. Wadsworth International Group, Belmont, CA (1984)
9. Carneiro, D., Guimarães, M., Carvalho, M., Novais, P.: Using meta-learning to predict performance metrics in machine learning problems. Expert Syst. **40**(1), e12900 (2023)
10. Chen, T., Guestrin, C.: XGBoost: a scalable tree boosting system. In: Proceedings of the 22nd ACM SIGKDD International Conference on Knowledge Discovery and Data Mining, pp. 785–794. Association for Computing Machinery, New York, NY, USA (2016)
11. Coignard, J., Janvier, M., Debusschere, V., Moreau, G., Chollet, S., Caire, R.: Evaluating forecasting methods in the context of local energy communities. Int. J. Electr. Power Energy Syst. **131**, 106956 (2021)
12. Cover, T., Hart, P.: Nearest neighbor pattern classification. IEEE Trans. Inf. Theory **13**(1), 21–27 (1967)
13. David, M., Boland, J., Cirocco, L., Lauret, P., Voyant, C.: Value of deterministic day-ahead forecasts of PV generation in PV + storage operation for the Australian electricity market. Sol. Energy **224**, 672–684 (2021)
14. Donti, P.L., Amos, B., Kolter, Z.: Task-based end-to-end model learning in stochastic optimization. In: Proceedings of the 31st International Conference on Neural Information Processing Systems, pp 5490–5500. Curran Associates Inc., Red Hook, NY, USA (2017)
15. Elmachtoub, A.N., Grigas, P.: Smart "predict, then optimize." Manage. Sci. **68**(1), 9–26 (2022)
16. Frahm, M., et al.: Occupant-oriented economic model predictive control for demand response in buildings, pp. 354–360. e-Energy '22, Association for Computing Machinery, New York, NY, USA (2022)
17. Fukushima, K.: Cognitron: a self-organizing multilayered neural network. Biol. Cybern. **20**(3–4), 121–136 (1975). https://doi.org/10.1007/BF00342633

18. Ghofrani, M., Alolayan, M.: Time series and renewable energy forecasting, pp. 77–92 (2017)
19. Granger, C.W.J.: Prediction with a generalized cost of error function. OR **20**(2), 199–207 (1969)
20. Haben, S., Ward, J., Vukadinovic Greetham, D., Singleton, C., Grindrod, P.: A new error measure for forecasts of household-level, high resolution electrical energy consumption. Int. J. Forecast. **30**(2), 246–256 (2014)
21. Heidrich, B., et al.: pyWATTS: python workflow automation tool for time series (2021). arXiv:2106.10157
22. Khabibrakhmanov, I., Lu, S., Hamann, H.F., Warren, K.: On the usefulness of solar energy forecasting in the presence of asymmetric costs of errors. IBM J. Res. Dev. **60**(1), 7:1–7:6 (2016)
23. Kuster, C., Rezgui, Y., Mourshed, M.: Electrical load forecasting models: a critical systematic review. Sustain. Urban Areas **35**, 257–270 (2017)
24. Li, G., Chiang, H.D.: Toward cost-oriented forecasting of wind power generation. IEEE Trans. Smart Grid **9**(4), 2508–2517 (2018)
25. Murphy, A.H.: What is a good forecast? an essay on the nature of goodness in weather forecasting. Weather Forecast. **8**(2), 281–293 (1993)
26. Pedregosa, F., et al.: Scikit-learn: machine learning in python. J. Mach. Learn. Res. **12**, 2825–2830 (2011)
27. Platt, J.: Probabilistic outputs for support vector machines and comparisons to regularized likelihood methods. Adv. Large Margin Classif. **10**(3), 61–74 (1999)
28. Putz, D., Gumhalter, M., Auer, H.: The true value of a forecast: assessing the impact of accuracy on local energy communities. Sustain. Energy Grids Networks **33**, 100983 (2023)
29. Ratnam, E.L., Weller, S.R., Kellett, C.M., Murray, A.T.: Residential load and rooftop PV generation: an Australian distribution network dataset. Int. J. Sustain. Energ. **36**(8), 787–806 (2017)
30. Sossan, F., Namor, E., Cherkaoui, R., Paolone, M.: Achieving the dispatchability of distribution feeders through prosumers data driven forecasting and model predictive control of electrochemical storage. IEEE Trans. Sustain. Energy **7**(4), 1762–1777 (2016)
31. Talagala, T.S., Hyndman, R.J., Athanasopoulos, G.: Meta-learning how to forecast time series. Monash Econometrics and Business Statistics Working Papers 6/18, Monash University, Department of Econometrics and Business Statistics (2018)
32. Vapnik, V.N.: The Nature of Statistical Learning Theory, 2nd edn. Springer, New York (2000). https://doi.org/10.1007/978-1-4757-3264-1
33. Wächter, A., Biegler, L.T.: On the implementation of an interior-point filter line-search algorithm for large-scale nonlinear programming. Math. Program. **106**, 25–57 (2006)
34. Wang, C., Bäck, T., Hoos, H.H., Baratchi, M., Limmer, S., Olhofer, M.: Automated machine learning for short-term electric load forecasting. In: 2019 IEEE Symposium Series on Computational Intelligence (SSCI), pp. 314–321. IEEE, Xiamen, China (2019)
35. Wang, X., Smith-Miles, K., Hyndman, R.: Rule induction for forecasting method selection: meta-learning the characteristics of univariate time series. Neurocomputing **72**(10), 2581–2594 (2009)
36. Wang, Y., Wu, L.: Improving economic values of day-ahead load forecasts to real-time power system operations. IET Gener. Trans. Distrib. **11**(17), 4238–4247 (2017)

37. Werling, D., Beichter, M., Heidrich, B., Phipps, K., Mikut, R., Hagenmeyer, V.: The impact of forecast characteristics on the forecast value for the dispatchable feeder. In: Companion Proceedings of the 14th ACM International Conference on Future Energy Systems, pp. 59–71. e-Energy '23 Companion, Association for Computing Machinery, New York, NY, USA (2023)

38. Werling, D., Heidrich, B., Çakmak, H.K., Hagenmeyer, V.: Towards line-restricted dispatchable feeders using probabilistic forecasts for PV-dominated low-voltage distribution grids. In: Proceedings of the Thirteenth ACM International Conference on Future Energy Systems, pp. 395–400. e-Energy '22, Association for Computing Machinery, New York, NY, USA (2022)

39. Zhang, H.: The optimality of naive Bayes. In: Proceedings of the Seventeenth International Florida Artificial Intelligence Research Society Conference (FLAIRS 2004). AAAI Press, Miami Beach, Florida, USA (2004)

40. Zhang, J., Wang, Y., Hug, G.: Cost-oriented load forecasting. Electric Power Syst. Res. **205**, 107723 (2022)

41. Zhao, C., Wan, C., Song, Y.: Cost-oriented prediction intervals: on bridging the gap between forecasting and decision. IEEE Trans. Power Syst. **37**(4), 3048–3062 (2022)

Data-Driven Smart Buildings

Early Stage Design Methodology for Energy Efficiency in Buildings Using Asynchronous Distributed Task Queues Framework

Aviruch Bhatia[1]([✉])(iD), Shanmukh Dontu[2](iD), Vishal Garg[1,2](iD), Philip Haves[3], and Reshma Singh[3](iD)

[1] Plaksha University, Mohali, India
aviruchbhatia@gmail.com
[2] International Institute of Information Technology, Hyderabad, India
[3] Lawrence Berkeley National Laboratory, Berkeley, USA

Abstract. Energy consumption in the building sector is about 40% of total energy consumed globally and is trending upwards, along with its contribution to greenhouse gas (GHG) emissions. Given the adverse impacts of GHG emissions, it's crucial to integrate energy efficiency into building designs. The most significant opportunities for enhancing energy performance are present during the initial phases of building design, which are less impacted by other design constraints. Various tools exist for simulating different design options, providing feedback in terms of energy consumption and comfort parameters. These simulation outputs must then be analyzed to derive design solutions. This paper presents an innovative approach that utilizes user input parameters, processes them through cloud computing, and outputs easily understandable strategies for energy-efficient building design. The methodology employs Asynchronous Distributed Task Queues (DTQ)-a scalable and reliable alternative to conventional speedup techniques-for conducting parametric energy simulations in the cloud. The goal of this approach is to assist design teams in identifying, visualizing, and prioritizing energy-saving design strategies from a range of possible solutions for each project.

Keywords: Asynchronous Distributed Task Queues · Parallel Simulations · Building Energy Analysis

1 Introduction

Rapid urbanization around the globe is driving energy demand and the associated greenhouse gas emissions. The buildings and construction sector accounts for 36% of final energy use and 39% of energy- and process-related emissions worldwide. In 2021, about 28% of the total U.S. energy consumption was associated with residential and commercial buildings [1]. As per the Global Construction 2030 report, the volume of construction output is expected to grow by

B. N. Jørgensen et al. (Eds.): EI.A 2023, LNCS 14467, pp. 119–134, 2024.
https://doi.org/10.1007/978-3-031-48649-4_7

85% to USD 15.5 trillion worldwide by 2030, with China, the U.S. and India leading the way and accounting for 57% of all global growth [2]. Much of the energy use in buildings is wasted because of "poor design, inadequate technology and inappropriate behavior" [3]. At the beginning of the design process, it is relatively simpler and less expensive to make design changes to arrive at the desired solution. The design process is generally phased sequentially as follows: conceptual design, schematic design, design development and construction documents. The early design phases provide more flexibility as there are fewer constraints imposed by other design decisions. There are a number of design parameters, primarily related to building form, that need to be considered during early design. Echenagucia et al. [4] discussed the importance of decisions taken in early design phase, asserting that this critical phase presents the greatest opportunity to obtain a high-performance solution for the building.

A number of building design analysis tools are currently available with varying features and functionality that can be used to explore building energy consumption, including EnergyPlus [5], DOE-2 [6] and IES-VE [7]. Some of these tools can be used with different external User Interface (UI) interfaces, For example, EnergyPlus, which is a whole building simulation tool developed by the U.S. Department of Energy (DOE), is included with OpenStudio [8], DesignBuilder [9] and Simergy [10], eQUEST [11] includes DOE-2.2, a derivative of DOE-2, and Green Building Studio [12] can serve as an interface to both DOE-2.2 and EnergyPlus. IES-VE includes both a simulation engine and a user interface. Despite the substantial number of building simulation tools available, the application of these tools is mostly restricted to the later design phases [13].

However, a number of authors have explored the use of building performance simulations in early design. One of the findings of Kristoffer Negendahl [14] emphasized that most tools and methods used in the early design stages are not sufficient to provide valid feedback while at the same time being flexible enough to accommodate a rapidly changing design process. Tian et al. [15] have compared seven energy optimization tools that can be used to achieve energy efficiency in the conceptual design phase. The results show that existing techniques are not able to fully address the architect's needs in the conceptual design stage and, therefore, further research and development are needed. Ostergard et al. [16] have presented a robust review of building simulation tools and addressed integration challenges for early design. These challenges are time-consuming modelling, rapid changes in design, and conflicting requirements.

The following points outline the limitations of the existing tools:

– Some of the tools require the user to have programming expertise
– Some tools use input files to provide the freedom to change variables but require considerable user expertise to understand the file content and format
– Only a few of the tools harness cloud servers and task queues
– None of the tools produce outputs that can be readily explicated as rules or clusters that are easily understandable by humans.

There appears to be no existing tool that is free of all these limitations. The use of available simulation tools in early design stage requires expertise in energy simulation. Also, if there is a requirement to run a large number of parametric simulations, the computation time is very high. For example, if there are five parameters and each parameter needs to be simulated with five variations, then there will be over three thousand combinations. Processing and data management in such cases is difficult for users who do not have expertise in running large numbers of simulations. An additional key issue is the ineffective display of simulation results to visualize the relative performance of design alternatives. Ideally, effective visualization would result in insights into the underlying causes of performance differences.

In this paper, a methodology has been presented having the following novel features:

- Presentation of results in the form of design constraints for building energy efficiency. These restrictions are easily understandable by designers, in particular, by architects.
- Distributed Task Queue (DTQ) cloud computing for modeling and processing of energy simulation results

In the following sections, details of the methodology for conducting early design simulations and finding strategies are presented. Following this, a concluding section is provided.

2   Methodology

A methodology has been developed to make energy-efficient decisions in the early stages of building design. The methodology can be divided into seven steps, as shown in Fig. 1, it consists of getting input ranges for building design variables from the user, creating simulation models and running these using task queues in the cloud. The simulation results are used to identify design strategies that result in performance in the lowest energy consumption range; the results are presented graphically to enable strategies to be visualized by users. Users can then refine the ranges to get more insights into design flexibility [17].

Step 1: User Inputs
The step 'User Input' identifies early design parameters. Some parameters can be fixed and some can be variable. The range of each variable parameter needs to be defined for parametric simulations to be performed. Key design attributes and the corresponding design parameters are listed in Table 1.

Fixed and Variable Input Parameters. Input parameters can be divided into two categories - fixed parameters and variable parameters. In some cases, the parameter may be fixed permanently; for example, orientation and/or aspect ratio may be fixed by the constraints of the site. In some cases, certain parameters may be fixed in the earliest stages of the analysis to focus computational resources on other aspects of the design.

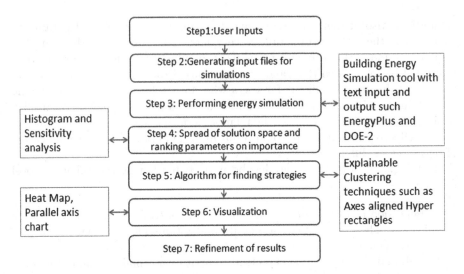

Fig. 1. Seven-step methodology for early stage building energy design.

Table 1. Building parameters.

Fixed Parameters	Variable Parameters
Location	Window to Wall Ratio (WWR)
Building type	Orientation
HVAC system	Glass type
Total built-up area	Aspect Ratio
Number of floors	Overhang
Window type	
Cool roof	
Daylight controls	
Heating Set Point	
Cooling Set Point	

An illustration of fixed and variable parameters for a typical project is presented in Table 1. In some cases, parameters such as Heating Ventilation and Air Conditioning (HVAC) type or presence of a cool roof may need to be variable rather than fixed in order to determine how comfort can be best obtained at a lower cost. For example, some cooling systems, such as radiant systems, may be inherently more efficient but have lower capacity than conventional air-based systems. In this step, input parameters are identified that are going to be used in further processing. Typical ranges for the parameters are shown in Table 2.

Table 2. Range of variable input parameters.

Parameter	Minimum Value	Maximum Value	Units
Aspect Ratio	1	10	Ratio
Orientation	0	360	Degree
Overhang	1	45	Degree
WWR	1	90	Percentage

Step 2: Generating Input Files for Simulations

The next step is to generate relevant combinations to run energy simulations. It starts with entering user inputs into templates to generate input data files - text files with a predefined structure, such as the EnergyPlus Input Data File (IDF) and DOE-2 input file. A template is a text file with parameters specified as variables, which is then used to generate a separate input file for each combination of parameter values. The number of input files depends on the potential parameter variations - for example, if there are eight parameters and each has five possible values, then a total of 32,768 input files will be generated. More details of the EnergyPlus IDF can be found in the EnergyPlus [5].

Step 3: Performing Energy Simulations

Each combination needs to be simulated using a building energy simulation tool. The simulation tool provides energy consumption for each combination. To handle a large number of simulations, parallel computing can be used. Garg et al. [18] have presented an approach to break annual simulation in several segments of smaller run period and each handled by a separate processor. The elapsed time is reduced by using multiple processors for each run. Speed gain of 3 x to 6 x was achieved in the study. Another study performed by Giannakis et al. [19] investigated simplifications in geometries and the use of co-simulation and achieved a reduction in runtime of 80%. Abhilash et al. [20] used regression to reduce computation by simulating some of the selected combinations and estimating the rest of them. Researchers have explored various techniques to handle multiple EnergyPlus simulations like multi-threading, multi-processing and parallel computing but reliable software architecture and the application of DTQ in building energy simulations still needs recognition.

In this methodology, DTQ are used for the simulations which is considered as a standard technique to perform tasks on multiple computational cores asynchronously. It is based on producer-consumer architecture. Producer en-queues the tasks in the message queue and consumers de-queues it, process it and updates the result in database. This work achieves novelty by introducing DTQ to run CPU-intensive EnergyPlus programs on the web by developing scalable and fault-tolerant application. A DTQ web application is deployed on the cloud, this application can also be deployed in research labs, universities, offices, etc for better cost savings in energy simulations. There are various software libraries for DTQs in different programming languages such as Huey, Celery [21], and

Resque. Open source python library "Celery" is opted in this work having multiple support for programming languages, brokers and monitoring tools which focuses on real-time operation but supports scheduling as well. Apart from this, it provides clean software implementation documentation and has wide user base across the globe [22].

The supervisor [23] is a client/server that provides a platform for users to monitor and control numerous processes in Linux based operating systems. An administrator is given the privilege of controlling Django, flower and celery app in any system/computer using this tool. This can be configured in a way which can start any program at boot time, it makes the system persistent. In the parametric simulations, only annual energy consumption is generated as the output. Annual energy consumption is expressed in terms of the Energy Performance Index (EPI), which is calculated by dividing the annual total energy consumption of the building by its gross floor area.

Step 4: Spread of Solution Space

It is helpful for the user to look at the spread of simulation results to get an idea about range of energy consumption. This is achieved by providing a solution histogram. Sensitivity analysis helps the user to understand the impact of design parameters on building energy performance.

Solution Histogram. Plotting the distribution of energy consumption of the of how energy consumption is divided over an entire range of values. A sample histogram is shown in Fig. 2, plotted for Energy Performance Index (EPI). This plot shows that most of the solutions lie in the lower energy range.

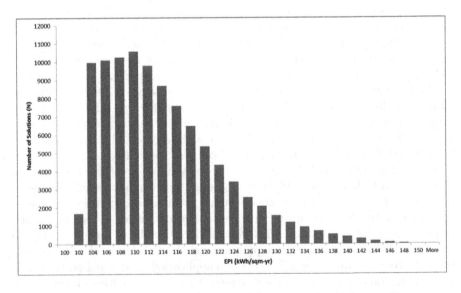

Fig. 2. Frequency distribution of EPI for energy simulation results.

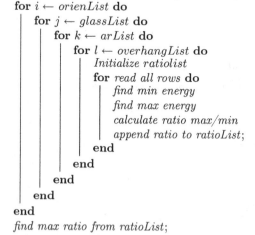

Input: A data file file containing all energy simulation results
Output: Imapact ratio

Read the data from the input file containing all simulation results

Initialize parameterlist with list of variables from the input data
paramter impact for wwr variable

  append orienList with unique values of orientation
  append glassList with unique values of glass
  append arList with unique values of aspectratio
  append overhangList with unique values of overhang
for $i \leftarrow$ *orienList* **do**
   for $j \leftarrow$ *glassList* **do**
      for $k \leftarrow$ *arList* **do**
         for $l \leftarrow$ *overhangList* **do**
            Initialize ratiolist
            for *read all rows* **do**
               find min energy
               find max energy
               calculate ratio max/min
               append ratio to ratioList;
            end
         end
      end
   end
end
find max ratio from ratioList;
return *max ratio*;

Algorithm 1: Algorithm to find impact factor for a given variable

Impact of Parameters. Sensitivity analysis helps the user understand the impact of design parameters on building energy performance. It shows the change in energy consumption resulting from a change in the value of one design parameter at a time, while keeping the other design parameters constant. This is equivalent to one-parameter-at-a-time sensitivity analysis at a selected point in the design space. An algorithm 1 is used to generate parameter impact.

Step 5: Finding Strategies

Energy simulation tools provide a large amount of output data. Careful selection of the data is required to reach useful conclusions. Once the simulations are completed, the next step is to select low-energy solutions from the design space. These selected solutions are then clustered to identify the design strategies. Clustering has become a very popular machine-learning technique for identifying groups of data points with common features in a set of data points. Lemley et al. [24] provided an algorithm for finding hyper-rectangles in high dimensional data that runs in polynomial time with respect to the number of dimensions.

An algorithm has been developed to provide parameter strategies that generate design solutions 2. The one-parameter strategy determines the range of values for each parameter for which each of the other parameters can take any value within its input range. For example, for a particular climate, if $WWR \leq 30\%$, any value of orientation, overhang, glass type, or aspect ratio can be chosen without any constraint, within the specified input ranges. This example is a special case, in that the performance of a building with a relatively small amount of glazing will be insensitive to the other envelope parameters; whether this solution is acceptable architecturally is a broader question for the designer. Glass type depends on the thermal conductance of glass, Solar Heat Gain Coefficient (SHGC) and Visible Light Transmittance (VLT).

Input: A data file containing all energy simulation results
Output: List of strategies
Read the data from the input file containing all simulation results

Initialize parameterlist with list of variables from the input data

Initialize threshold for energy
for *read all rows in csv* **do**
    if *energy < threshold* **then**
      | update value ← true.
    end
    else
      | update value ← false
    end
end
for $i \leftarrow$ *parameterlist* **do**
    uniqueList ← unique i;
    for $j \leftarrow$ *uniqueList* **do**
      Initialize count = 0
      for *read all rows* **do**
        if *value == false* **then**
          | *count = count + 1;*
        end
      end
      if *count = 0* **then**
        | *append i,j to singlevariable list;*
      end
    end
end
return *singlevariable list;*

Algorithm 2: Algorithm to find strategies from the energy simulation input data

The design sub-space defined by glazing type and window-to-wall ratio populated with solutions that satisfy a particular maximum energy consumption criterion is shown in Fig. 3.

Figures 4a, 4b show the data points with two, and three clusters identified using the K-Means algorithm [25]. These clusters do not provide design strategies

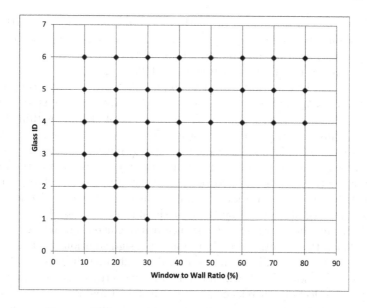

Fig. 3. Design subspace for Glass Type and WWR

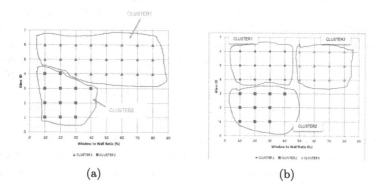

Fig. 4. Design subspace with two and three clusters

that can be communicated to the user. For example, Cluster 2 contains points with $WWR < 40$ and $GlassID < 4$. However, choosing low WWR should give freedom to the user to choose any Glass ID; this information is not getting captured in any cluster.

The clusters identified by distance-based clustering algorithms provide information about the effectiveness of combinations of values of different design parameters but the limitation is that they do not provide design strategies or provide information about design freedom, i.e. which design parameters have little effect on energy performance and so can be set based on other criteria [26]. For example, if low SHGC is chosen, then the user should be able to choose any WWR, but the sets of solutions identified by regular clustering algorithms do not capture this, so some form of synthesis is required. How, or whether, this synthesis should be performed depends on; whether non-energy criteria are to be incorporated, even in an implicit and qualitative way.

The stipulated criteria for clusters are as follows [26]:

Clusters must be explicable through simple rules such as $a_1 \leq feature_1 \leq b_1$, $a_2 \leq feature_2 \leq b_2$, and $a_n \leq feature_n \leq b_n$. Moreover, the clusters should be capable of adapting to scenarios where the number of clusters within the given space is initially uncertain and necessitates a discovery process. They are also expected to accommodate instances of overlapping clusters and account for data points that may not be categorized into any cluster. Furthermore, the methodology should arrange clusters according to their sizes, establishing a ranking based on this particular criterion. To amplify user control, the selection of clusters above a threshold defined by the user should also be feasible.

To overcome the limitation of distance-based clustering, an algorithm has been developed that identifies combinations of design solutions that can be used as strategies by designers. Referring to Fig. 4b, combining clusters 1 and 2 generates the strategy Low WWR, which results in low energy consumption whatever Glass Type is selected, whereas combining Clusters 1 and 3 generates the strategy High-Performance Glazing, which results in low energy consumption whatever WWR is selected. Cluster 1 may be undesirable for non-energy reasons: High-Performance Glazing is more expensive and low WWR may be undesirable in terms of view, daylighting and particular aesthetics. In projects where these considerations apply, there are then two strategies that incorporate other, non-energy criteria: Use Low-Performance Glazing if Low WWR is acceptable (Cluster 2) Use High-Performance Glazing if High WWR is required (Cluster 3) Cluster 1 will have the best energy performance but the improvement over Cluster 2 or Cluster 3 may be modest and not enough to justify the extra cost or compensate for the reduced amenity. By use of algorithm-1, the single and double variable strategies can be identified. This is also a type of clustering in which we are fixing one dimension, which will provide Axis Aligned Hyper Rectangle (AAHR) of remaining variables, which makes for easier communication with the user.

Figures 5 and 6 show six clusters from the algorithm. The data points shown in Figs. 5 and 6 are the points for which energy consumption is less than 10 % above the minimum energy consumption. These six clusters can later be merged into two clusters. The result can be easily converted into strategies that can be communicated to the user.

The six clusters are $WWR10\%$, $WWR20\%$, $WWR30\%$, $GlassID4$, $GlassID5$, and $GlassID6$. These six clusters can be combined in two clusters $WWR \leq 30$ and Glass ID 4, 5, and 6. This is very easy to communicate and understand. Let X, Y and Z be three axes in the design space and start with this three-dimensional subspace fully populated for each step of X, Y and Z. If there is a set of low energy consumption solutions that occupy a certain region of the design space that contains no other, higher energy consumption, solutions, then this set can be considered to represent a low energy design strategy.

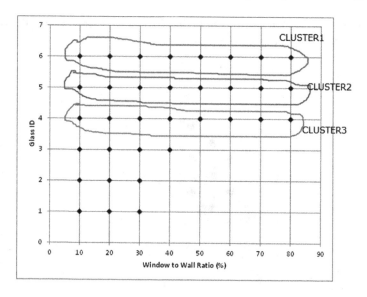

Fig. 5. Points with three clusters for Glass ID

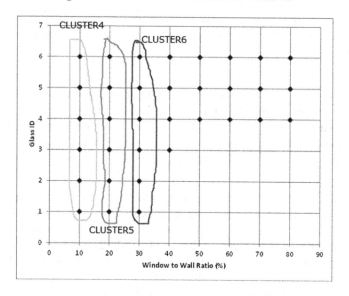

Fig. 6. Points with three clusters for WWR

If these solutions are constrained by, i.e. are either close to or bounded by, a plane parallel to the Y-Z plane (X=a, say), they constitute a single variable strategy ($X = a$ or $X \geq a$ or $X < a$). Figure 7 illustrates the case where the constraint X=a defines the strategy. If there are two constraints, e.g. $X = a$ and $Y > b$, then the low energy solutions are located in the region of the X=a plane defined by $Y > b$, as shown in Fig. 8. If the Y constraint were Y=b, the solutions would lie on the line defined by $X = a, Y = b$.

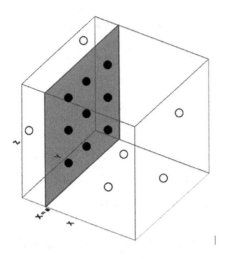

Fig. 7. Representation of one variable strategy; the solutions form a plane at X=a. Low energy solutions are represented by solid spheres and a sampling of higher energy solutions is represented by hollow spheres

If there are three constraints, corresponding to a three-variable design strategy, they can be represented graphically as follows:

Three identity constraints: $X = a$, $Y = b$, $Z = c$ define a point in the design subspace Two identity constraints and a limit constraint, e.g. $X = a$, $Y = b$, $Z > c$ define a line segment, as shown in Fig. 9.

Step 6: Visualization
Energy simulation tools provide a large amount of output data. Care is required in selecting the data required to reach useful conclusions. Researchers presented different data analysis and visualization techniques that can be used in the early stage of design decision-making. Yarbrough I. et al. [27] used heat maps to show energy demand in a campus. Ignacio Diaz Blano et al. [28] used a histogram for energy analytics in public buildings. Shweta Srivastava et al. [29] provided a review of different visualization techniques used in building simulations.

Parallel Coordinate Graph. Parallel coordinates plots are one way to visualize high-dimensional data. A six-dimensional graph is shown in Fig. 10. This figure shows a parallel coordinate graph for five design parameters and the resulting energy consumption; for this, six equally spaced vertical lines, are plotted. There are a number of software tools and libraries available to generate such graphs, such as D3 [30] and python Matplotlib [31]. This type of graph

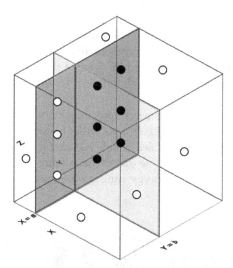

Fig. 8. Representation of a two-variable strategy defined by an identity constraint, $X = a$, and a limit constraint, $Y > b$; the solutions occupy part of a plane. Low energy solutions are represented by solid spheres and a sampling of higher energy solutions is represented by hollow spheres

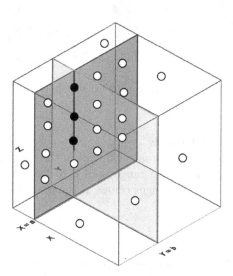

Fig. 9. Representation of a three-variable strategy defined by two identity constraints, X=a and Y=b, and a limit constraint, $Z > c$; the solutions occupy part of a line. Low energy solutions are represented by solid spheres and a sampling of higher energy solutions is represented by hollow spheres

can provide insights regarding the combination of design parameters that produce superior performance in terms of energy use. The user can also study the impact of various parameters on the performance of the building. Users can select ranges for different design parameters and see the impact on energy consumption. Parameters can be arranged in order of their sensitivity, e.g. with the most sensitive parameter at the right-hand side, to aid the interpretation of the graph.

Colour coding of the lines by energy consumption also aids interpretation. In Fig. 10, the blue lines indicate the solutions with the lowest energy consumption. Tracing these lines leftwards enables beneficial combinations of design parameters to be identified and provides one way of visualizing strategies. An interactive selection of lines of one colour/energy range, while hiding the others, can make the graph easier to interpret.

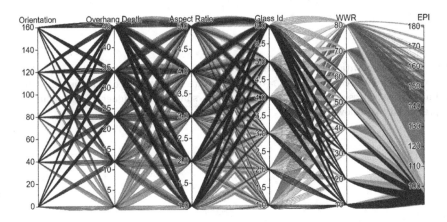

Fig. 10. Parallel Axis graph.(Color figure online)

Step 7: Refinement of Results
The user can review the results, make changes in the ranges, and look at more possibilities. Narrowing down the ranges can help the user to understand the output results. Fine-tuning of ranges comes at the cost of simulation time.

3   Conclusions

A novel methodology has been developed that can help architects and others select design parameters for energy-efficient buildings in the early stages of design. This methodology entails the assimilation of program prerequisites and various constraints, the generation of combinations of permissible design parameter values for simulation, analysis of the simulation outputs, and subsequent guidance to the design team on parameter combinations yielding optimal energy performance. Furthermore, an algorithm has been developed to identify strategies that depend on a subset of design parameters, promoting energy performance while allowing design freedom to select the values of other parameters based on considerations external to energy. Leveraging the Asynchronous Distributed Task Queue architecture, any tool based on the methodology can provide scalable execution of a multitude of EnergyPlus simulations.

Acknowledgments. The U.S. Department of Energy (DOE) and the Department of Science and Technology (DST), Government of India (GOI) provided joint funding for work under the U.S.-India Partnership to Advance Clean Energy Research (PACE-R) program's "U.S.-India Joint Centre for Building Energy Research and Development" (CBERD) project. The authors would also like to acknowledge Amazon Web Services (AWS) for supporting this work through the AWS cloud credits research program and the Indorama Ventures Center for Clean Energy for their support in the ongoing development.

References

1. IEA: Data and statistics. https://www.iea.org/data-and-statistics?country=USA&fuel=Energyconsumption&indicator=TFCShareBySector
2. Global Construction 2030. Technical report (2010). 1011.1669. www.globalconstruction2030.com. http://arxiv.org/abs/1011.1669. https://doi.org/10.1088/1751-8113/44/8/085201
3. World Business Council for Sustainable Development: Transforming the Market: Energy Efficiency in Buildings (2009). https://doi.org/10.1108/EUM0000000002227
4. Méndez Echenagucia, T., Capozzoli, A., Cascone, Y., Sassone, M.: The early design stage of a building envelope: multi-objective search through heating, cooling and lighting energy performance analysis. Appl. Energ. **154**, 577–591 (2015). https://doi.org/10.1016/j.apenergy.2015.04.090
5. Building technology program: EnergyPlus energy simulation software. https://energyplus.net/. Accessed 01 Aug 2020
6. DOE-2. http://doe2.com/doe2/
7. IES-VE. https://www.iesve.com
8. OpenStudio. https://www.openstudio.net/
9. DesignBuilder (2021). https://www.DesignBuilder.co.uk
10. Digital alchemy: Simergy - graphical user interface for EnergyPlus. Technical report. https://d-alchemy.com/html/products/DAProducts_Simergy.html
11. Hirsch, J.J.: & Associates: the quick energy simulation tool (eQUEST). http://www.doe2.com/equest/
12. Autodesk: green building studio. https://gbs.autodesk.com/GBS/. Accessed 02 Jan 2021
13. Hopfe, C.J., Struck, C., Hensen, J.: Design Optimization During the Different Design Stages. In: 7th International Conference on Adaptive Computing in Design and Manufacture, Bristol, pp. 275–278 (2006)
14. Negendahl, K.: Building performance simulation in the early design stage: an introduction to integrated dynamic models. Autom. Constr. **54**, 39–53 (2015). https://doi.org/10.1016/j.autcon.2015.03.002

15. Tian, Z.C., Chen, W.Q., Tang, P., Wang, J.G., Shi, X.: Building energy optimization tools and their applicability in architectural conceptual design stage. Energ. Procedia **78**, 2572–2577 (2015). https://doi.org/10.1016/j.egypro.2015.11.288

16. Østergård, T., Jensen, R.L., Maagaard, S.E.: Building simulations supporting decision making in early design - a review. Renew. Sustain. Energy Rev. **61**, 187–201 (2016). https://doi.org/10.1016/j.rser.2016.03.045

17. Bhatia, A.: Early design methodology for energy efficient building design. PhD thesis, IIIT Hyderabad (2019)

18. Garg, V., Jawa, A., Mathur, J., Bhatia, A.: Development and analysis of a tool for speed up of EnergyPlus through parallelization. J. Build. Perform. Simul. **7**, 179–191 (2014). https://doi.org/10.1080/19401493.2013.808264

19. Giannakis, G., Pichler, M., Kontes, G.: Simulation speedup techniques for computationally demanding tasks. In: 13th Conference of International Building Performance Simulation Association, Chambéry, France, pp. 3761–3768 (2013). http://www.ibpsa.org/proceedings/BS2013/p_1500.pdf

20. Sangireddy, S.A.R., Bhatia, A., Garg, V.: Development of a surrogate model by extracting top characteristic feature vectors for building energy prediction. J. Build. Eng. **23**, 38–52 (2019). https://doi.org/10.1016/j.jobe.2018.12.018

21. Celery: distributed task queue. http://www.celeryproject.org/. Accessed 6 June 2021

22. Dontu, S.: Distributed task queues for parametric EnergyPlus simulations on the web, MS Thesis, IIIT Hyderabad (2020)

23. Supervisor: a process control system. http://supervisord.org/. Accessed 6 June 2020

24. Lemley, J., Jagodzinski, F., Andonie, R.: Big holes in big data: a monte carlo algorithm for detecting large hyper-rectangles in high dimensional data. In: Proceedings - International Computer Software and Applications Conference, vol. 1, pp. 563–571 (2016). 1704.00683. https://doi.org/10.1109/COMPSAC.2016.73

25. Macqueen, J.: Some methods for classification and analysis of multivariate observations. In: Proceedings of the Fifth Berkeley Symposium on Mathematical Statistics and Probability, vol. 1, pp. 281–297 (1967). doi:citeulike-article-id:6083430

26. Bhatia, A., Garg, V., Haves, P., Pudi, V.: Explainable clustering using hyper-rectangles for building energy simulation data. ASIM **238**, 012068 (2018)

27. Yarbrough, I., Sun, Q., Reeves, D.C., Hackman, K., Bennett, R., Henshel, D.S.: Visualizing building energy demand for building peak energy analysis. Energ. Build. **91**, 10–15 (2015). https://doi.org/10.1016/j.enbuild.2014.11.052

28. Díaz Blanco, I., Cuadrado Vega, A.A., Pérez López, D., Domínguez González, M., Alonso Castro, S., Prada Medrano, M.Á.: Energy analytics in public buildings using interactive histograms. Energ. Build. **134**, 94–104 (2017). https://doi.org/10.1016/j.enbuild.2016.10.026

29. Srivastav, A., Tewari, A., Dong, B.: Baseline building energy modeling and localized uncertainty quantification using Gaussian mixture models. Energ. Build. **65**, 438–447 (2013). https://doi.org/10.1016/j.enbuild.2013.05.037

30. Bostock, M., Ogievetsky, V., Heer, J.: D3 data-driven documents. IEEE Trans. Visual Comput. Graphics **17**(12), 2301–2309 (2011). https://doi.org/10.1109/TVCG.2011.185

31. Hunter, J.D.: Matplotlib: a 2D graphics environment. Comput. Sci. Eng. **9**(3), 90–95 (2007). https://doi.org/10.1109/MCSE.2007.55

A Real-Time Non-Invasive Anomaly Detection Technique for Cooling Systems

Keshav Kaushik$^{(\boxtimes)}$ and Vinayak Naik

BITS Pilani, Sancoale, Goa, India
{p20180414,vinayak}@goa.bits-pilani.ac.in

Abstract. The cooling systems contribute to 40% of overall building energy consumption. Out of which, 40% After identifying the anomalies, we find the cause of the anomaly. Based on the anomaly, the solution recommends a fix. If there is a technical fault, our proposed technique informs the technician regarding the faulty component, reducing the cost and mean time to repair. In the first stage, we propose a domain-inspired statistical technique to identify anomalies in cooling systems. We observe the Area Under the Curve of the Receiver Operating Characteristic ($AUC - ROC$) score of more than 0.93 in both simulation and experimentation. In the second stage, we propose using a rule-based technique to identify the anomaly's cause and classify it into three classes. We observe an $AUC - ROC$ score of 1. Based on the anomaly classification, in the third stage, we identify the faulty component of the cooling system. We use the Nearest-Neighbour Density-Based Spatial Clustering of Applications with Noise (NN-DBSCAN) algorithm with transfer learning capabilities to train the model only once, where it learns the domain knowledge using simulated data. The overall *accuracy* of the three-stage technique is 0.82 and 0.86 in simulation and experimentation, respectively. We observe energy savings of up to 68% in simulation and 42% during experimentation.

Keywords: Cooling systems · Fault Detection · IoT

1 Introduction

The cooling systems contribute to 40% of buildings' energy consumption [17]. They consume more energy when there are anomalous instances, and these instances occur due to faults in the cooling system. Faults in cooling systems lead to energy wastage of up to 40% of its overall lifetime energy consumption [10]. Anomalies and the cause behind these anomalies must be identified in real-time. Delay in detecting anomalies increases downtime, and energy wastage by the cooling system [13]. Real-time identification of anomalies suggests user to take necessary action when a fault occurs. It also reduces the wastage of energy consumption by cooling systems.

B. N. Jørgensen et al. (Eds.): EI.A 2023, LNCS 14467, pp. 135–151, 2024.
https://doi.org/10.1007/978-3-031-48649-4_8

The cooling systems are categorized into two categories – ducted-centralized cooling systems and ductless-split cooling systems. In a ducted-centralized cooling system, a compressor is connected to Air Handling Units (AHUs) using ducts. Here, the ducts transfer cold air from the compressor to the rooms. However, in the ductless split cooling systems, one compressor is connected to one AHU. The user decides on a particular cooling system based on the usage and building requirements. However, both types of cooling systems are prone to anomalies.

Real-time detection of anomalies in cooling systems is an important task, especially in critical systems where it is required to maintain the room's temperature throughout with minimum downtime. Detection of these anomalies comes under the category of time-series anomaly detection. The two primary techniques to detect such anomalies are the classical approach and the Deep Learning (DL) approach.

The techniques mentioned above are capable of identifying anomalies in time-series data. However, these techniques cannot explain the reason behind the anomalies. These techniques are data-sensitive and require a large amount of data. However, anomalies in real-world systems depend on various environmental and deployment factors. We do not have a large dataset at the initial stages of real-world deployment. Hence, these approaches are not suitable for such applications. For example, identifying an unusually significant change in energy consumption by the cooling systems. There are various reasons behind this unusual change in energy consumption for example – technical, incorrect set temperature, the AC degraded over time and is not capable of cooling the room now.

The commonly used solution requires professional assistance for Fault Detection and Diagnosis (FDD) in cooling systems [7]. Here, they deploy a large set of sensors on each physical part of the cooling system to observe the changes. For example, in [7], Li et al. proposed to detect faults using temperature sensors. These temperature sensors are deployed on the condensing unit, liquid line, suction line, and evaporating lines. Based on these data points, they proposed to identify faults. These techniques are accurate but require many sensors, which increases the cooling system's cost.

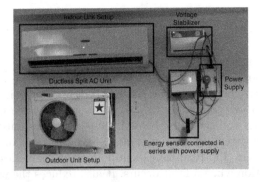

Fig. 1. An IoT-based sensor connected with AHU in series.

In this paper, we proposed an Internet of Things (IoT) and Machine Learning-based solution to identify anomalies and the cause of that anomaly in a real-world system. We collect temporal data using energy and temperature sensors in real-time. Using the collected data, we identify anomalous instances observed during the execution of the cooling system. Figure 1 shows the deployment of an IoT sensor connected with the AHU of the cooling system. It records the overall energy consumption of the cooling system.

We propose three staged non-invasive component-level anomaly detection techniques to identify the fault and its cause in real-time. Here, we do not connect sensors to each component of the cooling system separately, making the proposed approach non-invasive. At first, we use statistical inference to find the anomalous instances of energy consumption during the execution of the cooling system. Here, we use domain-inspired statistical inference to identify a significant change in energy consumption concerning the past data. Then, we define a set of rules based on domain knowledge to identify the cause of anomalous energy consumption instances. Once the anomaly is identified from stage one, it will only be forwarded to the second stage. Finally, we identify the faulty component. We use the overall energy consumption and environmental conditions of the cooling system and identify the faulty part without explicitly connecting a sensor to each component of the cooling system. Our proposed solution is out of the box and does not require being trained repeatedly with every new real-world deployment. It learns the percentage impact of each cooling system component and identifies the faulty component. From our knowledge, these two features are a big step forward from state-of-the-art.

For our proposed technique, detecting faults caused due to drainage, disposal of water, and clogged AHU due to dust is not feasible. The reason is that we use energy and temperature sensors to identify faults in cooling systems. However, the faults mentioned above do not cause any immediate change in energy consumption and temperature. The following are the significant contributions of this paper.

1. We propose the use of domain-inspired statistical inference for the real-time identification of anomalies in real-world systems. Here, we use $O(n)$ space to identify faults, reducing overhead.
2. We propose a rule-based method to identify the cause of anomalies in cooling systems. These rules are deduced based on domain knowledge.
3. If the cause of the anomaly is classified as a technical anomaly, we identify the faulty component of the cooling system. We propose a Nearest-Neighbour Density-Based Spatial Clustering of Applications with Noise (NN-DBSCAN) with a transfer learning framework to classify the faulty cooling system component.
4. We evaluate our proposed solution in a simulation environment using EnergyPlus, where we deployed more than forty faults and in an experimentation setup with six cooling systems in two different deployment scenarios. We observe energy savings of up to 68% and 42% in simulation and experimentation, respectively.

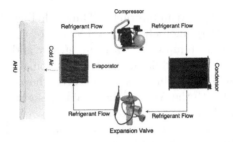

Fig. 2. The architecture of the cooling system, The compressor contributes the highest energy consumption, and the AHU the lowest.

2   Methodology

Cooling systems consists of five major components – compressor, condenser, evaporator, expansion valve, and AHU. Figure 2 shows a basic architecture of the cooling system.

To investigate whether faults have a discernible impact on temperature and energy consumption, we inject commonly observed faults [8] in each of the five components. We plot the measured temperature and energy values in Fig. 3. We see an opportunity to differentiate the faults from the measured values. There is, however, a need for an appropriate clustering technique to accurately identify the faults, which we address in this paper.

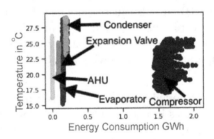

Fig. 3. Each faulty component has an impact on energy consumption and temperature. With an appropriate clustering technique, we can identify the faulty component.

Here are the definitions of the terms we use in our paper.

T_{set} : Set temperature of ductless-split cooling system (°C)
T_{room} : Current temperature of the room (°C)
T_{goal} : Desired final temperature of the room (°C)
$T_{external}$: External environmental temperature (°C)

τ : Change in temperature per unit time by ductless-split cooling systems ($^\circ$C)

P : Energy consumption per hour by the ductless-split cooling systems (W)

ΔT : Change in the room temperature ($^\circ$C)

Δt : Time interval between measurements (min)

PA : Past anomaly

ER : Energy Rating

P_{AP}: Energy consumption by the faulty component

AN : Anomaly cause

$AnomalyCause_i$: Anomaly Cause number i

2.1   Identifying the Anomalies

The cooling system's energy consumption follows a cooling cycle. Due to an anomaly generated by a fault or misconfiguration, the energy consumption by the cooling system fluctuates. This leads to a change in the cooling cycle of the cooling system. We propose to identify such changing patterns of the energy consumption of cooling systems due to the anomalies. We use the moving average of energy consumption by the cooling system in three cycles and compare the average value with data from the past non-anomalous cycle. In the first iteration, we take the ER specified on the data sheet of the AC. We declare an anomaly if the difference between the two values is more than 5%. The proposed anomaly detection technique does not require substantial space for identifying faults and anomalies compared to earlier proposed techniques discussed in [9]. The space complexity of our solution is $O(n)$. n is the number of sensory values input to the anomaly detection algorithm. We want to minimize the memory requirement so that the solution works on a low-cost IoT device. In [14], the authors use an $n \times n$ matrix to identify the anomalous instances, which takes $O(n^2)$ space. The time complexity of our solution is also $O(n)$.

2.2   Identifying a Cause of the Anomaly

The reason behind any change in energy consumption of the cooling system can be classified into three categories. 1) Wrong T_{set} – $AnomalyCause_1$, 2) Technical fault in the cooling system – $AnomalyCause_2$ and 3) Cooling requirements are not satisfied – $AnomalyCause_3$

In [4], the authors discussed important faults in cooling systems. We consider all of these and categorize them into three types based on the actions needed to fix them. In $AnomalyCause_1$, we consider faults due to incorrect cooling system ON/OFF modes with setpoint schedules. $AnomalyCause_2$ category consists of air duct leakage, AHU motor degradation, compressor flow, condenser fan, inefficient evaporator airflow, and sensors faults. $AnomalyCause_3$ identifies the faults due to oversized and undersized equipment design.

Table 1. Identifying a cause of the anomaly. Here, we use data collected from the environment and the cooling system. When there exists an anomaly, we identify its cause using these rules. These rules are based on domain knowledge. Using these rules, we conclude and suggest a fix. We measure these parameters every 2 min and use them in the algorithm. The parameters are for both types of cooling systems.

Anomaly Cause	Rule No.	Rule	Conclusion
$AnomalyCause_1$	Rule 1	$T_{room} < T_{goal}$	T_{set} of AC is high — Change T_{set}
	Rule 2	$T_{goal} < T_{room}$	T_{set} of AC is low — Change T_{set}
$AnomalyCause_2$	Rule 3	$\Delta T_{external} < \Delta T_{room}$	Cooling in T_{room} is less than $T_{external}$ — Identify faulty part
	Rule 4	$\Delta T_{room} < 0$	Unable to cool — Identify faulty part
	Rule 5	$PA > 4$	More than 4 continuous anomalies — Identify faulty part
$AnomalyCause_3$	Rule 6	$T_{room} < T_{set}$	No need to cool — Turn OFF cooling system
	Rule 7	$\Delta T_{room} \leq 0$ && $T_{set} = minimum$ && $T_{room} \leq T_{goal}$	Unable to reach the T_{goal} — Cooling system not sufficient

Anomaly Cause$_2$. The T_{set} of the cooling system is not according to the cooling requirements, and the cooling system cannot reach the T_{goal}. Here, either the T_{room} is below or above the desired levels. For both of the scenarios, the energy consumption pattern will change. When the T_{set} is less than T_{goal}, the system will consume more energy to cool the room. When the system's T_{set} is more than T_{goal}, the system will go into an issue called short cycling. Both issues are identified by observing a change in the patterns of energy consumption.

To detect a wrong T_{set}, we first identify whether it is possible to cool the room with the given cooling system. The cooling systems deployed in a room come with a cooling limit. We calculate the cooling requirements using the room's heat load and decide on the maximum cooling capacity of the system to be deployed in the room. To identify whether it is possible to cool or not, we use τ calculated as follows:

$$\Delta T = T_{goal} - T_{room} \tag{1}$$

ΔT represents the change in the room temperature in a given duration of time. The ΔT considers all dynamic heat loads inside the room, which change with time.

$$\tau = \frac{\Delta T}{\Delta t} \quad (°C \cdot min^{-1}) \tag{2}$$

τ represents the capacity of the cooling system. The cooling system's ability depends upon whether the system can bring the temperature down to the desired level and is checked by multiplying the τ by the time for which the system is executed. We consider the ideal continuous execution time of the cooling system ON cycle is 20 min [5]. Rule 1 and Rule 2 in Table 1 are to identify whether there exists an issue with the "$AnomalyCause_1$" type. We mention the rules in Table 1.

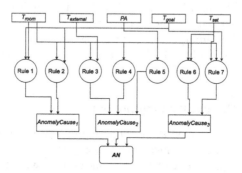

Fig. 4. Workflow for identifying the cause of the anomaly, we present the parameters which are being used by each rule and the flow of data and decisions.

Anomaly Cause₂. Detecting technical faults in the cooling system requires an expert's opinion. A trained engineer who is an expert in the domain uses a set of multi-meters and sensors to identify faults. Detecting these faults automatically is a non-trivial task. To detect these faults automatically, we propose to use the domain knowledge from the literature to construct a set of rules that help us identify the existence of technical faults in an AC. If the faults are not repaired, the cooling system will continue to waste energy.

The Rule numbers 3, 4, and 5 are deduced from the domain knowledge. We consider the impact of the cooling system in the environment where it is deployed. Using Rule 3, we identify If the cooling is less than the change in $T_{external}$, the cooling system consumes abnormal energy.

In Rule 4, if there is no change in the T_{room}, the cooling system cannot cool the room, which leads to disruption in the execution cycle of the cooling system. Rule 5 identifies that if the system has observed more than four anomalies continuously, it is a technical fault.

Anomaly Cause₂. The deployment of the cooling system is based on the static factors affecting the room's heat load. However, the real-world environment is not static. There are dynamic factors that change the heat load of the room over a duration of time. Even if we deploy a cooling system with sufficient cooling capacity, its cooling capacity reduces over time. To check the cooling systems' capabilities of satisfying the cooling requirements, we use Rules 6 and 7.

Rule 6 checks whether the T_{room} is already less than the T_{set}. In this scenario, we do not need to execute the cooling cycle. However, by default, the cooling system will try to turn ON the compressor and immediately turn it OFF, which causes the problem of short cycling. Rule 7 identifies anomalous instances as $AnomalyCause_3$ when the change in T_{room} is less than equal to 0, which represents the cooling system, can cool, and the T_{set} of the cooling system is set to a minimum. However, the room's T_{goal} is not reached, leading to continuous execution of the cooling system compressor at total capacity.

From the rule-based causal tree shown in Fig. 4, we get active high (1) or active low (0) values for each anomaly cause. When there is more than one active high anomaly, the particular type of anomaly is selected based on its priority. Here, the priority of $AnomalyCause_1$ is the highest, and for $AnomalyCause_3$ is the lowest. The priority is based on the chances of occurrence and the intensity of the anomaly.

2.3   Identifying the Faulty Component

When the anomaly is classified as $AnomalyCause_2$, we identify the component of the faulty AC to reduce the mean time to repair.

To identify the component of the cooling system with fault, we propose a machine learning technique, NN-DBSCAN. The NN-DBSCAN is based on the principle of DBSCAN. We have k independent and identically distributed samples $J = j_1, j_2, \ldots, j_k$ drawn from distribution F over $\mathbb{R}^D$. Using two hyper-parameters of DBSCAN, we find a set of n clusters with high empirical density for samples in J [15]. These hyper-parameters are eps and $minPts$. The eps is the maximum possible distance between the two samples to be considered a neighborhood. The $minPts$ is the minimum number of samples to be considered as a core point for a cluster. The DBSCAN is a clustering algorithm, not a classification algorithm, because it is an unsupervised approach. We use DBSCAN to classify the anomalies by taking the average of each cluster and comparing it with each cause's average from the data set. The cluster with the closest average is assigned to the particular cause.

To calculate the eps hyper-parameter, we use the Nearest Neighbour technique. We plot an elbow curve and select the value where the elbow occurs based on the distances obtained using the Nearest Neighbor. To calculate the second hyper-parameter $minPts$, the standard approach suggests selecting it to be twice the number of features. However, this approach does not always lead to an optimal value [16]. We use the gradient descent technique to get the optimal-$minPts$ by executing the DBSCAN algorithm multiple times [11].

The challenge with DBSCAN is that we need a large amount of data to obtain density-based clusters accurately. However, in the real world, the problem is that we do not have a significant amount of data that can classify the data points into clusters using DBSCAN. To deal with this challenge, we propose NN-DBSCAN with transfer learning capabilities. NN-DBSCAN requires training, which is performed using data from the simulation, and it is done once. In NN-DBSCAN, we train the model with transfer learning capabilities to be used in other deployments with the same application. During training, we calculate the initial cluster value, the centroid of the clusters formed during training. Then, we use these

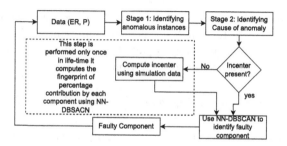

Fig. 5. The proposed techniques takes P and ER of the cooling system as input. If there is a technical anomaly, we use proposed NN-DBSCAN to identify faulty component. We train the model only once using simulated data. We transfer the model to any new cooling system using the later's ER.

Algorithm 1: NN-DBSCAN

1 **Input:** *Dataset, pretraining, P, ER, Ncluster, incenter[], minPts, eps*
   Result: FaultyComponent
2 **Initialization:** *Anomalous_Component[]*, FaultyPart, Dist[].
3 **if** *pretraining == 0* **then**
4 | /*When the *incenter[]* is empty*/
5 | *Accuracy = Accuracy*(DBSCAN(dataset with 50% test and train))
6 | *Nclusters =* number of clusters formed with DBSCAN() **for** $i \leftarrow 0$ **to** *Ncluster* **do**
7 | | *Anomalous_Part*.append(average value P for each cluster)
8 | | /*estimating fingerprint of each component*/
9 | | increment i
10 | **end**
11 | *pretraining = 1*
12 | **for** $i \leftarrow 0$ **to** *Ncluster* **do**
13 | | incenter.append(compute using Equation 4)
14 | | /*Computing energy fingerprint of each component for respective cooling system*/
15 | | increment i
16 | **end**
17 **else**
18 | **if** *Points in each cluster is* $\leq$ *minPts* **then**
19 | | Dist = EuclideanDistance(P to incenter)
20 | | /*Calculate the Euclidean distance from each point to the incenter*/
21 | | FaultyComponent = min(EuclideanDistance($P$to incenter))
22 | | /*Assign the point to the cluster with minimum Euclidean distance*/
23 | **else**
24 | | Run DBSCAN(*minPts,eps,P*)
25 | | FaultyComponent = P_C(*incenter[]*, P)
26 | | /*Function P_C finds the observed anomalous instance P is assigned to which cluster*/
27 | **end**
28 | return FaultyComponent
29 **end**

---

initial cluster values as domain knowledge in different deployments, enabling transfer learning. We allocate data to the cluster in different deployments based on the Euclidean distance between the observed point from the data set and the initial cluster value. Once we have the *minPts* in each cluster, the algorithm continues as DBSCAN. The Algorithm 1 represents the proposed NN-DBSCAN.

To obtain clusters' centers from the past data, we take the average energy consumption for each cluster, where each cluster represents a different anomalous component. We then calculate a fingerprint of a particular anomalous component concerning normal/usual energy consumption.

$$Anomalous\_Component = \frac{(ER + P_{AP})}{|ER|} \times 100 \qquad (3)$$

The Eq. 3 gives us a percentage contribution when a cooling system component is faulty. This percentage is the same for all the cooling systems, as the principle working of each is the same. So, we use the same percentage of fingerprints obtained during training for the initial cluster center assignment.

$$incenter_i = \frac{Anomalous\_Component_i \times ER}{100} \qquad (4)$$

Equation 4 computes the initial center for the cluster of a particular anomaly cause. Here, $i = 1, 2, ..., 5$ representing different components with the possible anomaly.

Each cooling system component is used for different functionalities with varying energy consumption. Further, we observe that the number of clusters formed with NN-DBSCAN equals the number of components present in the cooling system.

To identify the faulty component, our proposed NN-DBSCAN algorithm assigns each faulty component to one of the incenters of clusters, representing each component of the cooling system, based on the Euclidean distance between the observed point and the incenter. Once the number of instances in each cluster exceeds the $minPts$, the algorithm starts assigning the cluster based on the density. The calculation of the incenter is based on the percentage of energy consumed by each cooling system component when we simulate the faults for one cooling system model. Through transfer learning, we transform the learned model for other cooling systems. The transfer learning technique takes ER data from the datasheet as input and computes values for the incenters for the new model. Our use of transfer learning for NN-DBSCAN enables zero training requirements when deployed to the new cooling systems. Figure 5 shows a flowchart of the proposed three-stage solution.

3   Evaluation

This section describes our experimentation setup, simulation setup, and metrics we use to evaluate our proposed technique. We evaluate the proposed technique in an experimentation environment, by deploying a set of energy sensors and environmental sensors in the environment. These sensors provide the energy consumption by the cooling system and room temperature to a data server at intervals of every two minutes.

We evaluate our proposed solution in two different experiment scenarios. In the first deployment, the average heat load is about 47 megaJoules. In the second deployment, it is 63 megaJoules. Both setups consist of six ductless-split cooling systems.

In the experimental environment, it is challenging to deploy a large variety of faults that can occur in a cooling system. We perform simulations using the EnergyPlus simulator [3] to overcome this challenge. Here, we consider more than forty faults and use the proposed technique to identify faults with their cause. These faults are consequences of any fault in one of the five components of the cooling system and can lead to an increase in energy consumption by 60% [8]. To instrument these faults, we change the settings of cooling systems to act like faulty ones.

To generate anomaly cases in simulation and experiments. We collect data using the EnergyPlus simulator. Here, we inject faults in the cooling systems by changing the configuration and thresholds. The paper published by OSTI [8] details how to inject faults in the cooling systems using a simulator. For example, they reduce the flow rate of refrigerant in the compressor, which leads to a faulty compressor. In the experimentation setup, we use actual ACs with some of the faults we are studying. Our solution detected the anomalies which occurred due to these faults. The simulations consider all the possible faults.

Complexity Analysis: Stage 1 of the proposed solution uses a moving average, which takes $O(n)$ time. In stage 2, we use the rule-based technique that requires at most eight comparisons for every data point, which leads to a time complexity of $O(1)$. In stage 3, our proposed NN-DBSCAN has $O(5 * minPts)$ complexity, where 5 is the number of clusters. The number of $minPts$ is always less than n. Hence, the overall complexity of the proposed technique is $O(n)$. Here, n is the number of sensory values input to the anomaly detection algorithm.

We use $AUC - ROC$, $accuracy$, and F_1 scores for evaluating the proposed solution.

3.1   Simulation

Data Collection and Preparation. We deploy a ducted centralized cooling system and a ductless-split cooling system in a simulated building environment. In these cooling systems, we inject faults by changing the configuration and capacity of components. More than forty faults occur based on the changes in the configuration of the five major components of the AC. We collect simulation data in three environments, where $T_{external}$ ranges from 24°C to 42°C. We manually labeled the data set's fault cause and the faulty component, and this dataset is balanced. The data is collected at intervals of two minutes for one year using EnergyPlus. The simulation dataset consist of P, T_{room}, $T_{external}$, AN, and FaultyComponent. The training data for our proposed technique consists of 21,600 data points, out of which there are 12,600 data points representing more than 40 types of anomalies. To test our proposed technique, we used a simulated data set with 1,576,800 data points for anomalies in six different scenarios with a ductless-split cooling system and ducted-centralized cooling system in three different external environments where the $T_{external}$ ranges from 24°C to 42°C.

Preparation of Model. We use the data from the simulation with a ductless-split cooling system at an average $T_{external}$ of 38°C. We opt for the ductless-split cooling system because the principle working of both ductless-split and ducted-centralized cooling systems are the same, and the energy consumption ratio by each component is also the same. We split the data set into training and testing equally. We use a 50:50 split of the dataset for training with all types of anomalies, such that it can learn the fingerprint of each cooling system component. We have an equal number of instances in the dataset for each anomalous component. Any other split configuration leads to missing instances of a particular type of anomaly. Hence, the technique is unable to learn complete domain knowledge. To test the generalizability of the proposed approach, we perform testing with different datasets where no training is performed.

Identifying Anomalies. For this stage, we do not need to train the proposed approach before use. It is a statistical method that only needs energy consumption by the cooling system without anomaly as apriori. This apriori energy consumption we get from past data or the data sheet of the cooling system. Here, we observe an $AUC - ROC$ score of 0.95.

Identifying Cause of the Anomaly. At this stage, there is no training required. The proposed approach classifies the anomalies based on rules. In stage 2, we observed the $AUC - ROC$ score of 1 with the simulated data.

Identifying the Faulty Component. This stage requires training. Here, we first train the proposed NN-DBSCAN and then evaluate it with the help of test data. We compare the results obtained from the proposed NN-DBSCAN with other state-of-the-art techniques. These techniques are Neural Network (NN), XGBoost, CatBoost, DBSCAN, and LightGBM.

We construct a NN with one node at the input layer and two hidden layers, each with ten nodes. We opt for the softmax activation function and auto loss function [18]. We use XGBoost with multi:softprob loss function, CatBoost with MultiClass loss function, DBSCAN with same *eps* and *minPts* as NN-DBSCAN here, we assign causes to each cluster manually, and LightGBM with multi_logloss as loss function [1,2,6,15]. We compare the *accuracy* score and F_1 score of these state-of-the-art techniques with our proposed technique using NN-DBSCAN.

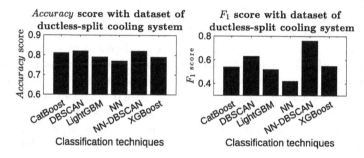

Fig. 6. NN-DBSCAN performs comparable to DBSCAN and better than all other standard state-of-the-art techniques in terms of *accuracy* and F_1 score.

Figure 6 compares the proposed NN-DBSCAN with other state-of-the-art classification approaches. Here, we observe that our proposed NN-DBSCAN outperforms compared to CatBoost, NN, XGBoost, and LightGBM. It performs as well as the standard DBSCAN. However, NN-DBSCAN stores relevant domain information that can be used in the future for transfer learning when deployed with another cooling system. We observe an *accuracy* score of 0.82 and F_1 score of 0.79 with NN-DBSCAN.

We compare these classification techniques in a new simulation deployment, where we have a ducted-centralized cooling system instead of a ductless-split cooling system. We do not perform any training. Our proposed NN-DBSCAN results in an *accuracy* score of 0.8 and F_1 score of 0.76. The closest state-of-the-art solution is DBSCAN, with an *accuracy* score of 0.67 and F_1 score of 0.64, and NN performed worst with an *accuracy* score of 0.28 and F_1 score of 0.42.

The NN works by applying mathematical operations and combinations to the dataset's features. In our case, we use a single feature 'P', for anomalous component identification, due to which the NN is unable to learn the pattern of the associated anomalous component. XGBoost, CatBoost, and LightGBM are tree-based classification techniques. These tree-based techniques are highly prone to small data variations, due to which tree generation varies and deviates from the correct classification. CatBoost performed better out of these. Density-based approaches, DBSCAN and NN-DBSCAN, perform better because of their ability to differentiate between clusters with high and low density.

From the above-discussed results, we observe that the *accuracy* of the proposed model and other state-of-the-art reaches a maximum of up to 82%. This is because the energy fingerprint of the three cooling system components is similar. These three components are – condenser, evaporator, and expansion valve. The condenser and evaporator are coils; they both have similar energy footprints. The working of the expansion valve is to control the flow to the evaporator, the energy footprint of the expansion valve is low, and due to a fault in the expansion valve, the evaporator does not perform its expected function. Hence, the footprint of the evaporator is added to the energy footprint of the expansion valve. These reasons make it difficult for the ML model to distinguish between the three with very high *accuracy*. Combining these three classes, we obtain an *accuracy* score of 1 with the proposed NN-DBSCAN.

We evaluated our proposed solution in the six deployment scenarios. we consider both ductless-split and ducted-centralized cooling systems with external temperatures of 26°C, 32°C, and 38°C. The performance of the proposed three staged techniques with an average *accuracy* score of 0.82 and an average F_1 score of 0.73 in six unique simulated deployments. Our proposed approach works with different cooling systems in different environments after a single training. With a confidence interval of 0.82 ± 0.02 for *accuracy* with a confidence level of 95%.

Case Study. We further evaluate our proposed technique concerning energy savings when the user takes the suggested action. Here, we observe the maximum energy savings of up to 68% with a mean energy savings of 34%. Early identification of faulty components leads to a reduction in repair and downtime of the cooling systems. It also saves the repair cost because the early identification prevents the complete damage of the faulty component.

3.2   Experimentation

Data Collection and Preparation. We collect energy and temperature data using sensors in a data server deployed at a remote location. The data is collected using Representational State Transfer (REST) APIs at an interval of two min. The data set features are T_{room}, $T_{external}$, P, and timestamp. The user provides the T_{set} and T_{goal}. We prepossess this time-series data. The data has been collected for more than two and a half years. We use data from the complaint management system (CMS) as the ground truth for an anomaly. The CMS contains information related to observed anomalies by the occupants. This CMS data includes the date and time when the anomaly was first identified, the timestamp of the complaint's resolution, and the technician's reason. These complaints are logged by an occupant or the room administrator based on changes in room temperature measured using a temperature sensor or high-temperature warning on servers. We collect this data from six different ductless-split cooling systems. The experimentation dataset contains 221,450 data points. Note that the model is pre-trained and is not connected to this data.

Model Preparation. We do not train the model again. The model learns domain-specific information during initial pretraining.

Identifying Anomalies. We use this stage's proposed domain-inspired statistical technique to identify the anomaly. Here, no pre-training is required. We observe an $AUC - ROC$ score of 0.93 in an experimentation deployment.

Identifying Cause of Anomaly. We observed a AUC score of 1 in the simulation with the rule-based technique. Similarly, in experimentation deployment, the AUC score obtained at this stage is 1.

Identifying Faulty Component. We do not perform any model pre-training for experimentation deployment. We take the model which is already pre-trained with simulated data. Here, our proposed NN-DBSCAN classifies the faulty components with an $AUC - ROC$ score of 0.88 and an F_1 score of 0.81, shown in Fig. 7. The significant increase in *accuracy* compared to simulation is due to anomalies from the evaporator, condenser, and expansion valve. It is rare in real-world experimentation. We evaluate the performance of the proposed technique and observations in five scenarios – 1. $AUC - ROC$ score of 0.93 for identifying anomalies, 2. $AUC - ROC$ score of 1 for identifying the anomaly's cause, 3. *accuracy* score of 0.88 with NN-DBSCAN for identifying faulty components, 4. an overall *accuracy* score of 0.86, and 5. overall F_1 score of 0.84. Here, the overall scores represent combining all three stages. The overall *accuracy* score of the proposed technique in experimentation deployment is 0.86. With a confidence interval of 0.86 ± 0.04 for *accuracy* with a confidence level of 95%.

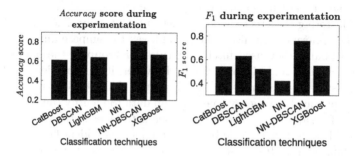

Fig. 7. *Accuracy* and F_1 score with the proposed approach during experimentation. We get an *accuracy* score of 0.88 and an F_1 score of 0.81. Our proposed technique outperforms the state-of-the-art.

Case Study. During experimentation, our proposed solution identifies anomalous instances of the cooling systems. Here, we observe maximum energy savings of up to 42% and mean energy savings of 30% with a downtime reduction of more than ten days when the action is taken immediately after identifying a faulty component by our proposed technique. Early identification of the faulty component using our proposed techniques saves up to 75% of repair costs as it prevents the complete damage of the faulty component. We observe a mean reduction of 60% repair cost of cooling systems.

We observe that NN-DBSCAN takes 0.031 s. The overall inference latency for identifying anomalies in the cooling system using our proposed three-staged anomaly detection technique is 0.05 s.

4   Related Work

The problem of anomaly detection is a focus of research. Some work focused on generalized techniques for any domain, while others focused on a specific domain. Yanfei et al.in [8] proposed a probabilistic framework to rank the faults in the Heating Ventilation and Cooling (HVAC) system using occupant comfort data. They identify only faults and not the faulty component. However, our proposed techniques identify the faulty part of the cooling system. Yang et al. in [19] proposed a Bayesian-based probabilistic technique to identify the faulty component inside AHU using 12 sensors with prior probability assigned to each fault. Our proposed technique uses only energy consumption data to identify the fault. Haroon et al. in [12] proposed to analyse the patterns of past energy consumption to identify faults. There, they used only energy consumption data collected using smart sensors. They achieved an AUC score of 0.89 for chillers. However, our proposed architecture not only identifies anomalies but also finds the cause of the anomaly.

Amer et al. in [9] proposed the use of ARIMA to predict future values of IoT data, using this data they identify faulty instances. There, they did not identify the cause or faulty component of the IoT system. Balakrishnan et al. proposed the Model Cluster and Compare framework in [10]. They used unsupervised clustering to detect the anomalies automatically. The first step was to identify the abnormal instances, the second was to compare and perform clustering, and finally, they used intelligent rules for grouping the anomalies. The proposed technique could identify faults. However, it did not identify the faulty part of the system. Haroon et al. in [13] proposed the UNUM rule-based technique on appliance-level energy consumption data to identify the behavior of the duty-cycle of an appliance. They used k-means to identify the ON-OFF state of the system. Lastly, using a rule-based technique, they identified whether there existed a fault or not. If we use their anomaly detection technique, it identifies anomalies, but it does not identify the cause of anomalies and the faulty part of the cooling system.

5   Conclusion

Identifying anomalies in real-world cooling systems is a significant concern. There are two types of cooling systems – ducted-centralized and ductless-split cooling systems. The cooling system is deployed in an enclosed environment based on its cooling needs. This paper proposes a novel, non-invasive component-level anomaly detection technique. It is a three-stage approach. In the first stage, we identify whether an anomaly exists or not. In the second stage, we classify the type of anomaly, and in the third stage, we identify the faulty component of the cooling system. We evaluate the generalizability of the proposed solution in different experiments and simulation environments. We observe *Accuracy* scores of 0.86 in experiments and 0.82 in simulations. Our solution identifies faulty components early leading to energy savings.

References

1. Chen, T., Guestrin, C.: XGboost: a scalable tree boosting system. In: KDD (2016)
2. Dorogush, A.V., Ershov, V., Gulin, A.: CatBoost: gradient boosting with categorical features support. CoRR abs/1810.11363 http://arxiv.org/abs/1810.11363 (2018)
3. EnergyPlus (2021). https://energyplus.net
4. Frank, S.M., Kim, J., Cai, J., Braun, J.E.: Common faults and their prioritization in small commercial buildings: February 2017 - December 2017 (2018). https://doi.org/10.2172/1457127, https://www.osti.gov/biblio/1457127
5. Kaushik, K., Agrawal, P., Naik, V.: A dynamic scheduling technique to optimize energy consumption by ductless-split ACs. In: ICOIN (2023)
6. Ke, G., et al.: LightGbm: a highly efficient gradient boosting decision tree. In: NIPS (2017)
7. Li, H., Braun, J.E.: Development, evaluation, and demonstration of a virtual refrigerant charge sensor. HVAC&R Res. **15**(1), 117–136 (2009)
8. Li, Y., O'Neill, Z.: An innovative fault impact analysis framework for enhancing building operations. Energ. Build. **199**, 311–331 (2019)
9. Malki, A., Atlam, E.S., Gad, I.: Machine learning approach of detecting anomalies and forecasting time-series of IoT devices. Alex. Eng. J. **61**(11), 8973–8986 (2022)
10. Narayanaswamy, B., Balaji, B., Gupta, R., Agarwal, Y.: Data driven investigation of faults in HVAC systems with model, cluster and compare (MCC). In: Buildsys (2014)
11. Ramadan, H.S., Maghawry, H.A., El-Eleamy, M., El-Bahnasy, K.: A heuristic novel approach for determination of optimal epsilon for DBSCAN clustering algorithm. J. Theor. Appl. Inf. Technol. **100**, 7 (2022)
12. Rashid, H., Singh, P.: Monitor: An abnormality detection approach in buildings energy consumption. In: IEEE CIC (2018)
13. Rashid, H., Singh, P., Stankovic, V., Stankovic, L.: Can non-intrusive load monitoring be used for identifying an appliance's anomalous behaviour? Appl. Energ. **238**, 796–805 (2019)
14. Sathe, S., Aggarwal, C.: Lodes: local density meets spectral outlier detection. In: SDM 2016
15. Schubert, E., Sander, J., Ester, M., Kriegel, H.P., Xu, X.: DBSCAN revisited, revisited: why and how you should (still) use DBSCAN. ACM Trans. Database Syst. **42**, 1–21 (2017)
16. Sefidian, A.M.: How to determine epsilon and minpts parameters of dbscan clustering (2021). http://www.sefidian.com/2020/12/18/how-to-determine-epsilon-and-minpts-parameters-of-dbscan-clustering/
17. Vishwanath, A., Chandan, V., Mendoza, C., Blake, C.: A data driven pre-cooling framework for energy cost optimization in commercial buildings. In: e-Energy (2017)
18. Zhao, X., Liu, H., Fan, W., Liu, H., Tang, J., Wang, C.: AutoLoss: automated loss function search in recommendations. In: KDD (2021)
19. Zhao, Y., Wen, J., Xiao, F., Yang, X., Wang, S.: Diagnostic Bayesian networks for diagnosing air handling units faults - part i: faults in dampers, fans, filters and sensors. Appl. Therm. Eng. **111**, 1272–1286 (2017)

A Novel Approach for Climate Classification Using Agglomerative Hierarchical Clustering

Sri Sanketh Uppalapati[1] , Vishal Garg[1,2] , Vikram Pudi[1] ,
Jyotirmay Mathur[3] , Raj Gupta[3] , and Aviruch Bhatia[2(✉)]

[1] International Institute of Information Technology, Hyderabad, India
[2] Plaksha University, Mohali, India
aviruchbhatia@gmail.com
[3] Malaviya National Institute of Technology, Jaipur, India

Abstract. Climate classification plays a significant role in the development of building codes and standards. It guides the design of buildings' envelope and systems by considering their location's climate conditions. Various methods, such as ASHRAE Standard 169, Köppen, Trewartha utilize climate parameters such as temperature, humidity, solar radiation, precipitation, etc., to classify climates. When establishing requirements in building codes and standards, it is crucial to validate the classification based on the building's thermal loads.

This paper introduces a novel methodology for classifying cities based on the number of similar days between them. It calculates similarity using daily mean temperature, relative humidity, and solar radiation by applying threshold values. A matrix of similar days is analyzed through agglomerative hierarchical clustering with different thresholds. A scoring system based on building thermal load, where lower scores signify better classification, is employed to select the best method.

The method was tested using U.S. weather data, yielding a lower score of 54.5 compared to ASHRAE Standard 169's score of 63.09. This suggests that the new approach results in less variation in thermal loads across cluster zones. The study used thresholds of $7\,^\circ$C for daily mean temperature, 45% for daily mean relative humidity, and 35 Wh/m^2 for daily mean solar radiation, which was found to yield the lowest score.

Keywords: Climate Classification · Building Energy Performance · Hierarchical Clustering

1 Introduction

The building sector plays a crucial role in achieving climate goals as it stands as the second-largest consumer of electricity. To promote energy efficiency in buildings, many countries have implemented mandatory regulations. Building energy regulations are based on climate zones and classifying a city into the correct climate zone is important. Franciso Jose et al. [1] provided a relation between

B. N. Jørgensen et al. (Eds.): EI.A 2023, LNCS 14467, pp. 152–167, 2024.
https://doi.org/10.1007/978-3-031-48649-4_9

climate zoning and its application to Spanish building energy performance. Various sets of methods are proposed in recent years for climate classification that can be utilized for use in building energy efficiency programs. Köppen-Geiger climate classification system [2], is the most widely used and referred model throughout the globe for defining climate zone. The Köppen climate classification divides climates into five main climate groups, with each group being divided based on seasonal precipitation and temperature patterns. This classification does not take into account some weather elements such as winds, precipitation intensity, amount of cloudiness and daily temperature extremes.

Briggs R. S. et al. [3,4] used Heating Degree Days (HDD) and Cooling Degree Days (CDD) based approach for the classification. ASHRAE has come up with a climate classification system [5] which classifies localities into climate zones based on temperature and precipitation basis. The thermal climate zone of a locality can range from 0–8. The moisture climate zone can be Marine, Dry or Humid. Monjur Mourshed [6] has also shown the importance of degree days that is used in ASHRAE classification.

There are many other classification approaches proposed such as Bansal and Minke [7] who have developed climate classification for India using mean monthly temperature and humidity values. Mayank B. et al. [8] have shown the classification of Indian cities using ASHRAE Standard 169 and compared it with Bansal and Minke's classification. ORNL researchers [9] used similarity methods for reimaging climate zones for the US. Cao Jingfu et al. [10] have considered cooling energy consumption to provide an efficient climate index for China. Zscheischler et al. [11] showed the value of unsupervised clustering for climate classifications. Hudson et al. [12] have provided climate classification for Colombia k-means clustering with multivariate climate data. Sathiaraj et al. [13] used k-means, DBSCAN, and BIRCH techniques for climate classification.

It was reported that DBSCAN shows less accuracy and effectiveness when applied for climate classification purposes.

Xiong Jie et al. [14] used hierarchical climatic zoning for China. Shin M et al. [15] have suggested using enthalpy based CDD instead of conventional CDD value that is based on outdoor dry-bulb temperatures that neglect the influence of latent heat on the total energy load. Giovanni Pernigotto [16] provided a classification of European climates using cluster analysis. Walsh A et al. [17] reported that most of the current classifications are oversimplified and not fit for building energy efficiency programs. One out of six areas analysed was misclassified while using ASHRAE classification criteria [18].

This study aims to develop a methodology to classify climate using a hierarchical clustering method based on the number of similar days between cities.

The methodology has been proposed with the following novel features -

- Classification is based on the number of similar days using climate data.
- The score is calculated using the thermal energy spread within a climate zone.

The upcoming sections will outline the methodology, followed by the data analysis for cities in the United States, the presentation of results, ensuing discussion, and finally the conclusion.

2   Methodology

2.1   Research Strategy

The strategy used for the study is mainly divided into three stages: preparation of data, clustering, and scoring.

In the first step, weather data files (EPW format) were downloaded for cities of the USA. EPW files are historical weather files used in climate analysis of cities and for use in simulation purpose. A total of 786 weather files from the USA were used after filtering based on anomalies for calculating mean daily temperature, mean daily relative humidity, and mean daily solar radiation data, which will be used in step two. A building model was built to perform energy simulations for all the weather files available. The resulting thermal load data (daily sensible cooling load, daily latent cooling load, daily total cooling load, and daily heating load) was then normalized using the z-score method for use in step three of the methodology.

In step two, the daily mean data of all the cities are used to identify the number of similar days between each and every city based on the maximum bipartite matching method considering different threshold values.

The similar days method takes into account daily data, allowing for a finer-grained analysis of climate patterns compared to traditional classification methods that often rely on monthly or annual averages.

Agglomerative hierarchical clustering is used for climate zoning based on the number of similar days present between the cities for all the threshold values as shown in Fig. 1.

In step three, scores were calculated based on the interquartile range of building thermal load (separately for sensible cooling, latent cooling, and total heating load) pattern for each cluster and added to get a final score for a threshold value. Based on the score achieved by each threshold value, the clusters with the lowest score were selected for further analysis. Also, the scores of clusters that were selected are compared with the scores achieved by the ASHRAE Standard 169 method. Details of the applied methods are presented in the following sections.

2.2   Preparation of Data

Weather Files. This methodology requires the use of typical meteorological year (TMY) data of different locations for the analysis. The data provides dry bulb temperature, dew point temperature, solar radiation, relative humidity and wind speed, etc. From these files, daily mean dry-bulb temperature, daily mean

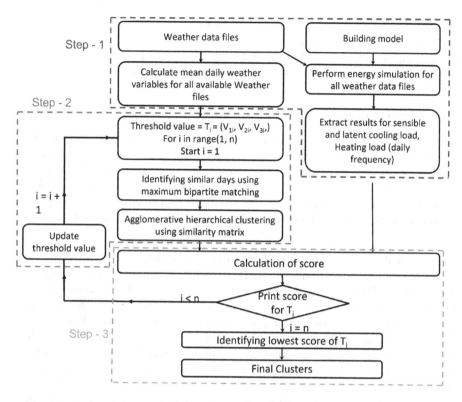

Fig. 1. Methodology for climate classification

relative humidity and daily mean solar radiation are extracted to calculate the 'similar' days between the two cities. The number of similar days between any two cities determines their 'closeness' which was used in the clustering approach.

Building Model. To calculate the thermal load characteristics of office buildings across the study area, a building model was first developed based on the relative building envelope present across the study area. Thermal load simulation for the model can be performed by any simulation software or tool such as EnergyPlus, IES-VE [22] and eQUEST [23] or any tool that provides hourly outputs based on weather files. Sensible cooling, latent cooling, and total heating energy are calculated using simulation and used for the calculation of score, considering similar internal load, and load generated using similar occupancy.

Data Pre-processing. To ensure consistency and comparability among the thermal load simulation results, the z-score method was utilized for normalization. This approach was adopted to align the data and assign equal importance to all attributes. Z-score normalization involves calculating the Z-score value, which indicates the deviation of each data point from the mean. By applying this technique, the values of a variable are rescaled to have a mean of 0 and a standard deviation of 1. This is achieved by subtracting the variable's mean from each value and dividing it by the standard deviation.

2.3 Clustering the Data

As the classification labels were not known prior, the unsupervised machine learning technique is used for the classification of climates. Unsupervised machine learning algorithms discover hidden patterns or data groupings from the given dataset. In this context, the agglomerative hierarchical clustering (AHC) algorithm was utilized. AHC is a connectivity-based algorithm that groups data points together based on their proximity or closeness to one another.

Agglomerative Hierarchical Clustering Algorithm. The algorithm begins by considering each location as an individual cluster. Subsequently, clusters that exhibit minor differences in climate conditions are combined to form new clusters. In the proposed method, the condition of merging is the cities with the highest number of similar days are grouped together to form a new cluster. The process is iterative and runs until the criteria to stop the merging is reached. The flow chart of the mentioned AHC algorithm is displayed in Fig. 2. Hierarchical cluster [20] analysis produces a unique set of nested clusters by sequentially pairing based on the criteria in the form of a dendrogram.

Since in the proposed method, there is a need to match/find similar days between two cities, the days should be matched uniquely, and maximum of such matching should occur. Therefore, maximum bipartite matching is used.

Maximum Bipartite Matching. A bipartite matching [21] is a set of edges in a graph chosen such that no two edges in that set will share an endpoint. The maximum matching is counting the maximum number of edges. The method uses a threshold value of each variable used to identify the number of similar days. The flow chart of the process for calculating similarity between cities using the maximum bipartite matching is shown in Fig. 3. Considering a brief example, we have five weather files labeled from "a" to "e". Each file encompasses data for 5 days regarding two weather variables, denoted as "V1" and "V2", as illustrated in Table 1. To determine the maximum count of similar days between all cities, specific thresholds are established for V1 and V2, which are 5 and 50 respectively. The outcomes are presented in a square matrix with dimensions n x n, where in this instance n = 5.

Once the maximum bipartite matching is performed, the resulting matrix is in a 5×5 format, as exemplified in Table 2. When comparing a weather file (WF) to itself, all days will match. If "a" is compared with "b", only 2 days meet the given threshold for similarity. Similarly, when "d" is compared with "e", 4 days fulfil the threshold for similarity, as depicted in Fig. 4.

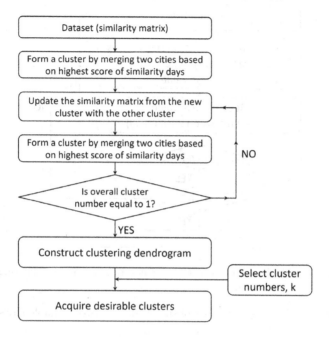

Fig. 2. AHC algorithm based clustering process

Table 1. Sample values from Weather file

	B1	B2	B3
A1	0.1	0.2	0.3
A2			
A3			

This matrix is used for Agglomerative hierarchical clustering. For this simple example, the number of clusters is set to three (k = 3). Agglomerative hierarchical clustering is used and the generated labels for the five cities are: [2 1 0 0 0]. It shows that the weather files "c", "d" and "e" are in one cluster and "a" and "b" are in two different clusters.

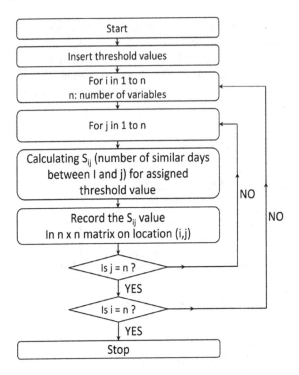

Fig. 3. Flow chart depicting the process of generating a matrix indicating the count of similar days between cities.

Table 2. Matrix of number of similar days between sample cities

	WF "a"	WF "b"	WF "c"	WF "d"	WF "e"
WF "a"	5	2	0	0	0
WF "b"	2	5	0	0	0
WF "c"	0	0	5	4	4
WF "d"	0	0	4	5	4
WF "e"	0	0	4	4	5

2.4   Calculation of Score

The scores are computed based on the sensible cooling, latent cooling, and total heating load present in each cluster, determined in the previous step. Since each cluster consists of a different number of cities or sites, all the cities within a cluster are taken into account when calculating the scores.

The score is defined by the interquartile range or spread of the box plot, which can be derived from the box plot diagram, as illustrated in Fig. 5, representing the total cooling load for all three clusters.

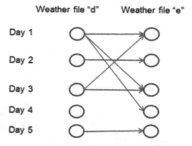

Fig. 4. Bipartite matching

The "spread score" of a zone for cooling and heating energy is determined by summing up the spreads across all the zones. This results in three "spread scores" for the variables: sensible cooling, latent cooling, and total heating, each of which has its own box plot.

To obtain a single representative "spread score" for a zone, these three individual spread scores are combined by simple addition. The objective is to minimize the spread among the cities within a zone, across the three energy variables. Equal weightage is assigned to all three energy variables during this process, allowing the reduction of the three scores into a single representative score.

Spread Score = SLCE + SSCE + STHE
where, SLCE = Spread of Latent Cooling Energy
SSCE = Spread of Sensible Cooling Energy
STHE = Spread of Total Heating Energy

The process is carried out for different threshold values and scores for each variation are recorded and the case with the lowest threshold value is considered for further analysis. The final "Spread Score" is then compared with the ASHRAE classification score.

3   Analysis of Climate Classification of USA

The ASHRAE Standard 169 is referred for the climate classification of the USA as shown in Fig. 5. The EPW files for the USA were extracted from EnergyPlus weather data source. These weather files are in typical meteorological year format and arranged by World Meteorological Organisation. For the analysis, the daily mean dry-bulb temperature, daily mean relative humidity, and daily mean solar radiation were extracted from the weather files for each city. These variables serve as inputs for the analysis. Figure 6 displays the geographic distribution of cities across the USA, representing their respective climate zones, which have been taken into account for the analysis.

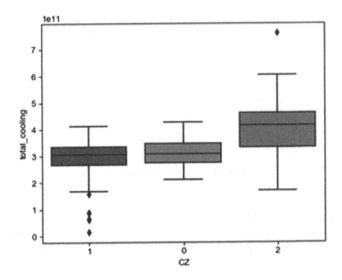

Fig. 5. Sample box plot

3.1   Clustering of Cities of USA

Daily values of the three parameters are utilized to calculate the 'similar' days between the cities, based on the maximum bipartite machine as per the flow diagram shown in Fig. 3. For the considered cities of the USA, the output matrix for similar days is of dimension 786×786. Various sets of threshold values were considered for calculating the number of similar days and some of the threshold values are listed in Table 4. Then the clustering analysis was performed for all the cities and divided the cities into 16 zones (Same as total zones of USA by ASHRAE Standard 169) and the cities were labeled with numbers ranging from 0 to 15. Figure 7 shows the weather data clusters with the proposed method. Figure 8 shows the frequency of cities in ASHRAE Standard 169 classification zones for the USA.

3.2   Building Energy Simulation

The EnergyPlus software was utilized to conduct building energy simulations. A typical core-perimeter zone office building with $400\,m^2$ floor area was prepared and used for the simulations. The developed model of the building is shown in Fig. 9. The simulations were performed for all 786 weather files in the USA.

From the simulation data, the energy consumption details are extracted i.e., daily latent cooling energy, daily sensible cooling energy, and daily total heating energy. Subsequently, z-score normalization was applied to the energy data, aligning the values by scaling them to have a mean of 0 and a standard deviation of 1.

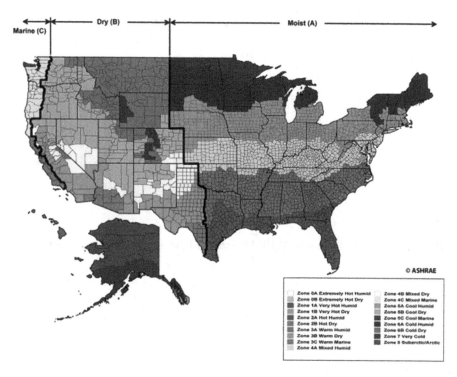

Fig. 6. United States climate zone map based on ASHRAE-169 [5]

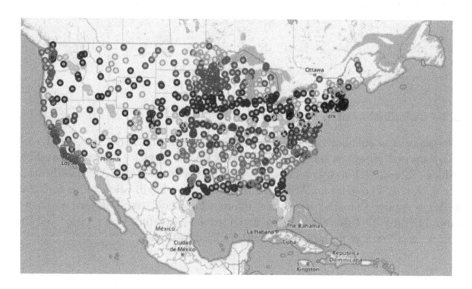

Fig. 7. Weather data clusters with proposed method

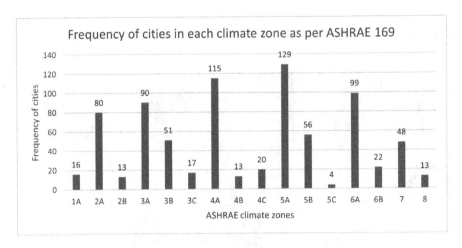

Fig. 8. Frequency of cities in ASHRAE Standard 169 classification zones for USA

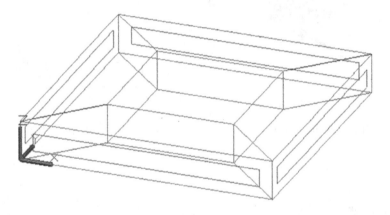

Fig. 9. EnergyPlus model

3.3   Calculation of Score

The score was calculated for both ASHRAE zones and zones generated with the proposed approach based on number of similar days for different threshold values. Table 3 elaborately shows how the final score of ASHRAE classification is calculated. The score for ASHRAE Standard 169 classification totals to 63.09, which is higher than the scores for different threshold combinations as shown later in Table 4. Table 4 has been arranged in ascending order based on the scores, as a lower score indicates a better classification.

Table 3. Calculated scores for ASHRAE Standard 169 classification

ZONE	SLCE	SSCE	STHE	SUM
1A	0.76	1.54	0.07	2.37
2A	1.8	1.51	0.44	3.75
2B	0.66	1.88	0.18	2.72
3A	1.16	1.13	0.74	3.03
3B	1.58	3.49	0.67	5.74
3C	0.85	1.2	0.28	2.33
4A	0.91	1.6	1.02	3.53
4B	0.86	1.51	0.92	3.29
4C	0.93	1.15	0.71	2.79
5A	1.89	1.69	1.31	4.89
5B	2.1	2.2	1.56	5.86
5C	0.22	0.31	0.11	0.64
6A	2.11	1.43	2.88	6.42
6B	0.91	0.79	1.25	2.95
7	2.31	1.19	2.2	5.7
8	1.45	0.53	5.11	7.09
SUM	20.5	23.15	19.45	63.09

Table 4. Threshold combinations and scores

Threshold combinations	Scores
7, 45, 35	54.5
9, 40, 35	54.59
6, 45, 35	55.17
8, 45, 35	55.76
4, 40, 30	56.06
5, 45, 35	56.06
ASHRAE	63.09

4 Results and Discussion

The findings demonstrate that the proposed method, utilizing the number of similar days and scoring techniques, achieves higher accuracy compared to ASHRAE Standard 169. Upon examining Table 4, it is evident that the most accurate classification is achieved when employing threshold values of 7°C for the daily mean dry-bulb temperature, 45% for the daily mean relative humidity, and 35 Wh/m^2 for the daily mean global horizontal radiation. Figure 10 and 11 shows the spread of sensible cooling and total cooling respectively for ASHRAE Standard 169 classification. Figure 12 shows the spread of sensible cooling and total cooling for our proposed classification.

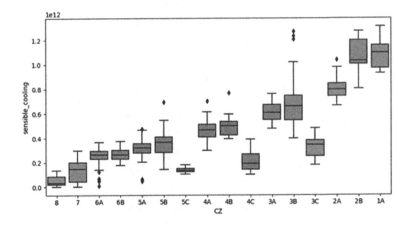

Fig. 10. ASHRAE climate zones and spread for sensible cooling

It can be observed from Figs. 10 and 11 that although Climate zone (CZ) 1 to 8 represents extreme hot to arctic, the mean cooling energy values are not in decreasing order. The climate zones 3C, 4C, and 5C of ASHRAE Standard 169 represent warm marine, mixed marine and cool marine respectively are not in order.

As zones are identified using unsupervised clustering; the zone numbers are not in order as per the energy consumption. Zone 13 is having highest cooling energy consumption can be referred to as an experimental hot climate and 0 can be an arctic zone.

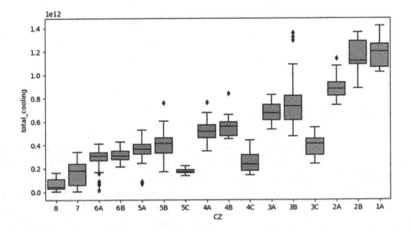

Fig. 11. ASHRAE climate zones and spread for total cooling

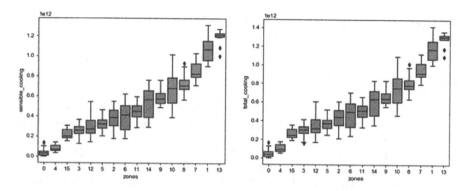

Fig. 12. Spread with new proposed clustering using agglomerative clustering

Upon looking at the distribution of cities in ASHRAE zones and the selected cluster classification based on the proposed method, more than 50% overlap was observed between the two. But a significant number of cities are distributed uniquely in the new classified zones.

4.1 Limitations

Our study relied on the availability of weather data for the selected U.S. cities. Limitations in data coverage and quality may influence the results. The choice of thresholds was based on careful consideration, but they may not be universally applicable to all regions or building types. Our study did not explicitly account for potential climate change effects, which can alter long-term climate patterns and impact building design considerations.

5   Conclusion

This study introduces a novel approach for climate classification of diverse cities by utilizing the number of similar days and employing a scoring system based on building load. The method aims to identify the most effective climate zoning among various combinations using different threshold values. Unsupervised learning is employed, utilizing mean daily weather data, to discover similarities between cities. The classification is then scored based on thermal energy, calculated through simulation tools. These scores are utilized to achieve more accurate zone classification. A lower score indicates a better classification in this context.

To test the proposed method, available weather files from the USA were employed. The climate of the USA was divided into 16 clusters using the developed method outlined in this research. Scores were computed for different combinations of threshold values to obtain improved zoning. The classification method presented in this study exhibits a superior score of 54.5, as compared to the ASHRAE Standard 169 classification score of 63.09. Furthermore, the method developed in this paper has the potential to be applied to other countries as it operates by identifying similarities among weather data.

References

1. Flor, F.J.S., Domínguez, S.Á., Félix, J.L.M., Falcón, R.G.: Climatic zoning and its application to Spanish building energy performance regulations. Energ. Build. **40**(10), 1984–1990 (2008)
2. Kottek, M., Grieser, J., Beck, C., Rudolf, B., Rubel, F.: World Map of the Köppen-Geiger climate classification updated. Meteorol. Zeitschrift **15**(3), 259–263 (2006)
3. Briggs, R.S., Lucas, R.G., Taylor, Z.T.: Climate classification for building energy codes and standards: part 1-development process. Trans. Soc. Heat. Refrig. Air Cond. Eng. **109**(1), 109–121 (2003)
4. Briggs, R.S., Lucas, R.G., Taylor, Z.T.: Climate classification for building energy codes and standards: part 2 - Zone definitions, maps, and comparisons. ASHRAE Trans. **109**, 122–130 (2003)
5. ANSI/ASHRAE Standard 169 Climate data for Building Design Standards
6. Mourshed, M.: Relationship between annual mean temperature and degree-days. Energ. Build. **54**, 418–425 (2012)
7. Bansal, N.K., Minke, G.: Climate Zones and Rural Housing in India. General Indian Corporation (1988)
8. Bhatnagar, M., Jyotirmay, M., Garg, V.: Reclassification of climate zones for Indian Cities. ISHRAE **19**, 34–43 (2016)
9. Kumar, J., Hoffman, F.M., New, R.J., Sanyal, J.: Reimagining climate zones for energy efficient building codes
10. Cao, J., Li, M., Zhang, R., Wang, M.: An efficient climate index for reflecting cooling energy consumption: Cooling degree days based on wet bulb temperature. Meteorol. Appl. **28**(3), 1–10 (2021)
11. Zscheischler, J., Mahecha, M.D., Harmeling, S.: Climate classifications: the value of unsupervised clustering. Procedia Comput. Sci. **9**, 897–906 (2012)
12. Hudson, R., Velasco, R.: Thermal comfort clustering; climate classification in Colombia, pp. 590–595 (2018)
13. Sathiaraj, D., Huang, X., Chen, J.: Predicting climate types for the continental United States using unsupervised clustering techniques. Environmetrics **30**(4), 1–12 (2019)
14. Xiong, J., Yao, R., Grimmond, S., Zhang, Q., Li, B.: A hierarchical climatic zoning method for energy efficient building design applied in the region with diverse climate characteristics. Energ. Build. **186**, 355–367 (2019)
15. Shin, M., Do, S.L.: Prediction of cooling energy use in buildings using an enthalpy-based cooling degree days method in a hot and humid climate. Energ. Build. **110**, 57–70 (2016)
16. Pernigotto, G., Gasparella, A., Hensen, J.L.M.: Assessment of a weather-based climate classification with building energy simulation Free University of Bozen-Bolzano, Italy Eindhoven University of Technology, Eindhoven, The Netherlands Abstract Key Innovations, pp. 853–860 (2021)
17. Walsh, A., Cóstola, D., Labaki, L.C.: Comparison of three climatic zoning methodologies for building energy efficiency applications. Energ. Build. **146**, 111–121 (2017)

18. Walsh, A., Cóstola, D., Labaki, L.C.: Validation of the degree-days method for climatic zoning- initial results based on the mean percentage of misplaced areas. In: USIM (2018)

19. Macqueen, J.: Some methods for classification and analysis of multivariate observations. In: Proceedings of the Fifth Berkeley Symposium on Mathematical Statistics and Probability, vol. 1, no. 233, pp. 281–297 (1967)

20. Bridges, C.C.: Hierarchical cluster analysis. Psychol. Rep. **18**(3), 851–854 (1966)

21. Hopcroft, J.E., Karp, R.M.: An algorithm for maximum matchings in bipartite graphs. SIAM J. Comput. **2**(4), 225–231 (1973)

22. IES-VE: "IES-VE."

23. Hirsch, J.J.: & Associates: the quick energy simulation tool (eQUEST) (2016). http://www.doe2.com/equest/

24. Python software foundation. https://www.python.org/

25. Hunter, J.D.: Matplotlib: a 2D graphics environment. Comput. Sci. Eng. **9**(3), 90–95 (2007)

26. Pedregosa, F., et al.: Scikit-learn: machine learning in Python. J. Mach. Learn. Res. **12**, 2825–2830 (2012)

Smart Data-Driven Building Management Framework and Demonstration

Jing Zhang[1], Tianyou Ma[1], Kan Xu[1], Zhe Chen[1], Fu Xiao[1,2(✉)], Jeremy Ho[3], Calvin Leung[3(✉)], and Sammy Yeung[3]

[1] Department of Building Environment and Energy Engineering,
The Hong Kong Polytechnic University, Hong Kong, China
21038117r@connect.polyu.hk, linda.xiao@polyu.edu.hk
[2] Research Institute for Smart Energy, The Hong Kong Polytechnic University, Hong Kong, China
[3] Electrical and Mechanical Services Department (EMSD), E&M AI Lab, Hong Kong, China
leungkf@emsd.gov.hk

Abstract. The building sector holds a significant impact over global energy usage and carbon emissions, making effective building energy management vital for ensuring worldwide sustainability and meeting climate goals. In line with this objective, this study aims to develop and demonstrate an innovative smart data-driven framework for building energy management. The framework includes semantic multi-source data integration schema, AI-empowered data-driven optimization and predictive maintenance strategies, and digital twin for informative and interactive human-equipment-information building management platform. A case study was conducted in a typical chiller plant on a campus located in Hong Kong, China. The results show that the deployment of the proposed smart data-driven framework achieves chiller sequencing control in a more robust and energy-efficient manner. Specifically, the proposed control strategy achieves energy savings of 5.9% to 12.2% compared to the conventional strategy. This research represents an important step forward in the development of smarter and more sustainable building management practices, which will become increasingly critical as we strive to reduce our environmental impact and combat climate change.

Keywords: Building Energy Management · Data-driven models · Digital Twin

1 Introduction

Improving building energy efficiency is crucial for achieving sustainable development on a global scale, given that buildings are significant energy consumers. The building sector accounts for about 30% of global energy consumption and 27% of energy-related greenhouse gas emissions [1], making it a key area for achieving climate objectives. Green buildings are crucial for decarbonization and reducing global greenhouse gas emissions. To achieve carbon neutrality, smart energy management technologies are vital to enhancing energy efficiency and intelligence in the building sector.

Today's buildings are not only energy-intensive but also data and information intensive. Data are continuously generated during the lifetime of the building, and mainly stored in Building Information Models (BIMs) and Building Automation Systems (BASs). BIMs store the static and spatial design and construction data, while BASs store the dynamic/temporal operation data. They provide a complete spatio-temporal description of a building. It is an effective way to understand and improve the building operation by analyzing and utilizing these valuable data. Numerous efforts have been made to effective data integration between BIMs and BAS, including directly linked data and ontology-linked data. Directly linked data method uses standardized naming formats such as Construction-Operations Building information exchange protocol (COBie) [2], Open Messaging Interface (O-MI) and the Open Data Format (O-DF) [3]. Ontology-linked data methods effectively store data in the data lake that is accessible through a common data management system. This method establishes a link between decoupled ontology and time-series databases, making data accessible to applications through a query process. With the development of ontology in the building sector, including Semantic Sensor Network (SSN) ontology [4], Building Automation and Control Systems (BACS) ontology [5], Building Topology Ontology (BOT) [6], ifcOWL ontology [7] and Brick Schema [8], semantic web technologies have gained popularity for integrating multi-source data due to their rich semantic description, interoperability, scalability, and query ability.

Most of the existing building energy management strategies are implemented in BAS, which are not informative, with limited visualization capability, and only support very limited and simple interactions between equipment and facility management staff. Digital Twin (DT) is considered a promising solution to address these challenges as it offers a more advanced and holistic approach to building energy management [9]. Chen et al. [10] developed a BIM-based digital twin which can improve decision-making in facility management by providing automatic scheduling of maintenance work orders. Chen et al. [11] developed a digital twin that enabled monitoring of indoor environments, indoor navigation, and predictive maintenance. By leveraging digital twin technology along with Mixed Reality (MR), IoT, Artificial Intelligence (AI), and other cutting-edge technologies, it is possible to establish an informative and interactive human-equipment-information building management platform. This platform can significantly enhance the efficiency of building operation and maintenance by creating a digital replica of the physical building and its equipment, enabling real-time monitoring and analysis of critical data.

Heating, ventilation and air conditioning (HVAC) systems often consume the most energy in buildings. Compared with conventional physics-based methods, data-driven methods require less information and understanding of buildings and their energy systems [13]. Advanced machine learning algorithms and models have achieved promising success in various applications concerning energy demand prediction [14], fault detection and diagnosis [15], energy benchmarking [16], and occupant behavior prediction [17].

This study aims to develop a smart data-driven building management framework for environmental and sustainability applications to improve building energy performance. The proposed framework includes several key components, such as developing a semantic model to integrate data from multiple sources, deploying optimization and predictive maintenance strategies empowered by AI algorithms, and developing a digital twin platform designed to manage building equipment and information comprehensively and interactively. To demonstrate the effectiveness of the proposed framework, a case study was conducted on a typical campus chiller plant.

2 Methodology

2.1 Overview of the Proposed Framework

Figure 1 shows the proposed framework for smart data-driven building management.

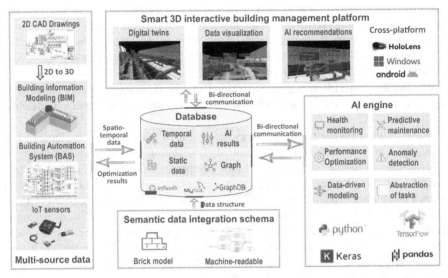

Fig. 1. Proposed framework for smart data-driven building management

Data from multiple sources across different stages of the building lifecycle are extracted and organized using a semantic model as a standardized data integration schema. These data are then stored in a database which provides real-time data to an AI engine. The AI engine is comprised of various environmental and sustainability application packages that can provide recommendations for energy savings and predictive maintenance (e.g., optimal settings, equipment warnings, etc.) to the building. These AI recommendations stored in the database will then be sent to both the smart 3D interactive building management platform for monitoring by building managers and operators, as well as the BAS for optimal control.

The combination of the semantic model, AI engine, and digital twin offers several benefits. Semantic model empowers machine-readable capabilities, enabling the AI engine and digital twin to access data in a building-independent way while maintaining semantic consistency. This facilitates intelligent analysis and decision support by comprehending and inferring data with semantic relationships and enables cost-effective deployment of AI algorithms through its flexibility and scalability. In addition, the collaboration between the AI engine and digital twin enhances operational efficiency and maintenance processes. By synchronizing the digital twin with the real system in real-time, it enables efficient and reliable monitoring, operation, and maintenance, leading to improved operational efficiency and reduced costs.

2.2 Multi-source Data Available in Buildings

Static data. 2D drawings and 3D building information model (BIM) contain the static data at the design and construction stage. They contain primarily semantic, geometric and parametric data of building elements (e.g., wall, window, room, equipment, etc.), for example, the name, type, height, width, orientation and materials of building walls and windows, the name and location of air ducts as well as the design thermal temperature of spaces and rooms. In addition, they can also provide relationships between different building elements, for example, each VAV box entity has an association relationship with its supply duct and the room it serves.

Temporal Data. Building automation system (BAS), also known as building management system (BMS), contains the temporal data at the building operation stage. Building operational data in BAS are typically multivariate time series data, including energy consumption data, operating variables (e.g., real-time indoor temperature), environmental parameters (e.g., outdoor air temperature), and miscellaneous [18]. With the radical evolution of internet of things (IoT) networks, more environmental data from IoT sensors [19] and occupant feedback [20] are also available for building operation management.

2.3 Semantic Data Integration Schema

In this study, the static data are extracted from BIM model using the COBie plug-in in Revit software, enabling the inclusion of building elements and their relationship information to develop the building semantic model. This semantic model is then stored in a graph database, which is a specialized data management system designed for efficient storage and querying of graph data. In graph database, nodes represent the building elements, while edges represent their relationships. Properties of building elements, such as wall materials and orientations, are stored in the static database alongside their corresponding unique identifiers within the semantic model. Temporal data from the BAS and IoT sensor network are collected by Building Automation and Control Networks (BACnet) protocol. This protocol is a commonly used data communication protocol and enables data communication among various equipment, devices, and sensors. The collected temporal data are then stored in the temporal database, with each measurement assigned a unique identifier. Within the semantic model, each identifier is stored as a node and linked to the corresponding element using the "hasreferenceId" relationship to achieve spatio-temporal data integration with semantic consistency.

2.4 AI Engine

The AI engine is designed to be a collection of diverse application packages focused on energy savings or predictive maintenance of buildings. These packages can provide a comprehensive view of building operations and offer recommendations for building management such as optimal control strategies, health monitoring, predictive maintenance strategies, anomaly detection, etc. This enables building managers to make informed decisions on how to optimize energy usage, reduce maintenance costs, and improve occupant comfort.

2.5 Smart 3D Interactive Building Management Platform

A digital twin-based building management platform is developed by Unity3D and can be published to cross-platform including Windows, IOS, Android and Mixed Reality devices, etc. The spatial and static data are mainly extracted from BIM for the development of digital twins. For aging buildings, preliminary BIM can be automatically recovered from 2D drawings [21] and serve as the foundation for creating a digital twin. The platform receives real-time operational data and AI recommendations from the database, which are then presented to building managers and operators for further review and analysis.

3 Case Study

This section elaborates the setup and results of the case study. In Sect. 3.1, the target chiller plant is introduced. Section 3.2 illustrates the development of the digital twin and semantic model. Section 3.3 presents the chiller sequencing results/

3.1 Introduction of the Target Chiller Plant

The target chiller plant is located in the Hong Kong Polytechnic University. The schematic diagram of the chiller plant is shown in Fig. 2. The chiller plant consists of 5 water-cooled chillers (WCC1-5) rated at 650 RT (Refrigeration Tons) each, one water-cooled chiller (WCC6) rated at 325 RT, and two air-cooled chillers (ACC1-2) rated at 325 RT each. The total cooling capacity is 4,225 RT. Primary chilled water pumps (PCHWPs) are connected in parallel. PCHWP4-9 serve WCC1-5 and the others serve three 325 RT chillers. Condenser water pumps (CDWPs) 1–6 and cooling towers (CTs) 1–5 serve WCC1-5, while CDWP7-8 and CT6 serve three 325 RT chillers. PCHWPs and CDWPs are equipped with one redundant for safety. All PCHWPs, CDWPs, and CTs are operated under fixed speed, and the normal power values are listed in Table 1. When a chiller is staged, a set of PCHWP, CDWP, and CT will also be switched. Therefore, it is important to determine the optimal number of chillers, i.e., optimal chiller sequencing control, to reduce unnecessary energy consumption by pumps and CTs.

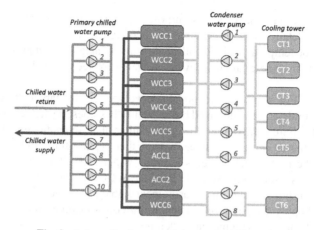

Fig. 2. Schematic diagram of the target chiller plant

Table 1. Nominal power of the equipment

Equipment	Power (kW)
PCHWP 1-3,10	30
PCHWP 4-9	55
CDWP 1-6	75
CDWP 7-8	45
CT 1-4	30
CT 5	18.5
CT 6	15

3.2 Development of Digital Twin and Semantic Model

As shown in Fig. 3, a digital twin is developed for the target chiller plant.

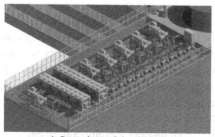 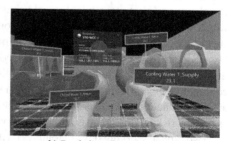

a) Overview of the digital twin b) Real-time data visualization

Fig. 3. Digital twin developed for the target chiller plant

The necessary static data for this purpose are extracted from BIM, encompassing comprehensive details about chillers, pumps, cooling towers, pipes, and other relevant components. The temporal data are collected from the integrated database that contains operational data from BAS and IoT devices as well as AI recommendations from the AI engine.

As shown in Fig. 4, a semantic model is developed for the target chiller plant. The static and temporal data are integrated based on the "hastimeseriesId" relationship in the semantic model. Figure 4(a) shows the entire chiller plant semantic model, with points representing different entities and lines showing their relationships. Figure 4(b) demonstrates a specific part of the model where the chiller "KC-POLYU-BCF-RF-HVAC-WCC-01" has a sensor point "POLYU-BCF-RF-WCC-01-CHWAST". The "hastimeseriesId" relationship connects this measurement with the identifier point "VSD WCC-1. Chilled Water Supply Temperature", indicating the corresponding temporal data is stored in the temporal database with the same identifier.

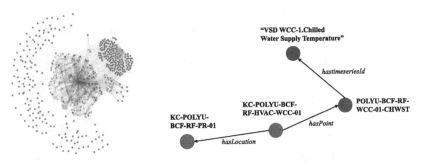

a) Overview of the semantic model   b) Zoomed-in view of the semantic model

Fig. 4. Semantic model developed for the target chiller plant

3.3 Test of AI-Enabled Chiller Sequencing Control Strategy

This study proposes and tests an AI-enabled robust chiller sequencing control strategy based on probabilistic cooling load prediction [22]. For comparison purposes, a conventional sequencing strategy widely used in building management systems was introduced, which makes sequencing decisions based on measured cooling load and chilled water supply temperature. Although effective in providing a stable and reliable cooling supply [23], unnecessary chillers may be staged by this reference control strategy because it does not consider future changes in cooling loads. The proposed strategy considers cooling load uncertainty to make sequencing actions more robust. An online risk-based actions evaluation scheme is designed to determine the number of operating chillers and assess the risks in the process and the reliability of the strategy simultaneously.

Two typical working days (Mondays) with similar outdoor air temperature and relative humidity were selected to compare the performance of two different chiller sequencing strategies. The first day, May 22nd, 2023, was used to test the conventional sequencing strategy, while the proposed sequencing strategy was tested on June 12th, 2023.

The conventional strategy was built into the building energy management system. The outdoor air temperature and relative humidity were recorded, as shown in Fig. 5. The outdoor temperature and relative humidity were very close in both trend and average levels. Therefore, the comparison of the sequencing strategies on these two days allows for a fair assessment of their performance.

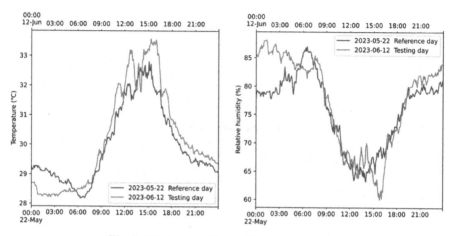

Fig. 5. Weather conditions of the two testing days

The chiller sequencing results of the conventional and proposed strategies are shown in Fig. 6a) and b), respectively. Two major differences can be identified. Firstly, when the conventional strategy was adopted from 8:00 am to 9:00 am, the chilled water supply temperatures were above 14 °C, leading to thermal discomfort in the occupied zones. This dissatisfaction occurred because the conventional strategy failed to provide sufficient cooling capacity when the previously unoccupied zones became occupied, after heat accumulation during midnight with only one chiller in operation. The proposed strategy, in contrast, staged on the second chiller earlier at 6:00 am and kept the chilled water supply temperature water at an acceptable level. The second difference is the temperature between the chilled water supply and the return temperature. The average temperature difference adopting the conventional strategy is only 3.2 °C, compared to the 3.5 °C adopting the proposed strategy. The low temperature difference can increase the energy consumption of pumps, resulting in decreased system performance.

The energy consumption of two testing days adopting the conventional strategy and the proposed strategy is shown in Table 2. Compared with the reference day, the proposed strategy achieves a 5.9% reduction in energy consumption for chillers. In terms of PCHWPs, CDWPS, and CTs, the proposed strategy leads to 12.2%, 8.9%, and 8.4% reduction in energy consumption, respectively. Overall, when comparing the total energy consumption of the two strategies, the proposed strategy saves 7.1% in energy consumption. These energy savings indicate that the proposed chiller sequencing strategy is more efficient and can help reduce energy usage in chilled water systems.

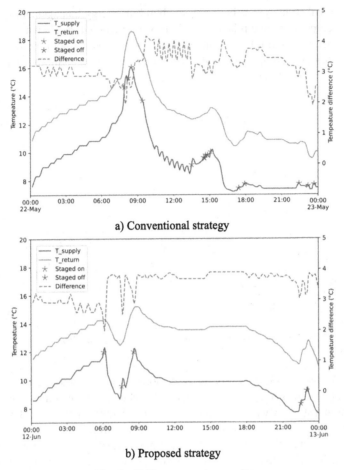

a) Conventional strategy

b) Proposed strategy

Fig. 6. Chiller sequencing results

Table 2. Comparison of energy consumption (kWh)

	Chillers	PCHWPs	CDWPs	CTs	Total
Conventional strategy	29334.8	4474.6	5878.8	2035.5	41723.7
Proposed strategy	27614.3	3927.9	5356.3	1865.5	38764.0
Energy saving (%)	5.9%	12.2%	8.9%	8.4%	7.4%

4 Conclusion

This study proposed a novel smart data-driven building management framework for environmental and sustainability applications. The proposed framework includes several key components, such as developing a semantic model to integrate data from multiple sources, deploying optimization and predictive maintenance strategies empowered by AI algorithms, and creating a digital twin platform designed to manage building equipment and information comprehensively and interactively.

The proposed framework was demonstrated in a chiller plant in Hong Kong. Through the deployment of this framework, chiller sequencing control was achieved in a robust and energy-efficient manner. The results show energy savings ranging from 5.9% to 12.2% compared to conventional strategies.

As one of the largest consumers of energy, the building sector has a significant impact on the environment and global carbon emissions. The proposed framework can be further improved and fine-tuned to better suit other types of buildings and facilities. By leveraging these technologies and strategies, substantial energy savings can be achieved, contributing to global sustainability efforts, and helping to achieve climate goals in the building sector.

Acknowledgement. The authors gratefully acknowledge the support of this research by the Innovation and Technology Fund (ITP/002/22LP) of the Hong Kong SAR, China, the Hong Kong Polytechnic University Carbon Neutrality Funding Scheme and the E&M AI Lab of Electrical and Mechanical Services Department (EMSD) of Hong Kong SAR, China.

References

1. IEA (2022), Buildings, IEA, Paris https://www.iea.org/reports/buildings, License: CC BY 4.0
2. East E W. Construction operations building information exchange (COBie)[R]. Engineer Research and Development Center Champaign Il Construction Engineering Research Lab (2007)
3. Dave, B., Buda, A., Nurminen, A., et al.: A framework for integrating BIM and IoT through open standards. Autom. Constr.. Constr. **95**, 35–45 (2018)
4. Compton, M., Barnaghi, P., Bermudez, L., et al.: The SSN ontology of the W3C semantic sensor network incubator group. J. Web Semant. **17**, 25–32 (2012)
5. Terkaj, W., Schneider, G.F., Pauwels, P.: Reusing domain ontologies in linked building data: the case of building automation and control. In: 8th International work-shop on formal ontologies meet industry. 2017, 2050
6. Rasmussen, M.H., Lefrançois, M., Schneider, G.F., et al.: BOT: The building topology ontology of the W3C linked building data group. Semantic Web **12**(1), 143–161 (2021)
7. Terkaj, W., Šojić, A.: Ontology-based representation of IFC EXPRESS rules: an enhancement of the ifcOWL ontology. Autom. Constr.. Constr. **57**, 188–201 (2015)
8. Balaji, B., Bhattacharya, A., Fierro, G., et al.: Brick: Metadata schema for portable smart building applications. Appl. Energy **226**, 1273–1292 (2018)
9. Jiang, F., Ma, L., Broyd, T., Chen, K.: Digital twin and its implementations in the civil engineering sector. Autom. Constr. **130**, 103838 (2021)
10. Chen, W., Chen, K., Cheng, J.C., Wang, Q., Gan, V.J.: BIM-based framework for automatic scheduling of facility maintenance work orders. Autom. Constr. **91**, 15–30 (2018)

11. Chen, W., Chen, K., Cheng, J.C.: From building information modeling to digital twin: the core for sustainable smart campus at HKUST. In: Research Companion to Building Information Modeling, pp. 671–696. Edward Elgar Publishing (2022)
12. Wang, S., Burnett, J.: Online adaptive control for optimizing variable-speed pumps of indirect water-cooled chilling systems. Appl. Therm. Eng. 21(11), 1083–1103 (2001)
13. Chen, Z., Xiao, F., Guo, F., Yan, J.: Interpretable machine learning for building energy management: A state-of-the-art review. Advances in Applied Energy, 100123 (2023)
14. Zhang, L., et al.: A review of machine learning in building load prediction. Appl. Energy 285, 116452 (2021)
15. Mirnaghi, M.S., Haghighat, F.: Fault detection and diagnosis of large-scale HVAC systems in buildings using data-driven methods: a comprehensive review. Energy Build. 229, 110492 (2020)
16. Ding, Y., Liu, X.: A comparative analysis of data-driven methods in building energy benchmarking. Energy Build. 209, 109711 (2020)
17. Jin, Y., Yan, D., Chong, A., Dong, B., An, J.: Building occupancy forecasting: a systematical and critical review. Energy Build. 251, 111345 (2021)
18. Xiao, F., Fan, C.: Building information modeling and building automation systems data integration and big data analytics for building energy management. Research Companion to Building Information Modeling, pp. 525–549 (2022)
19. Javed, A., Larijani, H., Ahmadinia, A., Emmanuel, R., Mannion, M., Gibson, D.: Design and implementation of a cloud enabled random neural network-based decentralized smart controller with intelligent sensor nodes for HVAC. IEEE Internet Things J. 4(2), 393–403 (2017)
20. Abdelrahman, M.M., Chong, A., Miller, C.: Personal thermal comfort models using digital twins: preference prediction with BIM-extracted spatial–temporal proximity data from Build2Vec. Build. Environ. 207, 108532 (2022)
21. Pan, Z., Yu, Y., Xiao, F., Zhang, J.: Recovering building information model from 2D drawings for mechanical, electrical and plumbing systems of ageing buildings. Autom. Constr. 152, 104914 (2023)
22. Liao, Y., Huang, G.: A hybrid predictive sequencing control for multi-chiller plant with considerations of indoor environment control, energy conservation and economical operation cost. Sustain. Cities Soc. 49, 101616 (2019)
23. Sun, S., Wang, S., Shan, K.: Flow measurement uncertainty quantification for building central cooling systems with multiple water-cooled chillers using a Bayesian approach. Appl. Therm. Eng. 202, 117857 (2022)

Advances in Machine-Learning Based Disaggregation of Building Heating Loads: A Review

Synne Krekling Lien[1](✉), Behzad Najafi[2], and Jayaprakash Rajasekharan[1]

[1] Department of Electric Energy, Norwegian University of Science and Technology, Trondheim, Norway
Synne.k.lien@ntnu.no
[2] Department of Energy, Politecnico di Milano, Milan, Italy

Abstract. This review article investigates the methods proposed for disaggregating the space heating units' load from the aggregate electricity load of commercial and residential buildings. It explores conventional approaches together with those that employ traditional machine learning, deep supervised learning and reinforcement learning. The review also outlines corresponding data requirements and examines the suitability of a commonly utilised toolkit for disaggregating heating loads from low-frequency aggregate power measurements. It is shown that most of the proposed approaches have been applied to high-resolution measurements and that few studies have been dedicated to low-resolution aggregate loads (e.g. provided by smart meters). Furthermore, only a few methods have taken account of special considerations for heating technologies, given the corresponding governing physical phenomena. Accordingly, the recommendations for future works include adding a rigorous pre-processing step, in which features inspired by the building physics (e.g. lagged values for the ambient conditions and values that represent the correlation between heating consumption and outdoor temperature) are added to the available input feature pool. Such a pipeline may benefit from deep supervised learning or reinforcement learning methods, as these methods are shown to offer higher performance compared to traditional machine learning algorithms for load disaggregation.

Keywords: Load disaggregation · non-intrusive load monitoring · Smart Meter Analytics · Machine learning · Space Heating · Building Energy Use

1 Introduction

In 2021, the operation of buildings was responsible for 30% of final global energy consumption and 27% of total energy sector emissions (out of which 8% is related to direct emissions from buildings, while 19% refers to emissions from generation of heat and electricity consumed by buildings) [1]. The electrification of buildings has been identified as a key alternative to achieve a more sustainable energy system and mitigate the corresponding emission of gases that result in climate change [2]. The

B. N. Jørgensen et al. (Eds.): EI.A 2023, LNCS 14467, pp. 179–201, 2024.
https://doi.org/10.1007/978-3-031-48649-4_11

Norwegian building sector is a special case as its heating supply is highly electrified, due to historically low electricity prices; the building stock was accordingly responsible for approximately 37% of delivered energy and 55% of delivered electricity [3] in 2021. This has a significant effect on the peak electricity use and, consequently, the peak experienced by the grid coincides with the coldest hours of the year. Therefore, as the transport and industrial sector are becoming electrified, electricity peaks are expected to rise, increasing the strain on the electricity grid. A substantial share of grid investments will be made to avoid bottlenecks that are expected to occur for only a few hours each year [4]. To limit the growth in the peak load that is expected in the green transition with increased electrification, and the resulting cost to society and consumers, further knowledge is needed about buildings' electricity use behind the main meter. Electricity meters only show how much electricity is delivered to the customer, but not how the electricity is used or how different loads and appliances drive the peaks. By separating the electricity consumption specifically for heating purposes from the overall electricity consumption in buildings, one can attain a deeper understanding of both the proportion of total energy consumption and the increase in peak load attributable to heating. This approach not only enhances our comprehension of the influence of various heating appliances and types of buildings on the peak load, but also provides valuable data for optimising grid planning and facilitating more efficient demand management within buildings. Consequently, this practice can result in cost savings for building occupants and reduce the need for investments in the grid, thereby benefiting society at large. As a consequence, this paper aims to investigate previous research on disaggregation of heating loads from the total electricity load of buildings. The goal is to gain insight into the most promising methodologies and to identify any existing research gaps in the domain of heating load disaggregation.

2 Background

By 2019, Norway mandated the installation of smart electricity meters for all electricity consumers as part of advanced metering systems (AMS) [5]. These meters record customers' hourly electricity usage and transmit data to grid companies. Moreover, the meters can provide high frequency (seconds) and medium frequency (minutes) data on electricity usage, as well as information on active and reactive power, voltage and frequency through the Home Area Network gate (HAN-gate). This allows for collection of aggregate electricity consumption data. However, to gain a deeper understanding of the total peak load and how to limit it, it is necessary to disaggregate the load to specific appliances, particularly those corresponding to heating systems [6].

One way to perform load disaggregation is by using intrusive metering, which involves installing separate meters for each appliance or in each building. However, this approach can be expensive due to costs associated with the manufacturing, installation, maintenance and monitoring of the required measurement devices. It can also be inconvenient for building residents, and new meters would have to be installed for every new appliance or installation, making it impractical and challenging to scale [7]. An alternative load disaggregation method is non-intrusive load monitoring (NILM), which involves using software tools to analyse power signals and disaggregate total energy load into individual loads or appliances from a single point of measurement. The concept of NILM was first proposed by Hart in the 1980s [8]. The objective of NILM techniques is to determine the individual power consumption or on/off state of electrical loads. These methods rely solely on measuring the aggregate energy consumption of these loads. NILM has various applications, including monitoring energy use in residential and service buildings, as well as in the industrial sector. Typically, NILM techniques are classified into two categories: 'low-frequency approaches' that use data or features at a frequency lower than the AC base frequency in buildings, or 'high-frequency approaches' with higher frequencies [9, 10]. The AC base frequency is usually 50 Hz or 60 Hz for AC power systems in Europe, Asia and North America.

Traditionally, NILM approaches for building loads involve 4 steps: data acquisition, appliance and feature extraction, inference and learning, and finally, load disaggregation and classification Several techniques have been studied for NILM [12], linear regression models and unsupervised methods. Optimisation and regression techniques are computationally efficient and can yield good results with small datasets. However, in recent years there has been significant research into other machine learning (ML) methods, particularly supervised learning techniques, which have gained substantial attention. These methods include Bayesian classifiers [13], support vector machines [14] and K-nearest neighbours [15], among others. Approaches used in unsupervised training instead include blind source separation [16], and the most researched method, which is hidden Markov models (HMM) [17, 18]. In addition, Deep Neural Networks (DNNs) have seen tremendous success in the domains of vision and natural language processing in recent years. Accordingly, since 2015 there has been a rapid increase in the number of DNN-based approaches and applications for building load disaggregation [9, 19].

With the increasing number of disaggregation techniques, applications and research, the NILM toolkit (NILMTK) was developed in an effort to create reproducible NILM experiments that serves as a reference library for dataset parsers and benchmark algorithm implementations [20]. The original NILMTK library comes with implemented methods for combinatorial optimisation (CO), mean regression, factorial hidden Markov models (FHMM), and the original algorithm by Hart from 1985. The toolkit can be used to disaggregate any dataset which has been structured as an NILMTK dataset, either manually or through a simple API, and the results can be reviewed using the performance measures implemented. Furthermore, the NILMTK-Contrib repository is an extension of the NILMTK toolkit that offers additional disaggregation algorithms, such as recurrent neural networks (RNN), FHMM, sequence-to-sequence models (Seq2Seq), and more [21]. Another toolkit that is an extension of NILMTK is Torch-NILM, which offers a suite of tools for training deep neural networks in the task of energy disaggregation [22].

In the Norwegian case, it is assumed that heating loads/heating technologies are responsible for the majority of the annual electricity consumption, as well as the electric peak load in buildings [23]. A deeper knowledge of how this varies for different building categories, and how the heating loads can be disaggregated from hourly measurements from the AMS meters, is missing. Disaggregation approaches are usually applied, trained and validated on datasets with labelled data for energy use in buildings. In some cases, these datasets have separate measurements for space heating units of buildings, and NILM techniques are used to identify and disaggregate heating loads from the total electricity load in buildings. The experience from these studies can help to gain more knowledge about disaggregation of heating loads in buildings, the nature of electricity used for heating in all electric buildings in cold climates, and insights on how to limit the growth in the peak electricity demand in Norway.

2.1 Scope

The scope of this review is to look into methods used specifically for disaggregation of space heating technologies and space heating demand from the total electric load of both commercial and residential buildings. This is particularly relevant for the Norwegian case, as the peak demand load is mainly caused by electrical heating in buildings. When we talk about heating loads in this paper, we specifically mean electricity used for space heating and heating of ventilation air. When talking about heating appliances, we consider all electrical appliances that can be used for space/ventilation heating, including heat pumps (air-to-air, ground-source, air-to-water, etc.), electric space heaters, electric heating batteries, electric floor heating and electrical boilers.

This paper explores methods that utilise both traditional learning methods, as well as deep supervised learning and reinforcement learning (RL) approaches, and outlines the data requirements for load disaggregation of the space heating demand in all electric, and partially electric, buildings, with recommendations for further work. The paper also looks into and provides an overview of building energy measurement datasets used for developing disaggregation methods. Finally, the paper briefly examines the suitability of NILMTK for disaggregation of heating technologies from low frequency electricity use in all electric buildings.

In this paper, the resolution of different datasets and approaches are referred to either as frequency given in Hz or as per time unit, given as seconds/minutes/hours. These units are used interchangeably, but essentially 1 Hz is the same as 1/s, meaning that a dataset with the resolution of one Hz has measurements with 1-s resolution. In this review paper, we also consider datasets and methods which are applied to datasets with resolution in the seconds domain to be of high resolution, while datasets with measurements in the minute or hour domain are considered to be of low resolution.

2.2 Related Works and Contributions

Several review studies have examined NILM and disaggregation techniques that employ machine learning to disaggregate individual appliances. A selection of these are summarised in Table 1. Some studies have partly examined methods for disaggregating heating appliances' electricity use from the building's aggregate load. However, there is a lack of a systematic overview of techniques that specifically address disaggregation of heating loads in buildings. Such a review is essential to determine the research gaps in the disaggregation field regarding heating loads and heating appliances and can contribute to increasing the knowledge of how heating loads contribute to peak loads in all-electric buildings and the building stock.

Other recently conducted reviews and relevant articles focus on disaggregation of building energy loads and/or machine learning approaches in the disaggregation research field. Rafati et al. [24] performed a review of NILM used for fault detection and efficiency assessment of HVAC systems. This review considered different methods of NILM applied to building HVAC systems with different measurement durations and sampling frequencies and showed that, even though NILM could be successfully implemented for Fault Detection and Diagnosis (FDD) and the energy efficiency (EE) evaluation of HVAC, and enhance the performance of these techniques, there are many research opportunities to improve or develop NILM-based FDD methods to deal with real-world challenges. Huber et al. [9] reviewed NILM approaches that employ deep neural networks to disaggregate appliances from low-frequency data, i.e. data with sampling rates lower than the AC base frequency. The study looked at around 100 studies in which deep learning approaches were used for NILM. Energy use for heat pumps was disaggregated in ten of the studies examined that investigated deep learning methods on the AMPds-datasets [25], while two studies disaggregated electric heaters. The study also found that the number of deep neural network approaches to solve NILM problems has increased rapidly since 2015. Himeur et al. [26] looked into machine learning methods for anomaly detection of energy consumption in buildings using machine learning. The method briefly reviewed ML-based NILM for anomaly detection of energy consumption in buildings and concluded that even though the performance of NILM to identify abnormal consumption is not yet as accurate as using sub-metering feedback, its performance could be further improved, to allow a robust identification of faulty behaviour. Himeur et al. (2) [27] made a second review of recent trends in smart NILM frameworks (event-based, non-event-based), as well as a more technical review describing sensors and devices utilised to collect energy consumption data in residential and public buildings before applying NILM. They also reviewed real-life applications of NILM systems. Angelis et al. [28] undertook a more general literature review about commonly used methodology and applications of NILM for building energy consumption. Earlier, Ruano et al. [29] reviewed NILM methods specifically for Home Energy Management Systems (HEMS) and Ambient Assisted Living (AAL).

Table 1. Overview of other review articles on disaggregation of building energy use.

Reference	Scope	Building category and appliances	References	Disaggregation approaches
Rafati et al. 2022 [24]	Fault detection, energy efficiency assessment	HVAC systems in residential and commercial buildings	53	All kinds
Huber et al. 2021[9]	DNN for NILM applications	Mostly residential. Electrical appliances, some including HVAC and HP	190	DNN
Himeur et al. 2021(1) [26]	ML approaches for anomaly detection of energy consumption, including ML for disaggregation	Energy consumption for all appliances	7 specifically about disaggregation out of 264	ML, supervised, unsupervised, DNN
Himeur et al. 2021(2) [27]	Overview of event and non-event based NILM-methods. Applications of NILM-systems	Residential and public buildings, all appliances	200	Both ML and other
Angelis et al.2022 [28]	General overview of NILM methods and applications for building energy use	Residential and public buildings	237	Both ML and other
Ruano et al. 2019 [29]	Review of NILM methods, focusing particularly on recent proposals and their applications, particularly in the areas of Home Energy Management Systems (HEMS) and Ambient Assisted Living (AAL)	Residential, all appliances	152	NILM specifically for HEMS and AAL. Some discussion of ML methods. No special attention to heating.

To the best of the authors' knowledge, this review article is the first review to specifically look into the scientific literature on disaggregation of space heating appliances/space heating loads from the aggregate building load. In contrast to other review papers that concentrate on the disaggregation of all household appliances, including electrical heating devices among them, there is reason to believe that heating appliances could potentially benefit from more tailored methodologies. This assertion is grounded in the relation with outdoor temperature, building characteristics and heating appliance usage patterns. The primary contribution of this paper is to investigate this proposition and to assess the effectiveness of machine learning advancements in the specific context of disaggregating heating loads.

2.3 Outline of the Paper

The paper is structured into different sections. Section 3, entitled "Methodology", explains the approach taken in the literature search. Additionally, it offers an overview of commonly used datasets within the NILM/disaggregation field, together with insights into the availability of separate meters for heating appliances in these datasets.

Proceeding to Sect. 4, "Disaggregation of Buildings' Heating Loads", the main findings from the literature review are presented. This section includes details of various disaggregation studies, categorised as traditional methods, deep supervised learning approaches and reinforcement learning methods.

Section 5 provides an evaluation of the data requirements essential for the development of effective disaggregation approaches.

Finally, in Sect. 6, the paper concludes by summarising the key findings and insights.

3 Methodology

The aim of this article is to conduct a literature review of proposed methods of disaggregation of building heating loads and the advances of machine learning methods within this field. This literature review looks into three main categories of literature: 1) other relevant review studies on disaggregation of building loads; 2) documented datasets for energy use in buildings used in NILM/disaggregation research; and 3) methods and results of disaggregation approaches for building heating loads.

To conduct this review, a literature search was executed on Google scholar, Elsevier library and IEEE Xplore using various combinations of key words: "disaggregation", "NILM", "HVAC", "space heating", "machine learning", "buildings", "deep learning", in January/February 2023. This resulted in a total of 1,970 articles being extracted, of which around 200 articles were screened and marked as relevant for the topic of disaggregation of energy use in buildings. An additional step in the literature search was conducted using Connectedpapers.org for articles which appeared to be specifically relevant, e.g. datasets containing measurements of heating technologies or disaggregationmethods utilising these datasets. This search describes citations within each article and points to other articles where the article in question is cited.

During the work with this article, the authors also tested NILMTK [20] and the extension NILMTK-Contrib [21] to get a better overview of the datasets used for NILM approaches, and some of the methods used for NILM. To get a better understanding of the requirements and limitations of NILM-Toolkit and commonly used datasets, NILMTK and NILMTK-Contrib were tested by following the user guide accessible through GitHub, using the IAWE [30], UK-DALE [31] and AMPds [25] datasets. The toolkit was also tested to give better insights into the NILM methodology and results. The toolkit was tested by writing a dataset converter and using the authors' proprietary dataset with hourly measurements of energy use in two Norwegian school buildings. Metadata for the datasets which are compatible with NILMTK was examined within the toolkit itself by accessing the information in the NILMTK GitHub repository [32] giving supplementary information about the datasets.

3.1 Datasets

To train, test and benchmark various disaggregation techniques, a variety of datasets are used in the literature. While some researchers gather and utilise proprietary datasets for their novel disaggregation approaches, acquiring high-resolution data on multiple buildings and appliances necessitates a significant investment of time and resources. As a result, most disaggregation methods are built, tested and benchmarked using existing datasets. Understanding these widely utilised datasets and their content is critical for gaining insight into which approaches have been utilised for disaggregating heating loads and technologies in buildings. Some of the datasets most frequently referenced in this paper include the datasets AMPDs [25], UK-Dale [31], IAWE [30] and REFIT [33] among others. AMPDs (Almanac of Minutely Power dataset) is a public dataset for load disaggregation and eco-feedback research and is a record of energy consumption of a single house in Vancouver with 21 sub-meters for an entire year (from April 1, 2012 to March 31, 2013) at one minute read intervals [31]. UK-Dale (UK recording Domestic Appliance-Level Electricity) is an open access dataset of disaggregated energy use data from 5 houses in the UK, measured over 655 days [31]. REFIT is another UK dataset he with electrical load measurements of 20 houses with nine individual appliance measurements at 8-s intervals per house, collected continuously over a period of two years [33]. The IAWE (Indian Dataset for Ambient Water and Energy) contains measurements of 73 days in 2013 of energy and water use data for a single family house [30]. Table 2 gives an overview of these datasets and other datasets for building energy use which are used in research on load disaggregation. The table indicates the location, building category and number of buildings in the datasets, as well as the measurement duration, sampling rate and available measured quantities. The availability of separate measurements for heating loads and heating technologies within the dataset, as well as NILMTK-compatibility, are also indicated in the table. A list of abbreviations is given at the end of the table.

Other recently conducted reviews and relevant articles focus on disaggregation of building energy loads and/or machine learning approaches in the disaggregation research field. Rafati et al. [24] performed a review of NILM used for fault detection and efficiency assessment of HVAC systems. This review considered different methods of NILM applied to building HVAC systems with different measurement durations and sampling frequencies and showed that, even though NILM could be successfully implemented for Fault Detection and Diagnosis (FDD) and the energy efficiency (EE) evaluation

Table 2. Overview of different datasets containing energy measurements for building loads.

Dataset	Location	Buildings	Duration	Sampling rate	Meters	Appliances	NILMTK compatibility
UK-DALE [31]	UK	5 SFH	2.5 years	16 kHz, 6s	P	H1: TOT, BOIL, STP, 50 EA H2: TOT, 19 EA H3: TOT, EH, 3 EA H4: TOT, OBOIL, 4 EA H5: TOT, 24 EA	Yes
REFIT [33]	UK	20 SFH	2 years	8 sec	P	H1, H9, H15: EH 19 EA (up to 9 per house)	Yes
REDD [34]	USA	3 SFH, 3 APT	3-19 days	0,33 Hz-15kHz	V, P	H2, H3: EH 10-20 EA per house	Yes
ECO [35]	Switzerland	6 SFH	8 months	1 Hz	V, I, P, Q, ✦	5-8 EA per house	Yes
SynD[36]	Austria	2 SFH	180	5 Hz	P	EH and 20 EA	Yes
ENERTALK [37]	Korea	22 SFH	29-122 days	15 Hz	P, Q	1-7 EA+TOT per building	Yes
AMPds(2)[25]	Canada	1 SFH	1 year (AMPds) 2 years (AMPds2)	1 min	V, I, f, pf, P, Q, S, E	Several EA, including HP. Electricity, water, natural gas.	Yes
HES[38]	United Kingdom	26 (year) 224 (month) RES	1 year/1 month	1/600 Hz	I, V, P, T	Only total consumption + recording of which appliances that were on/off	Yes
PLAID[39]	USA	Lab and 64 RES	5 seconds	30 kHz	V, I	TOT. 1876 appliances, mostly AE, 17 types. 15 EH (not in aggregate measurements). 27 AC.	Unknown
BLUED[40]	USA	1 SFH	8 days	12 kHz	V, I, P	TOT, 43 EA	Unknown
Tracebase [41]	Germany	-	1 day	1 Hz	P	122 EA	Unknown
BERDS[42]	USA	1 COM	1 year	20s	P, Q, S	Unknown #EA, HVAC	Unknown
iAWE[30]	India	1 SFH	73 days	1 Hz, 6s	V, I, f, P, Q, S, E, ✦	33 sensors, inc. EWH and AC	Yes
GREEND[43]	Austria/Italy	9 SFH	1 year	1 Hz	P	9 EA per house, TOT	Yes
DRED[44]	Netherlands	1 SFH	6 months	1 Hz, 1 s	P, T	11 EA, 1 CH	Yes
Dataport[45]	USA	722 RES	3.5 years	1 Hz-1min		<10 meters per house, mostly EA. EH and HWH present in very few houses.	Yes
RAE [46]	Canada	2 SFH	72 days	1 Hz	V, P, Q, S, f, E	20 EA, HP, EB	Yes
I-BLEND[47]	India	7 UNI	1 year	1 Hz, 1 min	V, P, f, I, Pf	No single appliances. Only per building and aggregate (7 buildings). Includes occupancy data.	Unknown
IRISE[48]	France	100 households	1 year	10 min, 1 hour	E	Unknown EA, 3 houses with HWH, EH	Unknown
Smart*[49]	USA	3 SFH	3 months	1 Hz	V, f, P, S	H1: 19 EA/rooms, 1 gBoil H2: 28 EA/rooms, 1 gBoil H3: 19EA/rooms, 2 Boilers (unknown fuel)	Yes
COMBED[50]	India	6 UNI (same as I-BLEND) 1 MFH (student housing)	1 Month	30s	P, Pf, f, E	No heating. Unknown # EA.	Yes
EIDeK [51]	Norway	75 RES+500 apps.	1 year	1 hour (households), 1 min (appliances)	P, E	500 appliances, inc. heaters	No
treASURE[52]	Norway	316 in 10 building categories (2 res and 8 com)	1-4 years	1 hour	P, E	Electricity, District heating (disaggregated to SH and DHW)	No
Denmark SMDH [53]	Denmark	2460 SFH, 564 MFH, 8 Service, 97 unclear	3 years	1 hour	P, E, T	District heating smart meter data	No

Abbreviations

Services/appliances

TOT	Aggregated electric load
EA	electrical appliances (all electric appliances such as TV and kitchen appliances not used for SH, DHW, HVAC)
BOIL	solar thermal pump
STP	Solar pump
EH	Electric heater
gBOIL	Gas boiler
AC	Air conditioning
EWH	Electric water heater
CH	Central heating

Building category

RES	Residential buildings, SFH and/or MFH where this is not specified.
SFH	single family house (detached, semi-detached,
MFH	Multifamily house (apartments)
COM	Commercial
UNI	University building

Measurements

P	Active power
Q	Reactive power
S	Apparent power
E	Energy
f	Frequency
Pf	Power Factor
✦	Phase angle
V	Voltage
I	Current
T	Temperature

of HVAC, and enhance the performance of these techniques, there are many research opportunities to improve or develop NILM-based FDD methods to deal with real-world challenges. Huber et al. [9] reviewed NILM approaches that employ deep neural networks to disaggregate appliances from low-frequency data, i.e. data with sampling rates lower than the AC base frequency. The study looked at around 100 studies in which deep learning approaches were used for NILM. Energy use for heat pumps was disaggregated in ten of the studies examined that investigated deep learning methods on the AMPds-datasets [25], while two studies disaggregated electric heaters. The study also found that the number of deep neural network approaches to solve NILM problems has increased rapidly since 2015. Himeur et al. [26] looked into machine learning methods for anomaly detection of energy consumption in buildings using machine learning. The method briefly reviewed ML-based NILM for anomaly detection of energy consumption in buildings and concluded that even though the performance of NILM to identify abnormal consumption is not yet as accurate as using sub-metering feedback, its performance could be further improved, to allow a robust identification of faulty behaviour. Himeur et al. (2) [27] made a second review of recent trends in smart NILM frameworks (event-based, non-event-based), as well as a more technical review describing sensors and devices utilised to collect energy consumption data in residential and public buildings before applying NILM. They also reviewed real-life applications of NILM systems. Angelis et al. [28] undertook a more general literature review about commonly used methodology and applications of NILM for building energy consumption. Earlier, Ruano et al. [29] reviewed NILM methods specifically for Home Energy Management Systems (HEMS) and Ambient Assisted Living (AAL).

4   Disaggregation of Buildings' Heating Loads

This section presents the literature review on methods for disaggregation of heating loads from aggregate building electricity loads. All investigated methods are summarised in Table 3 at the end of the section. The section is divided into three sub-sections based on the main machine learning class used in the different articles – namely "Traditional methods and shallow-algorithms", "Deep supervised learning" and "Reinforcement learning".

4.1   Traditional Methods and Shallow Algorithms

The first disaggregation methods were based on rule-based algorithms, statistical methods, and shallow learning algorithms, such as combinatorial optimisation, clustering and regression models. In this article, shallow learning refers to non-deep machine learning methods or traditional machine learning methods. These methods are still prevalent today due to their simplicity, interpretability and computational efficiency, making them well-suited for real-time monitoring and control applications. For instance, optimisation and linear regression models can be trained on small datasets, making them useful when data is limited or expensive to collect.

   Liu et al.'s method, which is based on Affinity propagation clustering (AP) and time-segmented state probability (TSSP), was proposed as a fast working algorithm for real time disaggregation in 2021 [54]. This method was tested on the AMPds dataset and offered an average load state identification accuracy of over 96% and power decomposition accuracy of over 89%, while including all appliances. The state recognition accuracy for heat pumps was notably lower than corresponding average accuracy obtained for all appliances, although it maintained a high power composition accuracy.

Another method that is based on optimisation was proposed by Balletti et al. [55], with a novel penalty-based binary quadratic programming formulation with appliance-specific as well as an optimisation-based automatic state detection algorithm to estimate power levels of appliances and their respective transient behaviour. Their approach was trained and tested on AMPds, UKDALE and REFIT and its capability to disaggregate many appliances with high accuracy was demonstrated. However, in the training procedure, some issues were faced for heat pumps, as the same unit is employed for cooling in summer and for heating in winter. The latter situation resulted in the wrong parameters for the heat pump in summer when the model is trained on winter data. To overcome this challenge, the parameters were re-estimated using two weeks for training and one for validation immediately before the test week.

Several methods have also been proposed for low resolution (1 h) data in this area. One statistical method developed in 2013 by Morch et al. [56] used linear regression to segment hourly electricity loads from households into weather-dependent (e.g. space heating) and weather-independent loads. This method considers the dependency of energy consumption on current and past-day temperatures. Lien et al. [57] also use linear regression, seasonality and temperature dependency to generate average profiles for domestic hot water heating (DHW) in buildings based on heat load and outdoor temperature measurements. However, this method is only tested on heating loads and not electricity loads, and it is best used for generating average load profiles, rather than disaggregating total heating loads in single buildings.

Other works have investigated unsupervised methods for disaggregating heating and cooling loads from hourly energy data. Zaeri et al. [58] used unsupervised time-series decomposition to disaggregate hourly aggregate electricity load into corresponding heating and cooling loads by decomposing the total signal into trend, seasonality and residuals before comparing with submeter data. The study showed promising results, but the results are difficult to interpret and replicate, as the type and characteristics of the office building's heating system are not provided in the article. Amayri et al. [59] developed NILM methods based on random forest to disaggregate flexible electricity use in three houses. The method aimed to classify whether the hot water heater and electric heater were on or off and were shown to perform well for two of the houses, but not the third one.

Najafi et al. [60] proposed another method for disaggregation of air-conditioning load from smart meter data, in which an extended pool of input features was extracted from both smart meter data and the corresponding weather conditions' dataset. Input features included calendar-based variables and features inspired by buildings' thermal behaviour (e.g. outdoor temperature in previous timestamps), along with statistics-based, regression-based and pattern-based features that were originally proposed by Miller et al. [61] for building characterisation. A feature selection algorithm was then employed to identify the most promising set of features and an optimisation process was utilised to determine the most promising algorithm (showing that extra trees algorithm offers highest performance). The method achieved an average R2 score of 0.905 for disaggregating cooling load and thus demonstrated the utility of the proposed set of features and the fact that high-frequency data or appliance-wise measurements are not always necessary to achieve high accuracy. However, this approach was tested on a relatively small dataset and should be tested on a larger set of buildings to further assess its generalisability.

Overall, shallow learning algorithms and rule-based algorithms can be useful for building load disaggregation when interpretability and computational efficiency are needed. However, if the data is highly complex and non-linear, and a large dataset is available, deep learning models may provide better accuracy and performance.

4.2 Deep Supervised Learning

In the past years, deep learning methods have been increasingly utilised for disaggregation of building energy use. Models based on deep supervised learning require more computational power compared to traditional methods, although they can provide better accuracy, scalability and performance compared to regression models in disaggregation applications, specifically while dealing with complex and non-linear relationships between the aggregate electricity consumption and appliance usage. Deep learning methods consist of a range of different models such as Convolutional Neural Networks (CNN), Residual Network (ResNet), Seq2Seq and Generative Adversarial Network (GAN), alone or in combination with each other and/or mechanisms such as Gated Recurrent Units (GRU) and Denoising Autoencoder (dAE).

Most of the proposed deep-learning based approaches for the disaggregation of heating loads that have been reviewed in this sub-chapter are designed for disaggregation of datasets with a resolution of 1 min or more. Considering the information that can be extracted from the measurement data with such resolution, these methods are typically designed to recognise patterns in different appliances' consumption and their states. In this context, Kaselimi et al., 2019 [62] introduced a Bayesian-optimised bidirectional Long Short-Term Memory (LSTM) method for energy disaggregation of household aggregate load. The method was evaluated using the AMPds dataset. In general, the model was shown to have a higher performance than the one achieved using other methods such as LSTM, CNN, CO and FHMM, but the proposed method performed significantly worse on disaggregating the heat pump's load compared to other appliances such as the dryer, the dishwasher and the oven. Methods based on LSTM were also examined by Xia et al. [63], who proposed a composite deep LSTM for load disaggregation. The method was not tested on any heating appliances, but it was tested on an air conditioner from the Dataport dataset with 1 min's resolution. The air conditioner was used frequently in the training period and the method performed better than all traditional methods and the DAE method for disaggregation of the air conditioner's load. Wang et al. [64] proposed an ensemble-based deep learning method for NILM, which used both LSTM and feed forward NN. The model used the real power readings from the dataset and considered sliding window data and additional attributes such as month and time of day for disaggregation of six appliances from the AMPds-dataset, including the heat pump and HVAC. The method achieved 93.9% accuracy for the heat pump disaggregation.

Davies et al. [65] proposed some CNN models for appliance classification, trained and tested on a PLAID dataset. Results showed that appliance classification is possible to some extent at low "smart meter"-like sampling frequencies, but performance increases greatly with sampling resolution. In general, their CNN architectures showed good separation of appliances on a PLAID dataset, but the models performed poorly on electric heater class, however, which was confused with the hairdryer. This is because heater onset events are generated by a single heating element turning on, corresponding to a simple step shaped transient. Such appliance classes are very difficult to separate since they contain a heating element whose onset appears as a plain step.

Li et al. [66] proposed a fusion framework using an integrated neural network for NILM with two tasks: load identification and power estimation. The foundation of load identification is event detection, achieved by using the CUSUM method. Experimental results on an AMPds dataset with 1 min's resolution showed that the proposed model could be used for NILM on datasets using low sampling-rate power data, and the method achieved 98.5% accuracy for identification of the heat pump.

Wang et al. [67] proposed an end-to-end method to identify individual appliances from aggregated data using a combination of DAE and LSTM networks on an AMPds dataset. The method was trained on aggregated data and tested on synthesised data. The results of the model showed that it had high performance for some appliances, but low performance on reconstructing appliances with continuous states (as opposed to on/off-appliances), such as a washing machine and a heat pump.

Harell et al. [68] proposed a causal 1-D CNN, inspired by WaveNet, for NILM on low-frequency data on the AMPds dataset. The study found that when implementing current, active power, reactive power and apparent power the model showed faster convergence and higher performance for NILM, but the study does not, however, present any results specifically for the heat pump or any other appliance.

Xia et al. [69] proposed sequence-to-sequence methods for NILM based on a deep delated convolution residual network. The original power data from UK-DALE and Dataport was normalised before sliding window was used to create input for the residual network. The method can improve disaggregation efficiency and the accuracy of disaggregation of electrical appliances with low usage. The method was not tested on any heating appliances, but on an air conditioner with promising performance, but the authors argue that other methods such as KNN, DEA, CNN, seq-2-point, and their own method based on DA-ResNet [70], offered just as high performance on the disaggregation of the air conditioner.

Kaselimi et al. [71] proposed a contextually adaptive and Bayesian optimised bidirectional LSTM model for modelling different household appliances' consumption patterns in a NILM operational framework. The model showed low accuracy in detecting the HPE appliance (AMPds), mainly due to recurring signal changes caused by external (seasonal) contextual conditions. Later in the same year, Kaselimi et al. [72] investigated the suitability of a GAN-based model for NILM. GAN-based models can generate longer instances of the signal waveform, thereby enhancing NILM modelling capability. The model includes a seeder component and generates specific appliance signatures in accordance with an appliance operation, and should accurately detect events occurring (e.g. switch-on events) during a day. The method was tested on two buildings, including one with a heat pump (from AMPds), with measurements performed for one month (17/5–17/6), when heat pumps are rarely in use. The model shows promising results for NILM on most appliances, performing as well or better than traditional and other deep learning methods for all appliances tested, but the study also shows that out of all appliances, all methods performed the worst for disaggregating the heat pump compared to other appliances (not for heating). This model was improved by Kaselimi in [73] by including a deep learning classifier in the discriminator component of GAN, which gave a slight improvement in disaggregation performance of the heat pump compared to [72].

Liu et al. [74] proposed a deep learning method for NILM, which used a GRU, as well as multi-feature fusion. The method considers the coupling relationship between the electrical signals of different appliances, as well as water and gas use, meaning that correlations between working states of appliances were considered in the disaggregation. They used an AMPds-dataset, which has a significant correlation between the working states of heat pump and furnace. The method improved the F1 score and accuracy greatly compared to methods that do not consider the relationship between the electricity use of the appliances, as well as the gas and water use.

Kianpoor et al. [75] proposed a deep adaptive ensemble filter based on various signal processing tools integrated with an LSTM for NILM. Their framework searches ensemble filtering techniques, including discrete wavelet transform, low-pass filter and seasonality decomposition, to find the best filtering method for disaggregating different flexible loads (e.g. heat pumps). The discrete wavelet transform gave best results for the heat pump combined with LSTM. Their study showed that using LSTM greatly improved performance compared to traditional methods, such as linear regression, and that introducing adaptive filtering improved the results even more, although the peaks of the heat pump power consumption are still not perfectly captured.

Zou et al. [76] introduced a method based on CNN and bidirectional LSTM (BiL-STM). In this approach, periodical changes in total demand (e.g. daily, weekly and seasonal variations) are disaggregated into corresponding frequency components and are correlated with the same frequency components in meteorological variables (e.g. temperature and solar irradiance), allowing selection of the combinations of frequency components with the strongest correlations as additional explanatory variables. Their study found that heating and lighting loads were identified with greater accuracy when the correlated frequency components were used as additional information during the disaggregation.

All of the research mentioned within this field has looked at datasets with resolutions of 1 min or higher. In 2022, Hosseini [77], however, suggested an LSTM-based method for disaggregating heating demand from the aggregated load profiles, with 15 min resolution, belonging to houses equipped with electric space heaters and water heaters. Their proposed method aims to identify major appliances by first extracting overall heating demand from the aggregated load before extracting the remaining appliances. To extract the electric space heaters, an LSTM network is used, with a sliding window that considers the past 7 instances of aggregated load and the past 8 instances of energy for the electric space heaters. It is worth noting that ambient conditions were not considered as input features in the latter disaggregation procedure. The remaining load is disaggregated through an unsupervised clustering procedure (Density-Based Spatial Clustering of Applications with Noise).

Deep supervised learning methods can be more difficult to interpret compared to traditional models and they require larger amounts of data and computational resources to train. To overcome the latter, reinforcement learning RL may be suitable for disaggregation of heating loads with high performance and less data.

4.3 Reinforcement Learning

Deep learning approaches typically require large datasets in the training procedure. Although many labelled datasets exist for developing and testing disaggregation techniques, providing a large amount of perfectly labelled training data for specific application may not always be feasible. RL and deep RL is an alternative data-driven approach which requires no labelled training data. In projects with data collection of energy use measurements in buildings, it can take a long time to acquire a full set of representative data. Algorithms developed for disaggregation of heating loads can benefit strongly from having data corresponding to more than one year, as the heating demand may vary greatly from one year to another. Considering ambient conditions, such as the outdoor temperature, could in addition improve the recognition of heating loads. With RL, one can start training the algorithm on a small dataset and continue to improve the learning algorithm as the dataset grows.

Only a few methods for disaggregation of heating loads in buildings based on RL have been proposed in the literature. Li [78] proposed an NILM recognition method based on adaptive K-nearest neighbours RL (AD-KNN-RL) and compared it to other models, such as the conventional KNN, genetic algorithm (GA) and Hidden Markov Model (HMM). The method was applied to an AMPds dataset and aimed at state recognition of 5–8 different appliances, including a heat pump. It proved that the accuracy of the state recognition of electrical appliances with simple state changes such as lamps and heat pumps is higher than for other electrical appliances, but that the accuracy of electrical identification is generally low for multi-state continuous changes. AD-KNN-RL proved to have the highest performance, while HMM performed the worst.

Zaoali et al. [79] used LSTM-based reinforcement Q-learning to disaggregate the REDD dataset. The experiment showed that the accuracy of the disaggregation was significantly improved by using this method, compared to using the deep learning approach, TFIDF-DAE, achieving an accuracy of 85%. The buildings 1, 2, 3, 4 and 6 from the REDD dataset were used for training of the model, while building number 4 was used to test the algorithm. Building numbers 2 and 3 have electric heaters, while building number 4 does not, so that the disaggregation of electric heaters from the aggregate load using this approach was not tested here.

Table 3. Overview of methods used for disaggregation of building electricity load in the literature.

	Ref	Year	method	B.cat	N buildings	Location	Dataset	Res	Relevant appliance	NILM-TK
Traditional methods and shallow algorithms	Liu et al. [54]	2022	Affinity propagation clustering (AP) and time-segmented state probability (TSSP)	SFH	1	Canada	AMPds	1 min	Heat pump	No
	Morch et al. [56]	2013	Linear regression with temperature dependency	Residential	75	Norway	EIDeK	1 h	Space heating	No
	Lien et al. [57]	2020	Linear regression to find average DHW consumption	Apartment and hotels	78	Norway	treASURE	1h	Space heating	No
	Najafi et al. [60]	2020	Feature selection, Extra trees regressor	Houses	20	TX, USA	Dataport	1h	Air conditioning	No
	Zaeri et al . [58].	2022	Unsupervised Time-series decomposition	Office	1	Ottawa, Canada	Original	1h	Unknown heating and cooling	No
	Amayri et al. [59]	2022	RF (NILM and interactive learning)	Houses	3	France	IRISE	1h and 10 min	HWH, EH and clothes dryer	No
	Balletti et al. [55]	2022	Mixed Integer Optimization	SFH	1	Canada, UK	AMPds, UKDALE (h1 and h2) and REFIT (h3 and H9)	1 min	Heat pump (AMPds)	No
Deep supervised learning	Kaselimi et al.[62]	2019	Bayes-Bi-LSTM	Residential	1	Canada	AMPds	1 min	HP	No
	Wang et al.[64]	2019	LSTM-RNN and LSTM-FF	Residential	1	Canada	AMPds	1 min	HP+HVAC	No
	Davies et al[65]	2019	CNN, FF	Residential	55	USA	PLAID	30 kHz	HVAC + heater	No
	Li et al.[66]	2019	CNN	SFH	1	Canada	AMPds	1 min	HP	No
	Wang et al.[67]	2019	LSTM-dAE	SFH	1	Canada	AMPds	1 min	HP	No
	Harell et al[68]	2019	CNN-wn	SFH	1	Canada	AMPds	1 min	HP	No
	Xia et al.[69]	2019	CNN-seq2seq	Residential	Unknown	UK, USA	UK-DALE, dataport	6s, 1 min	Air conditioner	No
	Xia et al. [70]	2019	CNN, DA-ResNet	Residential	Unknown	UK, USA	UK-DALE, dataport	6s, 1 min	Air conditioner	No
	Kaselimi et al. [71]	2020	CoBiLSTM	SFH	1	Canada	AMPds, REDD and REFIT	6s	HP	No
	Kaselimi et al. [72]	2020	CNN-dAE-GAN	SFH	Unknown. Results for 6 appliances presented.	Canada, UK	AMPds, REFIT	1 min	HP	Yes, for benchmarking
	Kaselimi et al. in [73]	2020	CNN-dAE- GRU-GAN	SFH	Unknown. Results for 6 appliances presented.	Canada, UK	AMPds, REFIT	1 min	HP	Yes, for benchmarking
	Xia et al.[63]	2020	CNN-LSTM	Residential	Selected appliances from 4 buildings	USA	REDD, dataport	1 min	HVAC	No
	Liu et al. al [74]	2021	GRU and multi feature fusion	Residential	1	Canada	AMPds	1 min	Heat pump and gas boiler	No
	Zou et al. [76]	2021	CNN-BiLSTM	Residential	6	Canada, UK	AMPds, UK-DALE and proprietary	1 min	Heat pump (AMPds)	Yes
	Hosseini [77]	2022	LSTM	SFH	10	Quebec	Original	15min	ESH (8-10 per house)	No
	Kianpoor et al.al [75]	2023	AEF LSTM	Residential	1	Canada	AMPds	1 min	Heat pump	No
RL	Li [78]	2020	AD-KNN-RL	SFH	1	Canada	AMPDS	1 min	1 HP and 7 EA	No
	Zaoali et al. [79]	2022	recurrent LSTM-RL-Q-learning	SFH/MFH	6	USA	REDD	0,33 Hz-15kHz	EH	No

5 Evaluation of Datasets and Requirements

The datasets described in Table 2 are both widely used and sometimes rarely used for the development of methods for disaggregation of building heating appliances, as shown in Sect. 4. The content of the datasets can be summarised as follows:

Building Category: 24 datasets are investigated. Four include measurements from commercial buildings and 22 include measurements from residential buildings – mostly from single-family houses but also some multi-family houses.

Sampling Rate: Most of the datasets have a frequency of 1 Hz or higher, while a few datasets have only very low resolution, of minutes or per hour.

Duration: The duration of the datasets varies between 1 day and several years, with a median value of 180 days.

Locations: The datasets are from different locations – 11 datasets are from buildings in Europe, 8 from North America, 3 from India and 1 from Korea. The datasets together represent buildings from both cold and warm climates.

Appliances: 12/24 datasets contain buildings with single measurements of heating appliances or heating loads, while the rest of the datasets have no measurements connected to space heating load.

Measurements: All contain measurements of power (active) or hourly energy use (apparent). Several datasets also contain corresponding measurements with current, voltage, phase factor, reactive power and phase angle.

NILMTK Compatibility: The majority of the datasets in Table 2 are available in the NILMTK format as hdf5 files and with available converters.

Most of the datasets investigated include high-resolution data (1 s or lower). However, for real world applications, energy measurement data is usually available at a much lower resolution (15–60 min). Hosseini [77] shows that their suggested model performs efficiently with low-resolution data (15 min) in identifying most of the ESH loads (electric heaters), although the model performs inadequately in capturing the peaks and causing unwanted variations in lower demand. Najafi et al. [60], however, achieved a high R2 value for recognising AC loads through the use of feature selection. High-resolution data measurements are widely used for development of disaggregation methods, but may not be applicable to hourly datasets, which are far more available and more commonly used in real-life applications.

Space heating loads are highly dependent on outdoor temperature, season, time of day, type of day (weekday/end) and building metadata (such as building type, heating appliances and energy efficiency, etc.) [6]. Buildings with electrical heating typically exhibit significant fluctuations in their load profiles. These fluctuations stem from the varying outdoor temperatures, which can differ substantially from year to year. Consequently, datasets with extended time spans prove exceptionally valuable. Most of the datasets in Table 2 contain less than one year of data.

Given the notable difference between information that is available in measured load profiles with low and high resolution, the corresponding pipelines benefit from being treated differently. The methods proposed for disaggregating high-resolution load profiles are typically designed to recognise patterns in different appliances and their states, while this information is often lost when moving into low resolution (15 min to 1 h). For the specific case of disaggregating the heating loads from low-resolution datasets, the pipeline may benefit from generating and employing features that are inspired by the thermal behaviour of buildings (e.g. the lagged values of ambient conditions such as outdoor temperature and the corresponding seasonality) to capture additional information that is not available in the load measurement's data.

Some datasets in Table 2 include measurements for heating appliances, but these are typically one single heating appliance per building. In the Norwegian setting, it is common to have more than one heating appliance per building, e.g. combinations of electric floor heating, electric panel heaters, air-to-air heat pump, electric boilers, electric water heaters, ground source heat pumps, etc. [80]. Several of these electric heating appliances and their combinations are not found in the existing datasets.

The availability of metadata varies for different datasets. The heating appliances and heating distribution system in a building greatly affect the use of electric heating appliances. An electric boiler used for both heating of domestic hot water and space heating typically has a different user pattern compared to an electric boiler solely used for one of these purposes. An air-to-air heat pump is typically used differently in a single-family house that also has access to non-electric heating options. The heating systems of the buildings in the different datasets are not always available to users, but could provide useful information for the disaggregation of the heating appliances.

While some datasets like AMPds contains hourly climate data, several of the datasets investigated include climate/ambient data or district heating data, in addition to measured electricity consumption. Space heating is highly dependent on outdoor temperature and climate conditions. This is rarely considered in traditional disaggregation approaches implemented in NILMTK. Although NILMTK can take in temperature and gas measurements, it is not utilised in the implemented methods. However, NILMTK currently does not support heating measurements from district heating.

6 Conclusion

This review paper has investigated existing approaches for disaggregation of space heating loads and appliances from buildings' total energy load that utilise traditional methods, shallow learning methods, deep supervised learning and RL methods. Previous research shows that several approaches have disaggregated single heating appliances from total electricity load. These methods are often applied to high-resolution energy measurements (50–60 Hz) from buildings, with varying durations of training datasets. Deep learning methods are shown to offer higher disaggregation performance compared to traditional and shallow learning methods such as FHMM, CO, Mean, etc. The review also shows that RL approaches for disaggregation are promising, but with a limited number of studies that can be further investigated in the future. Most of the disaggregation approaches investigated typically recognise and disaggregate single appliances, and the majority of them look at the heat pump from AMPds, or other single appliances such as heat pumps or electric space heaters from datasets with buildings with these appliances. However, few methods have been proposed in the literature for disaggregating total electricity use for space heating from the total electricity use in buildings with electric heating, or the loads of heat appliances in buildings with more than one heating appliance. At the same time, there is a demand for disaggregation algorithms tailored for cold climates that include electric heating from different heating options that work on low-frequency data. However, only a few methods have considered disaggregating the consumption of heating units based on features that are inspired from the thermal behaviour of buildings (e.g. lagged values of outdoor conditions or relationship between heating consumption and outdoor temperature). In most of the studies, power consumed by heating systems is commonly disaggregated using the same pipelines as those utilised for other appliances. Recommendations for future work include integrating deep supervised learning techniques with features inspired by building physics to develop pipelines for disaggregating heating loads from low-resolution aggregate electricity data, as this method shows significant promise, and as building energy data is mostly available as low-resolution data. Additionally, there remains a notable research gap in the disaggregation of heating loads in both commercial and public buildings, as well as in the application of reinforcement learning methods for this purpose.

Acknowledgment. This article has been written within the research project "Coincidence factors and peak loads of buildings in the Norwegian low carbon society" (COFACTOR). The authors gratefully acknowledge the support from the Research Council of Norway (project number 326891), research partners, industry partners and data providers.

References

1. IEA (2022). https://www.iea.org/reports/buildings
2. Energy Transitions Commission, 'Making Mission Possible', Health Prog. **76**(6), 45–7, 60 (2020)
3. SSB, 11561: Energibalanse. Tilgang og forbruk, etter energiprodukt 1990 - 2018 (2020). https://www.ssb.no/statbank/table/11561. Accessed 02 Jun 2023
4. Ødegården, L., Bhantana, S.: Status og prognoser for kraftsystemet 2018 rapportnr. 103–2018. NVE (2018). http://publikasjoner.nve.no/rapport/2018/rapport2018_103.pdf. Accessed 31 May 2023
5. NVE, NVE.no: Smarte strømmålere (AMS) (2022). https://www.nve.no/reguleringsmyndigh eten/kunde/strom/stromkunde/smarte-stroemmaalere-ams/
6. Lindberg, K.B.: Doctoral thesis Impact of Zero Energy Buildings on the Power System A study of load profiles, flexibility and Impact of Zero Energy Buildings on the Power System A study of load profiles , flexibility and system, vol. 6 (2017)
7. Carrie Armel, K., Gupta, A., Shrimali, G., Albert, A.: Is disaggregation the holy grail of energy efficiency? The case of electricity. Energy Policy **52**, 213–234 (2013). https://doi.org/10.1016/j.enpol.2012.08.062
8. Hart, G.W.: Nonintrusive appliance load monitoring. Proc. IEEE **80**(12), 1870–1891, (1992). https://doi.org/10.1109/5.192069
9. Huber, P., Calatroni, A., Rumsch, A., Paice, A.: Review on deep neural networks applied to low-frequency NILM. Energies **14**(9), Art. no. 9, Jan. 2021. https://doi.org/10.3390/en1409 2390
10. Zeifman, M., Roth, K.: Nonintrusive appliance load monitoring: Review and outlook. IEEE Trans. Consum. Electron. **57**(1), 76–84 (2011). https://doi.org/10.1109/TCE.2011.5735484
11. Makonin, S.: Approaches to Non-Intrusive Load Monitoring (NILM) in the Home APPROACHES TO NON-INTRUSIVE LOAD MONITORING (NILM) by Doctor of Philosophy School of Computing Science, no. October 2012, 2014

12. Kong, W., Dong, Z.Y., Hill, D.J., Luo, F., Xu, Y.: Improving nonintrusive load monitoring efficiency via a hybrid programing method. IEEE Trans. Ind. Inform. **12**(6), 2148–2157 (2016). https://doi.org/10.1109/TII.2016.2590359

13. Farinaccio, L., Zmeureanu, R.: Using a pattern recognition approach to disaggregate the total electricity consumption in a house into the major end-uses. Energy Build. **30**(3), 245–259 (1999). https://doi.org/10.1016/S0378-7788(99)00007-9

14. Figueiredo, M.B., De Almeida, A., Ribeiro, B.: An experimental study on electrical signature identification of non-intrusive load monitoring (NILM) systems. Lect. Notes Comput. Sci. Subser. Lect. Notes Artif. Intell. Lect. Notes Bioinforma., vol. 6594 LNCS, no. PART 2, pp. 31–40 (2011). https://doi.org/10.1007/978-3-642-20267-4_4

15. Nguyen, K.T., et al.: Event detection and disaggregation algorithms for NIALM system. In: NILM Workshop, June 2014, pp. 2–5 (2014)

16. Gonçalves, H., Ocneanu, A., Bergés, M.: Unsupervised disaggregation of appliances using aggregated consumption data. Environ (2011)

17. Wang, L., Luo, X., Zhang, W.: Unsupervised energy disaggregation with factorial hidden Markov models based on generalized backfitting algorithm. In: EEE International Conference of IEEE Region 10 (TENCON 2013) (2013)

18. Egarter, D., Bhuvana, V.P., Elmenreich, W.: PALDi: online load disaggregation via particle filtering. IEEE Trans. Instrum. Meas. **64**(2), 467–477 (2015). https://doi.org/10.1109/TIM.2014.2344373

19. Wu, Q., Wang, F.: Concatenate convolutional neural networks for non-intrusive load monitoring across complex background. Energies **12**(8) (2019). https://doi.org/10.3390/en12081572

20. Kelly, J., et al.: NILMTK v0.2: a non-intrusive load monitoring toolkit for large scale datasets: demo abstract. In: Proceedings of the 1st ACM Conference on Embedded Systems for Energy-Efficient Buildings, in BuildSys '14. Nov. 2014, pp. 182–183, Association for Computing Machinery, New York. https://doi.org/10.1145/2674061.2675024

21. Batra, N., et al. Towards reproducible state-of-the-art energy disaggregation. In: Proceedings of the 6th ACM International Conference on Systems for Energy-Efficient Buildings, Cities, and Transportation, Nov. 2019, pp. 193–202. ACM, New York. https://doi.org/10.1145/3360322.3360844

22. Virtsionis, N., Gkalinikis, C., Nalmpantis, Vrakas, D.: Torch-NILM: an effective deep learning toolkit for non-intrusive load monitoring in pytorch. Energies **15**(7), Art. no. 7, Jan. 2022. https://doi.org/10.3390/en15072647

23. Lindberg, K.B.: Impact of zero energy buildings on the power system, p. 192

24. Abbasi, A.R.: Fault detection and diagnosis in power transformers: a comprehensive review and classification of publications and methods. Electr. Power Syst. Res. **209**, 107990 (2022). https://doi.org/10.1016/j.epsr.2022.107990

25. Makonin, S., Ellert, B., Bajić, I.V., Popowich, F.: Electricity, water, and natural gas consumption of a residential house in Canada from 2012 to 2014. Sci. Data **3**(1), Art. no. 1, Jun. 2016. https://doi.org/10.1038/sdata.2016.37

26. Himeur, Y., Ghanem, K., Alsalemi, A., Bensaali, F., Amira, A.: Artificial intelligence based anomaly detection of energy consumption in buildings: a review, current trends and new perspectives. Appl. Energy **287**, 116601 (2021). https://doi.org/10.1016/j.apenergy.2021.116601

27. Himeur, Y., Alsalemi, A., Bensaali, F., Amira, A., Al-Kababji, A.: Recent trends of smart nonintrusive load monitoring in buildings: a review, open challenges, and future directions. Int. J. Intell. Syst.Intell. Syst. **37**(10), 7124–7179 (2022). https://doi.org/10.1002/int.22876

28. Angelis, G.-F., Timplalexis, C., Krinidis, S., Ioannidis, D., Tzovaras, D.: NILM applications: Literature review of learning approaches, recent developments and challenges. Energy Build. **261**, 111951 (2022). https://doi.org/10.1016/j.enbuild.2022.111951

29. Ruano, A., Hernandez, A., Ureña, J., Ruano, M., Garcia, J.: NILM techniques for intelligent home energy management and ambient assisted living: a review. Energies **12**(11), Art. no. 11, January 2019. https://doi.org/10.3390/en12112203

30. Batra, N., Gulati, M., Singh, A., Srivastava, M.B.: It's Different: insights into home energy consumption in India. In: Proceedings of the 5th ACM Workshop on Embedded Systems for Energy-Efficient Buildings, in BuildSys'13. November 2013, pp. 1–8. Association for Computing Machinery, New York, November 2013. https://doi.org/10.1145/2528282.252 8293

31. Kelly, J., Knottenbelt, W.: The UK-DALE dataset, domestic appliance-level electricity demand and whole-house demand from five UK homes. Sci. Data **2**(1), Art. no. 1, March 2015. https://doi.org/10.1038/sdata.2015.7

32. 'NILMTK: Non-Intrusive Load Monitoring Toolkit'. nilmtk, Feb. 27, 2023 . https://github.com/nilmtk/nilmtk. Accessed 28 Feb 2023

33. Murray, D., Stankovic, L., Stankovic, V.: An electrical load measurements dataset of United Kingdom households from a two-year longitudinal study. Sci. Data **4**(1), Art. no. 1, January 2017. https://doi.org/10.1038/sdata.2016.122

34. Kolter, J.Z., Johnson, M.J.: REDD: A Public Dataset for Energy Disaggregation Research'

35. Beckel, C., Kleiminger, W., Cicchetti, R., Staake, T., Santini, S.: The ECO dataset and the performance of non-intrusive load monitoring algorithms. In: Proceedings of the 1st ACM Conference on Embedded Systems for Energy-Efficient Buildings, Memphis Tennessee: ACM, pp. 80–89, November 2014. https://doi.org/10.1145/2674061.2674064

36. Klemenjak, C., Kovatsch, C., Herold, M., Elmenreich, W.: A synthetic energy dataset for non-intrusive load monitoring in households. Sci. Data **7**(1), Art. no. 1, April 2020. https://doi.org/10.1038/s41597-020-0434-6

37. Shin, C., Lee, E., Han, J., Yim, J., Rhee, W., Lee, H.: The ENERTALK dataset, 15 Hz electricity consumption data from 22 houses in Korea. Sci. Data **6**(1), 193 (2019). https://doi.org/10.1038/s41597-019-0212-5

38. Household Electricity Survey - Data Briefing

39. Medico, R., et al.: A voltage and current measurement dataset for plug load appliance identification in households. Sci. Data **7**(1), Art. no. 1, February 2020. https://doi.org/10.1038/s41 597-020-0389-7

40. Anderson, K.D., Ocneanu, A.F., Benitez, D., Carlson, D., Rowe, A., Berges, M.: BLUED: a fully labeled public dataset for event-based non-intrusive load monitoring research, August 2023

41. Reinhardt, A., et al.: On the accuracy of appliance identification based on distributed load metering data, p. 9 (2012)

42. Maasoumy, M., Sanandaji, B.M., Poolla, K., Vincentelli, A.S.: BERDS-BERkeley EneRgy Disaggregation Dataset. https://tokhub.github.io/dbecd/links/berds.html. Accessed 24 Jan 2023

43. Monacchi, A., Egarter, D., Elmenreich, W., D'Alessandro, S., Tonello, A.M.: GREEND: an energy consumption dataset of households in Italy and Austria. In: 2014 IEEE International Conference on Smart Grid Communications (SmartGridComm), pp. 511–516, November 2014. https://doi.org/10.1109/SmartGridComm.2014.7007698

44. Uttama Nambi, A.S.N., Reyes Lua, A., Prasad, V.R.: LocED: location-aware energy disaggregation framework. In: Proceedings of the 2nd ACM International Conference on Embedded Systems for Energy-Efficient Built Environments, Seoul South Korea: ACM, pp. 45–54, November 2015. https://doi.org/10.1145/2821650.2821659

45. Parson, O., et al.: Dataport and NILMTK: a building dataset designed for non-intrusive load monitoring. In: 2015 IEEE Global Conference on Signal and Information Processing (GlobalSIP), Orlando, FL, USA: IEEE, pp. 210–214, December 2015. https://doi.org/10.1109/Glo balSIP.2015.7418187

46. Makonin, S., Wang, Z.J., Tumpach, C.: RAE: the rainforest automation energy dataset for smart grid meter data analysis. Data **3**(1), 8 (2018). https://doi.org/10.3390/data3010008

47. Rashid, H., Singh, P., Singh, A.: I-BLEND, a campus-scale commercial and residential buildings electrical energy dataset. Sci. Data **6**(1), Art. no. 1, February 2019. https://doi.org/10.1038/sdata.2019.15

48. Basu, K., Debusschere, V., Bacha, S.: Residential appliance identification and future usage prediction from smart meter. In: IECON 2013 - 39th Annual Conference of the IEEE Industrial Electronics Society, pp. 4994–4999, November 2013. https://doi.org/10.1109/IECON.2013.6699944

49. Barker, S., Mishra, A., Irwin, D., Cecchet, E., Shenoy, P., Albrecht, J.: Smart*: an open dataset and tools for enabling research in sustainable homes. In: Proceedings of SustKDD, January 2012

50. Batra, N., Parson, O., Berges, M., Singh, A., Rogers, A.: A comparison of non-intrusive load monitoring methods for commercial and residential buildings (2014)

51. Sæle, H., Rosenberg, E., Feilberg, N.: State-of-the-art Projects for estimating the electricityu end-use demand (2010). Accessed 20 Mar 2023. https://www.sintef.no/globalassets/project/eldek/publisering/tr-a6999-state-of-the-art-projects-for-estimating-the-electricity-end-use-demand.pdf

52. Andersen, K.H., Krekling Lien, S., Byskov Lindberg, K., Taxt Walnum, H., Sartori, I.: Further development and validation of the "PROFet" energy demand load profiles estimator. In: presented at the 2021 Building Simulation Conference, September 2021. https://doi.org/10.26868/25222708.2021.30159

53. Schaffer, M., Tvedebrink, T., Marszal-Pomianowska, A.: Three years of hourly data from 3021 smart heat meters installed in Danish residential buildings. Sci. Data **9**(1), Art. no. 1, July 2022. https://doi.org/10.1038/s41597-022-01502-3

54. Liu, L., et al.: Non-intrusive load monitoring method considering the time-segmented state probability. IEEE Access **10**, 39627–39637 (2022). https://doi.org/10.1109/ACCESS.2022.3167132

55. Balletti, M., Piccialli, V., Sudoso, A.M.: Mixed-integer nonlinear programming for state-based non-intrusive load monitoring. IEEE Trans. Smart Grid **13**(4), 3301–3314 (2022). https://doi.org/10.1109/TSG.2022.3152147

56. Morch, A., Sæle, H., Feilberg, N., Lindberg, K.B.: Method for development and segmentation of load profiles for different final customers and appliances. In: ECEEE 2013 Summer Stud. Proc., 2013, Accessed: Mar. 20, 2023. https://www.eceee.org/library/conference_proceedings/eceee_Summer_Studies/2013/7-monitoring-and-evaluation/method-for-development-and-segmentation-of-load-profiles-for-different-final-customers-and-appliances/

57. Lien, S.K., Ivanko, D., Sartori, I.: Domestic hot water decomposition from measured total heat load in Norwegian buildings. SINTEF Academic Press, 2020. Accessed: Jan. 17, 2023. https://ntnuopen.ntnu.no/ntnu-xmlui/handle/11250/2684373

58. Zaeri, N., Gunay, H.B., Ashouri, A.: Unsupervised energy disaggregation using time series decomposition for commercial buildings. In: Proceedings of the 9th ACM International Conference on Systems for Energy-Efficient Buildings, Cities, and Transportation, Boston Massachusetts: ACM, pp. 373–377, November 2022. https://doi.org/10.1145/3563357.3566155

59. Amayri, M., Silva, C.S., Pombeiro, H., Ploix, S.: Flexibility characterization of residential electricity consumption: A machine learning approach. Sustain. Energy Grids Netw. **32**, 100801 (2022)

60. Najafi, B., Di Narzo, L., Rinaldi, F., Arghandeh, R.: Machine learning based disaggregation of air-conditioning loads using smart meter data. IET Gener. Transm. Distrib.Distrib. **14**(21), 4755–4762 (2020). https://doi.org/10.1049/iet-gtd.2020.0698

61. Miller, C., Meggers, F.: Mining electrical meter data to predict principal building use, performance class, and operations strategy for hundreds of non-residential buildings. Energy Build. **156**, 360–373 (2017). https://doi.org/10.1016/j.enbuild.2017.09.056

62. Kaselimi, M., Doulamis, N., Doulamis, A., Voulodimos, A., Protopapadakis, E.: Bayesian-optimized bidirectional LSTM regression model for non-intrusive load monitoring. In: ICASSP 2019 - 2019 IEEE International Conference on Acoustics, Speech and Signal Processing (ICASSP), Brighton, United Kingdom: IEEE, pp. 2747–2751, May 2019. https://doi.org/10.1109/ICASSP.2019.8683110

63. Xia, M., Liu, W., Wang, K., Song, W., Chen, C., Li, Y.: Non-intrusive load disaggregation based on composite deep long short-term memory network. Expert Syst. Appl. **160**, 113669 (2020). https://doi.org/10.1016/j.eswa.2020.113669

64. Wang, J., El Kababji, S., Graham, C., Srikantha, P.: Ensemble-based deep learning model for non-intrusive load monitoring. In: 2019 IEEE Electrical Power and Energy Conference (EPEC), pp. 1–6, October 2019. https://doi.org/10.1109/EPEC47565.2019.9074816

65. Davies, P., Dennis, J., Hansom, J., Martin, W., Stankevicius, A., Ward, L.: Deep neural networks for appliance transient classification. In: ICASSP 2019 - 2019 IEEE International Conference on Acoustics, Speech and Signal Processing (ICASSP), May 2019, pp. 8320–8324. doi: https://doi.org/10.1109/ICASSP.2019.8682658

66. Li, C., Zheng, R., Liu, M., Zhang, S.: A fusion framework using integrated neural network model for non-intrusive load monitoring. In: 2019 Chinese Control Conference (CCC), Guangzhou, China: IEEE, pp. 7385–7390, July 2019. https://doi.org/10.23919/ChiCC.2019.8865721

67. Wang, T.S., Ji, T.Y., Li, M.S.: A new approach for supervised power disaggregation by using a denoising autoencoder and recurrent LSTM network. In: 2019 IEEE 12th International Symposium on Diagnostics for Electrical Machines, Power Electronics and Drives (SDEMPED), Toulouse, France: IEEE, pp. 507–512, August 2019. https://doi.org/10.1109/DEMPED.2019.8864870

68. Harell, A., Makonin, S., Bajic, I.V.: Wavenilm: a causal neural network for power disaggregation from the complex power signal. In: ICASSP 2019 - 2019 IEEE International Conference on Acoustics, Speech and Signal Processing (ICASSP), Brighton, United Kingdom: IEEE, pp. 8335–8339, May 2019. https://doi.org/10.1109/ICASSP.2019.8682543

69. Xia, M., Liu, W., Wang, K., Zhang, X., Xu, Y.: Non-intrusive load disaggregation based on deep dilated residual network. Electr. Power Syst. Res. **170**, 277–285 (2019). https://doi.org/10.1016/j.epsr.2019.01.034

70. Xia, M., Liu, W., Xu, Y., Wang, K., Zhang, X.: Dilated residual attention network for load disaggregation. Neural Comput. Appl. **31**(12), 8931–8953 (2019). https://doi.org/10.1007/s00521-019-04414-3

71. Kaselimi, M., Doulamis, N., Voulodimos, A., Protopapadakis, E., Doulamis, A.: Context aware energy disaggregation using adaptive bidirectional LSTM models. IEEE Trans. Smart Grid **11**(4), 3054–3067 (2020). https://doi.org/10.1109/TSG.2020.2974347

72. Kaselimi, M., Voulodimos, A., Protopapadakis, E., Doulamis, N., Doulamis, A.: EnerGAN: a generative adversarial network for energy disaggregation. In: ICASSP 2020 - 2020 IEEE International Conference on Acoustics, Speech and Signal Processing (ICASSP), Barcelona, Spain: IEEE, pp. 1578–1582, May 2020. https://doi.org/10.1109/ICASSP40776.2020.9054342

73. Kaselimi, M., Doulamis, N., Voulodimos, A., Doulamis, A., Protopapadakis, E.: EnerGAN++: a generative adversarial gated recurrent network for robust energy disaggregation. IEEE Open J. Signal Process. **2**, 1–16 (2021). https://doi.org/10.1109/OJSP.2020.3045829

74. Liu, H., Liu, C., Tian, L., Zhao, H., Liu, J.: Non-intrusive load disaggregation based on deep learning and multi-feature fusion. In: 2021 3rd International Conference on Smart Power & Internet Energy Systems (SPIES), Shanghai, China: IEEE, pp. 210–215, September 2021. https://doi.org/10.1109/SPIES52282.2021.9633819

75. Kianpoor, N., Hoff, B., Østrem, T.: Deep adaptive ensemble filter for non-intrusive residential load monitoring. Sensors 23(4), Art. no. 4, Jan. 2023. https://doi.org/10.3390/s23041992

76. Zou, M., Zhu, S., Gu, J., Korunovic, L.M., Djokic, S.Z.: Heating and lighting load disaggregation using frequency components and convolutional bidirectional long short-term memory method. Energies 14(16), Art. no. 16, Jan. 2021. https://doi.org/10.3390/en14164831

77. Hosseini, S.S., Delcroix, B., Henao, N., Agbossou, K., Kelouwani, S.: A case study on obstacles to feasible NILM solutions for energy disaggregation in quebec residences. Power 2, 4 (2022)

78. Li, H.: A Non-intrusive home load identification method based on adaptive reinforcement learning algorithm. IOP Conf. Ser. Mater. Sci. Eng. 853(1), 012030 (2020). https://doi.org/10.1088/1757-899X/853/1/012030

79. Zaouali, K., Ammari, M.L., Bouallegue, R.: LSTM-based reinforcement q learning model for non intrusive load monitoring. In: Barolli, L., Hussain, F., Enokido, T. (eds.) Advanced Information Networking and Applications, pp. 1–13. Lecture Notes in Networks and Systems. Springer, Cham (2022). https://doi.org/10.1007/978-3-030-99619-2_1

80. NVE and SSB, Oppvarming i boliger. Kartlegging av oppvarmingsutstyr of effektiviseringstiltak i husholdningene. NVE Rapport 85–2014 (2014). Accessed 23 Mar 2023. https://publikasjoner.nve.no/rapport/2014/rapport2014_85.pdf

Incorporating Resilience into the IoT-Based Smart Buildings Architecture

Sera Syarmila Sameon[1]([⊠]) [iD], Salman Yussof[1] [iD], Asmidar Abu Bakar[1] [iD],
and Bo Nørregaard Jørgensen[2]

[1] Institute of Informatics and Computing in Energy, Universiti Tenaga Nasional, Kajang,
Malaysia
sera@uniten.edu.my
[2] Center for Energy Informatics, University of Southern Denmark Name, Odense, Denmark

Abstract. The design of IoT-based smart buildings places great emphasis on network infrastructure and the integration of resilience into the overall system. The research aims to develop a methodology that comprehensively integrates resilience into the design of IoT-based smart buildings. The study reviews the existing literature on IoT-based smart buildings, emphasizing energy efficiency through the design of resilient architecture platforms. Fundamental aspects of resilience architecture in IoT-based smart buildings are explored, along with an examination of current research efforts and challenges in IoT resilience. The methodology employed for integrating resilience into the architecture design is described, revealing the utilization of the Design Science Research (DSR) methodology to enhance the architecture's fault tolerance, survivability, and adaptability. The paper concludes with a summary of key findings and suggests future research directions for further enhancing the resilience of IoT-based smart building architectures.

Keywords: Resilience Architecture · Energy Efficiency · Smart Building

1 Introduction

One of the most significant and complex issues for smart cities is energy demand [1]. With the ever-growing standard of living, it is inevitable that energy consumption will continue to rise. The International Energy Agency (IEA), reports buildings are responsible for about one-third of global primary energy consumption and about one-third of total direct and indirect energy-related Greenhouse Gases (GHGs) emissions [2]. Not only that, but it also expected that energy demand in buildings will increase globally by 50% by 2050 based on projected growth in the absence of effective actions to improve building energy efficiency [3]. In the Southeast Asia region, there is an anticipated doubling of electricity demand by 2040 [4]. This persistent increase in energy demand, together with the limited supply of conventional energy reserves, necessitates a global effort to address these issues. One of the initiatives proposed on 30 November 2016 involves updating the Energy Performance of Buildings Directive (EPBD) with the aim of promoting the adoption of smart technology in buildings and monitor the energy performance of buildings throughout Europe [5]. Therefore, it is very important to design buildings to provide resilient infrastructure that can be adapted to environmental changes.

© The Author(s), under exclusive license to Springer Nature Switzerland AG 2024
B. N. Jørgensen et al. (Eds.): EI.A 2023, LNCS 14467, pp. 202–212, 2024.
https://doi.org/10.1007/978-3-031-48649-4_12

Smart buildings are defined as buildings that use information and communication technology to improve efficiency, performance, and sustainability and consider as ideal solution due to their focus on energy efficiency and the integration of sustainable and resilient infrastructure [6–9]. By integrating with other Internet of Things (IoT) technologies, energy consumption can be monitored through smart buildings and make necessary adjustments. In addition, smart buildings play an important role in resilient infrastructure development by enabling rapid response during natural disasters such as floods or earthquakes [10]. The lighting system in the building, for example, will be automatically switched off through a smart system in the event of a drastic change in the electricity source caused by a flood [11]. To mitigate potential losses, early intervention measures can be employed, such as the use of indoor sensors to detect and respond to incidents. Besides resilient architecture, several approaches and strategies have been studied focusing on energy efficiency in smart building IoT-based implementation. These includes passive design [12–14], Energy Management Systems (EMS) [15–17], energy-efficient Heating, Ventilation, and Air Conditioning (HVAC) systems [18, 19], Building Energy Management Systems (BEMS) [20, 21], energy-efficient lighting systems [18, 22, 23] and, advanced metering and energy monitoring [24].

Beginning in the late 1990s, building design began to be oriented around sustainable principles driven by strict standards. However, given the current effects of climate change, these sustainable practices alone are no longer sufficient. Simultaneously, resilient features have received significant attention in building design considerations [25]. The goal is to ensure the long-term durability of the building, resist extreme weather due to climate change [25], and minimize environmental impact [26]. Therefore, to ensure the operation efficiency and effectiveness of smart buildings, advanced technology like smart sensors must be integrated into the building [27].

The deployment of IoT plays a vital role in achieving these objectives. However, IoT consist of a variety of heterogeneous devices over IoT layers, which can grow in scale and complexity. Enabling IoT sensing technology in buildings presents challenges when it comes to merging and networking incompatible sensing and IoT devices, as well as ensuring data security.

Thus, an IoT network necessitates a resilience architecture that supports intelligent search, data recovery, failure detection, and dynamic and autonomous network maintenance [28]. There are a few parameters that have been considered when designing a resilience architecture smart building with IoT-based smart building such as redundant and diverse communication networks [29], robustness [27], interoperability and standardization [31, 32], edge computing [33] and local processing [34], real-time monitoring and analytics [35, 36], scalability and flexibility [31, 32], and, energy management and efficiency [28, 37, 38]. These parameters help ensure that the building can withstand and recover from disruptions while maintaining efficient and effective operations.

The aim of this research is to develop a methodology that comprehensively integrates resilience into the design of IoT-based smart buildings. This approach involves a thorough examination of network components and their interconnections, with a specific emphasis on guaranteeing both system resilience and energy efficiency. The rest of the paper is organized as follows. Section 2 provides a review of the literature on IoT-based smart buildings. Section 3 elaborates on the fundamental aspects of resilience architecture in the context of IoT-based smart buildings. Section 4 presents a discussion of the current state of research, including related work, challenge and effort in IoT resilience. Section 5 outlines the methodology employed to incorporate resilience into the architecture design. Finally, Sect. 6 concludes the study, summarizes the key findings, and proposes future research directions.

2   IoT-Based Smart Building

Figure 1 show the IoT architecture layer which serves as the fundamental framework for the IoT infrastructure. It enables the seamless integration of diverse systems and technologies, contributing to the enhanced efficiency and effectiveness of the smart building ecosystem.

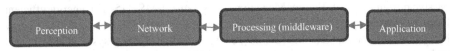

Fig. 1. IoT Architecture Layer

Based on the IoT architecture layer discussed above, [39, 40] proposes an IoT-based architecture for managing energy consumption and efficiency in smart buildings. This architecture incorporates a network of sensors and actuators that collect and measure data from various building systems. The collected data is then stored in a cloud database, allowing authorized parties to access and monitor the building's performance.

In the context of the smart building, continuous monitoring of energy consumption is prioritized to ensure occupant comfort and operational efficiency [41, 42]. IoT sensors and connected devices in smart buildings generate valuable data for analytics [43]. This data enables insights, optimization opportunities, and improvements in energy efficiency and user experience within the building. The transportation of data and instructions occurs through the building's data network. Therefore, two key elements are essential for a building to become smart: automation through a Building Management System (BMS) and connectivity facilitated by network infrastructure.

Findings by [44] also state that the use of IoT in smart buildings will generate several applications: (i) facilities management to maintain efficient services; (ii) energy management to manage energy consumption in optimizing the operational efficiency; and (iii) enhancement of interior comfort to ensure comfortable living conditions for building occupants.

By integrating the IoT-based architecture and leveraging the data generated by IoT sensors, smart buildings can efficiently manage energy consumption, ensure occupant comfort, and enhance operational efficiency.

3   The Fundamental of Resilience Architecture

According to author [45], "The resiliency of a system is defined by its capability (i) to resist external perturbance and internal failures; (ii) to recover and enter stable state(s); and (iii) to adapt its structure and behavior to constant change." In the context of network resilience, the study conducted by [46, 47] defines it as the ability to resist the degree of movement towards impaired service while maintaining an acceptable level of service. A challenge, is an event that triggers faults and errors, impacting the normal operation of the network [48]. If these errors propagate, it can ultimately lead to a network failure. The definitions provided by [46–48] shed light on the importance of resilience in both system and network contexts. Resilience involves the ability to withstand external disturbances and internal failures, recover effectively, and adapt to constant changes [2]. In the network realm, resilience is crucial in maintaining service levels and mitigating the impact of challenges that can disrupt normal network operations.

Resilience architecture enhances flexibility and adaptability [49], optimizing energy use based on real-time data in smart buildings. It integrates advanced monitoring and control systems for continuous energy consumption monitoring and optimization [18], enabling proactive maintenance and improving energy efficiency. Additionally, it facilitates rapid service recovery from disruptive events [50, 51], such as natural disasters or equipment failures. This capability helps minimize ensuring a quick return to normal operation and reduces the impact on energy efficiency [12].

The taxonomy of resilience, resilient architecture, and resilient mechanisms pertinent to IoT of previous and current research works were discussed by [52]. The large-scale deployment of IoT in buildings increases the chances of component faults, which can result in system malfunctions and unpredictable changes in network topology [53, 54]. Moreover, as the number of IoT devices continues to grow, several significant challenges may arise in the development of a robust IoT architecture. It is essential to anticipate and mitigate these challenges to ensure the successful integration and utilization of many IoT devices within smart building operation. By effectively addressing these challenges, the smartness of a building can be sustained, ultimately leading to the development of a resilient building over time.

4   Related Works on Challenges and Efforts in IoT Resilience

In response to these challenges, numerous efforts have been dedicated to developing resilience architecture for IoT-based smart building. Several specific solutions have been explored to tackle the complexity of IoT-based resilience architecture in different forms, focusing on enhancing its robustness and adaptability for effective implementation in diverse contexts.

The design of IoT smart buildings, with its focus on network infrastructure and resilience integration, aligns with the resilient strategy proposed by [47]. This strategy emphasizes key steps such as defend, detect, remediate, recover, and diagnose, refine $(D^2 R^2 + DR)$. It incorporates redundancy and diversity to prevent network failures and support changes in network topology. The challenge of network resilience, as defined in [55], involves providing a backup path within a minimal timeframe to ensure uninterrupted connectivity. Addressing this challenge requires swiftly establishing at least one backup path. Similarly, [28] emphasizes the need to determine the maximum number of failed nodes or links the network can withstand while still performing well. Another factor for sustaining network operation is having resilient traffic, as described in [56]—traffic resilience relates to how quickly a network can recover from service interruptions.

To effectively address this challenge, the focus should be on minimizing downtime and promptly restoring services. This involves the identification of critical network vertices based on latency-aware resiliency metrics. These metrics help determine the parts of the network that are most vital for swift recovery from disruptions, ensuring the network's resilience.

Meanwhile, [57] conducted research on a complex IoT process chain, emphasizing the significance of acknowledging interconnections within IoT systems when formally addressing resilience challenges. In this context, the researcher views the IoT system as a network consisting of interconnected activities, activity nodes, and links connecting these activities and processes. They also introduced a resiliency analysis approach using a graph-based mechanism and assessed the resilience of IoT chains by evaluating the performance and availability of the activity graph both before and after disruptions affecting critical components.

In response to the challenge posed by the expansion of the IoT, researchers in [58, 59] have introduced a framework for Wireless Sensor Networks (WSNs). This framework harnesses the resilience and coordination capabilities of IoT devices within WSNs. Meanwhile, Le et al. [60] suggest three different approaches that exhibit superior performance compared to the conventional Routing Protocol for Low-Power and Lossy Networks (RPL) solution. This innovation in routing protocols addresses critical challenges within the IoT and WSN domains, where conserving energy, reducing delays, ensuring reliable packet delivery, and balancing network loads are paramount concerns. To tackle the issue of unreliable communication in IoT services, an innovative architecture is suggested by [61]. This architecture aims to bolster the resilience of IoT infrastructure by incorporating trustworthy middleware. These advancements present promising opportunities to strengthen the reliability and efficiency of IoT and WSN systems.

Several studies have also been conducted that focused on enhancing the resilience of services in IoT networks to improve the reliability and robustness of IoT systems. Shammari et al. [28] developed a framework using Mixed Integer Linear Programming (MILP) to enhance service resilience in IoT networks, consequently improved network performance through optimized node and route selection. Basnayake et al. [62] introduced an AI-based smart building automation controller (AIBSBAC) that prioritizes user comfort, safety, and energy efficiency, with the added advantages of easy installation and plug-and-play compatibility.

Numerous studies have been dedicated to tackling the challenges of constructing a robust IoT infrastructure for efficient big data management. Bashir et al. [63] presents a reference architecture that emphasizes the importance of integrating real-time IoT data management, analytics, and autonomous control within smart buildings, utilizing the Integrated Big Data Management and Analytics (IBDMA) framework. Another publication [64] provides guidance on establishing and maintaining a comprehensive system featuring a resilient Data-Flow Path. This system effectively retrieves pertinent sensor data and handles abnormal data occurrences.

The existing literature falls short in providing concrete guidelines and comprehensive implementation architectures concerning the enhancement of the resilient network layer in IoT-based smart buildings. It is evident that additional research is essential to bridge this gap and generate practical solutions that offer clear and actionable guidance in designing and implementing robust and resilient architectural frameworks within the domain of smart buildings.

5 Incorporating Resilience into the Design

This section presents the proposed method for integrating resilience into the design. To create a resilient IoT smart building network, the study will employ the Design Science Research (DSR) methodology, which includes steps such as problem identification, design and development, evaluating outcomes, and reflection on the process, as shown in Fig. 2. This design will include $D^2R^2 + DR$ measures to increase system resilience by incorporating redundancy and diversity to prevent network failures and support changes in network topology. The research will focus on two important metrics, Betweenness Centrality (BC) and Closeness Centrality (CC), which are commonly used to analyze network resilience and robustness.

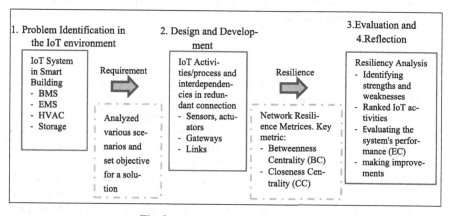

Fig. 2. DSR Methodology approach

BC identifies nodes that have a crucial role in maintaining efficient communication across the network. If these nodes become inaccessible, it can severely disrupt network traffic. In contrast, CC measures how fast a node can connect to all other nodes in the network. Nodes with low CC are closely connected to others, facilitating rapid information dissemination. Nodes with high CC help in quickly spreading information during emergencies or component failures, ensuring that critical data reaches its destination promptly. These two metrics were selected because, as per [57], IoT node activities are interdependent on each other and on the network links. Therefore, BC and CC are suitable for evaluating IoT network performance and availability.

The resilience analysis process commences with the definition of metric parameters. In this study, BC and CC have been selected as the resiliency metrics. Subsequently, after establishing these resilience metrics, the study proceeds to the resiliency assessment phase. During this stage, IoT activities (or services) are identified, and controlled disruptions are introduced to evaluate the strengths and weaknesses of the proposed design. This process contributes to the formulation of a resilience strategy, a key step in the subsequent phase of analysis, known as resiliency enhancement.

In the resiliency enhancement phase, IoT activities are ranked to assess their impact on resiliency. To facilitate this analysis, three levels of ranking have been identified. These levels include: (i) connected component analysis, (ii) end-to-end path analysis, and (iii) traffic management analysis. In evaluating the performance, Evaluation Criteria (EC) can be employed, as recommended by [63]. These criteria serve as guidelines for assessing the performance and effectiveness of the designed system. In the context of this study, a total of four specific criteria have been carefully identified and chosen. With the goal of achieving efficacy, the criteria encompass efficiency, reliability, functionality, and robustness. These criteria were selected primarily due to their direct relevance to the research objectives.

The performance of the network can be measured and evaluated under different scenarios. Design and performance analysis can be conducted using techniques such as graph-based modeling, mathematical calculations, and simulations. These approaches enable a comprehensive understanding of the network's behavior and assist in developing an efficient and resilient design.

6 Conclusion

In conclusion, the development of resilience architecture in IoT-based smart buildings is a crucial aspect in ensuring the robustness and adaptability of these systems. The integration of resilient features into the overall system design is essential for addressing potential disruptions and enhancing performance. However, several challenges need to be addressed, such as complex integration, compatibility of devices and protocols, data security and privacy concerns, and energy efficiency optimization.

Future work in this field should focus on proposing a comprehensive reference architecture that specifically addresses the resilience requirements of IoT-based smart buildings. This reference architecture should provide clear guidelines and implementation strategies for integrating resilient features into the system design. It should consider the unique characteristics of smart buildings, including diverse sensors and actuators, network connectivity, and data management.

By proposing a robust and comprehensive reference architecture, researchers can provide practical guidance for designing resilient IoT-based smart buildings. This will pave the way for the development of more efficient, reliable, and sustainable smart building systems that can effectively handle disruptions and ensure the long-term resilience of the infrastructure.

References

1. Mattoni, B., Gugliermetti, F., Bisegna, F.: A multilevel method to assess and design the renovation and integration of smart cities. Sustain. Cities Soc. **15**, 105–119 (2015). Accessed 13 July 2023
2. Amasyali, K., El-Gohary, N.M.: A review of data-driven building energy consumption prediction studies. Renewable Sustainable Energy Rev. **81**(January 2016), 1192–1205 (2018). https://doi.org/10.1016/j.rser.2017.04.095

3. Gunasingh, S., Wang, N., Ahl, D., Schuetter, S.: Climate resilience and the design of smart buildings. In: Smart Cities: Foundations, Principles, Applications, pp. 641–667 (2017)
4. The ASEAN Post Team. (2018, September 23). The cost of cooling down (2018). https://the aseanpost.com/article/cost-cooling-down. Accessed 13 July 2023
5. EC—European Commission. Buildings. https://ec.europa.eu/energy/en/topics/energy-effici ency/buildings. Accessed 1 Dec 2022
6. Amaxilatis, D., Akrivopoulos, O., Mylonas, G., Chatzigiannakis, I.: An IoT-based solution for monitoring a fleet of educational buildings focusing on energy efficiency. Sensors **17**, 2296 (2017)
7. Buckman, A.H., Mayfield, M., BM Beck, S.: What is a smart building? Smart Sustainable Built Environ. **3**, 92–109 (2014)
8. King, J., Perry, C.: Smart buildings: Using smart technology to save energy in existing buildings. Amercian Council for an Energy-Efficient Economy Washington, DC, USA (2017)
9. Metallidou, C.K., Psannis, K.E., Egyptiadou, E.A.: Energy efficiency in smart buildings: IoT approaches. IEEE Access **8**, 63679–63699 (2020)
10. Lokshina, I.V., Greguš, M., Thomas, W.L.: Application of integrated building information modeling, IoT and blockchain technologies in system design of a smart building. Procedia Comput. Sci. **160**, 497–502 (2019)
11. Al-Kodmany, K.: Sustainable high-rise buildings: toward resilient built environment. Front. Sustainable Cities **4**, 782007 (2022)
12. Casini, M.: Smart buildings: advanced materials and nanotechnology to improve energy-efficiency and environmental performance. Woodhead Publishing (2016)
13. Merabet, G.H., et al.: Intelligent building control systems for thermal comfort and energy-efficiency: a systematic review of artificial intelligence-assisted techniques. Renewable Sustainable Energy Rev. **144**, 110969 (2021)
14. Ochoa, C.E., Capeluto, I.G.: Strategic decision-making for intelligent buildings: comparative impact of passive design strategies and active features in a hot climate. Build. Environ. **43**, 1829–1839 (2008)
15. Al-Ghaili, A.M., Kasim, H., Al-Hada, N.M., Jørgensen, B.N., Othman, M., Wang, J.: Energy management systems and strategies in buildings sector: a scoping review. IEEE Access **9**, 63790–63813 (2021)
16. Lee, D., Cheng, C.-C.: Energy savings by energy management systems: a review. Renewable Sustainable Energy Rev. **56**, 760–777 (2016)
17. Salerno, I., Anjos, M.F., McKinnon, K., Gomez-Herrera, J.A.: Adaptable energy management system for smart buildings. J. Build. Eng. **44**, 102748 (2021)
18. Wei, C., Li, Y.: Design of energy consumption monitoring and energy-saving management system of intelligent building based on the Internet of things (2011)
19. Weng, T., Agarwal, Y., Computers, T.O.: From buildings to smart buildings—sensing and actuation to improve energy efficiency. IEEE Design **29**, 36–44 (2012)
20. Hannan, M.A., et al.: A review of internet of energy based building energy management systems: issues and recommendations. IEEE Access **6**, 38997–39014 (2018)
21. Ock, J., Issa, R.R., Flood, I.: Smart building energy management systems (BEMS) simulation conceptual framework. In: 2016 Winter Simulation Conference (WSC), pp. 3237–3245. IEEE (2016)
22. Chinchero, H.F., Alonso, J.M.: A review on energy management methodologies for LED lighting systems in smart buildings. In: IEEE International Conference on Environment and Electrical Engineering and 2020 IEEE Industrial and Commercial Power Systems Europe (EEEIC/I&CPS Europe), pp. 1–6. IEEE (2020)
23. Shankar, A., Vijayakumar, K., Babu, B.C.: Energy saving potential through artificial lighting system in PV integrated smart buildings. J. Build. Eng. **43**, 103080 (2021)

24. Naji, N., Abid, M.R., Benhaddou, D., Krami, N.: Context-aware wireless sensor networks for smart building energy management system. Information **11**, 530 (2020)

25. Moraci, F., Errigo, M.F., Fazia, C., Burgio, G., Foresta, S.: Making less vulnerable cities: resilience as a new paradigm of smart planning. Sustainability **10**, 755 (2018)

26. Felicioni, L.: Exploring Synergies in Sustainable, Resilient And Smart Buildings to Address New Design Paradigms In: The Next Generation Of Architecture (2022)

27. Venticinque, S., Amato, A.: Chapter 6 - Smart sensor and big data security and resilience. In: Ficco, M., Palmieri, F. (eds.) Security and Resilience in Intelligent Data-Centric Systems and Communication Networks, pp. 123–141. Academic Press (2018)

28. Al-Shammari, H.Q., Lawey, A.Q., El-Gorashi, T.E., Elmirghani, J.M.: Resilient service embedding in IoT networks. IEEE Access **8**, 123571–123584 (2020)

29. Anjana, M., Ramesh, M.V., Devidas, A.R., Athira, K.: Fractal iot: a scalable iot framework for energy management in connected buildings. In: Proceedings of the 1st ACM International Workshop on Technology Enablers and Innovative Applications for Smart Cities and Communities, pp. 10–17 (2019)

30. Xing, T., Yan, H., Sun, K., Wang, Y., Wang, X., Zhao, Q.: Honeycomb: An open-source distributed system for smart buildings. Patterns 3, (2022)

31. Kumar, A., Sharma, S., Goyal, N., Singh, A., Cheng, X., Singh, P.: Secure and energy-efficient smart building architecture with emerging technology IoT. Comput. Commun.. Commun. **176**, 207–217 (2021)

32. Lilis, G., Kayal, M.: A secure and distributed message oriented middleware for smart building applications. Autom. Constr.. Constr. **86**, 163–175 (2018)

33. Kim, H., Lee, E.A., Dustdar, S.: Creating a resilient IoT with edge computing. Computer **52**, 43–53 (2019)

34. Kim, H., Kang, E., Broman, D., Lee, E.A.: Resilient authentication and authorization for the Internet of Things (IoT) using edge computing. ACM Trans. Internet Things **1**, 1–27 (2020)

35. Carli, R., Cavone, G., Ben Othman, S., Dotoli, M.: IoT based architecture for model predictive control of HVAC systems in smart buildings. Sensors **20**, 781 (2020)

36. Shah, S.A., Seker, D.Z., Rathore, M.M., Hameed, S., Yahia, S.B., Draheim, D.: Towards disaster resilient smart cities: can internet of things and big data analytics be the game changers? IEEE Access **7**, 91885–91903 (2019)

37. Ha, Q., Phung, M.D.: IoT-enabled dependable control for solar energy harvesting in smart buildings. IET Smart Cities **1**, 61–70 (2019)

38. Plageras, A.P., Psannis, K.E., Stergiou, C., Wang, H., Gupta, B.B.: Efficient IoT-based sensor BIG Data collection–processing and analysis in smart buildings. Futur. Gener. Comput. Syst.. Gener. Comput. Syst. **82**, 349–357 (2018)

39. Metallidou, C.K., Psannis, K.E., Egyptiadou, E.A.: Energy efficiency in smart building: IoT approaches. Special Section on Future Generation Smart Cities Research: Services, Applications, Case Studies and Policymaking Considerations for Well-Being [Part II]., IEEE Access March 30 (2020)

40. Morabitoa, R., Petrolob, R., Loscric, V., Mittonc, N.: LEGIoT: a Lightweight Edge Gateway for the Internet of Things. Future Generation Computer Systems 81, October (2017)

41. Jia, M., Srinivasan, R.S., Raheem, A.A.: From occupancy to occupant behavior: an analytical survey of data acquisition technologies, modeling methodologies and simulation coupling mechanisms for building energy efficiency. Renewable Sustainable Energy Rev. **68**, Part 1, 525–540 (2017)

42. Horban, V.: A multifaceted approach to smart energy city concept through using big data analytics. In: 2016 IEEE First International Conference on Data Stream Mining & Processing (DSMP), pp. 392–396 (2016)

43. Bashir, M.R., Gill, A.Q.: Towards an IoT Big Data Analytics Framework: Smart Building Systems. IEEE Smart City 2016 (2016)

44. Daissaouia, A., Boulmakoulc, A., Karimd, L., Lbatha, A.: IoT and big data analytics for smart buildings: a survey. In: The 11th International Conference on Ambient Systems, Networks and Technologies (ANT), 6–9 April (2020)

45. Delic, K.A.: The internet of things on resilience of IoT systems. In: Ubiquity Symposium ACM Publication, February 2016

46. Sterbenz, J.P.G., et al.: Resilience and survivability in communication networks: strategies, principles, and survey of disciplines. Comput. Networks **54**(8), 1245–1265 (2010)

47. Hutchison, D., Sterbenz, J.P.G.: Architecture and design for resilient networked systems. Comput. Commun. **131**, 13–21, Elsevier, Science Direct (2018)

48. E.K. Çetinkaya, J.P.G. Sterbenz. "A taxonomy of network challenges" 9th IEEE/IFIP Conference On Design Of Reliable Communication Networks (DRCN), Budapest, April, 2013, pp. 322–330 (2013)

49. Li, R., et al.: Ten questions concerning energy flexibility in buildings. Build. Environ. **223**, 109461 (2022)

50. Elvas, L.B., Mataloto, B.M., Martins, A.L., Ferreira, J.C.: Disaster management in smart cities. Smart Cities Found. Principles Appl. **4**, 819–839 (2021)

51. Feng, Q., et al.: Time-based resilience metric for smart manufacturing systems and optimization method with dual-strategy recovery. J. Manuf. Syst. **65**, 486–497 (2022)

52. Berger, C., Eichhammer, P., Reiser, H.P., Domaschka, J., Hauck, F.J., Habiger, G.: A survey on resilience in the IoT: taxonomy, classification, and discussion of resilience mechanisms. ACM Comput. Surv. **54**, 7, Article 147 (September 2021)

53. Rajaram, K., Susanth, G.: Emulation of IoT gateway for connecting sensor nodes in heterogenous networks. In: IEEE International Conference on Computer, Communication, and Signal Processing: (ICCCSP 2017), pp. 1–5. IEEE. (2017)

54. Aguilar, L., Peralta, S., Mauricio, D.: Technological architecture for IoT smart buildings. In: Proceedings of the 2nd International Conference on Electrical, Communication and Computer Engineering (ICECCE). IEEE (2020)

55. Sterbenz, J.P.: Smart city and IoT resilience, survivability, and disruption tolerance: Challenges, modelling, and a survey of research opportunities 2017 9th International Workshop on Resilient Networks Design and Modeling, pp. 1–6. RNDM, IEEE (2017)

56. Abadeh, M.N., Mirzaie, M.: Ranking resilience events in IoT industrial networks. In: 2021 5th International Conference on Internet of Things and Applications, IoT, IEEE pp. 1–5 (2021)

57. Abadeh, M.N., Mirzaie, M.: Resiliency-aware analysis of complex IoT process chains, Computer Communications, Volume 192, 245–255 (2022)

58. Oteafy, S.M., Hassanein, H.S.: Resilient IoT architectures over dynamic sensor networks with adaptive components. IEEE Internet Things J. **4**, 474–483 (2016)

59. Shah, J., Mishra, B.: Customized IoT enabled wireless sensing and monitoring platform for smart buildings. Procedia Technol. **23**, 256–263 (2016)

60. Le, Q., Ngo-Quynh, T., Magedanz, T.: Rpl-based multipath routing protocols for internet of things on wireless sensor networks. In: International Conference on Advanced Technologies for Communications (ATC 2014), pp. 424–429. IEEE (2014)

61. Abreu, D.P., Velasquez, K., Curado, M., Monteiro, E.: A resilient Internet of Things architecture for smart cities. Ann. Telecommun.Telecommun. **72**, 19–30 (2017)

62. Basnayake, B., Amarasinghe, Y., Attalage, R., Udayanga, T., Jayasekara, A.: Technology: Artificial intelligence based smart building automation controller for energy efficiency improvements in existing buildings. Int. J. Adv. Autom. Sci. **40** (2015)

63. Bashir, M.R., Gill, A.Q., Beydoun, G., Mccusker, B.: Big data management and analytics metamodel for IoT-enabled smart buildings. IEEE Access **8**, 169740–169758 (2020)
64. Dharur, S., Hota, C., Swaminathan, K.: Energy efficient IoT framework for smart buildings. In: International Conference on I-SMAC (IoT in Social, Mobile, Analytics and Cloud) (I-SMAC), pp. 793–800. IEEE (2017)

Energy and Industry 4.0

Impact of Setpoint Control on Indoor Greenhouse Climate Modeling

Marie-Pier Trépanier$^{(\boxtimes)}$ (iD) and Louis Gosselin (iD)

Department of Mechanical Engineering, Université Laval, Québec, QC, Canada
marie-pier.trepanier.5@ulaval.ca

Abstract. Greenhouse agriculture is a crucial solution to global food security and sustainability challenges, as it provides a controlled environment for plant growth, resulting in higher yields and efficient resource utilization. Climate control plays a critical role in determining energy consumption and plant growth within greenhouse systems. The selection and optimization of control parameters have a significant impact on the overall performance. This study conducted simulations of a tomato greenhouse located in Montreal, Canada, with the aim of evaluating the effect of different control setpoints in the presence of high-pressure sodium (HPS) supplemental lighting and light-emitting diode (LED) supplemental lighting on greenhouse performance. To comprehensively assess the influence of each control setpoint, a sensitivity analysis (SA) was performed, systematically varying the control setpoints over a wider range than what is typically observed in tomato production. The SA utilized different control setpoints as inputs, while energy consumption and crop yield were considered as outputs. The setpoints for relative humidity and air temperature during the light period were identified as the most influential factors. This highlights the importance of accurate measurements and predictions of temperature and humidity to optimize environmental conditions in indoor greenhouses when implementing a predictive control strategy. The results obtained from this SA can contribute to the development of reduced-order models that focus on the most influential variables.

Keywords: Greenhouse · Energy consumption · Control

Nomenclature:

CO_2^{ppm}	Carbon dioxide (CO_2) concentration, ppm
I_{Glob}	Global solar radiation, W/m^2
p_{Band}	Tolerance band for control, -
RH	Relative humidity, %
$SumI_{Glob}$	Daily global solar radiation sum, MJ/m^2/day
T	Temperature, $\circ$C

Subscript

Air	Inside air
blScr	Black screen parameters

© The Author(s), under exclusive license to Springer Nature Switzerland AG 2024
B. N. Jørgensen et al. (Eds.): EI.A 2023, LNCS 14467, pp. 215–233, 2024.
https://doi.org/10.1007/978-3-031-48649-4_13

Dark	Period when the lamps are off
Day	Period from sunrise to sunset
Lamps	Lamps parameters
Light	Period when the lamps are on
Night	Period from sunset to sunrise
SP	Setpoint
thScr	Thermal screen parameters

1 Introduction

Greenhouses play a significant role in addressing the global food security and sustainability challenges. The world population is projected to reach 9.7 billion by 2050 [1], meaning food production will have to increase by at least 50% to meet demand [2]. This increased food production is also associated with increased energy consumption, resulting in a significant carbon footprint and environmental degradation.

Greenhouse farming is a key solution to this challenge, providing a controlled environment for plant growth, higher yields, and efficient use of resources, including water and energy. Greenhouses also provide access to fresh local produce year-round, regardless of the outside climate. However, the energy consumption required to maintain ideal conditions for plant growth in greenhouses is high, making energy efficiency a critical aspect of greenhouse agriculture.

Climate controls determine energy consumption and crop growth in a greenhouse. Studies have shown that the selection and optimization of control parameters significantly impact the overall performance of greenhouse systems. As mentioned by Rizwan et al., maintaining optimal control in a greenhouse environment is challenging due to the interconnected nature of its climate parameters [3]. However, growers are conservative in changing their control setpoints and tolerances.

Climate control research has focused on developing accurate greenhouse models and efficient controllers to regulate microclimate variables. These investigations range from simple air temperature models to complex models involving plant responses.

The literature reviews by [4] and [5] outline two primary categories of greenhouse control algorithms: conventional control and optimal control (see Fig. 1). Conventional control seeks to minimize deviations between setpoints and measured values. In contrast, optimal control considers greenhouse behavior, actuator capabilities, energy consumption, and crop response as inputs to the control strategy [4, 6]. To meet the crop requirements, advanced controllers combined with artificial neural networks have been proposed by many researchers for precise control and energy efficiency [5].

Figure 1 also illustrates the various control components and parameters in greenhouse control systems, where each component affects different parameters (e.g., the heating system affects temperature and humidity control) [5, 7]. These control components exhibit strong coupling among multiple parameters, going beyond pairwise interactions [5, 6].

Numerical simulations, primarily using MATLAB/Simulink, are the predominant method for investigating greenhouse control strategies, accounting for about 30% of the selected literature [5].

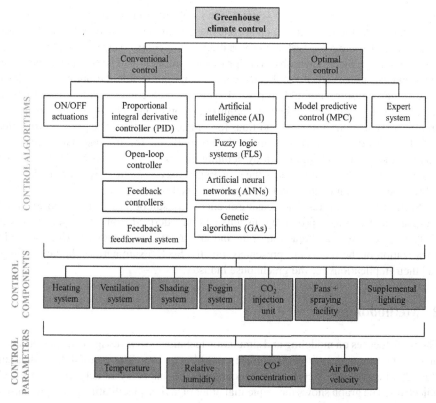

Fig. 1. Review of greenhouse control algorithms, components and parameters (adapted from [4] and [5]).

The primary focus of this research is to evaluate and analyze which control parameters have the most significant impact on greenhouse performance, specifically in terms of energy consumption and crop yield. By investigating and assessing various control parameters, such as temperature, humidity, carbon dioxide (CO_2), and lighting, this study aims to identify the key setpoint factors that significantly affect greenhouse performance.

In the long term, this research will allow to target the controls that would gain to be set dynamically, ensuring optimal, real-time adaptation to external conditions such as meteorological climate and energy markets. Such dynamic controls have the potential to significantly influence the operational costs and environmental impacts associated with greenhouse operations. By comprehensively investigating the influence of control parameters on energy consumption and crop yield, this research seeks to provide valuable insights into optimizing greenhouse systems, leading to improved sustainability, resource efficiency, and economic viability.

This study conducted a simulation of a tomato greenhouse located in Montreal, Canada. The purpose of the simulations was to evaluate the impact of different control setpoints on greenhouse performance. Greenhouses with high-pressure sodium (HPS) and light-emitting diode (LED) supplemental lighting were considered. To comprehensively assess the influence of each control setpoint, a sensitivity analysis (SA) was performed, involving the systematic variation of the control setpoints within a wider range than the typical range observed for tomato production. The inputs for the sensitivity analysis consisted of the diverse control setpoints, while the outputs considered were energy consumption and crop yield. This research contributes to a better understanding of the relationships between control setpoints, greenhouse performance, and optimization of environmental conditions for tomato production. The paper is structured as follows. Section 2 presents the methodology, outlining the approach and methods. It explains the model and simulation by defining the reference greenhouse and reference climate controls. It also introduces the sensitivity analysis method by defining the input values, the sampling method and the regression method.

Section 3 shows the results, focusing on energy consumption and crop yield. Section 4 presents the discussion, providing insights and data derived from the experiments and analysis. The control and reaction of the indoor climate, the energy contribution, and a linearization of the inputs are presented. Finally, Sect. 5 summarizes the key findings and their implications for the greenhouse industry.

2 Methodology

The work focuses on modeling and simulation techniques to investigate the performance of greenhouses under different climate control setpoints. The methodology diagram (Fig. 2) illustrates the step-by-step process used in this study to achieve the research objectives. The graph shows the sequential order of actions, facilitating a comprehensive understanding of the methodology.

Section 2.1 presents the model and simulation methodology used to evaluate the energy consumption and crop yield of a greenhouse in Montreal, Canada. Section 2.2 introduces the SA that was used to evaluate the effect of varying control setpoints (input parameters) on the energy consumption and yield (output variables) of the tomato greenhouse simulation. By systematically adjusting the control setpoints and observing the resulting changes, the study aimed to determine the sensitivity of the model outputs to the variations in the input parameters.

Fig 2 .Model Selection and Simulation Approach

The energy and growth simulations were performed using the GreenLight model [8], an open-source model designed for illuminated greenhouses with tomato crops (MATLAB code available at https://github.com/davkat1/GreenLight and run on MATLAB R2021a). GreenLight was chosen because the computational time is reasonable, and all codes are accessible, allowing transparency in the research. Initially, this model was designed to replicate an advanced Venlo-type greenhouse with a tomato crop and supplemental lighting. According to Katzin et al. [8], based on the dataset of an experimental trial, the error in predicting the annual heating needs is in the range of 1 to 12%.

Before any modification was made to the GreenLight model, it was verified against literature data and previous results to ensure its accuracy and reliability. Using the same methodology as Katzin et al. in [9], each step was validated and compared with the energy consumption results for Amsterdam, the Netherlands, given in the article (importing climate data, running scenarios, and post-analysis).

Reference Greenhouse. The reference greenhouse simulated in this research is a virtual state-of-the-art high-tech tomato greenhouse located in Montreal, Canada. The decision to focus on a modern high-tech greenhouse, rather than a conventional greenhouse commonly found in the region, was motivated by the goal of exploring future possibilities and potential advancements in greenhouse technology. By simulating a cutting-edge greenhouse, this study aims to evaluate the feasibility and potential benefits of implementing advanced dynamic climate control strategies in greenhouse operations. This research seeks to provide valuable insights for the development of future greenhouse designs that integrate dynamic control systems with real-time monitoring with multiple sensors.

This state-of-the-art greenhouse is based on products available from the major Dutch greenhouse manufacturers (Priva [10], Ridder [11], Dalsem [12], Certhon [13], and Havecon [14]). The most common advanced greenhouse for commercial use is the high-tech Venlo-type Dutch glasshouse [8, 15], which is designed to optimize plant growth and yield by controlling the environment in the greenhouse. This type of greenhouse has features such as automated climate control systems, advanced irrigation systems, supplemental lighting, humidification and dehumidification, CO_2 supplementation, and energy-efficient design (double glazing, energy curtains, etc.) [16]. The high-tech glass greenhouse is the most popular advanced greenhouse for commercial use in the Netherlands due to its efficiency, sustainability, and flexibility.

After analyzing the market related to tomato greenhouses, the reference greenhouse for the simulation is the one proposed by Katzin et al. [8] for the GreenLight model. In that study, a 4-hectare Venlo-type greenhouse, 200 m wide and long, with a gutter height of 6.5 m, a ridge height of 7.3 m and a roof slope of 22° was replicated. The roof was made of glass panels, with 1 in 6 panels having a ventilation window (1.40 m × 1.67 m) that can be opened to 60°. Thermal screens were installed at a height of 6.3 m. The path width was 1.6 m with a pipe rail system. This reference greenhouse is based on the Dutch greenhouse design described by Vanthoor et al. [17].

The GreenLight model was adapted considering the physical characteristics of the selected greenhouse and the meteorological data of the selected location. The meteorological data for Montreal, Canada, is retrieved from EnergyPlus (https://energyplus.net/weather). The database used is the Canadian Weather for Energy Calculations (CWEC), an hourly weather observation of a characteristic one-year period specifically designed for building energy calculations [18].

Based on the methodology of Katzin et al. [9], all simulations of this study are almost one year long (350 days) and start on September 27, which represents the planting date of the crops. The simulated crops are assumed to be mature. Growers typically have a tomato harvest season of 350 days because about two weeks are needed between harvests to change crops and wash the greenhouse. The cycle adds up to a full year and allows for better crop management.

Figure 3 illustrates the relations of the system designed to control the indoor climate of the greenhouse and presents the flow of information and control decisions within the system. The diagram is divided into five sections: Outdoor Weather, Indoor Climate, Crop, Controls and Outputs. Control decisions are based on outdoor weather conditions, the existing indoor climate, and the current state of the crop. The indoor climate is influenced by the outdoor weather, the controls, and the crop. The crop is influenced by the indoor climate. The key outcomes of this research are the yield (which depends on the crop) and the energy consumption (which depend on the controls).

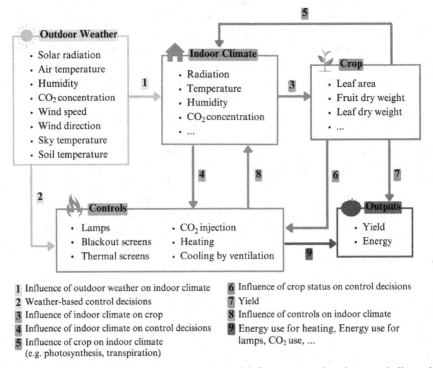

Fig. 3. Representation of the greenhouse system and influences (numbered arrows indicate the flow of information and control decisions) (adapted from [19]).

Reference Climate Controls. High-tech commercial greenhouses are equipped with advanced climate control systems. Therefore, the simulation of greenhouses must also account for the climate controls to provide the optimal environment according to the requirements of different growth stages of the crops. The climate controls included in GreenLight consider the following aspects: lamps, blackout screens, thermal screens, CO2 injection, heating, cooling by ventilation, and dehumidification [19].

As regulated by the reference climate controls, the lamps are on from midnight to 18:00, which represents 18 h of lighting, the ideal lighting time for tomato production [20]

[21]. However, during this time, the lamps are turned off depending on the solar radiation and the indoor temperature. Blackout screens are present to avoid light pollution, so they are closed at night, except when the indoor relative humidity or temperature is too high. Thermal screens contribute to the energy efficiency of greenhouses. They are closed when the external solar radiation and temperature are low. However, the screens are opened when ventilation is needed. CO_2 is injected during the light period (when the plants are exposed to light, either from the sun or lamps) when the concentration is below a certain setpoint.

The heating is set to a specific setpoint temperature, one for the light period and one for the dark period. Ventilation cooling of the roof windows is activated (windows open) when the indoor temperature is 5 °C above the setpoint. Ventilation dehumidification in the greenhouse is activated when the indoor relative humidity is too high. All the values and conditions of these different controls are listed in Table 1.

The climate was controlled using a smoothed proportional controller (defined by a sigmoid function). In the GreenLight program, the controller enables the definition of a setpoint and an acceptable tolerance band (*pBand*) for each parameter (Table 1). This function allows realistic control of the different variables since the desired values are not always attainable despite the setpoints.

Table 1. Climate controls and their conditions for the GreenLight simulation [19].

Control	Condition(s)	Setpoint	P_{Band}
Lamps	**On:** from 00:00 to 18:00 **Off** if: $(I_{Glob} > I_{Glob SP})$ OR $(T_{Air} > T_{Lamps SP})$ OR $(Night if blackout screens open)$ OR $(SumI_{Glob} > SumI_{Glob SP})$	$I_{Glob SP} = 400W/m^2$ $T_{Lamps SP} = 26.5°C$ $SumI_{Glob SP} = 10MJ/m^2/day$	
Blackout screens	**Closed** during the night *AND* **Open** during the day **Forced open** if: $\left(RH_{Air} > RH_{blScr SP} AND T_{Air} > T_{Air_{SP}} - 1°C\right)$ OR $(T_{Air} > T_{Lamps SP})$	$RH_{blScr SP} = 90\%$	$0.5°C(T)$ OR $0.5\%(RH)$
Thermal screens	**Closed** if: $\left(I_{Glob} < I_{Glob_{thScr} SP} AND T_{Out} < T_{thScr SP(Day)}\right)$ OR $\left(I_{Glob} > I_{Glob_{thScr} SP} AND T_{Out} < T_{thScr SP(Night)}\right)$ **Forced to open** if: $(T_{Air} > 2°C + T_{Air_{SP}})$ OR $\left(RH_{Air} > RH_{Air SP} AND T_{Air} > T_{Air_{SP}} - 1°C\right)$	$I_{Glob_{thScr} SP} = 50W/m^2$ $T_{thScr SP(Day)} = 18°C$ $T_{thScr SP(Night)} = 5°C$ $RH_{Air SP} = 85\%$	$1°C(T)$ OR $10\%(RH)$
CO_2 injection	**On** during the light period if: $(CO_2^{ppm} < CO_2^{ppm} SP)$	$CO_2^{ppm} SP = 1000ppm$	$100ppm$ (CO_2)
Heating	**Setpoint for heating:** Light period $(T_{Air SP(Light)})$ AND Dark period $(T_{Air SP(Dark)})$ **Heating on** only if: $(T_{Air} < T_{Air_{SP}} - 2°C)$	$T_{Air SP(Light)} = 19.5°C$ $T_{Air SP(Dark)} = 18.5°C$	$1°C(T)$
Cooling by ventilation	**Roof windows open** if: $(T_{Air} > 5°C + T_{Air_{SP}})$ OR $(RH_{Air} > 87\%)$		Open: $4°C(T)$ OR $50\%(RH)$

Table 2. Input parameters and range for the climate control SA.

Parameter	Minimum value	Maximum value	Units	Reference
$RH_{Air\,SP}$	50	95	%	[24]
$T_{Air\,SP(LightPeriod)}$	10	30	°C	[24, 25]
$T_{Air\,SP(DarkPeriod)}$	10	25	°C	[24, 25]
$T_{thScr\,SP(Day)}$	-32	25	°C	[25, 26]
$T_{thScr\,SP(Night)}$	10	25	°C	[26]
$CO_2^{ppm}{}_{SP}$	450	1500	ppm	[24]
$I_{Glob\,SP}$	150	500	W/m^2	[16, 19]
$SumI_{GLob\,SP}$	7	25	MJ / m^2/day	[20]

2.1 Sensitivity Analysis (SA)

In this study, a SA was performed to identify which input parameters have the most significant impact on the output variables, allowing for a better understanding of their relationships. Two sensitivity analyses were carried out, one with HPS supplemental lighting and one with LED supplemental lighting.

SA is the study of how uncertainty in the output of a model can be attributed to different sources of uncertainty in the model input [22]. An analysis of the control system makes it possible to better understand the peculiarities of the model and to discover which components have the largest influence on the greenhouse. SA is used to achieve several goals, such as validating the robustness of the model to check whether the model depends on weak assumptions, prioritizing future research by targeting factors that merit further analysis or measurement, and simplifying the model by holding certain factors constant or even removing them [23].

Input Values. The SA involved varying the values of the control setpoints over a range wider than the proposed "optimal" values for crop growth. Specifically, the control setpoints were adjusted to a minimum value reduced by 25% and a maximum value increased by 25%. The input variables of the SA are the different control setpoints listed in Table 2. The input ranges of the different variables were based on literature and realistic ranges with respect to existing tomato greenhouse controls. In total, eight input variables were considered in the SA

Sampling Method. The sampling method used for the SA is a modified latin hypercube sampling (LHS). The LHS is a method of sampling from a given probability distribution [27]. It ensures full coverage of the range of input variables. the LHS produces a pseudo-random sample that Mimics a random structure. This type of sampling is similar to stratified sampling. compared to simple random sampling, LHS requires a smaller sample size to achieve the same precision [23]. The LHS algorithm assumes that the input variables are independent [28].

For the regression-based sensitivity analysis used in this work (see next section), Nguyen and Reiter [29] suggest a sample size of 1.5 to 10 times the number of input variables. Eight input variables are considered in this project, so 80 samples were evaluated.

Regression Method. Different sensitivity analysis methods can be used depending on the features of a given problem [30]. Tian [31] presented an overview of sa techniques with their main characteristics. Their review, which focuses on the application of sa in the field of building performance analysis, analyzes the different sensitivity analysis methods that are possible.

With the approach based on linear regressions, the relationship between a dependent variable (y) and multiple independent variables (x_i) is represented by the following equation:

$$y = \beta_0 + \beta_1 x_1 + \beta_2 x_2 + \beta_3 x_3 + \ldots + \beta_i x_i + \ldots + \beta_n x_n + \varepsilon \qquad (1)$$

where β_0 is the intercept term (the value of y when all x_i are zero), β_i are the regression coefficients that represent the change in y that corresponds to a one-unit change in each respective x_i and ε is the error term that represents the unexplained variation in y that is not accounted for by the independent variables.

The goal of a linear regression is to estimate the values of β_i that minimize the sum of the squared differences between the observed values of y and the predicted values from the linear equation. The Standard Regression Coefficients (SRC) method, which is fast to compute and easy to understand, was chosen as the SA method in the present work. This method is suitable for linear or nearly linear models [29], so the first step is to validate the linearity of the outputs with the SCR method. This method also requires that the inputs be uncorrelated. In the SCR method, the coefficients β_i give an indication of the importance of the variable i [30] with respect to the output considered. These coefficients were determined using the Matlab function "regress" for multiple linear regressions (Matlab R2022b) [32]. Since the magnitude of β_i is affected by the units of measurement used for the corresponding regressor, a more robust strategy is to scale the model to generate standardized regression coefficients [33].

It is possible to calculate standardized value (y^*) of the output y (dependent variable) by subtracting the mean of y($\bar{y}$) from the observed value and then dividing it by the standard deviation (σ_y):

$$y^* = \frac{y - \bar{y}}{\sigma_y} \qquad (2)$$

Standardizing the values makes it easier to compare and interpret the data.

Similarly, standardized coefficients (β_i^*) of the input x_i (independent variable) can be obtained by multiplying the original coefficient (β_i) with the ratio of the standard deviation of the dependent variable (σ_y) to the standard deviation of xi (σ_{x_i}):

$$\beta_i^* = \beta_i \frac{\sigma_y}{\sigma_{x_i}} \qquad (3)$$

Standardizing the coefficients helps to compare the relative importance and impact of different independent variables in the regression model and to quantify the linearity of a model. The closer the sum of the squares of the β_i^* coefficients is to 1, the more linear and fit the model is [33]. Once the standardized regression coefficients are estimated, they provide information about the strength and direction of the relationship between the dependent variable (y) and each independent variable (x_i).

Evaluation Metrics. The methodology uses a comprehensive set of evaluation metrics to analyze the impact of the different independent lamp parameters (inputs, x_i). The primary outputs studied are the total energy consumption, which includes energy for lighting and heating, and the total yield, which is represented by the total fresh weight of harvested tomatoes (productivity). To facilitate comparisons with other studies, all metrics are calculated per square meter of greenhouse area. For each output, the standardized regression coefficients (β_i^*) of the inputs x_i (independent variables) are analyzed.

3   Results

In this results section, the two outputs studied (i.e., y in Eq. (1)) are the annual energy consumption and total fresh weight tomato yield. The objective of an optimal greenhouse is to reduce its energy consumption while increasing its total yield, therefore the analysis centers on these two outputs, with a focus on the impact of input parameters. The significant correlations and standardized regression coefficients, illustrating the importance of independent variables, are shown. In addition, a comparison between HPS and LED lighting is presented. These findings inform strategies for greenhouse optimization.

The total fresh weight tomato yield in kg per square meter of greenhouse floor area for a 350-day period for a greenhouse with HPS lamps in Montreal, Canada, is reported in Fig. 4 as a function of each input parameter independently (scatter plots) for the sample under consideration. In this scatter plot, each data point corresponds to a specific combination of SA input and tomato yield, and the color of each point indicates the yield, with blue representing higher yields and yellow representing lower yields. The color gradient allows for a clear distinction between better and worse yields.

From Fig. 4, the observed correlation between the air temperature setpoint and tomato yield highlights the importance of maintaining appropriate temperature in optimizing tomato production under HPS lighting conditions.

Similarly, the total energy consumption in MJ per square meter of greenhouse floor area is shown in Fig. 5. Again, a color gradient is used to distinguish the results. The best energy consumption values (lowest values) are represented in blue and the worst energy consumption values (highest values) are represented in yellow.

Figure 5 shows a correlation between the input control variable of relative humidity, and the total energy consumption. The distribution of the data points suggests that as the relative humidity setpoint increases, less energy is needed. This correlation is indicated by the clustering of the blue dots, representing lower energy, towards the higher values of relative humidity, while the yellow dots tend to be more prevalent at lower relative humidity values. Overall, Fig. 5 provides valuable visual evidence for the relationship between relative humidity and total energy, suggesting that manipulating relative humidity levels could be a potential strategy for reducing energy consumption in HPS lighting systems.

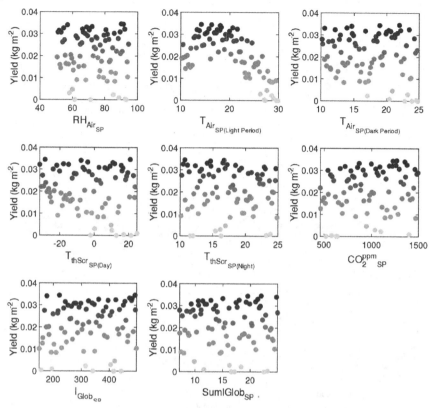

Fig. 4. Total fresh weight tomato yield as a function of the SA input variable (independent variable, x_i) for 350 days under HPS lighting (Colors indicate the yield: blue represents higher yields and yellow represents lower yields).

The same simulations were performed under LED lighting, and the results exhibited correlations similar to those shown in Figs. 4 and 5.

Figure 6 summarizes the key findings by showcasing the standardized regression coefficients (β_i^*) for each independent variable, providing a concise overview of the SA results. The standardized regression coefficients provide information on the strength and direction of the relationship between the input and output variables.

HPS LightingLED Lighting.

Positive values on the y-axis indicate a positive relationship, where an increase in the independent variable leads to an increase in the dependent variable. Conversely, negative values indicate a negative relationship, where an increase in the independent variable results in a decrease in the dependent variable. More importantly, the magnitude of the coefficients (β_i^*) reveals the relative importance of the independent variables. Larger coefficient values mean that the corresponding independent variables have a strong impact on the dependent variable, while smaller coefficient values indicate a weak influence.

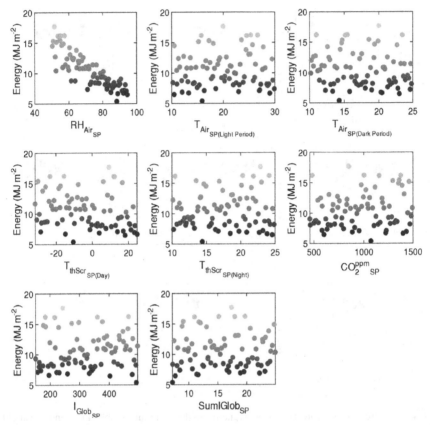

Fig. 5. Total energy consumption as a function of the SA input variable (independent variable, x_i) for 350 days under HPS lighting (Colors indicate the energy: blue represents lower energy and yellow represents higher energy).

The comparison between HPS and LED lighting conditions allows one to evaluate how the importance of each independent variable may differ based on the lighting system used. From the results in Fig. 6 we can conclude that there is no significant difference between the two types of lamps with that respect. For the main correlations (relative humidity setpoint for the total energy and air temperature setpoint during lighting period for the total yield), the standardized regression coefficients are slightly less dominant for greenhouses under LED lighting. For the total fresh weight tomato yield output, the standardized regression coefficient of the air temperature setpoint during light period is -0.8605 for HPS and -0.8266 for LED. For the total energy output, the standardized regression coefficient of the relative humidity is for -0.6349 HPS and -0.5521 LED.

For both HPS and LED lightings, the sum of the square standardized regression coefficient (β^{*2}) is higher for the total energy consumption than for the total fresh weight tomato yield. For energy, the sum is equal to 0.801 for HPS and 0.810 for LED, and for total yield, the sum is equal to 0.522 for HPS and 0.432 for LED.

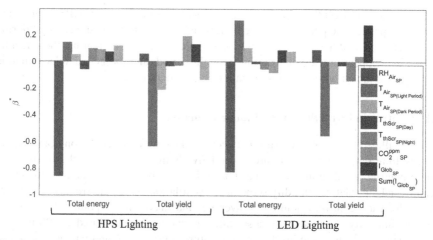

Fig. 6. Standardized regression coefficient (β^*) of each independent variable (inputs, x_i) for yearly energy consumption and yield, for both types of lamps (HPS and LED).

4 Discussion

Predictive control has emerged as a promising approach for maintaining optimal environmental conditions in various indoor settings, including greenhouses and controlled growth environments. The SA presented above shows that the setpoints of the control system that have the most impact on the energy consumption and tomato yield are the relative humidity and air temperature during the light period, respectively. According to Zhang et al. [5], most of the literature (approximately 60%) focuses on temperature and humidity as the regulated parameters in greenhouse climate control as these variables have a direct impact on crop yield and represent the primary contributors to energy consumption. This means that to implement a predictive control strategy, it is essential to have accurate measurements and predictions of temperature and humidity to optimize environmental conditions in indoor greenhouse settings.

Reliable predictions allow the control algorithm to anticipate environmental changes and adjust control actions accordingly. This adaptability helps maintain desired setpoints and prevents overshooting or undershooting, thereby improving system performance. Accurate prediction of temperature and humidity is challenging due to the complex nature of indoor environments. Data-driven approaches, such as machine learning and statistical techniques, offer the potential to improve temperature and humidity predictions. Integrating data from multiple sensors, including temperature, humidity, CO_2 levels, and solar radiation, can improve prediction accuracy. The key factors to focus on are those related to relative humidity and air temperature, according the present SA. However, as shown in Fig. 6, there are other factors at play depending on the type of lamps and the output. The three most influential factors in order of importance for the total energy consumption under HPS lighting are the relative air humidity setpoint, the air temperature setpoint during the light period, and the daily summed global solar radiation setpoint. Under LED lighting, the two main factors remain the same, but the third one is the air temperature setpoint during the dark period. For the total fresh weight tomato yield, the three most influential factors in order of importance under HPS lighting are the air temperature setpoint during the light period, the air temperature setpoint during the dark period, and the CO_2 concentration setpoint. Under LED lighting, these factors are the air temperature setpoint during the light period, and the global solar radiation setpoint, and the air temperature setpoint during the dark period.

4.1 Control and Reaction of the Indoor Climate

Figure 7 illustrates the relationship between the heating and ventilation controls and the resulting output air temperature and relative humidity for selected 24-h periods. These controls are determined by, but not limited to, the air temperature setpoint for heating and the relative humidity setpoint for ventilation. Three different scenarios are shown for each control, a minimum, average, and maximum setpoint value. For the sake of simplicity, the focus is on a specific day and is conducted under HPS lighting conditions. To illustrate the inside air temperature (Fig. 7 A, C, and E), the day shown is January 1 (winter), and to illustrate the relative air humidity (Fig. 7 B, D, and F), the day shown is July 1 (summer). The heating control activates the boiler. When the value is 100% the boiler works at full capacity. The ventilation control activates the opening of the roof windows. When the value is 100% the windows are fully open.

Figure 7 shows how changes in the control setpoints affect the environmental conditions. Throughout the day, the heating and ventilation commands vary based on the setpoints, indicating that the system is attempting to achieve the desired environmental conditions. It is important to note that although the setpoints vary, this does not necessarily mean that the system always achieves these specific values. Instead, the system tries to achieve the setpoints and the corresponding results are analyzed. In Fig. 7 B, D and F, the boiler control is low because the day shown is in summer. However, it demonstrates increased energy consumption when the control setpoint of relative humidity is lower. This is likely because the vents are more open, resulting in the activation of heating when the outside air temperature is lower during nighttime hours. This analysis shows oscillations in the boiler control of Fig. 7 A and C. This should be adjusted in future work.

4.2 Energy Consumption Contribution

To better understand the energy dynamics of the simulation, additional details focusing on the breakdown of energy consumption is presented. Specifically, the division of energy usage between artificial lighting and greenhouse heating is highlighted. These details are presented in Fig. 8, covering the entire simulation period and offering a comprehensive view of energy utilization patterns for three different relative air humidity control setpoints. In these three simulations, all controls are identical except for the value relative air humidity setpoint.

For all simulations, during winter, the energy is at its highest for heating and for artificial lighting. This is due to the cold outside conditions and low outside light period in Montreal, Canada. During winter, the energy for heating dominates and the opposite happens during summer as the energy for lighting is higher.

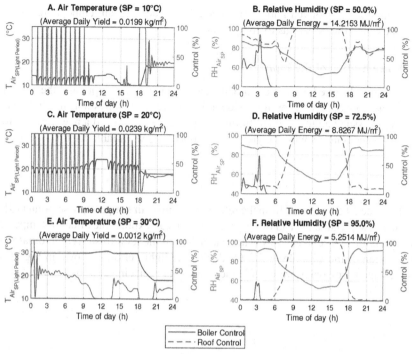

Fig. 7. Heating (boiler) control and output air temperature over one day (January 1) with an air temperature setpoint control of 10 °C (A), 20 °C (C), 30 °C (E) for HPS lighting. Heating (boiler) and ventilation (roof) controls and output relative air humidity over one day (July 1) with a relative air humidity setpoint control of 50% (B), 72.5% (D), 95% (F) for HPS lighting.

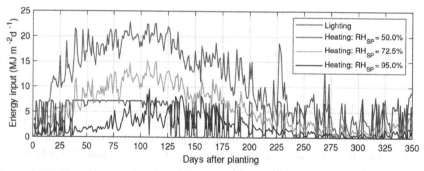

Fig. 8. Daily energy input related to lamp use and heating for 350 days (day of planting is September 27) under HPS lighting for a different relative air humidity control setpoint.

The energy for lighting does not vary with the relative humidity control setpoint. On the other hand, heating energy varies considerably, especially during the winter months (mid-November to March / 50–150 days after planting). The main solution to reduce humidity is roof ventilation. However, this reduces the air temperature inside the greenhouse and the boiler has to compensate.

4.3 Linearization of the Inputs

In Fig. 4, we observed a correlation between the temperature input and the total fresh weight tomato yield; however, it is evident that the relationship is not strictly linear. To address this issue and to facilitate further analysis, we introduced a new variable to try to linearize the relation with the yield. The proposed new variable for this linearization is:

$$x_{T_{Air}} = \left| T_{Air_{SP(LightPeriod)}} - 19.5°C \right| \tag{4}$$

The value 19.5 °C comes from the reference optimal air temperature setpoint [19]. By using the new variable instead of $x_{T_{Air}}$ directly, we can express the effect of temperature on the yield in a more linear way. The scatter plot of the total fresh weight tomato yield as a function of the variable of Eq. (4) during the light period is shown in Fig. 9. The SAs presented previously were performed again but replacing $x_{T_{Air}}$ by Eq. (4).

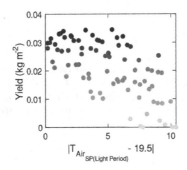

Fig. 9. Linearization of total fresh weight tomato yield in function of the air temperature control during light period under HPS lighting (Colors indicate the yield: blue represents higher yields and yellow represents lower yields).

For HPS lighting, the new standardized regression coefficient is -0.6932 compared to -0.6349 without the linearization. For LED lighting, the coefficient is now -0.7831 compared to -0.5521. The difference is more important under LED lighting. In both cases the air temperature setpoint during light period is the most influential inputs for total fresh weight tomato yield. With the new variable, the sum of the square standardized regression coefficient (β^{*2}) becomes 0.567 (HPS) and 0.656 (LED) compared to 0.522 and 0.432 before. This means that with this new variable, it is possible to explain an even higher percentage of the variance with the regression.

4.4 Limitation of the Model

The accuracy and realism of the results depends on the model employed in the simulation, which contain limitations. The model provides only a limited set of humidity and temperature values, lacking details on how these conditions vary across the greenhouse. This restricts our ability to analyze spatial differences in the indoor climate, as the model precludes a more granular analysis of spatial variations. Also, the precision of the research is inherently tied to the model's accuracy, meaning that any limitations in the model may affect the accuracy of our results [19]. Furthermore, to ensure the model's reliability, it would be beneficial to validate it by comparing its predictions to real-world data under different control conditions. This would help confirm that the model accurately represents the physical processes at play. The scope of this research is confined to the specific sequence of controls integrated into the model, predominantly reliant on predefined setpoints and control band parameters. This limitation prevents us from evaluating the potential of more advanced control strategies, such as model predictive control.

5 Conclusion

This study investigated the impact of setpoint control on indoor greenhouse climate modeling. By performing a SA on greenhouse control setpoints, the setpoints for relative humidity and air temperature during the light period were identified as the most influential factors.

To further understand and optimize greenhouse performance, the implementation of a digital twin could be explored. A digital twin would provide a virtual replica of the greenhouse, allowing real-time monitoring and simulation of control strategies. The results of the SA could help to obtain reduced order models focusing on the most influential variables. In addition, the adoption of more dynamic variable control approaches could help improve the accuracy of climate modeling. While the current study focused primarily on setpoint control, it would be interesting to expand the analysis to include other variables and their impact on greenhouse climate control. By considering additional factors, such as permissive band control rules, a more complete understanding of the complex interplay of variables could be gained and control strategies refined accordingly. However, it is important to recognize that the GreenLight model used in this study has limitations. The accuracy and realism of greenhouse climate modeling depends on the model. By exploring better control strategies, it is possible to achieve more efficient and sustainable greenhouse cultivation practices.

References

1. United Nation, World Population Prospects 2019: Highlights, Department of Economic and Social Affairs (2019). https://population.un.org/wpp/Publications/Files/WPP2019_10KeyFindings.pdf
2. Food and Agriculture Organization of the United Nations, Ed., The future of food and agriculture: trends and challenges. Rome: Food and Agriculture Organization of the United Nations, 2017
3. Rizwan, A., Khan, A.N., Ahmad, R., Kim, D.H.: Optimal environment control mechanism based on OCF connectivity for efficient energy consumption in greenhouse. IEEE Internet Things J. 10(6), 5035–5049 (2023). https://doi.org/10.1109/JIOT.2022.3222086

4. Duarte-Galvan, C., et al.: Review. Advantages and disadvantages of control theories applied in greenhouse climate control systems. Span J. Agric. Res. **10**(4), 926 (2012)https://doi.org/10.5424/sjar/2012104-487-11

5. Zhang, S., Guo, Y., Zhao, H., Wang, Y., Chow, D., Fang, Y.: Methodologies of control strategies for improving energy efficiency in agricultural greenhouses. J. Clean. Prod. **274**, 122695 (2020). https://doi.org/10.1016/j.jclepro.2020.122695

6. Chimankare, R.V., Das, S., Kaur, K., Magare, D.: A review study on the design and control of optimised greenhouse environments. J. Trop. Ecol. **39**, e26 (2023). https://doi.org/10.1017/S0266467423000160

7. Soussi, M., Chaibi, M.T., Buchholz, M., Saghrouni, Z.: Comprehensive review on climate control and cooling systems in greenhouses under hot and arid conditions. Agronomy **12**(3), 626 (2022). https://doi.org/10.3390/agronomy12030626

8. Katzin, D., van Mourik, S., Kempkes, F., van Henten, E.J.: GreenLight – an open source model for greenhouses with supplemental lighting: evaluation of heat requirements under LED and HPS lamps. Biosys. Eng. **194**, 61–81 (2020). https://doi.org/10.1016/j.biosystemseng.2020.03.010

9. Katzin, D., Marcelis, L.F.M., van Mourik, S.: Energy savings in greenhouses by transition from high-pressure sodium to LED lighting. Appl. Energy **281**, 116019 (2021). https://doi.org/10.1016/j.apenergy.2020.116019

10. Priva I Smart horticulture & building management solutions, Priva. https://www.priva.com/. Accessed 25 May 2023

11. Ridder I Innovative technical solutions for protected horticulture I Inside greenhouse technology for profitable horticulture, Ridder. https://ridder.com/ (Accessed 25 May 2023)

12. Complete Greenhouse Projects - Dalsem, Dalsem. https://www.dalsem.com/en (Accessed 25 May 2023)

13. Certhon Growing anything, anywhere. For everyone., Certhon. https://certhon.com/ Accessed 25 May 2023)

14. Havecon I Horticultural Projects, Havecon. https://havecon.com/en/. Accessed 25 May 2023

15. Payne, H.J., Hemming, S., Van Rens, B.A.P., Van Henten, E.J., Van Mourik, S.: Quantifying the role of weather forecast error on the uncertainty of greenhouse energy prediction and power market trading. Biosys. Eng. **224**, 1–15 (2022). https://doi.org/10.1016/j.biosystemseng.2022.09.009

16. Stanghellini, C. van't Ooster, B. Heuvelink, E.: Greenhouse horticulture, Technology for optimal crop production. The Netherlands: Wageningen Academic Publishers (2019)

17. Vanthoor, B.H.E., Stanghellini, C., Van Henten, E.J., De Visser, P.H.B.: A methodology for model-based greenhouse design: Part 1, a greenhouse climate model for a broad range of designs and climates. Biosys. Eng. **110**(4), 363–377 (2011). https://doi.org/10.1016/j.biosystemseng.2011.06.001

18. EnergyPlus. https://energyplus.net/weather/sources#CWEC. Accessed 08 Jun 2023

19. Katzin, D.: Energy saving by LED lighting in greenhouses : a process-based modelling approach. Wageningen University (2021). https://doi.org/10.18174/544434

20. Turcotte, G. :Production de la tomate de serre au Québec, Syndicat des producteurs en serre du Québec, p. 297, Apr. 2015

21. Palmitessa, O.D., Pantaleo, M.A., Santamaria, P.: Applications and development of LEDs as supplementary lighting for tomato at different latitudes. Agronomy **11**(5), 835 (2021). https://doi.org/10.3390/agronomy11050835

22. Saltelli, A. (ed.): Sensitivity Analysis in Practice: a Guide to Assessing Scientific Models. Wiley, Hoboken, NJ (2004)

23. Saltelli, A., Ed., Global Sensitivity Analysis: The Primer. Chichester, England ; Hoboken, NJ: John Wiley (2008)

24. Dorais, M.: PLG-3207-H23: Cultures en serre (17896, 17897). Université Laval
25. Kim, R., Kim, J., Lee, I., Yeo, U., Lee, S., Decano-Valentin, C.: Development of three-dimensional visualisation technology of the aerodynamic environment in a greenhouse using CFD and VR technology, part 1: development of VR a database using CFD. Biosys. Eng. **207**, 33–58 (2021). https://doi.org/10.1016/j.biosystemseng.2021.02.017
26. EnergyPlus. https://energyplus.net/weather. Accessed 25 May 2023
27. Latin Hypercube Sampling vs. Monte Carlo Sampling – Data Science Genie. https://datasc iencegenie.com/latin-hypercube-sampling-vs-monte-carlo-sampling/. Accessed 08 Jun 2023
28. Petelet, M., Iooss, B., Asserin, O., Loredo, A.: Latin hypercube sampling with inequality constraints. AStA Adv. Stat. Anal. **94**(4), 325–339 (2010). https://doi.org/10.1007/s10182-010-0144-z
29. Nguyen, A.-T., Reiter, S.: A performance comparison of sensitivity analysis methods for building energy models. Build. Simul. **8**(6), 651–664 (2015). https://doi.org/10.1007/s12273-015-0245-4
30. Gagnon, R., Gosselin, L., Decker, S.: Sensitivity analysis of energy performance and thermal comfort throughout building design process. Energy and Buildings **164**, 278–294 (2018). https://doi.org/10.1016/j.enbuild.2017.12.066
31. Tian, W.: A review of sensitivity analysis methods in building energy analysis. Renew. Sustain. Energy Rev. **20**, 411–419 (2013). https://doi.org/10.1016/j.rser.2012.12.014
32. Multiple linear regression - MATLAB regress, Matlab. https://www.mathworks.com/help/stats/regress.html. Accessed 25 May 2023
33. Grégoire, F., Gosselin, L., Alamdari, H.: Sensitivity of carbon anode baking model outputs to kinetic parameters describing pitch pyrolysis. Ind. Eng. Chem. Res. **52**(12), 4465–4474 (2013). https://doi.org/10.1021/ie3030467

A Modifiable Architectural Design for Commercial Greenhouses Energy Economic Dispatch Testbed

Christian Skafte Beck Clausen⬛, Bo Nørregaard Jørgensen⬛, and Zheng Ma(✉)⬛

SDU Center for Energy Informatics, Maersk Mc-Kinney Moeller Institute,
The Faculty of Engineering, University of Southern Denmark, Odense, Denmark
{csbc,zma}@mmmi.sdu.dk

Abstract. Facing economic challenges due to the diverse objectives of businesses, and consumers, commercial greenhouses strive to minimize energy costs while addressing CO_2 emissions. This scenario is intensified by rising energy costs and the global imperative to curtail CO_2 emissions. To address these dynamic economic challenges, this paper proposes an architectural design for an energy economic dispatch testbed for commercial greenhouses. Utilizing the Attribute-Driven Design method, core architectural components of a software-in-the-loop testbed are proposed which emphasizes modularity and careful consideration of the multi-objective optimization problem. This approach extends prior research by implementing a modular multi-objective optimization framework in Java. The results demonstrate the successful integration of the CO_2 reduction objective within the modular architecture with minimal effort. The multi-objective optimization output can also be employed to examine cost and CO_2 objectives, ultimately serving as a valuable decision-support tool. The novel testbed architecture and a modular approach can tackle the multi-objective optimization problem and enable commercial greenhouses to navigate the intricate landscape of energy cost and CO_2 emissions management.

Keywords: Modifiability · architecture · economic dispatch · testbed · greenhouse energy systems

1 Introduction

Commercial greenhouses confront economic challenges stemming from the dynamic objectives of businesses, consumers, and policymakers [1]. From a business standpoint, greenhouses aim to minimize energy costs, while from a societal perspective, stakeholders such as consumers and policymakers strive to reduce CO_2 emissions [2]. These challenges are intensified by escalating energy costs and the global urgency to curb CO_2 emissions [3]. The landscape is further complicated by fluctuating energy prices and CO_2 emissions dependent on specific energy technologies. Commercial greenhouses operating in cold and low-light climates utilize heterogeneous energy systems to meet plant

© The Author(s), under exclusive license to Springer Nature Switzerland AG 2024
B. N. Jørgensen et al. (Eds.): EI.A 2023, LNCS 14467, pp. 234–252, 2024.
https://doi.org/10.1007/978-3-031-48649-4_14

growth demands by providing supplemental heat and electricity [4]. In the prevailing scenario, greenhouse operators determine daily optimal energy system operation based on fluctuating energy prices, climate data, and plant information. This economic dispatch procedure, typically executed in spreadsheets, is both costly and error-prone, involving models that are difficult to adapt to evolving business, consumer, and policymaker objectives.

Therefore, to address these dynamic economic challenges, this paper aims to present an architectural design for a testbed focused on the modifiability of energy economic dispatch in commercial greenhouses, addressing the associated challenges.

The paper is organized as follows. Section 1.1 describes related research. Section 2 describes the methodology. Section 3 identifies stakeholders and high-level requirements. Section 4 describes the experimental setup. Section 5 presents the results. Section 6 discusses the results. Section 7 concludes the paper and lists future work.

1.1 Related Works

Economic dispatch is a regular method in energy systems that aims to dispatch instructions to generation units while minimizing costs given the constraints of load demands [5]. Costs include all relevant economic aspects in the domain. Economic dispatch has been applied in e.g., power systems [6–8], demand response [9], and greenhouses [10, 11]. In essence, economic dispatch is an optimization problem and can be implemented in numerous ways; merit order dispatch [12, 13], multi-objective optimization [3, 6, 14], genetic algorithms [15–18], and particle swarm optimization [19] to mention a few. Each method has inherent advantages/disadvantages.

The economic dispatch algorithm must be verified before deploying it to operation. The verification methods apply the dispatch instructions on generation units in a simulated environment. The type of environment depends on the application's needs, but examples include discrete-event and real-time simulation environments [20]. The purpose is to verify the performance of the dispatcher in open- or closed-loop control systems. The control loop requires models of the generation units under the system environment conditions. White-, grey-, and black-box methods are applied to deriving models that describe the reality of the systems. Recent approaches include digital twins that utilize the Internet of Things (IoT) to (i) mimic the behavior of the physical twins and (ii) operate the physical twin through its inherent cognitive abilities [21].

In-the-loop paradigms can utilize the virtual model or digital twin at various development stages. Software-in-the-loop (SIL) is applied at the early stage to assess the feasibility of the dispatch strategy [22, 23]. The benefit of SIL is that the control logic can be reused throughout the lifetime of the system. This enables rapid feedback cycles that lower costs and reduce risks before deploying the controller logic to production.

To manage and reduce the cost of software changes, flavors of this quality have been proposed: Modifiability, modularity, changeability, flexibility, adaptability, maintainability, and extensibility. Modifiability is a fundamental quality of software systems because changing requirements cause software evolution over the entire lifetime [24]. Therefore, software needs to be modifiable in places that are likely to change. The modifiability parameters involve modularization, increasing cohesion, and reducing coupling.

These parameters can be realized to address changes at different points in time. For example, a change may be manifested during coding-, build-, deployment-, initialization-, or runtime. The existing literature on economic dispatch focuses mostly on the optimization methodology rather than software modifiability and changing needs. The authors in [25], however, demonstrated a climate control application with the ability to add and remove independently developed objectives through a global lookup registry called a blackboard architecture. This paper contributes to the existing literature by suggesting an architectural testbed for economic dispatch for greenhouse energy systems. In contrast to the existing literature, this paper includes (i) an analysis of the architectural issues, (ii) integrates Functional Mock-up Units (FMU) to mimic individual energy production units, (iii) and demonstrates the consequence of various decision-making strategies among Pareto-optimal solutions.

This paper consequently uses the term modifiability to describe the degree to which the system can be changed (add/delete/modify) to meet new requirements [26]. This requires the identification of foreseeable changes through module decomposition which will reduce the change's cost impact.

2 Methodology

This paper applies software engineering principles to design the architecture for the energy economic dispatch in commercial greenhouses with a focus on modifiability. The approach follows Attribute-Driven Design (ADD) proposed by Bass et al. [27]. The goal of ADD is to propose an initial architecture that enables iterative refinement. This method is depicted in Fig. 1. The Attribute-Driven Design (ADD) methodology. The driver of ADD is Architectural Significant Requirements (ASRs) i.e., the important functional and non-functional requirements. The ASRs are derived from high-level stakeholder- and business requirements. These requirements are used to sketch the core architecture where solutions to each architectural element are designed in subsequent iterations. The design must be verified by using appropriate techniques. This paper verifies the design by using a generic energy system of a greenhouse. Experimentation with physical energy production systems exposes the business to significant risks. Therefore, this paper operates on virtual models of energy production systems.

The paper extends previous research in [28, 29] and by applying a Java-based modular multi-objective optimization framework developed at the SDU Center for Energy Informatics [30]. This framework was developed with core design guidelines that focus on modularity. Other Multi-objective Evolutionary Algorithm (MOEA) frameworks are available e.g., jMetal, and MOEA Framework, but they do not satisfy the requirements of (i) providing decision making strategies to select ideal solutions from the Pareto-front and (ii) out-of-the-box integration with Functional Mock-up Interfaces (FMI) and Functional Mock-up Units (FMU). This includes the separation of algorithm configuration, decision variables, objectives, and decision-making strategies. Furthermore, it is important that the framework is interoperable with upstream and downstream systems to function with in-the-loop control approaches.

The chosen framework provides a multi-objective genetic algorithm (MOGA) The MOGA is an evolutionary heuristic search algorithm that progresses in iterations. In the

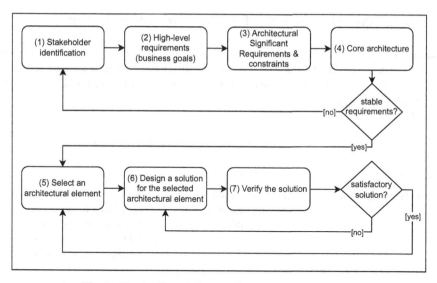

Fig. 1. The Attribute-Driven Design (ADD) methodology.

first iteration, a population of candidate solutions is randomly generated. Each solution is evaluated against the set of objectives and the evaluation yields metrics to compare the optimality of a solution against other solutions. Since objectives may conflict, the currently best solutions found by the MOGA are stored in a Pareto-optimal set. In the subsequent iterations, the MOGA progresses by selecting parent solutions from the Pareto-set. Based on the parents, new candidates are created by applying the MOGA operators of crossover and mutation. Crossover selects genes from each parent, and mutation alters the value of a gene to a random value to diversify the population. Crossover also enables the MOGA to escape local minima. The MOGA terminates upon reaching a termination criterion which in this case is temporally determined. MOGA provides the advantages of being intuitive to understand, fast to implement, and enabling separate modification of objectives during compilation- and runtime. The modification of multiple objectives is possible because the objective does not interfere. This property enables an architecture where objectives can be plugged in/out. The significant disadvantage of MOGA is the high computational cost. This is an important factor for real-time applications, and the application designer must decide whether the computational cost can be afforded. For this paper, the computational window for decision-making is at least 10 min. This window is dictated by the control of the physical equipment. Furthermore, greenhouse climate operators prefer slow ramp-ups/downs of their equipment because it is empirically cost-efficient. This gives time for the MOGA to converge towards optimality.

The paper applies Functional Mock-up Units (FMU) for modeling the energy system dynamics. An FMU is an executable unit that encapsulates the design and behavior of a system as a black box simulation. FMUs provide the necessary interfaces and code to exchange dynamic simulation models of the greenhouse's energy systems. The FMUs in this paper were developed in Dymola/Modelica.

3   High-Level Stakeholders' Requirements Identification

Based on the business ecosystem mapping concept introduced in [31], the stakeholders and their interests were identified through coordinated meetings and seminars. The result is shown in Table 1. The stakeholders and interests are important factors in scoping the architecture through ASRs.

Table 1. Stakeholders, descriptions, and their interests.

Stakeholder	Description	Concerns
Greenhouse business owner	Owns the greenhouse and is therefore responsible for achieving its overall goal	To meet the business goals and the economic aspects of: • Maximizing revenue • Minimizing expenses • Complying with regulatory requirements
Greenhouse grower	The grower is responsible for nurturing the plants including (1) watering, (2) applying fertilizer and retardation, (3) moving plants between conveyors, and (4) logging events for regulatory authorities	• To comply with the expected plant quality (size, number of leaves, etc.)
Greenhouse climate operator	The greenhouse climate operator is responsible for creating ideal growing conditions by monitoring and controlling the indoor environment. For example, artificial lights, curtains, temperature, and CO_2	• To operate the indoor climate while complying with the growing conditions of the plants
Customer	The customer buys the plants	• To buy plants of the expected quality and price
Policy maker	Makes international, national, or local policies that are motivated by social and political factors	• To make and enforce regulations
External data provider	The external data provider is responsible for providing services or data that support the greenhouse business operation	• To provide relevant data of a certain quality (including resolution) that can help the growers in the decision-making process

(*continued*)

Table 1. (*continued*)

Stakeholder	Description	Concerns
Energy Systems Engineer	The energy systems engineer provides the virtual models to simulate the dynamics of the greenhouse energy systems	• To provide virtual models that mimic the real-world properties of the greenhouse energy systems
Systems Engineer	The systems engineer manages and digitalizes the greenhouse business processes to help the business owner achieve their goals	To develop a system that: • Meets the expectations of all stakeholders • To minimize the development effort by managing complexity • To enable rapid development cycles to meet the need for frequent changes in the greenhouse operation
Researcher	The role of the researcher is to advance research within the optimization of energy systems	To have an architectural testbed that enables experimentation through: • Crisp interfaces and abstractions • Analysis of algorithmic output • Translation of business goals into algorithmic objectives

The use of the system is two-folded since the system aims to address research-related- and business-related challenges. Ideally, the energy dispatch algorithms developed on the architectural testbed can be effortlessly deployed on the real system. Figure 2 shows a high-level development process of this ideal. The architecture must support the software-in-the-loop paradigm by operating on virtual models that comply with the interfaces and behavior of the real system. To realize this, the researcher, systems engineer, and energy systems engineer collaborate to realize the control software during early development in stage 1. The control software operates in a closed-loop mode to verify that the controller operates as expected. In stage 2, the virtual models are substituted with a digital twin of the energy systems. This enables verification of the real-time properties of the closed-loop controller. Furthermore, it enables the climate operator to test the decision support tools using the digital twin. Due to high investment costs and physical space requirements, it is infeasible to test the control software on actual hardware using hardware-in-the-loop in a lab. Testing on a digital twin lowers investment costs and enables rapid development cycles. When the test in Stage 2 is satisfactory, the controller software is configured to operate on the real hardware in Stage 3.

The users of the architectural testbed are researchers and climate operators. The researcher's use case is to utilize the architectural testbed to provide a feasible method of economic dispatch. The climate operator use case is decision-making support by using

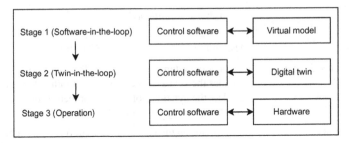

Fig. 2. Development stages using software-in-the-loop and digital twins in process control.

the output of the economic dispatch algorithm to operate the energy systems. Based on the stakeholder analysis and verification requirements, a set of high-level requirements was formulated as presented in Table 2.

Table 2. High-level system requirements.

ID	Description	Requirement type
Requirement 1	The system must address the economic dispatch problem by providing tradeoffs between conflicting business objectives	Functional
Requirement 2	The system must provide monitoring, scheduling, and decision-making features to assist the climate operator in decision-making	Functional
Requirement 3	The system must provide a testbed for developing economic dispatch control strategies. This includes the possibility of algorithmic performance evaluation	Functional
Requirement 4	The system must be modifiable to address the challenge of research-based activities and continuous change throughout the greenhouse operation's lifetime	Non-functional
Requirement 5	The system must support interoperability with test facilities and existing infrastructure e.g., forecasts services, virtual models, digital twins, and SCADA systems	Non-functional

3.1 Architectural Design

Following the ADD method, this section presents a high-level view of the core system architecture (Fig. 3) and subsequently narrows the focus to the economic dispatch optimizer. The design intends to satisfy the requirements by applying the process-control [32, 33] and in-the-loop paradigms. Therefore, the core design must hold throughout the three development stages.

The architecture is decomposed into four subsystems: 1) External inputs, 2) an optimizer, 3) an emulator, and 4) a graphical interface. This decomposition draws a natural

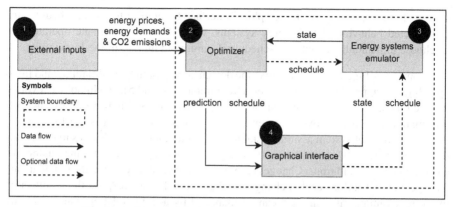

Fig. 3. Architectural design of the economic dispatch testbed.

boundary between the external data providers and the internal system. Furthermore, the architecture enables flexibility, and design choices can be delayed until the refinement of each subsystem. From a functional perspective, it gives the following properties:

- The optimizer isolates the economic dispatch optimization problem to accommodate experimentation with control strategies and performance evaluation. Furthermore, the optimizer can be executed on dedicated computational resources to improve performance using horizontal or vertical scaling.
- The emulator exposes a black box process with controls and the state of the energy system. The emulator can be developed independently by an energy systems engineer in any environment. This assumes that the optimizer and emulator models are interoperable. Furthermore, the emulator can be substituted by the real cyber-physical system.
- The graphical interface can be used by the climate operator for monitoring and decision support purposes. The exact usability requirements and technicalities can be delayed. But for example, it enables isolated development, and optional programming environment or thin clients for mobile units.

The execution of the economic dispatch algorithm is described on a high level as follows:

1. The optimizer is instantiated with a configuration of the multi-objective optimization problem. This includes forecast inputs and the state of the energy system.
2. The optimizer executes until a termination criterion is met. The output is a vector that consists of setpoints for each energy system in a certain resolution (hourly, minutely, …). Essentially, this is a prescription intended to control the energy systems and to inform the climate operator.
3. The optimizer sends the schedule (the current set of setpoints) and the prediction (the predicted result of actuating the setpoints) to the graphical interface. Optionally, the optimizer can send the schedule to the emulator when operating in closed-loop mode.

4. The climate operator uses the graphical interface to monitor the state, schedule, and predicted behavior of the energy systems. Furthermore, the climate operator can choose to manually actuate the schedule if running in human-in-the-loop mode.

From a non-functional perspective, the design aims to satisfy modifiability and interoperability at appropriate system levels (Requirements 4 and 5). Modifiability involves the identification and management of foreseeable changes. Interoperability involves information exchange between systems. On a system level, changes are localized to their respective subsystem assuming stable subsystem interfaces. Changes may cascade if the interoperability assumptions are wrong, i.e., data, sequencing, timing, endpoints, and pre-and post-conditions. Changes regarding interoperability within the boundary are manageable, but unforeseeable changes to the external inputs expose the architecture to wrong assumptions. This risk can be managed by accommodating interoperability through a modifiable architecture.

In the next step of the ADD, the internal structure of the optimizer (Fig. 4) is analyzed since this is the central subsystem of the architecture. The structure reflects the abstractions that need to be modifiable. Most abstractions are provided by the chosen MOEA framework [30] and need only to be specialized in subclasses. The 'External Inputs' module is responsible for upstream interoperability by fetching forecasts and states and making that data compatible with the framework. The 'Decision maker' module provides a configuration of how the 'best' decision from the Pareto-frontier must be selected. This can be used to select the setpoints in the closed-loop scenario with a Digital twin. The 'Output' module is responsible for downstream interoperability with the digital twin and the graphical interface.

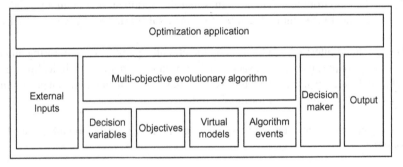

Fig. 4. Internal structure of the optimization application

The 'Multi-objective evolutionary algorithm' module consists of specialized decision variables, objectives, and the algorithm provided by the framework. Decision variables involve the encoding/decoding of the problem. The decision variables e.g., resolution, length, etc. are localized here. The objectives are responsible for evaluating the decision variables into scalar values using external input and the estimated response on the integrated virtual models. The virtual models are integrated into the optimizer as individual components (i.e., heat pumps, combined heat and power plant, gas boiler, district heating, and thermal energy storage). This design accommodates changes in the greenhouse energy system because the component composition can be reflected in code. For example, it can be used to experiment with up- or down-scaling or with heterogeneous energy production technologies. The framework emits algorithmic events that can be used to collect data for performance evaluation e.g., on each generation or upon termination.

4 Experimental Setup

The purpose of the experiment is to demonstrate the economic dispatch in a hypothetical greenhouse application built upon the modular architecture. The experiment includes the following setup:

4.1 Greenhouse Energy System Configuration

The case is based on a hypothetical greenhouse compartment with heterogeneous energy systems. The compartment's energy system was composed of virtual models and a block diagram of their relations is depicted in Fig. 5 where the corresponding symbols are defined in Table 3. The models were implemented in Dymola/Modelica and the models were exported to FMUs for integration with the optimizer's objective functions. The virtual models in this paper were derived with grey-box modeling techniques using on-site measurements from a commercial greenhouse in Denmark. White-box modeling is computationally expensive, and black-box modeling does not capture the physical properties of the system. Furthermore, black-box modeling relies on high-quality training data which were unavailable. The grey-box models approximate the system response using the collected measurements to tune the parameters of theoretical models. This approach is suitable for this paper where the focus is the architectural design and because the model precision can be tuned later. The system dynamics were simplified to linear equations and the thermal energy storage does not account for temperature gradients or heat loss.

The input vector used to instantiate the energy system is defined by

$$S_{init} = [LF_{chp}, LF_{gb}, LF_{hp}, T_{source}, T_{init}, P_{dh,req}, P_{gh}] \qquad (1)$$

where the output of each model is calculated. The heat output vector $P_{out} = [P_{h,chp}, P_{h,gb}, P_{h,hp}, P_{dh}]$ is used as input parameters of the TES. The TES operates analogous to a battery that can be charged and discharged but with heat instead of electricity. The TES enables flexible operation because heat can be stored when prices are low and drained when prices are high. The outputs $E_{out} = [P_{e,chp}, m_{chp}, m_{gb}, P_{e,hp}, P_{dh}]$ are used to calculate the economics of the energy system in terms of costs and CO_2 emissions.

4.2 Multi-objective Problem Definition

The energy dispatch schedule is represented as a decision vector that contains the energy systems load factors for each instant in the schedule:

$$S = [C_i, C_{i+1}, \ldots, C_{i+h}, G_i, G_{i+1}, \ldots, G_{i+h}, H_i, H_{i+1}, \ldots, H_{i+h}, D_i, D_{i+1}, \ldots, D_{i+h}]^T \qquad (2)$$

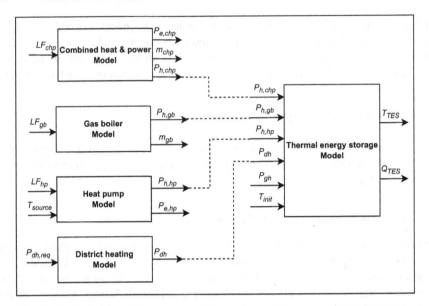

Fig. 5. Block diagram of the experimental greenhouse compartment's energy system.

where S is the schedule, i is an instant, C is the CHP load factor, G is the GB load factor, H is the HP load factor and D is the heat request to the DH provider. The number of instants i are configured depending on the application requirements.

The optimization problem is subject to minimizing the costs and CO_2 emissions of the schedule:

$$\min O_{cost}(S) = \sum_{i=1}^{h} cost_{gas,i} + cost_{el,i} + cost_{dh,i} - income_{el,i} \tag{3}$$

$$\min O_{CO2}(S) = \sum_{i=1}^{h} CO2_{gas,i} + CO2_{el,i} + CO2_{dh,i} \tag{4}$$

where h is the number of instants within the schedule. $Cost_{gas,i}$ is the price of gas consumed in the instant, $cost_{el,i}$ is the price of electricity consumed in the instant, and $cost_{dh,i}$ is the price of district heating consumed in the instant. The CHP produces electricity which needs to be deducted from $income_{el,i}$ in the instant. $CO2_{gas,i}$ is the emissions of gas consumed by the CHP and GB. $CO2_{el,i}$ is the emissions of electricity consumed by the HP. $CO2_{dh,i}$ is the emissions caused by district heating.

The optimization is subject to the following objective space constraints:

$$C_{electricity}(S) = \forall i \in S : P_{gh,i} + P_{e,hp,i} \leq P_{grid\_capacity} \tag{5}$$

$$C_{TES}(S) = \forall i \in S : T_{TES,min} \leq T_{TES,i} \leq T_{TES,max} \tag{6}$$

$C_{electricity}(S)$ states that the greenhouse power demand and the HP power consumption must not exceed the grid capacity in any instant. $C_{TES}(S)$ states that the temperature of the TES must be within the minimum and maximum values in any instant.

Table 3. Block diagram symbols and descriptions.

Symbol	Unit	Interval	Description
LF_{chp}	[-]	[0, 1]	Load factor of the combined heat & power (CHP) model
LF_{gb}	[-]	[0, 1]	Load factor of the gas boiler (GB) model
LF_{hp}	[-]	{0, 1} (binary)	Load factor of the heat pump (HP) model. Either on or off
T_{source}	[°C]	[20, 50]	Water temperature at the inlet of the evaporator of the HP
$P_{h,chp}$	[MW]	[0, 2.8]	Heat power produced by the CHP
$P_{h,hp}$	[kW]	[0, 500]	Heat power produced by the HP
$P_{h,gb}$	[MW]	[0, 7]	Heat power produced by the GB
$P_{dh,req}$	[MW]	[0, 6]	The district heating (DH) power request from the DH network
P_{dh}	[MW]	[0, 6]	Obtained district heating power from the DH network
P_{gh}	[MW]	[0, 10]	Greenhouse heat demand
T_{init}	[°C]	[0, 90]	The initial temperature of the thermal energy storage (TES)
$P_{e,chp}$	[MW]	[0, 1.2]	Electric power produced by the CHP
m_{chp}	[kg/s]	[0, 12]	Gas mass flow rate consumed by the CHP
mgb	[kg/s]	[0, 194]	Gas flow rate consumed by the GB
Pe,hp	[kW]	[0, 125]	Electric power consumed by the HP
T_{TES}	[°C]	[0, 90]	Water temperature of the TES
Q_{TES}	[MWh]	[0, 65]	Stored energy in the TES

The optimization is subject to the following decision space constraints to reduce the size of the decision space.

$$C_{CHP}(S) = \forall C_i \in S : (0 \leq C_i \leq 1) \wedge (C_i mod C_r = 0) \tag{7}$$

$$C_{GB}(S) = \forall G_i \in S : (0 \leq G_i \leq 1) \wedge (G_i mod G_r = 0) \tag{8}$$

$$C_{DH}(S) = \forall D_i \in S : (0 \leq D_i \leq D_{max}) \wedge (D_i mod D_r = 0) \tag{9}$$

$$C_{HP}(S) = \forall H_i \in S : H_i = 0 \vee H_i = 1 \tag{10}$$

$C_{CHP}(S)$ states that the load factor C_i must be between 0 and 1 while being divisible by the resolution C_r. $C_{GB}(S)$ and $C_{DH}(S)$ have similar properties but with separate resolutions G_r and D_r. C_{HP} state that the load factor H_i must be exactly 0 (turned off) or 1 (turned on).

4.3 Optimization Configuration

Table 4 shows the parameters of the optimizer. The TES was configured with an initial temperature T_{init} to enable immediate flexible use. For the experiment, it must not be economically feasible to drain the TES completely in the last instants of the schedule as the optimizer would regard the initial TES contents as free energy. Therefore, an additional objective constraint was created to avoid this case:

$$C_{TES\_end\_temperature}(S) = \forall i \in S : T_{init} \leq T_{TES,h} \tag{11}$$

where T_{init} is the initial temperature of the TES and $T_{TES,h}$ is the temperature in the last instant.

Table 4. Optimization parameters.

Scope	Parameter	Value	Unit
MOGA	Schedule length	168	[h]
	Termination criteria	1	[h]
	Crossover rate	50	[%]
	Mutation operator	Random resetting	[-]
	Crossover operator	Single-point crossover	[-]
	Mutation rate	5	[%]
$C_{electricity}(S)$	$P_{grid\_capacity}$	$12 \cdot 10^6$	[W]
	Electricity Tariff and Fee	0.185	[EUR/kWh]
$C_{TES}(S)$	$T_{TES,min}$	43.96	[°C]
	$T_{TES,max}$	79.84	[°C]
$C_{CHP}(S)$	C_r	$\frac{1}{20}$	[-]
$C_{GB}(S)$	G_r	$\frac{1}{20}$	[-]
$C_{DH}(S)$	D_r	10^4	[-]
	D_{max}	$6 \cdot 10^6$	[W]
TES Model	T_{init}	50	[°C]
HP Model	T_{source}	20	[°C]

4.4 External Inputs

Given the architectural boundary, it is assumed that the external inputs are available as forecasts. The forecasts consist of the greenhouse energy demands (electricity and heat), electricity-, gas-, and district heating prices, and CO_2 emissions for each technology. The forecasted greenhouse demands are depicted in Fig. 6. The forecasted energy demands are based on optimal climate and historical energy consumption records [29] The electricity wholesale price signal was retrieved from Nordpool in the Danish area DK1 and tariffs were retrieved from Energinet. The gas price signal was retrieved from the next day's index of the Exchange Transfer Facility (ETF) at the European Energy Exchange (EEX). The energy prices are depicted in Fig. 7. The CO_2 emissions for electricity are available in a 5-min resolution at Energinet. The 5-min resolution was aggregated into an hourly resolution to satisfy the optimization constraints. CO_2 emissions for district heating are declared as a yearly average and were retrieved from the Danish provider Fjernvarme Fyn. The CO_2 emissions for gas are estimated to be 204 kg CO_2 / MWh by the Danish Energy Agency. The estimated CO_2 emissions are depicted in Fig. 8.

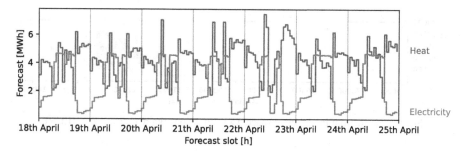

Fig. 6. Greenhouse heat and electricity forecast.

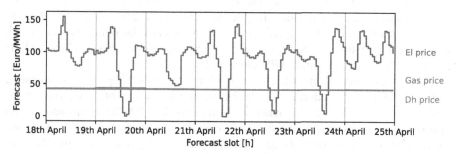

Fig. 7. Energy price forecast.

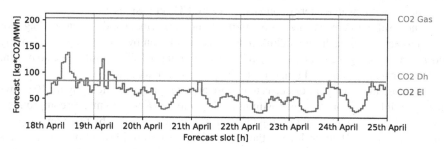

Fig. 8. Estimated CO_2 emissions forecast.

5 Results

The results were conducted on a workstation with an AMD Ryzen 9 5900X 12-core (24 threads) processor, 64 GB DDR4–3200 RAM, NVIDIA GeForce RTX 3060, and a Samsung 970 EVO NVMe drive. The termination criterion was set to 1 h to match the lowest sample resolution from the external inputs. The data was exported in CSV format by using the built-in framework interfaces `GenerationFinishedListener` and `TerminationListener`.

Figure 9 depicts the resulting Pareto-front as a scatter plot of the objective space with CO_2 emissions [kg*CO_2] on the x-axis and costs [EUR] on the y-axis. The gray dots are invalid solutions while the red dots are valid solutions.

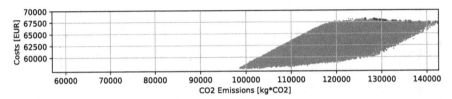

Fig. 9. Pareto-front in objective space; CO_2 emissions [kg*CO_2] vs. costs [EUR].

A solution is valid if the constraints of $C_{electricity}(S)$, $C_{TES}(S)$, and $C_{TES\_end\_temperature}(S)$ are satisfied. The number of invalid solutions is caused by the implementations of the constraints. To guide the MOGA in the objective space, the constraints were implemented as objectives that return a scalar value of the distance to each constraint. The distance is the sum of hours of unsatisfied electricity and heat, and the Euclidean distance to the target TES temperature.

The plot indicates an almost linear relationship between kg*CO_2 and costs indicating CO_2 emissions can be reduced without significantly increasing the costs. This can be explained by the constant CO_2 emission factors [kg*CO_2/MWh] of gas and district heating. Naturally, an increased energy consumption leads to increased CO_2 emissions. This explanation holds true for the gas and district heating CO_2 emissions signals because they are constant. However, CO_2 emissions for electricity consumption does not have this linear relationship, and therefore, the total emission depends on the fraction of energy produced by renewable energy sources with zero CO_2 emissions.

The resulting Pareto-front can be used for automated/manual decision-making. For the automated approach, the optimizer selects one solution by prioritizing or balancing costs or CO_2 using the built-in `DecisionMaker` interface. The result can also be sent to the climate operator for human-in-the-loop decision-making.

Suppose that the operator needs to choose an appropriate solution. Figure 10 shows three possible decision strategies: Minimize CO_2, minimize costs or make a compromise. This can be achieved by configuring the decision-making strategy by first removing the invalid solutions. Then, following the approach suggested in [34], all objective scores are normalized for comparison and have a social welfare metric applied. The minimum CO_2 and cost objectives are computed using an elitist metric, while the compromise is computed using the utilitarian metric. Simply put, the elitist metric selects the lowest value in either dimension. The utilitarian metric sums the normalized objectives scores and selects the solution with the overall lowest value.

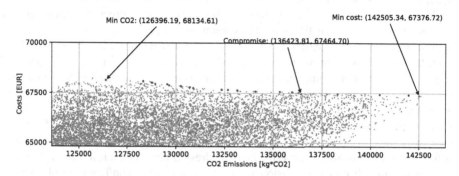

Fig. 10. Decision-making strategies within the Pareto-front.

Table 5 shows a comparison of the three strategies. In the given experiment it is possible to reduce the costs by 757.89 [EUR] (1.11%) but this increases CO_2 emissions by 16109,15 [kg*CO2] (12.74%) over a 168-h period. 16 tons CO_2 corresponds approximately to the average CO_2 emissions of one US citizen in a year.

Table 5. Decision-making strategy comparison.

Strategy	CO_2 [kg*CO_2]	Costs [EUR]	CO_2 index	Costs index
1	126,396.19	681,34.61	100	100
2	136,423.81	674,64.70	107.93	99.02
3	142,505.34	673,76.72	112.74	98.89

6 Discussion

The paper extended the research in [30] by utilizing the modifiable architecture. The CO_2 objective was integrated by adding a new objective that operated on the original set of decision variables in the greenhouse domain. Changes to the CO_2 objective (add/remove/modify) are localized and do not interfere with the cost objective. The external inputs for CO_2 emissions were similarly added to the modular architecture by adhering to the hourly resolution in the domain. The CO_2 objective is limited in a few ways. Firstly, the district heating estimated CO_2 emission is a yearly constant. The objective space would change significantly if the estimates were more precise. Furthermore, there is a risk that averaging the 5-min CO_2 input to an hourly rate skews the optimization results. For example, the CO_2 emissions might increase tremendously in a 5-min period but decrease for the remaining hour. This information is lost when averaging. Secondly, the computational performance can suffer if the resolution is increased from hourly to 5-min intervals, because the solution space increases drastically. Therefore, it is important to adjust the optimization resolution for real-world application needs. Thirdly, the FMUs could have a localized model that reflected CO_2 emissions more precisely depending on the efficiency of the production unit. The computational performance of the algorithm is limited by the FMU integration. FMUs consist of native C-code that must be called from Java when a decision vector is evaluated in the objective. To speed up the performance, a local cache was implemented. The cache stores the computed FMU output on a given decision vector. There is a high probability that equivalent decision vectors are generated due to the stochastic nature of MOEA. Tests showed that implementing the FMUs as linear functions could speed up the objective evaluation by a factor of 50. This computational cost associated with FMU integration is a serious trade-off consideration. A few limitations within the experiment are addressed next. There is a lack of demonstrating modifiability in the decision vector. Changes to the configuration of energy production units require the decision vectors to reflect these changes. There is a tight coupling between the decision vectors, objectives, and FMUs that must be addressed to lower modification costs further. Ideally, these modifiability changes could be made by the climate operator in a domain-specific language or user interface that focuses on usability. The results in hourly resolution should also be compared with decision-making frequencies that reflect the greenhouse domain, for example, to schedule the operation daily or weekly.

7 Conclusion and Future Work

This paper proposes an architectural design for a testbed for energy economic dispatch in commercial greenhouses. This includes the identification of stakeholders and their requirements along with an architectural design. The architecture demonstrated modifiability to the extent that the incoming change request for including CO_2 emissions in the decision-making process can be supported. Furthermore, the architecture separates the core modules in the optimizer to enable economic dispatch experimentation. For example, to experiment with other decision-making strategies, tuning, etc. The architecture aims to accommodate the foreseeable requirements of in-the-loop testing by applying the process-control paradigm. The paradigm separates the decision variables and optimization from the controlled process. This separation promotes modifiability and reusability of the controller in later in-the-loop stages. The proposed novel testbed architecture and a modular approach can tackle the multi-objective optimization problem and enable commercial greenhouses to navigate the intricate landscape of energy cost and CO_2 emissions management. Future work might consider (i) including a demonstration of modifiability in the decision vector and lowering the inherent coupling to the objectives. (ii) Assessing the costs of reconfiguring the energy system by adding new production units or removing obsolete units. (iii) Identifying more operation objectives such as favoring certain production units for impairment or maintenance reasons. (iv) The real-time capability of the core architecture should be tested at the subsequent development stages. Furthermore, (v) the demonstration must involve the graphical decision-making support tool and the digital twin of the greenhouse energy system.

Acknowledgements. This paper is part of the IEA-IETS Annex XVIII: Digitization, artificial intelligence and related technologies for energy efficiency and reduction of greenhouse gas emissions in industry project, funded by EUDP (project number: 134–21010) and the Greenhouse Industry 4.0 project funded by the Danish Energy Technology Development and Demonstration Program (EUDP Project no 64019–0018).

References

1. Ma, Z., Jørgensen, B.N.: Energy flexibility of the commercial greenhouse growers: the potential and benefits of participating in the electricity market. In: 2018 IEEE Power & Energy Society Innovative Smart Grid Technologies Conference (ISGT) (2018)

2. Howard, D.A., Ma, Z., Jørgensen, B.N.: Digital twin framework for energy efficient greenhouse industry 4.0. In: Novais, P., Vercelli, G., Larriba-Pey, J.L., Herrera, F., Chamoso, P. (eds.) Ambient Intelligence – Software and Applications: 11th International Symposium on Ambient Intelligence, pp. 293–297. Springer International Publishing, Cham (2021). https://doi.org/10.1007/978-3-030-58356-9_34

3. Howard, D., et al.: Optimization of energy flexibility in cooling process for brewery fermentation with multi-agent simulation. In: 6th IEEJ International Workshop on Sensing, Actuation, Motion Control, and Optimization. Shibaura Institute of Technology, Tokyo, Japan (2020)

4. Christensen, K., et al.: Agent-based modeling for optimizing CO_2 reduction in commercial greenhouse production with the implicit demand response. In: 6th IEEJ International Workshop on Sensing, Actuation, Motion Control, and Optimization (SAMCON2020). IEEJ Digital Library: Tokyo, Japan, p. 6 (2020)

5. Chowdhury, B.H., Rahman, S.: A review of recent advances in economic dispatch. IEEE Trans. Power Syst. **5**(4), 1248–1259 (1990)

6. Abido, M.A.M.I.: Environmental/Economic power dispatch using multiobjective evolutionary algorithms. IEEE Trans. Power Syst. **18**(4), 1529–1537 (2003)

7. Xia, X., Elaiw, A.M.: Optimal dynamic economic dispatch of generation: a review. Electric Power Syst. Res. **80**(8), 975–986 (2010)

8. Kunya, A.B., Abubakar, A.S., Yusuf, S.S.: Review of economic dispatch in multi-area power system: state-of-the-art and future prospective. Electric Power Syst. Res. **2023**(217), 109089 (2022)

9. Kjaergaard, M.B., et al.: Demand response in commercial buildings with an assessable impact on occupant comfort. In: 2016 IEEE International Conference on Smart Grid Communications, SmartGridComm **2016**, 447–452 (2016)

10. Van Beveren, P.J.M., et al.: Optimal utilization of a boiler, combined heat and power installation, and heat buffers in horticultural greenhouses. Comput. Electron. Agric. **162**, 1035–1048 (2019)

11. Sørensen, J.C., Jørgensen, B.N.: An extensible component-based multi-objective evolutionary algorithm framework, pp. 191–197 (2017)

12. Hanafi, I.F., Dalimi, I.R.: Economic load dispatch optimation of thermal power plant based on merit order and bat algorithm. In: 2nd IEEE International Conference on Innovative Research and Development, ICIRD **2019**(2), p. 4–8 (2019)

13. Ongsakul, W.: Real-time economic dispatch using merit order loading for linear decreasing and staircase incremental cost functions. Electric Power Syst. Res. **51**(3), 167–173 (1999)

14. Shi, B., Yan, L.X., Wu, W.: Multi-objective optimization for combined heat and power economic dispatch with power transmission loss and emission reduction. Energy **56**, 135–143 (2013)

15. Montana, D., et al.: Genetic algorithms for complex, real-time scheduling. Proc. IEEE Int. Conf. Syst. Man Cybern. **3**, 2213–2218 (1998)
16. Chiang, C.L.: Genetic-based algorithm for power economic load dispatch. IET Gener. Transm. Distrib. **1**(2), 261–269 (2007)
17. Bisht, V.S., et al.: A review on genetic algorithm and its application in power system engineering. In: Malik, H., et al. (eds.) Metaheuristic and Evolutionary Computation: Algorithms and Applications, pp. 107–130. Springer Singapore, Singapore (2021)
18. Qu, Q., et al.: A comprehensive review of machine learning in multi-objective optimization. In: 2021 IEEE 4th International Conference on Big Data and Artificial Intelligence (BDAI) (2021)
19. Mahor, A., Prasad, V., Rangnekar, S.: Economic dispatch using particle swarm optimization: a review. Renew. Sustain. Energy Rev. **13**(8), 2134–2141 (2009)
20. Christensen, K., et al.: Agent-based modeling of climate and electricity market impact on commercial greenhouse growers' demand response adoption. In: 2020 RIVF International Conference on Computing and Communication Technologies (RIVF) (2020). Ho Chi Minh City, Vietnam: IEEE (2020)
21. Negri, E., et al.: Field-synchronized digital twin framework for production scheduling with uncertainty. J. Intell. Manuf. **32**(4), 1207–1228 (2021)
22. Demers, S., Gopalakrishnan, P., Kant, L.: A generic solution to software-in-the-loop. Proceedings - IEEE Military Communications Conference MILCOM (2007)
23. Osadcuks, V., Galins, A.: Software in the loop simulation of autonomous hybrid power system of an agricultural facility. Latvia University Agriculture, Faculty Engineering, institute for Mechanics (2012)
24. Bachmann, F., Bass, L., Nord, R.: Modifiability Tactics. Software Engineering Institute - Technical Report (2007) (CMU/SEI-2007-TR-002)
25. Rytter, M., et al.: Advanced model-based greenhouse climate control using multi-objective optimization. Acta Hort. **2012**(957), 29–35 (2014)
26. Oquendo, F., Leite, J., Batista, T.: Designing modifiability in software architectures. In: Oquendo, F., Leite, J., Batista, T. (eds.) Software Architecture in Action, pp. 127–141. Springer International Publishing, Cham (2016). https://doi.org/10.1007/978-3-319-44339-3_9
27. Bass, L., et al.: Software Architecture in Practice, 4th Edition (2021). Addison-Wesley Professional
28. Howard, D.A., Ma, Z., Veje, C., Clausen, A., Aaslyng, J.M., Jørgensen, B.N.: Greenhouse industry 4.0 – digital twin technology for commercial greenhouses. Energy Inf. **4**(2), 1–13 (2021). https://doi.org/10.1186/s42162-021-00161-9
29. Qu, Y.: A digital twin framework for commercial greenhouse climate control system (2023), University of Southern Denmark (The Maersk Mc Kinney Moller Institute)
30. Clausen, C.S.B., Sørensen, J.V.: Architectural refinement of a multi-objective multi-issue optimization framework (2021). University of Southern Denmark (The Maersk Mc Kinney Moller Institute)
31. Ma, Z., Christensen, K., Jorgensen, B.N.: Business ecosystem architecture development: a case study of Electric Vehicle home charging. Energy Inf. **4**, 37 (2021)
32. Åström, K.J., Wittenmark, B.: Computer-Controlled Systems: Theory and Design, Third Edition. Dover Books on Electrical Engineering (2011). Dover Publications
33. Shaw, M.: A software design paradigm based on process control (1994)
34. Anders, C., et al.: Impact of social welfare metrics on energy allocation in multi-objective optimization. Energies **13**, 1–19 (2020)

Business Models for Digitalization Enabled Energy Efficiency and Flexibility in Industry: A Survey with Nine Case Studies

Zhipeng Ma[1]([⊠]) [ID], Bo Nørregaard Jørgensen[1]([⊠]) [ID], Michelle Levesque[2], Mouloud Amazouz[3], and Zheng Ma[1]([⊠]) [ID]

[1] SDU Center for Energy Informatics, Maersk Mc-Kinney Moller Institute,
The Faculty of Engineering, University of Southern Denmark, 5230 Odense, Denmark
{zma,bnj,zhma}@mmmi.sdu.dk
[2] CanmetMINING-Sudbury, Natural Resources Canada, 1079 Kelly Lake Road, Sudbury,
ON P3E 5P5, Canada
michelle.levesque@NRCan-RNCan.gc.ca
[3] CanmetENERGY Varennes, Natural Resources Canada, 1615 Lionel-Boulet Blvd., Varennes,
QC J3X 1S6, Canada
mouloud.amazouz@NRCan-RNCan.gc.ca

Abstract. Digitalization is challenging in heavy industrial sectors, and many pilot projects facing difficulties to be replicated and scaled. Case studies are strong pedagogical vehicles for learning and sharing experience & knowledge, but rarely available in the literature. Therefore, this paper conducts a survey to gather a diverse set of nine industry cases, which are subsequently subjected to analysis using the business model canvas (BMC). The cases are summarized and compared based on nine BMC components, and a Value of Business Model (VBM) evaluation index is proposed to assess the business potential of industrial digital solutions. The results show that the main partners are industry stakeholders, IT companies and academic institutes. Their key activities for digital solutions include big-data analysis, machine learning algorithms, digital twins, and Internet of Things developments. The value propositions of most cases are improving energy efficiency and enabling energy flexibility. Moreover, the technology readiness levels of six industrial digital solutions are under level 7, indicating that they need further validation in real-world environments. Building upon these insights, this paper proposes six recommendations for future industrial digital solution development: fostering cross-sector collaboration, prioritizing comprehensive testing and validation, extending value propositions, enhancing product adaptability, providing user-friendly platforms, and adopting transparent recommendations.

Keywords: Industry 4.0 · Digitalization · Energy Efficiency · Energy Flexibility · Business Model

B. N. Jørgensen et al. (Eds.): EI.A 2023, LNCS 14467, pp. 253–270, 2024.
https://doi.org/10.1007/978-3-031-48649-4_15

1 Introduction

The industry sector accounts for 25.6% of the energy consumption in the European Union (EU) in 2021 [1], where both the industrial process and non-process-related operations contribute to this energy usage. It is crucial to improve energy efficiency and flexibility in the industry to combat global climate change. In this context, digitalization has emerged as a promising technology to achieve these goals in Industry 4.0 [2].

Energy efficiency [3] refers to the capacity of decreasing energy consumption while maintaining production quality. It involves employing technologies, practices, and systems that minimize energy waste and maximize the output obtained from the energy consumed [4]. On the other hand, energy flexibility [5] pertains to the capability of an energy system to adapt its energy production or consumption patterns in response to fluctuations in energy supply or demand conditions. This flexibility allows the system to efficiently balance the energy generated or consumed with the changing needs and availability of energy resources [6].

Digitalization enables the collection and analysis of large-scale data from industrial processes, equipment, and operations for the research of energy efficiency and flexibility through various technologies such as Artificial Intelligence (AI), Machine Learning (ML), Internet of Things (IoT), Digital Twins (DT), Cloud Computing, etc. [7]. These technologies can be leveraged to identify energy consumption patterns [8] and optimize energy usage [9] in industry. Moreover, industrial processes can be optimized to minimize energy usage and maximize production quality with Optimization models and ML algorithms [10]. They can be employed to identify energy-efficient operating conditions [11], adjust setpoints [3], and optimize process parameters [12]. Furthermore, the intelligent system can offer recommendations for optimizing key devices regarding energy efficiency or flexibility by utilizing explainable AI frameworks [13]. These frameworks provide transparency and comprehensibility in the decision-making process, enabling users to understand and interpret the provided recommendations.

Numerous projects have emerged to leverage the benefits of digitalization by employing digital tools to assist industrial stakeholders in attaining their energy consumption goals [14]. However, the process of industrial digitalization is intricate and influenced by various factors [15]. Consequently, developing tailored strategies that cater to distinct requirements and minimize individual risks becomes essential [16].

Prior to the development of industrial digital solutions, it is crucial to conduct a comprehensive survey of existing cases and understand their strengths and drawbacks. The Business Model Canvas (BMC) is a strategic management tool that visually represents key value blocks, outlining the core aspects of a business model [17]. By using the BMC, a systematic overview of industrial digitalization cases can be obtained, enabling individuals to identify potential gaps, opportunities, and areas for innovation within their products, which facilitates more effective decision-making and strategic planning processes. Four business models based on BMC have been developed in [15] to investigate the building participation in energy aggregation market by analyzing building owners' requirements to develop feasible market access strategies for different types of buildings. An evaluation tool [18] is proposed to access the business model for smart cities with the potential to be extend for evaluating all BMCs for digital solutions.

So far, only a few studies have surveyed industrial digitalization cases for energy efficiency and flexibility and employed the BMC to analyze the cases. To fill the research gap, this paper utilizes the BMC to analyze nine cases of digitalization-enabled energy efficiency and flexibility in the industry. Moreover, their values in different BMC blocks are analyzed in detail and an evaluation index is proposed to assess the value of potential business models of industrial digital solutions.

The remainder of the paper is organized as follows. Section 2 reviews the literature on digital solutions and relevant business models for energy efficiency and flexibility. Section 3 introduces the data collection and analysis methods. Section 4 presents the results of the BMC on nine cases in industrial digitalization and Sect. 6 discusses the potentials and challenges of digitalization for energy efficiency and flexibility. Section 7 concludes the study and makes recommendations for future research.

2 Related Works

2.1 Digital Solutions for Energy Efficiency and Flexibility

Advancements in digitalization technologies, such as Artificial Intelligence (AI), Machine Learning (ML), the Internet of Things (IoT), Digital Twin (DT), and Cloud Computing, have provided unique opportunities for augmenting the performance of energy applications. The fusion of these diverse methodologies often results in a more precise and resilient analysis.

For instance, a study in [19] introduces an innovative ML-based optimization framework to tweak the pivotal parameters affecting bioenergy production, with the objective of enhancing energy efficiency. This study leverages a neural network (NN) for predicting energy consumptions and production yield with a high accuracy.

In another research [8], a kCNN-LSTM framework is put forward to yield accurate predictions on building energy consumption. The research employs k-means clustering to decipher energy consumption patterns; utilizes Convolutional Neural Networks (CNN) to unravel complex features that influence energy consumption; and uses Long Short Term Memory (LSTM) to capture long-term dependencies by modeling temporal information in time series data. This framework's implementation at both the electricity network and user levels could significantly assist in informed decision-making, effective demand management, and improving energy efficiency.

Furthermore, [20] employs a multi-agent-based simulation to probe into the potential of energy flexibility in the Danish brewery sector. The research indicates that Danish breweries could reduce their electricity expenses by 1.56% annually, maintain operational security, and decrease their greenhouse gas (GHG) emissions by approximately 1745 tons. Moreover, [21] applies a life cycle assessment (LCA) model to evaluate the carbon footprint in the food processing industry. Here, the k-means clustering technique is used to discern the optimal production flow that results in lower energy consumption. The study's findings suggest that the most energy-efficient temperature at the end of the production line is -25 °C, with a tolerance of $\pm$ 2 °C.

2.2   Business Models for Energy Efficiency and Flexibility

Business models play an important role in digital technology analysis, which is helpful to facilitate, configure, and broker system innovation [22]. [23] discusses the business model innovation to address salient bottlenecks in the European energy transition. The results show that digital technologies for cost reduction are often more impactful than digital technologies for adding value.

The study in [24] indicates that eight dimensions in business models should be considered when analyzing industrial digitalization, including resource, network, customer, market, revenue, manufacturing, procurement, and financial. The summary and comparison demonstrate that digitalization has a positive impact on sustainable manufacturing. Furthermore, [25] introduces a digital business model innovation ladder that helps to enhance understanding of the social and environmental values associated with industrial digitalization. The higher up business models are on the innovation ladder, the greater value they create for the energy system but fewer benefits for users.

Existing business models typically focus on analyzing either digital solutions or energy efficiency studies. However, this study introduces a novel business model that specifically analyzes industrial digital solutions aimed at improving energy efficiency and enhancing energy flexibility. The details of this model will be presented in the following section.

3   Methodology

3.1   Data Collection

This study is aimed at gathering cases of digitalization adoption and implementation in industries across multiple sectors. To achieve this, a survey methodology is employed, where industrial stakeholders and IT technology providers offer essential information on base details, technology implementation, and other key takeaways. The data collection process involves a questionnaire with open-ended questions to gather the necessary information from the partners.

The questionnaire comprises four sections: basic information, technology development, market segment, and additional information. The basic information section encompasses both the company's and project's brief descriptions. The technology development section gathers information regarding technology applications, such as implemented solutions, partners involved, and associated implementation costs. The market segment section focuses on the anticipated value proposition and potential implementation challenges. Lastly, the additional information section covers key takeaways and lessons learned.

3.2   Data Analysis – Business Model Canvas

Business Model Canvas. The business model canvas (BMC) [17] is a strategic management tool that provides a visual framework for describing, analyzing, and designing business models, which comprises nine key components, including key partners, key activities, key resources, value propositions, customer relationships, channels, customer segments, cost structure, and revenue streams.

Figure 1 demonstrates the business model for industrial digitalization for energy efficiency and flexibility based on the nine cases. Academic and industry partners play distinct roles when developing industrial digital solutions and contribute different expertise. Academic partners primarily provide theoretical support and state-of-the-art technology, while industry partners contribute data and assist in tool testing and validation. Value proposition represents the unique values that a system offers to meet the specific needs and demands of its target customers. In the context of energy efficiency and flexibility, the industry focuses on achieving goals such as reducing energy consumption and GHG emissions. Moreover, there is also a need to decrease operational costs and enhance production quality.

In the customer relationship perspective, the system provider should offer customized service after selling their products, because most industrial digital solutions are customized. Hence, both communication channels and revenue streams are also negotiated between providers and customers. Moreover, the customer segments involved can vary significantly due to distinct targets in different cases.

Key Partners	Key Activities	Value Propositions	Customer Relationships	Customer Segments
• Academic stakeholders • Industrial stakeholders	• Big-data analysis • AI	• Energy efficiency • Energy flexibility	• Consultation • Maintenance service	• Production data management • R&D
	Key Resources • Skilled Professionals • Software/Platform		**Channels** • Online platforms • Telephonic service	
Cost Structure • Fix costs • Variable costs			**Revenue Streams** • Financial inflow	

Fig. 1. Business model of digital solutions for energy efficiency and flexibility in industry.

3.3 Evaluation Index for Business Models

An evaluation index is developed to assess the value of potential business models based on the evaluation tools in [15, 18]. All components affecting business models as well as technology readiness levels (TRLs) and Relevance-Breadth (RB) are included in Eq. (1). This evaluation index can be utilized in all technology-related business model analyses to investigate their value potential. The value 0.3 in Eq. (1) is aimed at avoiding negative results by shifting the VBM (Value of business model) value. The TRL and RB are set as two independent factors while the remaining parameters are parts in a sum, because the TRL and RB directly relate to commercialization potential whereas the others are support factors in the evaluation [15].

$$VBM = TRL \times RB \times (EPR + RID + RA + NCP + CAD + NS + FA - RIC + 0.3) \quad (1)$$

TRLs are a method for estimating the maturity of technologies during the acquisition phase of a program [26]. In 2013, the TRL scale was further canonized by the International Organization for Standardization (ISO) with the publication of the ISO 16290:2013 standard. Table 1 shows the definition of the TRL scale in the European Union (EU). The TRL level 1–9 is also the value of parameter TRL in Eq. (1).

Table 1. The definition of TRL [27].

TRL	Definition
1	Basic principles observed
2	Technology concept formulated
3	Experimental proof of concept
4	Technology validated in the laboratory
5	Technology validated in a relevant environment
6	Technology demonstrated in a relevant environment
7	System prototype demonstration in an operational environment
8	System complete and qualified
9	Actual system proven in an operational environment

The RB metric indicates the applicability of the tool in various domains. A score of 1 signifies that the system can be applied across multiple domains and targets, while a score of 0.5 indicates that the tool is specific to a particular domain or target. Furthermore, a score of 0.1 implies that the system is customized for a specific company. The rest of the parameters in VBM are defined in Table 2.

Based on the definition of each parameter and their value ranges, the range of VBM is (0, 64.8]. A large value represents a more significant commercial potential of the business model. The VBM value can be assigned to three different levels as Table 3 shows.

The low level denotes that the business model has little commercial value. The threshold 7.5 is calculated by setting TRL at 5, RB at 0.5, NS at 0.2, and all of the rest parameters at 0.5. An industrial digital solution with a TRL under 5 is still undergoing laboratory testing and validation, and real-world application tests have not yet been conducted. RB at 0.5 indicates that such a product has the potential to be sold to similar companies in the market. Moreover, more participating segments may lead to higher collaboration risks. For instance, it becomes challenging to reach a consensus where every segment involved is completely satisfied.

Table 2. Description of evaluation index for the business model.

Components from Business Model Canvas	Criteria	Value Explanation
Key Partners	External partner reliability (EPR)	1: none or small collaboration with external partners 0.5: external partners are necessary 0.1: mainly rely on external partners
Key Activities	Relative implementation difficulty (RID)	1: easy to implement 0.5: can be design and implemented by in-house expertise 0.1: requires external expertise to design and implement
Key Resources	Resource accessibility (RA)	1: existing resources 0.5: new but easy to reach 0.1: new and hard to reach
Value Propositions	Relative Benefits (RB)	1: significant benefits in multiple areas 0.5: significant benefits in one area, or minor benefits in multiple areas 0.1: minor benefits in one area
Customer Relationships	New customer potential (NCP)	1: easy to extend new customers 0.5: hard to extend new customers 0.1: aimed at keeping existing customers
Channels	Channel access difficulty (CAD)	1: an existing channel 0.5: new but easy to build 0.1: new and hard to build
Customer Segments	Number of Segments (NS)	1/(number of segments) range: (0,1] More segments may lead to more interest confliction
Cost Structure	Relative Implementation Cost (RIC)	1: high, and detailed economic feasibility analysis is required 0.5: relatively average, and usually requires a first-order economic feasibility analysis 0.1: limited to no cost involved to implement the opportunity

(continued)

Table 2. (*continued*)

Components from Business Model Canvas	Criteria	Value Explanation
Revenue Streams	Familiarity and affordability (FA)	1: familiar to customers and companies 0.5: partly familiar to customers and companies 0.1: totally new to customers and companies

The medium level refers to a system that has limited commercial value in the market and several barriers to be applied in multiple areas, whereas the high level represents that the products have high commercial value in multiple areas. The threshold 21.9 is calculated by setting TRL at 7, RB at 1, NS at 1/3, and the rest of the parameters at 0.5. A product with a TRL above 7 is mature enough to be sold in the market. RB at 1 indicates that such a product has the potential to be sold to companies in different areas.

Table 3. Level of VBM values.

Range of the VBM value	Level
(0, 7.5]	Low
(7.5, 21.9]	Medium
(21.9, 64.8]	High

4   Case Studies

This research paper analyzes nine diverse instances of industrial digitalization, each one strategically implemented for the enhancement of energy efficiency and flexibility. These nine case studies are derived from nine distinct projects associated with the IEA-IETS Annex XVIII. This Annex is concerned with the integration of digitization, artificial intelligence, and other associated technologies to optimize energy efficiency and reduce greenhouse gas emissions within various industrial sectors [28].

A comprehensive analysis of all nine cases has been conducted using the business model canvas outlined in Fig. 1. This strategic management template is utilized to analyze each case's business model and understand their structure and strategies in detail. In addition to this, the commercial potential of each case is further assessed by computing their respective VBM values. This process provides valuable insights into the individual commercial viability and success potential of each case.

Furthermore, Table 4 provides an overview of the general information pertinent to the nine case studies. More detailed descriptions and findings for each case can be found in the referenced document [28].

Table 4. General information on the nine cases.

No	Company name	Sector	Topic
1	ArcelorMittal	Steel manufacturing	Scheduling a Galvanizing Line Using Ant-Colony Optimization to Minimize Costs and Energy Consumption
2	CanmetENERGY/NRCan	Pulp and paper mill	Online Paper Machine Operation Optimization and Inefficiencies Diagnosis
3	Christonik	Transportation	Structured Data Collection and Analytics for Reduced Carbon Footprint Mobile
4	KMD A/S	General Production	Energy Key Production Insight
5	MayaHTT	Pulp and paper production	Pulp & Paper Production Quality Prediction
6	SDU-CEI	Horticulture	Digital Twin of Greenhouse Energy System
7	SDU-CEI	Horticulture	Digital Twin of Greenhouse Production Flow
8	Software AG	General Production	KI4ETA - Artificial Intelligence for Energy Technology and Applications in Production
9	Tata Steel B.V	Steel manufacturing	SMEAT: Smart Heat Management

5 Results

The nine cases are analyzed based on BMC in Sect. 3.2, and the case information regarding the nine BMC blocks is summarized and compared in the following subsection. Their VBM scores are presented in this section as well.

5.1 Business Model Analysis

Key Partners. Table 5 illustrates the key partnerships in the selected cases, involving academic and industry stakeholders. These partnerships serve unique roles in developing and implementing industrial digital solutions, each contributing their distinct expertise. Academic partners are typically responsible for providing theoretical backing and contributing cutting-edge technology. On the other hand, industry partners supply necessary data and lend support in the testing and validation of digital tools.

Only a third of the cases involved academic partners, mainly due to the fact that the project leads hailed from academic institutions and were equipped to tackle theoretical challenges independently. Industrial partners are further divided into three categories: IT service providers, industry decision-makers and end-users, and investors. IT service providers support in establishing the IoT architecture, resolving hardware issues, and crafting software solutions. Industry decision-makers and end-users contribute real-world processing data and specific application requirements. Lastly, investors comprise of both investment companies and funding agencies.

Table 5. Summary and comparison of key partners in the nine cases.

Key partners	Case 1	Case 2	Case 3	Case 4	Case 5	Case 6	Case 7	Case 8	Case 9
Academic partners	✓	✓					✓		
IT service providers		✓	✓		✓			✓	✓
Industry decision maker and end-user		✓			✓	✓	✓	✓	✓
Investor				✓					

Key Activities. The key activities across the nine cases, as summarized in Table 6, demonstrate the range of technologies employed to create and deliver value in this study. These technologies include big data analytics, artificial intelligence (AI), machine learning (ML), Internet of Things (IoT), and digital twins (DT). Big data analytics methods are utilized to process raw industrial data, aimed at enhancing data quality and operational efficiency. ML and deep learning (DL) algorithms are employed as state-of-the-art AI technologies for prediction, decision-making, optimization, and recommendation across many domains. DT serves as a digital replication of a physical system, used to simulate the performance of the physical counterpart, leading to efficiency, productivity, and performance improvements. IoT pertains to a network of physical objects equipped with sensors and software that allow them to collect and exchange data over the internet.

Table 6. Summary and comparison of key activities in the nine cases.

Key activities	Case 1	Case 2	Case 3	Case 4	Case 5	Case 6	Case 7	Case 8	Case 9
Big data		✓	✓		✓				
ML/DL	✓	✓		✓	✓			✓	✓
DT		✓				✓	✓		
IoT			✓		✓			✓	

Key Resources. Key resources include the vital assets and infrastructures required to deliver value propositions, such as skilled professionals, hardware/software facilities, and intellectual property rights. Within the context of industrial digitalization, the expertise of professionals and the software or platforms used for programming and simulation are considered critical resources.

Value Propositions. The value propositions of the nine cases are shown in Table 7. In the energy efficiency domain, the primary objectives are to reduce GHG emissions and minimize energy consumption. This involves implementing technologies that enhance energy resource utilization, such as equipment upgrades and energy-saving practices. By reducing energy waste and improving overall efficiency, the purpose is to mitigate the environmental impact associated with energy generation and consumption.

In the energy flexibility domain, the focus shifts toward identifying and implementing optimal practices in industrial processing. The goal is to optimize processes efficient energy resource utilization, leading to reduced energy costs and production time. While reducing energy costs and production time are key targets in the energy flexibility domain, it's important to consider other value propositions as well. Operational costs play a significant role in determining industrial best practices, so any improvements in energy efficiency or flexibility should aim to minimize these costs. Additionally, the production quality is crucial in ensuring the reliability and performance of industrial systems, and it should be considered alongside other factors when designing and implementing industrial digital solutions for energy efficiency and flexibility in industry.

Table 7. Summary and comparison of value propositions in the nine cases.

Value propositions	Case 1	Case 2	Case 3	Case 4	Case 5	Case 6	Case 7	Case 8	Case 9
Improve energy efficiency		✓	✓	✓			✓	✓	✓
Reduce GHG emissions		✓	✓	✓	✓	✓			✓
Reduce energy cost					✓	✓			
Reduce production time					✓				
Optimize process	✓				✓	✓	✓	✓	
Improve production quality	✓							✓	

Customer Relationships. The term 'customer relationships' denotes the interaction and services exchanged between system providers and customers. In the context of energy efficiency and flexibility, industrial digital solutions are customized to meet unique demands. Consequently, technology providers are expected to offer timely consultation and regular maintenance services.

Channels. To facilitate smooth customer interaction, service providers must establish a stable and easily accessible communication channel. This could be through online platforms or telephonic services, enabling efficient and convenient exchanges.

Customer Segments. Table 8 summarizes the customer segments in the cases. These groups are categorized based on their roles in the project. This study focuses on the technical segments of digitalization system implementation, while excluding the management and financial departments from its scope. Initially, the IT department responsible for production data management should be involved to provide top-tier data, thereby ensuring accurate analysis and informed decision-making. Typically, this data collection and management process is led by the technology departments. Subsequently, IT departments also infuse their industry-specific knowledge into the project, offering valuable insights on technical aspects, standards, regulations, and best practices related to the industrial digital solutions. Finally, the Research and Development (R&D) department illuminates the challenges and optimization necessities within the production workflow, leveraging their expertise to identify inefficiencies, bottlenecks, and areas for improvement.

Table 8. Summary and comparison of customer segments in the nine cases.

Customer segments	Case 1	Case 2	Case 3	Case 4	Case 5	Case 6	Case 7	Case 8	Case 9
R&D Dept	✓	✓							✓
Energy Dept		✓						✓	✓
IT Dept. Technology	✓		✓	✓	✓	✓	✓		

Cost Structure. Table 9 demonstrates the cost structure of the cases. It's crucial to identify all significant costs and expenses tied to the operation of your business, including fixed and variable costs, economies of scale, and resource allocation. When managing a business for digitalization systems, it is essential to consider both fixed and variable costs. The fixed costs encompass expert hours for system development and the licensing costs of software and platforms. On the other hand, variable costs relate to devices and expert hours required for system updates and maintenance.

Revenue Streams. Within the context of this study, revenue streams are defined as the various modes of financial inflow. These streams epitomize the agreed upon forms of remuneration, carefully negotiated and established between system providers and

Table 9. Summary and comparison of the cost structure in the nine cases.

Cost structure	Case 1	Case 2	Case 3	Case 4	Case 5	Case 6	Case 7	Case 8	Case 9
Expert hours	✓	✓		✓	✓	✓	✓	✓	✓
License			✓			✓	✓	✓	✓
System update/maintenance	✓	✓	✓	✓	✓	✓	✓	✓	✓

customers. These arrangements not only underscore the business' profitability but also reflect the value proposition offered to the consumers.

5.2 Value of Business Model Evaluation

The data illustrated in Table 10 reveals that six out of the nine industrial digital solutions occupy a medium position, signifying that a majority of the industrial digital solutions hold commercial potential, but require additional verification. Primarily, in most instances, the Technology Readiness Levels (TRLs) of these systems are classified at level 6. This indicates that these industrial digital solutions have undergone successful validation and demonstration in a context that is relevant to their designed functions. However, to enhance the TRLs, it's necessary to undertake further testing in a real-world operational environment.

Moreover, although these industrial digital solutions bring significant advantages in certain areas, their applicability in different domains tends to be restricted, leading to a Relevance-Breadth (RB) score of 0.5. To illustrate, the software deployed in the third case study has successfully enhanced energy efficiency by up to 20%. However, its ability to be adapted to optimize different objectives, such as operational cost, or its applicability in other industrial sectors, might be constrained. Therefore, its VBM level is medium as shown in Table 10.

Table 10. Evaluation scores of parameters in VBM

Cases	TRL	RB	EPR	RID	RA	NCP	CAD	NS	FA	RIC	VBM	Level
1	9	1	1	0.5	0.1	1	0.5	0.2	0.5	0.1	**36**	**High**
2	6	0.5	0.5	0.5	0.1	0.1	0.5	1	0.5	0.1	**10.2**	**Medium**
3	8	0.5	0.1	1	0.5	1	0.5	1	0.5	0.1	**19.2**	**Medium**
4	6	0.5	1	0.1	0.5	0.1	0.5	1	0.5	0.5	**10.5**	**Medium**
5	7	1	0.5	1	0.1	0.5	0.5	1	0.5	0.5	**27.3**	**High**

(continued)

Table 10. (*continued*)

Cases	TRL	RB	EPR	RID	RA	NCP	CAD	NS	FA	RIC	VBM	Level
6	6	0.5	0.5	1	1	0.1	0.5	1	0.5	0.5	**13.2**	Medium
7	6	0.5	0.5	1	1	0.1	0.5	0.5	0.5	0.1	**12.9**	Medium
8	6	1	0.1	0.5	0.1	0.5	0.5	1	0.5	0.5	**18**	Medium
9	3	0.1	0.5	0.5	0.5	0.1	0.5	0.33	0.5	0.1	**0.94**	Low

6   Discussion

6.1   Strengths and Weaknesses

The nine cases in this paper are all specifically designed with a focus on enhancing energy efficiency and flexibility within various industries. Given the European Union's ambitious objective of a 55% reduction in GHG emissions by 2030 [29], there is a significant potential for growth in the market for industrial digitalization tools geared towards decreasing energy consumption and GHG emissions.

Current industrial digital solutions have demonstrated their proficiency in offering solutions for improving energy efficiency and reducing operational costs. For example, the digitalization framework in case 2 helps the pulp and paper mill company save about 11% energy. This is achieved through the deployment of advanced digitalization methodologies including Machine Learning/Deep Learning (ML/DL), Digital Twins (DT), and the Internet of Things (IoT). Additionally, these industrial digital solutions often offer customization to suit specific partners and objectives, thus facilitating flexible requirements from the client's end. Moreover, the development cost of these digital solutions is relatively manageable, usually entailing expenses such as expert personnel salaries, licensing fees for specific software or platforms, and certain hardware devices.

Despite these strengths, there are limitations that must be acknowledged. Firstly, the discrete scale used in the VBM metric is derived from [10, 12], which might not be the optimal scale for evaluation as how close to a specific value is not defined. Secondly, except for cases 1 and 3, the remaining digital solutions are still in developmental phases, not yet primed for commercial applications. They necessitate extensive real-world testing to ensure reliability and effectiveness. In addition, digital systems also contribute to GHG emissions through electricity consumption by servers, computing equipment, and cooling systems. Achieving net energy savings in both the industry system and digitalization tools is therefore paramount. Moreover, the discussed industrial digital solutions were sector-specific, limiting their applicability. Therefore, tech providers should broaden product adaptability across sectors, potentially expanding their customer base, supporting commercial success, and advancing energy efficiency and GHG reduction goals.

6.2   Relationships Between BMC Components

The results show that there are differences in key partners key activities, customer segments from value proposition perspective as shown in Table 11, but not in the other

BMC components. Commonly, timely information exchange with customer departments is crucial for discussing requirements and maintenance services in the development of industrial digital solutions. Therefore, it is essential to establish a stable and accessible communication channel. Furthermore, careful calculation and discussion of costs and budget between the system provider and customer, along with negotiation of financial inflow, are critical for ensuring successful system development. Moreover, both industrial and academic partners can contribute to the big-data analysis and AI frameworks in distinct aspects. Such methods are leveraged in some software or hardware platforms by skilled professionals, which are the key resources.

Table 11. Relationships between BMC components

Value propositions	Improve energy efficiency	Reduce GHG emissions	Optimize process	Improve production quality	Reduce energy cost	Reduce production time
Key partners	Industry decision maker and end-user; IT service providers					
	Academic partners					
	Investor					
Key activities	Big data; Machine learning; IoT					
	DT				DT	
Customer segments	IT Department					
	R&D Department; Energy Department					

6.3 Recommendations on Digital Solution Development for Enabling Energy Efficiency and Flexibility in Industry

This paper presents an improved and comprehensive set of recommendations designed to enhance the effectiveness and value proposition of industrial digital solutions, with a particular focus on big data-driven tools and services:

- Fostering cross-sector collaboration: Cross-sector collaboration is a pivotal strategy for developing digitalization solutions [30]. Industry stakeholders should emphasize the collection and integration of high-quality, multi-sourced data, as well as the use of advanced data analytics technologies in their operations. This requires forging partnerships with IT companies offering AI-integrated, data-driven products and services. Additionally, collaboration with research institutes can offer access to state-of-the-art solutions, fostering knowledge sharing and further enhancing data utilization.
- Prioritizing comprehensive testing and validation: The operational effectiveness of industrial digital solutions relies heavily on extensive testing and validation in real-world environments [31]. Such practices ensure the systems can reliably handle real-life situations, identify potential bottlenecks or weaknesses before full-scale deployment. This can lead to a more secure, reliable, and efficient system.

- Extending value propositions: The value proposition of digital solutions should not be solely technology-focused [32]; it should also include aspects like operational costs and production quality. In a competitive industrial environment, organizations should strive to enhance efficiency and product quality, two key performance indicators directly influenced by digitalization.
- Enhancing product adaptability: Digital solution providers should focus on improving the adaptability of their systems for wider application scenarios [33]. This broadens the customer base by catering to diverse industry requirements, which subsequently enhances the commercial viability and impact of the solutions.
- Providing user-friendly platforms: From the customer's perspective, it's vital to have a user-friendly platform that provides accurate analyses [34]. The ease of use and precision of insights significantly influence customer satisfaction, facilitating more informed decision-making and promoting adoption of the solution.
- Adopting transparency: Service providers should offer clear and understandable recommendations to clients [35]. Hence, the application of explainable AI technologies is highly recommended in these systems. Such transparency fosters trust between providers and users, making it easier for clients to understand the value of the solution and how it contributes to their operations.

7 Conclusion

This study conducted an in-depth analysis and provided a critical discussion surrounding digital solutions designed for energy efficiency and flexibility within the industrial sector. Primary data on nine pertinent cases was meticulously compiled via survey methods, which were subsequently evaluated and compared through the lens of the Business Model Canvas framework. In a novel approach, an evaluative index known as the Value of Business Model (VBM) was introduced with the purpose of assessing the business viability and potential of these digital solutions.

Our findings underscore the necessity for extensive real-world testing and validation to elevate the technical robustness of these digital solutions. Additionally, to optimize energy efficiency and flexibility in industry, operational costs and product quality should be elevated to the status of key metrics, alongside traditional considerations of energy consumption and GHG emissions. It is equally vital that the digital solutions possess a degree of extensibility to enable their adoption across wider scenarios, consequently broadening the potential customer base. A system's inherent flexibility and scalability, therefore, are paramount attributes that enable adaptation to diverse needs and accommodate future expansion.

In summary, it is of utmost importance to orchestrate symbiotic, intelligent digital solutions capable of informing and guiding decisions concerning energy efficiency and energy flexibility. Drawing on the insights gleaned from the case studies featured in this study, future research endeavors can further refine and enhance industrial digital solutions. It is recommended to design digital solutions that are user-friendly, transparent, and possesses the ability to maximize potential for application across a range of contexts. This approach will not only improve usability but also foster a wider acceptance and implementation of digital solutions in various industrial sectors.

Acknowledgements. This paper is part of the IEA IETS Task XVIII: Digitalization, Artificial Intelligence and Related Technologies for Energy Efficiency and GHG Emissions Reduction in Industry, funded by the Danish funding agency, the Danish Energy Technology Development and Demonstration (EUPD) program, Denmark (Case no.134–21010), and the project "Data-driven best-practice for energy-efficient operation of industrial processes - A system integration approach to reduce the CO2 emissions of industrial processes" funded by EUDP (Case no.64020–2108).

References

1. Final energy consumption in industry - detailed statistics (2023). https://ec.europa.eu/eurostat/statistics-explained/index.php?title=Final_energy_consumption_in_industry_-_detailed_statistics#:~:text=Since%201990%20electricity%20and%20natural,in%202021%20(%2D22.5%20%25)

2. Gao, D., Li, G., Yu, J.: Does digitization improve green total factor energy efficiency? Evidence from Chinese 213 cities. Energy **247**, 123395 (2022)

3. Li, W., et al.: A novel operation approach for the energy efficiency improvement of the HVAC system in office spaces through real-time big data analytics. Renew. Sustain. Energy Rev. **127**, 109885 (2020)

4. Howard, D.A., Ma, Z., Jørgensen, B.N.: Digital twin framework for energy efficient greenhouse industry 4.0. In: Novais, P., Vercelli, G., Larriba-Pey, J.L., Herrera, F., Chamoso, P. (eds.) ISAmI 2020. AISC, vol. 1239, pp. 293–297. Springer, Cham (2021). https://doi.org/10.1007/978-3-030-58356-9_34

5. Howard, D.A., Ma, Z., Jørgensen, B.N.: Evaluation of industrial energy flexibility potential: a scoping review. In: 2021 22nd IEEE International Conference on Industrial Technology (ICIT). IEEE (2021)

6. Ma, Z., Jørgensen, B.N.: Energy flexibility of the commercial greenhouse growers: the potential and benefits of participating in the electricity market. In: 2018 IEEE Power & Energy Society Innovative Smart Grid Technologies Conference (ISGT) (2018)

7. Ma, Z., et al.: An overview of digitalization for the building-to-grid ecosystem. Energy Inform. **4**(2), 36 (2021)

8. Somu, N., MR, G.R., Ramamritham, K.: A deep learning framework for building energy consumption forecast. Renew. Sustain. Energy Rev. **137**, 110591 (2021)

9. Khan, T., Yu, M., Waseem, M.: Review on recent optimization strategies for hybrid renewable energy system with hydrogen technologies: state of the art, trends and future directions. Int. J. Hydrogen Energy **47**(60), 25155–25201 (2022)

10. Howard, D., et al.: Optimization of energy flexibility in cooling process for brewery fermentation with multi-agent simulation. In: 6th IEEJ International Workshop on Sensing, Actuation, Motion Control, and Optimization. Shibaura Institute of Technology, Tokyo, Japan (2020)

11. Subhan, S., et al.: Studies on the selection of a catalyst–oxidant system for the energy-efficient desulfurization and denitrogenation of fuel oil at mild operating conditions. Energy Fuels **33**(9), 8423–8439 (2019)

12. Dey, A., Hoffman, D., Yodo, N.: Optimizing multiple process parameters in fused deposition modeling with particle swarm optimization. Int. J. Interact. Design Manuf. (IJIDeM) **14**, 393–405 (2020)

13. Himeur, Y., et al.: A survey of recommender systems for energy efficiency in buildings: principles, challenges and prospects. Inf. Fusion **72**, 1–21 (2021)

14. Ma, Z., Asmussen, A., Jørgensen, B.N.: Industrial consumers' acceptance to the smart grid solutions: case studies from Denmark. In: Smart Grid Technologies - Asia (ISGT ASIA), 2015. IEEE Innovative (2015)

15. Ma, Z., Billanes, J.D., Jørgensen, B.N.: Aggregation potentials for buildings—business models of demand response and virtual power plants. Energies **10**(10), 1646 (2017)

16. Ma, Z., Christensen, K., Jorgensen, B.N.: Business ecosystem architecture development: a case study of Electric Vehicle home charging. Energy Inform. **4,** 37 (2021)

17. Osterwalder, A., Pigneur, Y.: Business model generation: a handbook for visionaries, game changers, and challengers, vol. 1. John Wiley & Sons (2020)

18. Díaz-Díaz, R., Muñoz, L., Pérez-González, D.: The business model evaluation tool for smart cities: application to SmartSantander use cases. Energies **10**(3), 262 (2017)

19. Jin, H., et al.: Optimization and analysis of bioenergy production using machine learning modeling: Multi-layer perceptron, Gaussian processes regression, K-nearest neighbors, and Artificial neural network models. Energy Rep. **8**, 13979–13996 (2022)

20. Howard, D.A., et al.: Energy flexibility potential in the brewery sector: a multi-agent based simulation of 239 Danish Breweries. In: 2022 IEEE PES 14th Asia-Pacific Power and Energy Engineering Conference (APPEEC). IEEE (2022)

21. Milczarski, P., et al.: Machine learning methods in energy consumption optimization assessment in food processing industry. In: 2021 11th IEEE International Conference on Intelligent Data Acquisition and Advanced Computing Systems: Technology and Applications (IDAACS). IEEE (2021)

22. Brown, D., Kivimaa, P., Sorrell, S.: An energy leap? Business model innovation and intermediation in the 'Energiesprong'retrofit initiative. Energy Res. Soc. Sci. **58**, 101253 (2019)

23. Loock, M.: Unlocking the value of digitalization for the European energy transition: a typology of innovative business models. Energy Res. Soc. Sci. **69**, 101740 (2020)

24. Maffei, A., Grahn, S., Nuur, C.: Characterization of the impact of digitalization on the adoption of sustainable business models in manufacturing. Procedia Cirp **81**, 765–770 (2019)

25. Hiteva, R., Foxon, T.J.: Beware the value gap: creating value for users and for the system through innovation in digital energy services business models. Technol. Forecast. Soc. Chang. **166**, 120525 (2021)

26. Héder, M.: From NASA to EU: the evolution of the TRL scale in public sector innovation. Innov. J. **22**(2), 1–23 (2017)

27. Technology readiness levels (TRL); Extract from Part 19 - Commission Decision C(2014)4995 (2014). ec.europa.eu

28. https://www.energyinformatics.academy/projects-iea-iets-xviii-sub-task3

29. Jäger-Waldau, A., et al.: How photovoltaics can contribute to GHG emission reductions of 55% in the EU by 2030. Renew. Sustain. Energy Rev. **126**, 109836 (2020)

30. Ma, Z., Jørgensen, B.N.: A discussion of building automation and stakeholder engagement for the readiness of energy flexible buildings. Energy Inform. **1**(1), 54 (2018)

31. Christensen, K., Ma, Z., Jørgensen, B.N.: Technical, economic, social and regulatory feasibility evaluation of dynamic distribution tariff designs. Energies **14**(10), 2860 (2021)

32. Christensen, K., et al.: Agent-based modeling of climate and electricity market impact on commercial greenhouse growers' demand response adoption. In: 2020 RIVF International Conference on Computing and Communication Technologies (RIVF). Ho Chi Minh City, Vietnam: IEEE (2020)

33. Ma, Z.: The importance of systematical analysis and evaluation methods for energy business ecosystems. Energy Inform. **5**(1), 1–6 (2022). https://doi.org/10.1186/s42162-022-00188-6

34. Tanev, S., Thomsen, M.S., Ma, Z.: Value co-creation: from an emerging paradigm to the next practices of innovation. In: ISPIM Innovation Symposium 2010. Quebec City, Canada: ISPIM (2010)

35. Grace Ma, Z., Asmussen, A., Jørgensen, B.N.: Influential factors to the industrial consumers' smart grid adoption. In: International Energy Conference (ASTECHNOVA 2016). Yogyakart, Indonesia: IEEE (2016)

Identifying Best Practice Melting Patterns in Induction Furnaces: A Data-Driven Approach Using Time Series K-Means Clustering and Multi-criteria Decision Making

Daniel Anthony Howard⬤, Bo Nørregaard Jørgensen⬤, and Zheng Ma$^{(\boxtimes)}$⬤

SDU Center for Energy Informatics, Maersk Mc-Kinney Moller Institute,
University of Southern Denmark, Odense, Denmark
{danho,bnj,zma}@mmmi.sdu.dk

Abstract. Improving energy efficiency in industrial production processes is crucial for competitiveness, and compliance with climate policies. This paper introduces a data-driven approach to identify optimal melting patterns in induction furnaces. Through time-series K-means clustering the melting patterns could be classified into distinct clusters based on temperature profiles. Using the elbow method, 12 clusters were identified, representing the range of melting patterns. Performance parameters such as melting time, energy-specific performance, and carbon cost were established for each cluster, indicating furnace efficiency and environmental impact. Multiple criteria decision-making methods including Simple Additive Weighting, Multiplicative Exponential Weighting, Technique for Order of Preference by Similarity to Ideal Solution, modified TOPSIS, and VlseKriterijumska Optimizacija I Kompromisno Resenje were utilized to determine the best-practice cluster. The study successfully identified the cluster with the best performance. Implementing the best practice operation resulted in an 8.6% reduction in electricity costs, highlighting the potential energy savings in the foundry.

Keywords: Energy Efficiency · Foundry Industry · Induction Furnace · Time-series K-means Clustering · Multi-criteria Decision Making

1 Introduction

The industrial sector accounts for approximately 40% of global energy consumption and represents the second-largest contributor of CO_2 emissions following power generation [1]. The iron and steel industry is categorized as the industry sub-sector with the highest CO_2 emissions, accounting for approximately 2.6 GtCO2 in 2020 [2]. In November 2021, the International Energy Agency (IEA) reported that the industry sector is not on track to meet the Net Zero Emissions by 2050 scenario [2].

Several strategies and recommended actions have been proposed to accelerate the industry's progress toward meeting the Net Zero Emissions by 2050 scenario targets. The strategies include increased direct and indirect electrification of processes and

B. N. Jørgensen et al. (Eds.): EI.A 2023, LNCS 14467, pp. 271–288, 2024.
https://doi.org/10.1007/978-3-031-48649-4_16

improved overall energy efficiency through best-practice operation and maintenance [2]. Within the iron and steel sub-sector, IEA emphasizes the need for energy efficiency measures by deploying the best available technologies [3]. Furthermore, data collection and transparency should be emphasized to facilitate performance benchmarking assessments.

The foundry industry is a vital sector of the manufacturing industry that produces metal castings for a wide range of applications, including automobiles, infrastructure, and consumer goods. As a result of high demand, crude steel production doubled between 2000 and 2021 [4]. A report on global steel production costs showed that the production cost of one tonne of steel had increased by an estimated 51% from 2019 to 2021. The report also identified that countries with low raw material and energy costs had lower production costs. As the foundry production process is highly energy-intensive and generates significant greenhouse gas emissions, there is an increasing need to improve energy efficiency and sustainability to increase the market competitiveness for European countries and meet the goals set forward by the IEA.

Denmark has proposed climate goals of reducing greenhouse gas emissions by 70% by 2030 compared to 1990 levels and being climate neutral by 2050 [5]. The 15 Danish foundries produced 90 Mt of castings in 2019 across the industry, accounting for 1.5% of Danish energy consumption and 3.2% of Danish industrial energy consumption [6, 7]. Furthermore, the Danish government has agreed to phase in a CO_2 tax starting from 2025, which all industries must pay based on their emissions [8]. The foundries constitute a significant part of Danish energy consumption, and for Denmark to meet the climate goals, the foundry industry must become increasingly sustainable. Furthermore, electrical consumers have been shown to have an increasing alertness toward electricity price and CO_2 emissions [9].

The process energy consumption associated with the foundry process presented in Fig. 1 is mapped according to the approximate distribution identified by [10]. As seen in Fig. 1, the melting process accounts for approximately 55% of the energy consumption in a casting process. Furthermore, the primary forming in the casting mold accounts for approximately 20% of the energy consumption. It is, therefore, essential to address the melting and casting processes to improve a foundry process's energy efficiency and flexibility. The top drivers for energy efficiency covering the Swedish aluminum and casting industry were described by [11]. The drivers included the desire to reduce power charge, avoid exceeding power peaks, and reduce costs due to lower energy usage and taxes associated with energy and carbon emissions.

Within the foundry industry, the operation is primarily based on the tacit knowledge of furnace operators [12]. To promote efficient operation, there is a need to identify the melting patterns that can be considered best practices. The diversity of melting patterns makes it difficult to categorize and analyze them effectively. Additionally, the lack of a systematic approach for evaluating and comparing the performance of different melting patterns hinders the identification of best practices. These factors highlight the need for a comprehensive, data-driven methodology to address these challenges. While previous studies have explored various aspects of energy efficiency and optimization in industrial processes, the specific problem of identifying best practice melting patterns in induction furnaces has not been adequately addressed in the literature.

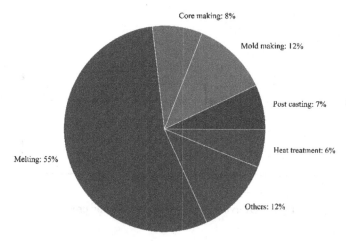

Fig. 1. Foundry industry energy consumption distribution based on [10]

Therefore, this paper aims to present a systematic method for identifying best-practice melting patterns in induction furnaces to enable energy-efficient operation. The method includes applying time-series K-means clustering to categorize melting patterns into clusters, calculating performance parameters for each cluster to assess their efficiency and environmental impact, employing multi-criteria decision-making methods to determine the best practice melting pattern cluster, and lastly evaluating the potential cost savings and energy efficiency improvements resulting from implementing the identified best practice pattern. The method is demonstrated in a case study of a Danish foundry.

The rest of this paper is structured as follows, initially, relevant background and literature is presented surrounding the current development of realizing energy efficiency in the foundry industry. Subsequently, the methodologies employed in this paper are outlined, providing an overview of the approach used to identify best practice melting patterns in induction furnaces. Afterward, the results are presented, showcasing the application of time series K-means clustering to categorize melting patterns and determine the ideal number of clusters using the elbow method. Next, relevant performance parameters are established for the clusters, along with the introduction of multi-criteria decision-making (MCDM) methods employed to evaluate and compare the performance of different clusters. Lastly, the potential cost savings and energy efficiency improvements resulting from implementing the best practice pattern are explored before discussing the results and concluding upon the findings with suggestions for further research.

2 Background

The fundamental process flow observed within a foundry production process can be shown in Fig. 2. As shown in Fig. 2, several production steps are involved in producing the final casting workpieces.

The foundry process shown in Fig. 2, is initiated with collecting and sorting melting material, primarily iron, and alloys, in different qualities, including the addition of scrap

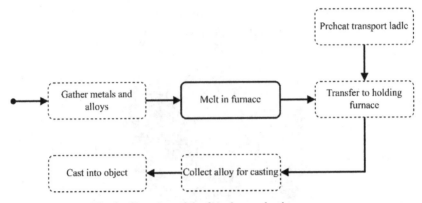

Fig. 2. Overview of the foundry production process

metal collected from the scrap metal pits. Subsequently, the iron is added to the induction furnace, where it is heated to the specified temperature adjusting for ferromagnetic losses. Once the melt has achieved the specified temperature, it is transferred to a pre-heated transfer ladle. In the transfer ladle, doping may be performed to achieve specific alloy capabilities adhering to the melt currently in the holding furnace. The melt is then transferred to a holding furnace, where it can be stored for a set period. The transfer to the holding furnace marks the completion of the melting part of the foundry process. Subsequently, the primary forming stage commences.

Once the primary forming starts, alloy of the required quality is collected from the holding furnace in a pre-heated transfer ladle. At this stage, doping can be performed again to meet customer-specific demands for alloy capabilities. Once the correct alloy has been achieved, it is transferred to one of the molding machines that perform the primary forming of the melt using sand-molded casting. The casting is subsequently transferred to a cooling line which marks the end of the primary forming of the casting.

2.1 Energy Efficiency in Foundry Production

Industrial production, foundry production, is usually a highly energy-intensive process that consumes large amounts of electricity, natural gas, and other fuels to melt and shape metal alloys [13]. Over the past few decades, there has been growing interest in improving the energy efficiency of industrial production to reduce energy consumption, greenhouse gas emissions, and costs [14].

Several studies have focused on identifying the primary energy consumption sources in foundry production, such as melting and casting operations, heat treatment, and material handling. For example, a study found that melting and casting processes accounted for the majority of energy consumption in a steel foundry [10, 15]. However, it was found that heat treatment and melting accounted for the majority of energy consumption, approximately 60%, in an aluminum foundry [16]. These studies have also identified various energy-saving opportunities, such as using more energy-efficient equipment, improving process control, and recycling waste heat.

Various strategies have been proposed to improve energy efficiency in foundries. One approach is to use more efficient equipment and technologies, such as induction melting and high-pressure die casting. Another strategy is to implement energy management systems and conduct energy audits to identify and address areas of inefficiency [16, 17].

Several studies have also applied advanced modeling and simulation techniques to optimize foundry production processes for energy efficiency. For instance, the use of computational fluid dynamics (CFD) and finite element analysis (FEA) have been used in several studies to optimize the design of melting and casting operations and to study the heat transfer processes within the furnace and mold, allowing for the identification of potential energy savings [18, 19]. Optimization techniques such as mathematical programming, artificial intelligence, and machine learning have also been reported to reduce energy consumption in the foundry process [20–23].

Foundry production process modeling and simulation have also been investigated to improve cost and energy efficiency. E.g., early foundry simulation efforts examined the impact of scheduled jobs in a foundry setting where each job should follow specific criteria relating to the number of castings needed and the weight of each casting [24]. Several studies have applied simulation in various aspects of the production process especially emphasizing molding, casting, and core shooting [12, 25–27].

Best-practice operations have been shown to enable substantial energy savings [28]. However, the concept of best practice operation in the context of foundries has not been sufficiently investigated in previous literature. Operational practices have been shown to impact the industry's performance and potential energy efficiency [29]. Previous studies have suggested that induction furnaces may experience up to 25–30% losses due to unfavorable operation [30], considering that the majority of energy consumption in the foundry is consumed in the melting process; this presents a significant gap in the literature for promoting energy-efficient operation in the foundry.

This paper proposes clustering to identify and group melting patterns in the induction furnace to distinguish operational practices. In the literature, clustering has been used to identify energy consumption patterns in production processes and group similar processes together based on their energy consumption profiles, e.g., [31]. This information has been used to identify opportunities for energy savings by optimizing the energy consumption of the production processes. Clustering has also seen use for benchmarking in energy regulation [32]. Clustering has also been used to group similar processes together based on their flexibility and responsiveness; to identify opportunities for process optimization and improvement. For instance, clustering can identify processes that can switch between energy sources or operate at different production rates, enabling them to respond to energy availability or demand changes, e.g., [33]. Lastly, clustering has seen use in identifying the optimal configuration of production processes to maximize energy efficiency and flexibility. Clustering can identify the optimal configuration of production processes by analyzing the relationships between different variables, such as energy consumption, production rates, and operating conditions, e.g., [33].

MCDM has been proposed for establishing best practices in various domains, such as quality management and selection of technologies [34, 35]. However, it has not seen in-depth investigation in establishing industry best practices. However, MCDM has seen usage for establishing energy efficiency practices [36]. Previous studies have examined the use of MCDM in the automotive industry to improve energy efficiency in automotive engineering and service center selection [37, 38]. Furthermore, in the beverage industry, MCDM has seen use for choosing energy improvement measures [39]. MCDM has also seen use in selecting locations for energy storage systems in combination with using K-means++, and for mapping industries for participation in electricity markets [40, 41]. In summary, it is evident that there is a need to establish best practice operations for furnace operation in foundries. Best practices have been established both through clustering and MCDM in various domains; however, there is little literature on combining the methods for providing industries with the identification of best practice operations. Utilizing a data-driven clustering approach ensures that the best practice adheres to the constraints of the process as the clusters build on historical data, while the MCDM allows the facility to prioritize the subjective weighting of what performance parameters indicate best practice.

3   Methodology

An overview of the methodology used in this paper can be seen in Fig. 3. To enable the clustering of operational practices and identification of the best practice cluster, the relevant clustering and MCDM algorithms are selected.

Data preparation and separation of practices

Clustering of operational practices

Evaluation of cluster performance

Identification of best practice cluster using MCDM

Fig. 3. Methodology for identifying best-practice melting patterns.

3.1   Clustering Algorithm Selection

As production processes often collect time-series data and experience variance in the processing time, the data requires specialized clustering algorithms that can handle the temporal nature of the data and capture the patterns and relationships within the time series. Therefore, time-series clustering is proposed, as time-series clustering is an unsupervised learning technique used to identify patterns and group similar data points based on their temporal behavior. Previous studies have compared various clustering algorithms; it was found that the K-means algorithm provided better performance while also being computationally efficient [42]. Time-series K-means clustering is a modified version of K-means clustering that considers the temporal nature of the data. This method involves representing each time series as a sequence of vectors and clustering these vectors using K-means clustering; the vectors may be established using dynamic time warping or Euclidian distance [43]. The resulting clusters represent similar patterns in the time-series data.

Compared to other clustering algorithms, time-series K-means clustering has several advantages. Previous comparisons have established that the performance of the K-means clustering algorithm outweighs other clustering algorithms, and furthermore, the implementation of K-means is faster compared to other algorithms [43–45]. This is further supported by the ability to scale with large datasets and guaranteed convergence [46]. Other clustering algorithms, such as Kernel K-means, and Kshape, have also been used for time-series clustering. However, these algorithms have limitations when dealing with the computation of cluster centroid and datasets of various lengths due to relying on cross-correlation of the cluster time series [43].

The elbow method is commonly used to determine the optimal K-means clustering cluster size [45]. The elbow method involves plotting the within-cluster sum of squares against the number of clusters and selecting the number of clusters at the "elbow" of the plot, where the rate of decrease in the within-cluster sum of squares slows down [47]. The within-cluster sum of squares measures the sum of the squared distances between each data point and its assigned cluster center. The idea behind the elbow method is to select the number of clusters that significantly decreases the within-cluster sum of squares while minimizing the number of clusters [47]. Increasing the number of clusters too much can lead to overfitting and loss of generalizability, while too few clusters may not capture all the underlying patterns in the data. Time series K-means clustering was utilized in this paper to identify clusters of similar profiles relating to the operation. By identifying clusters of operational patterns the performance of the various practices could be evaluated to identify efficient and inefficient operations.

3.2 Multi-criteria Decision Making

The performance of a specific operation may be evaluated across several parameters, and the goals and preferences of various foundries may vary. Therefore, there may not be a single solution that fits all foundries; therefore, MCDM algorithms are implemented to incorporate the goals and preferences of the foundry when evaluating a specific operational practice.

MCDM is a method used to select the best option from a set of alternatives based on multiple criteria or objectives [48]. There are several MCDM techniques available, such as Analytical Hierarchy Process (AHP), the Technique for Order Preference by Similarity to Ideal Solution (TOPSIS), and VlseKriterijumska Optimizacija I Kompromisno Resenje (VIKOR). The MCDM process involves identifying the criteria, weighing them according to their importance, and evaluating the alternatives against the criteria [48]. In the context of energy usage in industrial production processes, MCDM can be applied to support decision-making in various scenarios, such as production planning, resource allocation, and energy performance evaluation, e.g. [49]. The MCDM approach has several advantages, such as the ability to handle multiple criteria, the flexibility to incorporate subjective preferences, and the ability to evaluate alternatives comprehensively. However, MCDM also has some limitations, such as difficulty determining the appropriate weights for the criteria and the subjective nature of the decision-making process [50].

This paper has implemented a series of MCDM algorithms based on the work conducted in [51] and [52]. The MCDM algorithms utilized in this research are Simple Additive Weighting (SAW), Multiplicative Exponential Weighting (MEW), TOPSIS, Modified Technique for Order Preference by Similarity to Ideal Solution (mTOPSIS), and VIKOR. By utilizing multiple MCDM algorithms, the robustness of the final decision can be increased, and any differences in ranking can be examined [53].

4   Case Study

A large Danish foundry provides a case study for the application of the identification of best-practice operations. The Danish foundry is the largest in Northern Europe and produces 45,000 tonnes of casting products each year, exported to 25 different countries. The foundry has committed to reducing its greenhouse gas emissions and has actively implemented circular economy and sustainability as active goals in its business strategy. As a part of the foundry's sustainability efforts, the energy consumption of their production was mapped. The mapping revealed that 78.5% of their annual energy consumption is electricity, predominantly consumed by the melting and holding furnaces. As part of the energy mapping, it was shown that 0.5 tonnes of carbon dioxide emissions were emitted per tonne of produced casting.

The case study is ideal for identifying best-practice melting patterns due to their commitment to improving sustainable foundry practices and being a state-of-the-art facility utilizing induction furnaces with processes monitored through existing sensors. The production observed in the foundry case study follows the steps shown in Fig. 2. The facility includes an in-house factory where machining and surface treatment of casting workpieces can be undergone. In this study, only the foundry process is considered as this is the mandatory part of the production flow. This study focuses on the melting operation in the furnace, and the adjacent steps shown with dashed lines are not included.

5   Results

Based on the case study, data for one of the induction furnaces could be obtained. The period range of the obtained data was from the 11th of May 2022 to the 30th of May 2022. An overview of the parameters and data completeness can be seen in Fig. 4.

Before initiating the cluster identification, the data was cleaned and prepared. The cleaning involved removing the furnace state parameter and removing the rows of data with missing temperature measurements. The parameters collected in Fig. 4 include the melt temperature, melt weight, furnace voltage, furnace state, furnace power consumption, furnace isolation resistance, furnace frequency, furnace current, and multiple measuring points for the cooling water temperature and flow.

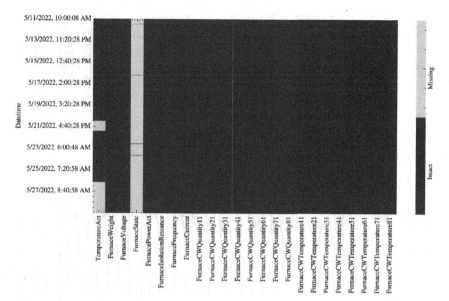

Fig. 4. Induction furnace parameters and data completeness.

Using temperature to identify melting patterns in induction furnaces is driven by its significance in melting. Temperature is a fundamental parameter that directly impacts the physical and chemical transformations occurring within the furnace and provides a comprehensive representation of the thermal behavior of the furnace during the melting cycle. Examining temperature data over time enables the identification of distinct patterns in the melting process. These patterns can be associated with different operational conditions, such as the charging of materials, power input, or changes in furnace load. In contrast, parameters like power consumption may not capture the nuances of the melting process as effectively as temperature. Therefore, the temperature profiles were investigated and can be seen in Fig. 5.

As the obtained data is in a time-series format, an algorithm is necessary to separate the individual melts. The algorithm used to separate the time series data in this study can be seen in Fig. 6.

The algorithm seeks to identify the melting endpoints from which the starting points of the subsequent melt can be inferred. Using the index, the change in temperature from one time to the next can be calculated. As shown in Fig. 5, a significant decrease in temperature is observed at the end of a melt by tuning the minimum temperature, and the minimum change in temperature of the melts can be identified. The limits are imposed as changes in temperature can happen due to adding new material to the melt, and the change should hence occur under a set temperature limit, indicating that the melt has been completed. Ninety-three individual melts were identified for the period.

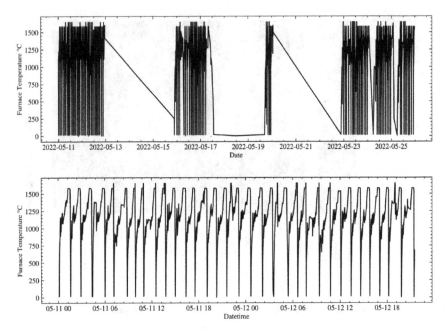

Fig. 5. Time-series overview of the melt temperature from the furnace computer for the whole period and for a segment of the period

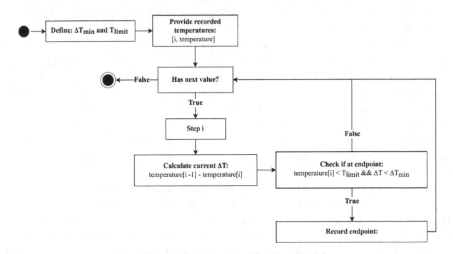

Fig. 6. Melting pattern identification algorithm.

5.1 Time-Series K-means Clustering of Melting Profiles

Timeseries K-means clustering was performed to identify similar melting profiles. As seen in Fig. 7, the number of clusters was determined based on the elbow method with a comparison of the inertia, distortion, and silhouette scores for finding the optimal K.

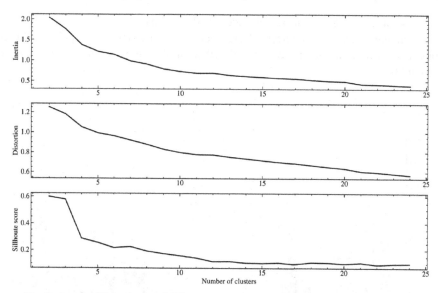

Fig. 7. Inertia, Distortion, and Silhouette score in response to the number of clusters

As shown in Fig. 7, the inertia and distortion do not yield a distinct elbow. Examining the silhouette score shows an elbow at K = 12. Subsequently, the time series K-means clustering was performed using the number of clusters determined from the silhouette score. The result of the clustering can be seen in Fig. 8.

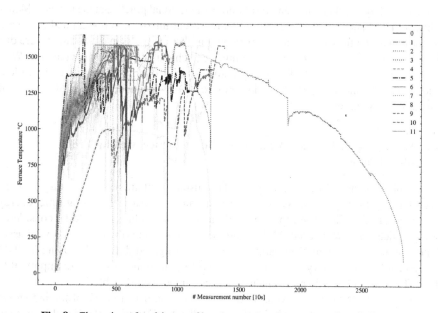

Fig. 8. Clustering of melting profiles showcasing the average of each cluster.

As seen in Fig. 8, 12 clusters are identified, with each cluster plot line showing the mean temperature of all current cluster members at a given time step. Each cluster consists of several melting profiles; the distribution of melting profiles in each can be seen in Fig. 9.

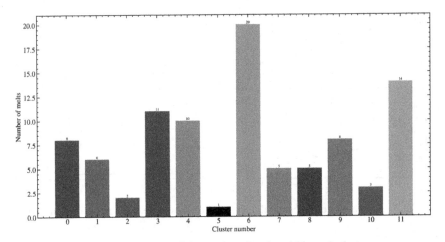

Fig. 9. Distribution of the number of melts within each cluster

As seen in Fig. 9, the melts were distributed in 12 clusters, with cluster no.6 containing the highest number of melts. The clusters containing the highest number of melts (e.g., no. 3, 4, 6, and 11) represent the common operational practice at the furnace. Meanwhile, other clusters, e.g., no. 2, 5, and 10 represent uncommon operational practices. According to the furnace operators' explanation, the few melts in cluster no.2 were due to changing the furnace's refractory lining, i.e., scheduled furnace maintenance. With further collaboration with the furnace operators, specific operational practices were identified within the identified clusters, aiding in explaining and understanding the observed cluster melting pattern.

5.2 Multi-criteria Decision Making for Best Practice Melting Profile Identification

As established in the previous chapter, the clusters contain similar melting profiles. Each melting profile has an associated performance in terms of melting time, energy consumption, etc. Therefore, to sufficiently assess which cluster should be considered best practice, MCDM is used. MCDM allows assessing an array of options with associated parameters, where each parameter may be weighted differently. Using MCDM hence enables the foundry to emphasize the performance metrics that are important to them. The cluster-specific performance metrics can be seen in Table 1.

Several MCDM methods were used to compare the performance of the individual clusters. Table 2 shows the ranking of each of the MCDM methods. Equal weighting was assumed between each performance parameter.

Table 1. Cluster-specific performance parameters

Cluster	Average production time [s]	Average electricity consumption [kWh]	Average energy-specific performance [kWh/tonne]	2030 Carbon tax [DKK]
0	5346.25	5186.90	554.83	509.44
1	5251.67	5111.82	552.55	552.57
2	20515.00	5364.75	573.80	643.60
3	4332.73	4858.24	522.00	338.01
4	5221.00	4980.30	551.26	496.16
5	12870.00	6368.12	664.31	803.86
6	4892.00	4880.48	541.03	396.21
7	6216.00	5236.36	554.28	493.01
8	5886.00	5028.03	550.13	368.42
9	7370.00	5027.46	563.93	404.34
10	11820.00	5260.52	605.99	410.19
11	5218.57	5065.82	545.92	421.69

Table 2. Cluster-specific MCDM ratings

Cluster	SAW	MEW	TOPSIS	mTOPSIS	VIKOR
0	0.25783	0.25160	0.82853	0.82853	0.30858
1	0.26195	0.25443	0.79901	0.79901	0.35786
2	0.40147	0.37967	0.17793	0.17793	0.83386
3	0.21649	0.20874	1.00000	1.00000	0.00000
4	0.25162	0.24555	0.84409	0.84409	0.26624
5	0.38969	0.38676	0.37868	0.37868	1.00000
6	0.23199	0.22617	0.93427	0.93427	0.11052
7	0.26293	0.25968	0.81689	0.81689	0.29767
8	0.23903	0.23532	0.90686	0.90686	0.16566
9	0.25763	0.25636	0.82027	0.82027	0.25173
10	0.30212	0.29815	0.59682	0.59682	0.50407
11	0.24141	0.23617	0.90259	0.90259	0.16635

As can be seen from the table above, cluster three shows the overall best performance as it scores best across all MCDM methods. Hence, cluster three is selected as the cluster representing the best-practice operation.

5.3 Energy Efficiency Potential for Best-Practice Operation

The identified best-practice cluster performance was assumed across all melts in the investigated period to assess the impact of using best-practice operations, assuming 100% adherence to the best-practice operation. I.e. the average performance of the melts in the best practice cluster were assumed for all other clusters in the dataset. Using the recorded start times of the melts in the other clusters the corresponding electricity cost and CO_2 emissions could be calculated subject to the best practice performance. The foundry is assumed to follow the spot market electricity price and CO_2 emissions. The implication of utilizing best practice operations can be seen in Table 3.

Table 3. Comparison of current operation and implementation of best practice operation

Operating Mode	Electricity Cost [DKK]	2030 Carbon Cost [DKK]	CO2 Emissions [kg]	Total Electricity Cost [DKK]
Current practice	602913.00	40761.88	54349.18	643674.89
Best practice	551041.56	37321.17	49761.56	588362.73
Percentage change	8.60%	8.44%	8.44%	8.59%

6 Discussion

To identify best-practice melting patterns in induction furnaces, the following four steps have been conducted:

1. Application of the time series K-means clustering to categorize melting patterns into clusters
2. Calculation of the performance parameters for each cluster to assess their efficiency and environmental impact
3. Deployment of the multi-criteria decision-making methods to determine the best practice melting pattern cluster,
4. Evaluation of the potential cost savings and energy efficiency improvements resulting from implementing the identified best practice pattern.

In accordance with the presented method, the obtained data was prepared and separated into individual melts. The application of time-series K-means clustering enabled the identification and categorization of melting patterns in the induction furnace, leading to the determination of an optimal number of clusters using the elbow method, as seen in Fig. 7. Examining the distribution of clusters from Fig. 9 and the cluster patterns in Fig. 8 furthermore enabled identification of specific operations within the furnace, e.g., change of refractory lining. The cluster distribution furthermore showed that the melts adhering to the best practice operation only occur around 12% of the time. As seen in Table 1, the performance parameters calculated for each cluster, such as melting time, energy-specific performance (kWh/tonne), and carbon cost, provided insights into different patterns' energy efficiency and cost-effectiveness. Using MCDM methods, SAW, MEW, TOPSIS, mTOPSIS, and VIKOR, facilitated comparing and selecting a cluster representing the best-practice performance seen in Table 2. The foundry could achieve cost savings by implementing the identified best practice melting pattern, with an estimated reduction of approximately 8.6% in electricity costs.

7 Conclusion

This paper has addressed the challenge of identifying best practice melting patterns in induction furnaces through a data-driven methodology utilizing time-series K-means clustering and multi-criteria decision-making (MCDM) methods. The cluster representing the best practice performance could be identified by categorizing melting patterns into clusters and evaluating their performance based on various parameters such as melting time, energy-specific performance, and carbon cost.

The implications of the findings are significant for the foundry industry, as implementing the identified best practice melting pattern can lead to substantial cost savings and improved energy efficiency. The estimated electricity cost savings of approximately 8.6% demonstrate the tangible benefits of improving melting practices.

Building on the findings presented in this paper, there is potential for exploring further research. The findings in this paper build on the investigation of a single furnace within the foundry, which could be extended to include other furnaces. Furthermore, limited information was available on the alloy composition within the furnace; for future research, it would be beneficial to include the alloy composition to investigate the impact of alloy composition on best practice operation.

From the methodology perspective, investigating the scalability and applicability of the methodology for the identification of best practice melting patterns across different foundries and regions would aid in verifying the robustness of the methodology. Furthermore, the applicability of the methodology outside of the foundry domain could be investigated to examine the potential for the identification of best-practice operations in other domains. Lastly, the implementation of the best practice operation is subject to underlying uncertainties present in production processes; therefore, it would be beneficial to develop a simulation model that can accurately represent the process flow and evaluate any unforeseen consequences due to the best practice operation to provide a more nuanced understanding of the best practice implications.

Acknowledgment. This paper is part of the "IEA-IETS Annex XVIII: Digitization, artificial intelligence and related technologies for energy efficiency and reduction of greenhouse gas emissions in industry" (Case no. 134-21010), and "Data-driven best-practice for energy-efficient operation of industrial processes - A system integration approach to reduce the CO2 emissions of industrial processes" (Case no. 64020-2108) funded by the Danish Energy Technology Development and Demonstration (EUPD) program, Denmark.

References

1. International Energy Agency. World Energy Outlook 2021 (2021)
2. International Energy Agency. Tracking Industry 2021. Paris (2021)
3. International Energy Agency. Iron and Steel (2021)
4. m'barek, B.B., Hasanbeigi, A., Gray, M.: Global steel production costs. In: A Country and Plant-Level Cost Analysis (2022)
5. Danish Energy Agency. Danish Climate Policies (2023)
6. The World Foundry Organization. Census of World Casting Production (2019)
7. Energistyrelsen. Kortlægning af energiforbrug i virksomheder (2015)
8. Danish Ministry of Finance. Regeringen indgår bred aftale om en ambitiøs grøn skattereform (2022). https://fm.dk/nyheder/nyhedsarkiv/2022/juni/regeringen-indgaar-bred-aftale-om-en-ambitioes-groen-skattereform/. Accessed 26 June 2023
9. Ma, Z.G., et al.: Ecosystem based opportunity identification and feasibility evaluation for demand side management solutions. In: 2023 IEEE Conference on Power Electronics and Renewable Energy (CPERE), pp. 1–6 (2023)
10. Paudel, S., Nagapurkar, P., Smith, J.: Improving Process Sustainability and Profitablity for a Large U.S. Gray Iron Foundry (2014)
11. Haraldsson, J., Johansson, M.T.: Barriers to and drivers for improved energy efficiency in the Swedish aluminium industry and aluminium casting foundries. Sustainability 11(7) (2019)
12. Dawson, C., Lindahl, H.: Production Flow Simulation Modelling in the Foundry Industry (2017)
13. Ma, Z., et al.: Energy flexibility potential of industrial processes in the regulating power market. In: The 6th International Conference on Smart Cities and Green ICT Systems (2017)
14. Ma, Z., Jørgensen, B.N.: Energy flexibility of the commercial greenhouse growers: the potential and benefits of participating in the electricity market. In: 2018 IEEE Power & Energy Society Innovative Smart Grid Technologies Conference (ISGT) (2018)
15. Futaš, P., Pribulová, A., Pokusova, M.: Possibilities reducing of energy consumption by cast iron production in foundry. Mater. Sci. Forum 998, 36–41 (2020)
16. Salonitis, K., et al.: Improvements in energy consumption and environmental impact by novel single shot melting process for casting. J. Clean. Prod. 137, 1532–1542 (2016)
17. Salonitis, K., et al.: The challenges for energy efficient casting processes. Procedia CIRP 40, 24–29 (2016)
18. Horr, A.M., Kronsteiner, J.: On numerical simulation of casting in new foundries: dynamic process simulations. Metals 10(7), 886 (2020)
19. Chiumenti, M., et al.: Numerical simulation of aluminium foundry processes. In: Modeling of Casting, Welding and Advanced Solidification Processes, pp. 377–384 (2003)
20. Popielarski, P.: The conditions for application of foundry simulation codes to predict casting quality. In: Materials Research Proceedings, pp. 23–30 (2020)
21. Ganesh, H.S., et al.: Improving Energy Efficiency of an Austenitization Furnace by Heat Integration and Real-Time Optimization. In: Miclea, L., Stoian, I. (eds.) Proceedings of the 2018 IEEE International Conference on Automation, Quality and Testing, Robotics (AQTR 2018) – THETA, 21st edn, pp. 1–6. Institute of Electrical and Electronics Engineers Inc. (2018)
22. Manojlović, V., et al.: Machine learning analysis of electric arc furnace process for the evaluation of energy efficiency parameters. Appl. Energy 307 (2022)
23. Howard, D.A., Ma, Z., Jørgensen, B.N.: Evaluation of Industrial Energy Flexibility Potential: A Scoping Review (2021)
24. Decker, R.L., et al.: Foundry: A Foundry Simulation (1979)

25. Peter, T., et al.: Coupled simulation of energy and material flow - a use case in an aluminum foundry. In: Proceedings of the Winter Simulation Conference, pp. 3792–3803 (2017)
26. Mardan, N., Klahr, R.: Combining optimisation and simulation in an energy systems analysis of a Swedish iron foundry. Energy **44**(1), 410–419 (2012)
27. Solding, P., Thollander, P.: Increased energy efficiency in a Swedish iron foundry through use of discrete event simulation. In: Proceedings - Winter Simulation Conference, pp. 1971–1976 (2006)
28. Lunt, P., Levers, A.: Reducing energy use in aircraft component manufacture - applying best practice in sustainable manufacturing. In: SAE Technical Papers. SAE International (2011)
29. Demirel, Y.E., et al.: Selection of priority energy efficiency practices for industrial steam boilers by PROMETHEE decision model. Energy Efficiency **14**(8) (2021)
30. Trauzeddel, D.: Energy Saving Potential of Melting Cast Iron in Medium-Frequency Coreless Induction Furnaces, pp. 79–85 (2006)
31. Al Skaif, A., Ayache, M., Kanaan, H.: Energy consumption clustering using machine learning: K-means approach. In: 2021 22nd International Arab Conference on Information Technology (ACIT 2021). Institute of Electrical and Electronics Engineers Inc. (2021)
32. Dai, X., Kuosmanen, T.: Best-practice benchmarking using clustering methods: application to energy regulation. Omega (United Kingdom) **42**(1), 179–188 (2014)
33. Sun, L., et al.: A clustering-based energy consumption evaluation method for process industries with multiple energy consumption patterns. Int. J. Comput. Integrat. Manuf. 1–29 (2023)
34. Sin, K.Y., Jusoh, M.S., Mardani, A.: Proposing an Integrated Multi-criteria Decision Making Approach to Evaluate Total Quality Management Best Practices in Malaysia Hotel Industry. Institute of Physics Publishing (2020)
35. AbdulBaki, D., Mansour, F., Yassine, A., Al-Hindi, M., Abou Najm, M.: Multi-criteria decision making for the selection of best practice seawater desalination technologies. In: Naddeo, V., Balakrishnan, M., Choo, K.-H. (eds.) Frontiers in Water-Energy-Nexus—Nature-Based Solutions, Advanced Technologies and Best Practices for Environmental Sustainability. ASTI, pp. 489–492. Springer, Cham (2020). https://doi.org/10.1007/978-3-030-13068-8_122
36. Christensen, K., Ma, Z., Jørgensen, B.N.: Technical, economic, social and regulatory feasibility evaluation of dynamic distribution tariff designs. Energies **14**(10), 2860 (2021)
37. Vujanović, D.B., Momcilović, V.M., Vasić, M.B.: A hybrid multi-criteria decision making model for the vehicle service center selection with the aim to increase the vehicle fleet energy efficiency. Therm. Sci. **22**(3), 1549–1561 (2018)
38. Castro, D.M., Silv Parreiras, F.: A review on multi-criteria decision-making for energy efficiency in automotive engineering. Appl. Comput. Inf. **17**(1), 53–78 (2018)
39. Sittikruear, S., Bangviwat, A.: Energy efficiency improvement in community – scale whisky factories of Thailand by various multi-criteria decision making methods. Energy Procedia **52**, 173–178 (2014)
40. Yilmaz, I., Adem, A., Dağdeviren, M.: A machine learning-integrated multi-criteria decision-making approach based on consensus for selection of energy storage locations. J. Energy Storage **69** (2023)
41. Fatras, N., Ma, Z., Jørgensen, B.N.: Process-to-market matrix mapping: a multi-criteria evaluation framework for industrial processes' electricity market participation feasibility. Appl. Energy **313**, 118829 (2022)
42. Finazzi, F., et al.: A comparison of clustering approaches for the study of the temporal coherence of multiple time series. Stoch. Env. Res. Risk Assess. **29**(2), 463–475 (2015)
43. Towards Data Science. Time Series Clustering — Deriving Trends and Archetypes from Sequential Data (2021). https://towardsdatascience.com/time-series-clustering-deriving-trends-and-archetypes-from-sequential-data-bb87783312b4. Accessed 31 Mar 2023

44. McInnes, L., Healy, J., Astels, S.: Comparing Python Clustering Algorithms (2016). https://hdbscan.readthedocs.io/en/latest/comparing_clustering_algorithms.html. Accessed 31 Mar 2023

45. Jessen, S.H., et al.: Identification of natural disaster impacted electricity load profiles with k means clustering algorithm. Energy Informatics 5(4), 59 (2022)

46. Google. k-Means Advantages and Disadvantages (2022). https://developers.google.com/machine-learning/clustering/algorithm/advantages-disadvantages. Accessed 31 Mar 2023

47. Vatsal, P.: K-Means Explained (2021). https://towardsdatascience.com/k-means-explained-10349949bd10. Accessed 31 Mar 2023

48. Thakkar, J.J.: Multi-criteria Decision Making, 1st edn, vol. 336. Springer, Singapore (2021)

49. Singh, S., et al.: Analysis of mango drying methods and effect of blanching process based on energy consumption, drying time using multi-criteria decision-making. Clean. Eng. Technol. 8 (2022)

50. Marttunen, M., Lienert, J., Belton, V.: Structuring problems for multi-criteria decision analysis in practice: a literature review of method combinations. Eur. J. Oper. Res. 263(1), 1–17 (2017)

51. Akestoridis, D.-G.: MCDM (2022). https://github.com/akestoridis/mcdm. Accessed 31 Mar 2023

52. Christensen, K.: Multi-agent based simulation framework for evaluating digital energy solutions and adoption strategies. In: SDU Center for Energy Informatics the Maersk Mc-Kinney Moller Institute. University of Southern Denmark (2022)

53. Vassoney, E., et al.: Comparing multi-criteria decision-making methods for the assessment of flow release scenarios from small hydropower plants in the alpine area. Front. Environ. Sci. 9 (2021)

Machine Learning Applied to Industrial Machines for an Efficient Maintenance Strategy: A Predictive Maintenance Approach

Bruno Mota⬤, Pedro Faria$^{(\boxtimes)}$ ⬤, and Carlos Ramos⬤

GECAD - Research Group on Intelligent Engineering and Computing for Advanced Innovation and Development, LASI; Polytechnic of Porto, Rua Dr. António Bernardino de Almeida 431, 4200-072 Porto, Portugal
{bamoa,pnf,csr}@isep.ipp.pt

Abstract. Maintenance activities are crucial in manufacturing environments to reduce machine breakdowns and maintain product quality. However, traditional maintenance strategies can be expensive, as they can lead to unnecessary maintenance activities. As a result, Predictive Maintenance (PdM) can be a great way to solve these issues, as it enables the prediction of a machine's condition/lifespan allowing for maintenance-effective manufacturing. This paper aims to address these issues by proposing a novel methodology to improve the performance of PdM systems, by proposing a machine learning training methodology, an automatic hyperparameter optimizer, and a retraining strategy for real-time application. To validate the proposed methodology a random forest and an artificial neural network model are implemented as well as explored. A synthetic dataset, that replicates industrial machine data, was used to show the robustness of the proposed methodology. Obtained results are promising as the implemented models can accomplish up to 0.97 recall and 93.15% accuracy.

Keywords: Data Preprocessing · Hyperparameter Optimization · Predictive Maintenance

1 Introduction

Several changes have been happening in the energy sector, namely with the implementation of the smart grid concept [1], having more active participation of electricity consumers in demand response programs [2, 3]. Booming innovation in Big data, data analytics, and Internet of Things (IoT) has resulted in a shift in traditional industrial maintenance strategies to systems capable of forecasting machine lifespan [4, 5]. Furthermore, taking into account energy usage is also critical for optimizing production lines in industrial environments, because machine health can have a significant impact on a machine's energy efficiency capabilities [6, 7]. Accordingly, it is in these industries' best interests to implement these systems to minimize energy consumption, reducing not only costs but also contributing to a sustainable future through energy savings. There has been the development of two new maintenance concepts for detecting abnormalities in

B. N. Jørgensen et al. (Eds.): EI.A 2023, LNCS 14467, pp. 289–299, 2024.
https://doi.org/10.1007/978-3-031-48649-4_17

the production environment: prognostic and health management, as well as condition-based maintenance [8]. Predictive Maintenance (PdM), which analyzes past data to forecast behavior patterns, is frequently used with these two principles in mind, either with prognosis and health management or condition-based maintenance, and in some circumstances, the application of both [9]. The use of predictive systems to determine when maintenance activities are required is critical in a manufacturing environment, not only to avoid wasteful expenses and cut potential Greenhouse gas emissions but also to enhance product quality. According to [10], maintenance expenses can represent 15% to 70% of the cost of manufactured products. Predictive maintenance enables continuous monitoring of the machine's integrity, allowing maintenance to be performed only when absolutely needed, reducing unnecessary maintenance costs. Moreover, PdM prevents, to some extent, machine breakdowns, which are responsible for the emission of Greenhouse gas emissions in some industrial sectors [11]. Prediction systems that use statistical inference, historical data, engineering methods, and integrity factors allow for early abnormalities detection [12]. Forecasting a machine's condition and/or lifespan can be done through a variety of techniques, such as Artificial Neural Networks (ANNs) [13–15], Random Forests (RFs) [16–18], deep learning [19], digital twins [20], support vector machines [21], k-means [22], gradient boosting [23], naive bayes [24], and decision trees [25]. Other noteworthy techniques are presented in [12] as well as in [26].

This paper focuses on the implementation as well as the exploration of the advantages and disadvantages of the two most popular machine learning approaches, according to [12], for PdM: ANNs (27% model employment) and RFs (33% model employment). The prominent use of RF in PdM systems, due to its performance and easy implementation, is the main reason for the exploration of this model in the present paper. Nevertheless, an ANN model has the potential to outperform an RF, both in recall and context adaption, when its hyperparameters are adequately optimized. Furthermore, unlike the RF model, ANNs have the advantage of backpropagation (i.e., fine-tuning of the network's weights based on the error rate), allowing a current model to be constantly fed with data and improve over time without the need to recreate the model every time there is new training data, which is ideal for manufacturing environments.

The work in [13] proposes an ANN for PdM using the mean time to failure values and backpropagation for adjusting the neuron's weights. A PdM system for air booster compressor motors is proposed in [14] that employs an ANN with optimized weights and bias by using a particle swarm optimization algorithm. Also using an ANN, the proposed work in [15] focuses on a PdM system for induction motors that optimizes hyperparameters (e.g., number of hidden layers and neurons) to improve performance in the model. For RF, the work in [16] proposes a real-time PdM system for production lines using IoT data. A new PdM methodology, using RF, is proposed in [17] to allow dynamic decision rules to be imposed for maintenance management. A data-driven PdM system applied to woodworking is proposed in [18] using an RF that takes advantage of event-based triggers.

Of the above-cited works, none tackle, to the extent of the present paper, the main problem plaguing PdM problems, imbalanced data. Furthermore, with the exception of the works in [14] and [15], there is little to no optimization regarding hyperparameters, which can improve model performance significantly primarily in imbalanced datasets.

Finally, only the work in [16] considers real-time deployment and only the work in [13] takes advantage of the backpropagation feature for retraining. As such, the premise of this paper is to contribute to the progression of the current state-of-art by proposing:

- An innovative machine learning training approach for PdM that aims to improve model performance while also taking into account imbalanced and irrelevant/erroneous data.
- An automatic hyperparameter optimization strategy, used to determine the optimal hyperparameters for the ANN and RF, hence enhancing the models' performance even further.
- The application in real-time of both implemented models, by taking into account model retraining and user application.

This paper structure is divided into five sections. After this introductory and state-of-art section, Sect. 2 describes the training and testing dataset used to validate the proposed methodology. Section 3 describes the proposed methodology for PdM on an ANN and RF, while Sect. 4 presents the obtained results of the implemented models, as well as a discussion regarding such a topic. The conclusions are presented in Sect. 5.

2 Training/Testing Dataset

The PdM dataset used for training and testing of the proposed methodology was made available from the University of California in Irvine, Machine Learning Repository [27].

The PdM dataset from 2020, labeled "AI4I 2020 Predictive Maintenance Dataset Data Set," is freely accessible in [28]. The synthetic dataset has 10,000 data points where 339 represent failures and 9661 non-failures data points (i.e., a ratio of 1:28), as presented in Fig. 1. The machine data is the following:

- Air temperature–defines the exterior temperature of the machine, in Kelvin (K);
- Process temperature − defines the temperature produced within the machine, in Kelvin (K);
- Rotational speed–defines the rotational speed of the tools inside the machine, in Revolutions per minute (rpm);
- Torque–defines the force required to rotate the machine's tools, in Newton-meters (Nm);
- Tool wear–defines the amount of deterioration of the tools inside the machine, in minutes until breakdown (min);
- Machine failure–defines a machine failure status by assuming the value 0 for non-failure and 1 for failure.

The correlation heatmap between the used dataset features is described in Fig. 2.

It demonstrates that there is a medium positive correlation between machine failure and the features torque (0.190 positive correlation) and tool wear (0.110 positive correlation). On the other hand, the lowest correlation found to machine failure was the rotational speed (0.044 negative correlation) and process temperature (0.036 positive correlation).

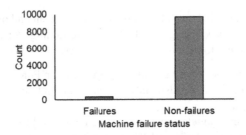

Fig. 1. Machine failure status bar chart of the used dataset.

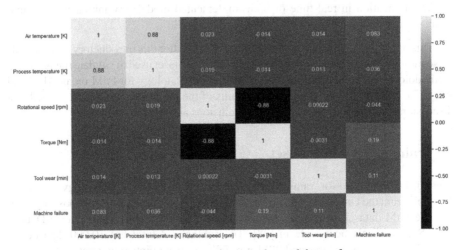

Fig. 2. Correlation heatmap between the used dataset features.

3 Proposed Methodology

Two machine learning models, an ANN and an RF model, are implemented and explored for PdM. In the proposed methodology, training of the implemented models can be done in batches, mini-batches, or continuous data streaming. Before real-time training, an initial model is constructed through a dataset, and only then, the training process is carried out in real-time via data streaming or mini-batches.

The initial model for the ANN or RF is constructed using:

- The dataset described in Sect. 2;
- The Holdout method, 80% for training and 20% for testing;
- A Min-Max approach for data normalization;
- A newly added dataset feature, machine temperature difference (i.e., process temperature − air temperature), replaces the process and air temperature features. It focuses on improving model performance, by reducing the number of inputs for less complexity and better correlation between temperature and machine failure;
- A data balancing method, 5% oversampling on failure data and a majority undersampling strategy on non-failure data. To achieve this, the imbalanced-learn [29] library was used;

- A 5-fold cross-validation splitting strategy to search for the best hyperparameters.

It is worth mentioning that, the Holdout method and the 5-fold cross-validation splitting strategy described above were employed as safe measures to prevent overfitting of the models.

The proposed methodology for real-time training begins by obtaining the most recent machine data, described in Sect. 2, from machine databases in the facility. Afterward, prior to training, a data preprocessing phase is employed, which can be divided into six sequential subphases:

1. Data aggregator–combines all acquired data into a single data file;
2. Data normalization–standardizes data units and types between machines, using a Min-Max technique with the MinMaxScaler method [30] from the Scikit-Learn library [31];
3. Data imputation–fills missing values on the obtained data, through a k-Nearest Neighbors imputation approach with the KNNImputer method [32] from the Scikit-Learn library;
4. Data filtering–removes any potentially incorrect or irrelevant data, by detecting outliers using the Z-score with the SciPy stats Z-score method [33] from the SciPy library [34];
5. Data engineering–creates or removes features to better depict the underlying problem;
6. Data balancing–balances machine data failure and non-failure points, with the imbalanced-learn library [29].

Then, the preprocessed data is used to train the machine learning models (i.e., ANN or RF), wherein the ANN neuron weights are adjusted due to the back-propagation feature, or, in the case of the RF, the model has to be reconstructed from the start using the new and past data.

The methodology for real-time application of the implemented machine learning models in a machine can be divided into three phases:

1. Data acquisition–obtains the necessary machine data from the machine to be inspected;
2. Data preprocessing–applies data normalization, imputation, filtering, and engineering on the obtained data;
3. Machine failure status prediction–uses one of the models, designated by the user, to predict the machine failure status (0 for non-failure and 1 for failure).

3.1 Artificial Neural Network Training

The ANN was trained using an automatic hyperparameter optimizer, which focuses on finding the optimal hyperparameter values to obtain a high-performing model. This is achieved by using the GridSearchCV [35] method available from the Scikit-Learn library. The automatic hyperparameter optimizer works by exploring each hyperparameter's possible values, at random, in order to find a high-performing ANN model, which contains the optimal values for each hyperparameter. Table 1 presents the possible and found optimal hyperparameter values for the ANN model. However, some hyperparameters were predefined, as there was no need to find the optimal value, such as the loss function, defined with binary cross-entropy function, metrics with binary accuracy, the number of input neurons as 4 (temperature difference, rotational speed, torque, tool wear), the number of output neurons as 1 (machine failure), the output layer activation function defined with a sigmoid function, and a normal weight initialization in the hidden layers.

For the ANN classifier, the KerasClassifier [36] from the Keras [37] library was used. It operates through rules created during the training phase to achieve the lowest possible accuracy error in contrast to the training classes. The model is ready to generate predictions once it has been properly fitted using training data.

Table 1. Artificial neural network hyperparameters possible and optimal values.

Hyperparameter	Possible Values	Optimal Value
Batch Size	10, 20, 40, 60, 80, 100, 200, 500, 1000, 2000, or 5000	5000
Dropout Regularization on Hidden Layers	0%, 5%, 10%, 20%, 30%, 35%, 40%, 50%, 60%, 70%, 80%, or 90%	35%
Dropout Regularization on Input Layer	0%, 5%, 10%, 20%, 30%, 40%, 50%, 60%, 70%, 80%, or 90%	0%
Epochs	10, 50, 100, 150, 200, 300, 500, 1000, 2000, 5000, 8000, or 10000	5000
Neuron Activation Function	Hard Sigmoid, Linear, Relu, Sigmoid, Softmax, Softplus, Softsign, or Tanh	Relu
Hidden Layers Neuron Composition	1 to 4 layers 5, 10, 15, 20, 25, or 30 neurons per layer	25 neurons in layer 1 20 neurons in layer 2 15 neurons in layer 3 15 neurons in layer 4
Optimizer	Adadelta, Adagrad, Adam, Adamax, Nadam, RMSprop, or SGD	Nadam
Weight Initialization in Input Layer	Glorot Normal, Glorot Uniform, He Normal, He Uniform, Lecum Uniform, Normal, Uniform, or Zero	Glorot Uniform

3.2 Random Forest Training

The RF was also trained using an automatic hyperparameter optimizer, aiming to find a robust RF model. This is accomplished through the RandomizedSearchCV [38] method. This method focuses on determining the optimal estimator to employ in the model by selecting one of the possible values for each hyperparameter at random and then assessing each estimator based on their accuracy scores. Each hyperparameter's possible values and optimal value for the RF model are shown in Table 2. The RandomForestClassifier [39] was used as the RF classifier.

Table 2. Random forest hyperparameters possible and optimal values.

Hyperparameter	Possible Values	Optimal Value
Bootstrap Sample	True or False	True
Criterion Function	Gini or Entropy	Gini
Max Depth	10 to 32	10
Max Features	Auto, Sqrt, or Log2	Log2
Min Samples Leaf	1, 2, 4, 6, 8, or 10	1
Min Samples Split	2, 5, 10, 20, or 30	2
Tree Amount	200 to 3000	511

4   Results and Discussion

Four metrics were used to validate the performance of the proposed machine learning models: recall, precision, f1-score, and accuracy. It is worth noting that, since PdM problems commonly have very imbalanced datasets that have a low number of failure data points, the recall metric was considered to be the most relevant performance metric to validate the proposed methodology. The ANN performance metrics using the optimal hyperparameters found in Table 1 and the performance of the RF model using the optimal hyperparameters in Table 2 are shown in Table 3.

Table 3. Performance metrics of the proposed machine learning models using their respective optimal hyperparameters.

Machine Learning Model	Recall	Precision	F1-score	Accuracy
Artificial Neural Network	0.97	0.15	0.27	83.65%
Random Forest	0.95	0.30	0.46	93.15%

According to the results presented in Table 3, each model has its own benefits and drawbacks, with the ANN being slightly better at predicting when there is about to be a machine breakdown, since it has the highest recall, and the RF excelling at lowering the number of false alarms (i.e., false positives), because of having the highest precision and accuracy scores. As a result, on one hand, if maintenance costs are inexpensive and undetected machine breakdowns can lead to dire consequences, the ANN is the preferred model to be employed. On the other hand, the RF model is better at reducing the number of false alarms, which reduces unnecessary maintenance activities when compared to the ANN. Nevertheless, both models have good accuracy scores, mainly the Random Forest model with 93.15%, for this type of problem, where imbalanced predictive maintenance datasets are common and negatively affect accuracy scores. Table 4 presents the ANN and RF confusion matrixes. It is noteworthy that there is a big trade-off between true positives and false positives between the two models, with the RF only having 1 more unsuccessful machine failure prediction but having 191 fewer false alarms than the ANN. Therefore, in general, even though the recall was considered to be the most relevant metric, the RF model has the best performance overall, since it does not fall behind too much on recall and all other metrics are much better than in the ANN model. It is worth mentioning that another work [40] utilized the same dataset as the current paper to justify the usage of a bagged trees ensemble classifier. However, cited work did not split the dataset for training and testing, resulting in an overfitted model and inflated results, because of this, no comparison was made to this work. Despite the fact that the cited work inflated their obtained results, it achieved a recall score of only 0.71, lower than the present paper's ANN model with a recall of 0.97 and RF with 0.95.

Table 4. Artificial neural network and random forest confusion matrix.

Predicted		Actual	
		Failure	Non-failure
Artificial Neural Network	Failure	59	325
	Non-failure	2	1614
Random Forest	Failure	58	134
	Non-failure	3	1805

5 Conclusion

To further reduce costs and improve product quality, the manufacturing industry has been investing in PdM strategies to cut down on unnecessary maintenance costs, as PdM systems are capable of predicting machine condition/lifespan allowing for maintenance-effective manufacturing.

The proposed methodology aims to improve performance in machine learning models for PdM problems by proposing a novel training methodology, an automatic hyper-parameter optimization strategy, and a new retraining method. To achieve this, an ANN and RF models are implemented and explored. A synthetic dataset for PdM, containing imbalanced data, is presented to validate the proposed methodology.

The obtained results show the robustness of the proposed methodology, with the ANN model accomplishing a recall of 0.97, a precision of 0.15, an f1-score of 0.27, and an accuracy of 83.65%. The RF model was able to excel even further by achieving a lower recall of 0.95, but having a much better precision of 0.30, an f1-score of 0.46, and an accuracy of 93.15%. In general, the RF model has better performance overall, nevertheless, it is clear that the ANN is slightly better at reducing true positives while the RF reduces false positives.

Future work will address the use of real-world data instead of a synthetic dataset, allowing to better evaluate the effectiveness of the proposed methodology in practical manufacturing environments. In addition model interpretability, through eXplainable Artificial Intelligence (XAI), will also be explored for the proposed ANN and RF models, in order to improve confidence in PdM systems.

Funding. This work has received funding from project MUWO (grant agreement No. 771066), through COMPETE program, under the PORTUGAL 2020 Partnership Agreement, through the European Regional Development Fund (ERDF/FEDER). Pedro Faria has Support from FCT trough project CEECIND/01423/2021. The authors acknowledge the work facilities and equipment provided by GECAD research center (UIDB/00760/2020) to the project team.

References

1. Ramos, D., Faria, P., Gomes, L., Vale, Z.: A contextual reinforcement learning approach for electricity consumption forecasting in buildings. IEEE Access. **10**, 61366–61374 (2022). https://doi.org/10.1109/ACCESS.2022.3180754
2. Faria, P., Vale, Z.: Distributed energy resource scheduling with focus on demand response complex contracts. J. Mod. Power Syst. Clean Energy **9**, 1172–1182 (2021). https://doi.org/10.35833/MPCE.2020.000317
3. Mashal, I., Khashan, O.A., Hijjawi, M., Alshinwan, M.: The determinants of reliable smart grid from experts' perspective. Energy Informatics. **6**, 1–23 (2023). https://doi.org/10.1186/S42162-023-00266-3/TABLES/5
4. Sharma, A., Yadava, G.S., Deshmukh, S.G.: A literature review and future perspectives on maintenance optimization (2011). https://doi.org/10.1108/13552511111116222
5. Faccio, M., Persona, A., Sgarbossa, F., Zanin, G.: Industrial maintenance policy development: a quantitative framework. Int. J. Prod. Econ. **147**, 85–93 (2014). https://doi.org/10.1016/j.ijpe.2012.08.018
6. Mota, B., Gomes, L., Faria, P., Ramos, C., Vale, Z., Correia, R.: Production line optimization to minimize energy cost and participate in demand response events. Energies (Basel). **14**, 462 (2021). https://doi.org/10.3390/en14020462
7. Ramos, C., Barreto, R., Mota, B., Gomes, L., Faria, P., Vale, Z.: Scheduling of a textile production line integrating PV generation using a genetic algorithm. Energy Rep. **6**, 148–154 (2020). https://doi.org/10.1016/j.egyr.2020.11.093
8. Garg, A., Deshmukh, S.G.: Maintenance management: literature review and directions (2006). https://doi.org/10.1108/13552510610685075
9. Shin, J.H., Jun, H.B.: On condition based maintenance policy. J. Comput. Des. Eng. **2**, 119–127 (2015). https://doi.org/10.1016/j.jcde.2014.12.006
10. Thomas, D.S.: The Costs and Benefits of Advanced Maintenance in Manufacturing, pp. 1–45. National Institute of Standards and Technology (2018). https://doi.org/10.6028/nist.ams.100-18
11. Rodriguez, P.C., Marti-Puig, P., Caiafa, C.F., Serra-Serra, M., Cusidó, J., Solé-Casals, J.: Exploratory analysis of SCADA data from wind turbines using the K-means clustering algorithm for predictive maintenance purposes. Machines **11**, 270 (2023). https://doi.org/10.3390/machines11020270

12. Carvalho, T.P., Soares, F.A.A.M.N., Vita, R., Francisco, R.daP., Basto, J.P., Alcalá, S.G.S.: A systematic literature review of machine learning methods applied to predictive maintenance. Comput. Ind. Eng. **137**, 106024 (2019). https://doi.org/10.1016/j.cie.2019.106024

13. Koca, O., Kaymakci, O.T., Mercimek, M.: Advanced predictive maintenance with machine learning failure estimation in industrial packaging robots. In: Proceedings of the 2020 15th International Conference on Development and Application Systems (DAS 2020), pp. 1–6. Institute of Electrical and Electronics Engineers Inc. (2020). https://doi.org/10.1109/DAS 49615.2020.9108913

14. Rosli, N.S., Ain Burhani, N.R., Ibrahim, R.: Predictive maintenance of air booster compressor (ABC) motor failure using artificial neural network trained by particle swarm optimization. In: 2019 IEEE Student Conference on Research and Development (SCOReD 2019), pp. 11–16. Institute of Electrical and Electronics Engineers Inc. (2019). https://doi.org/10.1109/SCO RED.2019.8896330

15. Kavana, V., Neethi, M.: Fault analysis and predictive maintenance of induction motor using machine learning. In: 3rd International Conference on Electrical, Electronics, Communication, Computer Technologies and Optimization Techniques (ICEECCOT 2018), pp. 963–966. Institute of Electrical and Electronics Engineers Inc. (2018). https://doi.org/10.1109/ICEECC OT43722.2018.9001543

16. Ayvaz, S., Alpay, K.: Predictive maintenance system for production lines in manufacturing: a machine learning approach using IoT data in real-time. Expert Syst. Appl. **173**, 114598 (2021). https://doi.org/10.1016/j.eswa.2021.114598

17. Paolanti, M., Romeo, L., Felicetti, A., Mancini, A., Frontoni, E., Loncarski, J.: Machine learning approach for predictive maintenance in Industry 4.0. In: 2018 14th IEEE/ASME International Conference on Mechatronic and Embedded Systems and Applications (MESA 2018). Institute of Electrical and Electronics Engineers Inc. (2018). https://doi.org/10.1109/ MESA.2018.8449150

18. Calabrese, M., et al.: SOPHIA: an event-based IoT and machine learning architecture for predictive maintenance in Industry 4.0. Information (Switzerland) **11**, 202 (2020). https://doi. org/10.3390/INFO11040202

19. Nguyen, K.T.P., Medjaher, K.: A new dynamic predictive maintenance framework using deep learning for failure prognostics. Reliab. Eng. Syst. Saf. **188**, 251–262 (2019). https://doi.org/ 10.1016/j.ress.2019.03.018

20. Haghshenas, A., Hasan, A., Osen, O., Mikalsen, E.T.: Predictive digital twin for offshore wind farms. Energy Informatics **6**, 1–26 (2023). https://doi.org/10.1186/S42162-023-00257-4/FIGURES/19

21. Chaudhuri, A.: Predictive Maintenance for Industrial IoT of Vehicle Fleets Using Hierarchical Modified Fuzzy Support Vector Machine (2018)

22. Wang, Q., Liu, J., Wei, B., Chen, W., Xu, S.: Investigating the construction, training, and verification methods of k-means clustering fault recognition model for rotating machinery. IEEE Access **8**, 196515–196528 (2020). https://doi.org/10.1109/ACCESS.2020.3028146

23. Udo, W., Muhammad, Y.: Data-driven predictive maintenance of wind turbine based on SCADA data. IEEE Access **9**, 162370–162388 (2021). https://doi.org/10.1109/ACCESS. 2021.3132684

24. Ahmad, B., Mishra, B.K., Ghufran, M., Pervez, Z., Ramzan, N.: Intelligent predictive maintenance model for rolling components of a machine based on speed and vibration. In: 3rd International Conference on Artificial Intelligence in Information and Communication (ICAIIC 2021), pp. 459–464. Institute of Electrical and Electronics Engineers Inc. (2021). https://doi. org/10.1109/ICAIIC51459.2021.9415249

25. Trivedi, S., Bhola, S., Talegaonkar, A., Gaur, P., Sharma, S.: Predictive maintenance of air conditioning systems using supervised machine learning. In: 2019 20th International Conference on Intelligent System Application to Power Systems (ISAP 2019). Institute of Electrical and Electronics Engineers Inc. (2019). https://doi.org/10.1109/ISAP48318.2019.9065995
26. Zonta, T., da Costa, C.A., da Rosa Righi, R., de Lima, M.J., da Trindade, E.S., Li, G.P.: Predictive maintenance in the Industry 4.0: a systematic literature review. Comput. Ind. Eng. **150**, 106889 (2020). https://doi.org/10.1016/j.cie.2020.106889
27. Frank, A., Asuncion, A.: {UCI} Machine Learning Repository (2010). https://archive.ics.uci.edu/ml/index.php
28. Matzka, S.: UCI Machine Learning Repository: AI4I 2020 Predictive Maintenance Dataset Data Set. https://archive.ics.uci.edu/ml/datasets/AI4I+2020+Predictive+Maintenance+Dat aset. Accessed 23 Jan 2022
29. Imbalanced-Learn Documentation — Version 0.9.0. https://imbalanced-learn.org/stable/. Accessed 20 Apr 2022
30. sklearn.preprocessing.MinMaxScaler — scikit-learn 1.1.2 documentation. https://scikit-learn.org/stable/modules/generated/sklearn.preprocessing.MinMaxScaler.html. Accessed 08 Sept 2022
31. scikit-learn: machine learning in Python — scikit-learn 1.0.2 documentation. https://scikit-learn.org/stable/index.html. Accessed 20 Apr 2022
32. sklearn.impute.KNNImputer — scikit-learn 1.1.2 documentation. https://scikit-learn.org/sta ble/modules/generated/sklearn.impute.KNNImputer.html. Accessed 08 Sept 2022
33. scipy.stats.zscore — SciPy v1.9.2 Manual. https://docs.scipy.org/doc/scipy/reference/genera ted/scipy.stats.zscore.html#scipy-stats-zscore. Accessed 11 Oct 2022
34. SciPy documentation — SciPy v1.9.2 Manual. https://docs.scipy.org/doc/scipy/index.html. Accessed 11 Oct 2022
35. sklearn.model_selection.GridSearchCV — scikit-learn 1.0.2 documentation. https://scikit-learn.org/stable/modules/generated/sklearn.model_selection.GridSearchCV.html. Accessed 20 Apr 2022
36. tf.keras.wrappers.scikit_learn.KerasClassifier | TensorFlow. http://man.hubwiz.com/docset/ TensorFlow.docset/Contents/Resources/Documents/api_docs/python/tf/keras/wrappers/sci kit_learn/KerasClassifier.html. Accessed 20 Apr 2022
37. Chollet, F., Keras, O.: The Python deep learning API. https://keras.io/. Accessed 25 Jan 2022
38. sklearn.model_selection.RandomizedSearchCV — scikit-learn 1.0.2 documentation. https:// scikit-learn.org/stable/modules/generated/sklearn.model_selection.RandomizedSearchCV. html. Accessed 20 Apr 2022
39. sklearn.ensemble.RandomForestClassifier — scikit-learn 1.0.2 documentation. https:// scikit-learn.org/stable/modules/generated/sklearn.ensemble.RandomForestClassifier.html. Accessed 20 Apr 2022
40. Matzka, S.: Explainable artificial intelligence for predictive maintenance applications. In: Proceedings of the 2020 3rd International Conference on Artificial Intelligence for Industries (AI4I 2020), pp. 69–74. Institute of Electrical and Electronics Engineers Inc. (2020). https:// doi.org/10.1109/AI4I49448.2020.00023

Author Index

B. N. Jørgensen et al. (Eds.): EI.A 2023, LNCS 14467, pp. 301–302, 2024.
https://doi.org/10.1007/978-3-031-48649-4

Printed in the United States
by Baker & Taylor Publisher Services